By
Recommendation
Only

Johanna Kaestner

By Recommendation Only

Party and Wedding Resource Guide
to the
Greater San Francisco Bay Area
including Monterey Bay

Seventh Edition

www.ByRecOnly.com

Tosca J. Clark
Regional Author

Adobe Creek Publishing
Redmond, Washington

ISBN 0-9627482-7-7

Printed in the United States of America

Adobe Creek Publishing
24439 NE 19th Street
Redmond, WA 98053

Disclaimer

Every effort has been made to ensure the accuracy of the information provided in this guide. However, no responsibility is assumed for any errors or inaccuracies, especially those due to changes made by the listed enterprises after the publication date.

CONTENTS

CONTENTS

The By Recommendation Only Seal of Approval

When you see this seal, you are assured that the vendor meets
the high standards of

By Recommendation Only

By Recommendation Only

on the World Wide Web!

www.ByRecOnly.com

The continuously updated BRO Website provides valuable information that complements this guide:

- story of the month
- wedding trends
- wedding planner
- how to hire a wedding professional
- how to survive the emotional demands
- vendor web pages and links

The BRO Website also has the most up-to-date information about all vendors in the guide, such as:

- change of phone number
- change of business address
- change of e-mail address

and much more!

You can also send your comments via e-mail to:

johanna@ByRecOnly.com

New

The BRO Marketplace

www.ByRecOnly.com/market.htm

In November 1998, the BRO Marketplace was launched to offer innovative resources for bride, groom, or anyone planning a wedding or looking for a tasteful selection of exquisite gifts. Our vision was to create a store in which it is fun to shop - a place to stretch your imagination and to find wonderful new ideas while planning this very special occasion.

By Recommendation Only has selected the artists and gifts with the same eye for the high quality found within the resource guide.

The Gallery features artists who have created beautiful and unique gift items and accessories:

· Jewelry · Textile Art · Paper Art · Food Art ·

The BRO Collection offers attractively designed items from around the world:

· Wedding & Reception Planning · Accessories · Gifts for Him ·
· Gifts for Her · Mementos · Personalized Ribbons ·

As we continue to add to our online catalogue, we encourage you to visit the site often to peruse our new offerings.

www.ByRecOnly.com/market.htm

BRO Song

(set to the melody of "Get me to the church on time!",
My Fair Lady)

When you're about to plan a wedding
And you are wond'ring what to do
Don't even bother
To look any farther
By Recommendation Only's for you.

The best and the brightest in the business
To help you to plan your special day
Are yours to discover
From cover to cover
From all around the San Francisco Bay.

They'll do the flowers
They'll do the cake
They'll help decide which photographs to take
They'll do the music
And the cuisine
And pick you up in a chauffeured limousine.

Oh, planning a wedding will be easy
For every groom and every bride
Whatever you desire
Is there for the hire
The people in the know
Are found in BRO
The Bay Area's party & wedding resource guide!

Sari August
All About You (page 355)

ACKNOWLEDGMENTS

This book is dedicated to all the industry professionals who have been committed to providing the level and quality of service on which this guide is based. Your professionalism has contributed to the success of many milestone events.

My heartfelt thanks to Johanna Kaestner, innovator of this unique, invaluable resource guide, for having both the vision to bring this book to life and the faith in my abilities to continue your endeavor into the next millennium.

To Sari, who brought me humor and sanity during the course of writing this guide, I extend my deepest gratitude. As editor and friend, you have been the glue and eyes of this guide.

Hats off to Kristi Pangrazio, the diplomat of our BRO team, for providing fresh ways to reinvent ourselves. The website and marketplace would not have succeeded without your creative energy and hard work.

My undying gratitude goes to Tom Clark, my husband, best friend and partner, for placing his life on hold to help me and playing Mr. Mom to our beautiful son Gavin Thomas. Your dedicated assistance was immeasurable; your integrity uncompromised. Our wonderful marriage and your faith in me are the reasons I have made planning and coordinating weddings my life's career. If I can help couples get started on the path to what we have, then our mission on this earth will be complete.

To Gavin, always know you are the air that I breathe. I love you, "caro mio."

Special thanks to all my family and friends who think I dropped off the face of the earth. I am back!

Tosca J. Clark

PUBLISHER'S NOTE

After nearly a decade of authoring and publishing the *By Recommendation Only* series of guides, this 7th edition is the first one for which I did not do all the legwork. My move to the Northwest necessitated the search for a local author. I was fortunate to have found Tosca Clark, whose dedication to the endeavor as well as her experience as a member of the event industry certainly enhanced the publication.

Working on his edition required heavy reliance on the "communication highway." With Tosca in Daly City, Sari August (my longtime editor and friend) in Monterey, and me in Redmond, we were able to exchange files as well as thoughts in a matter of seconds. We couldn't have done it without the Internet.

Taking further advantage of the Internet, we have included e-mail and website addresses, making it faster and easier to get in touch with the highly regarded group of vendors reviewed in the guide.

And, on one more Internet note, the BRO Website has been enhanced to include feature stories and the latest trends in weddings. Psychologist Amy Honigman's column offers answers to questions that may arise during the engagement or early marriage. Last, but not least, the new BRO Marketplace makes it easy for the bride to find tasteful specialty items, nowhere else to be found.

Take advantage of the multimedia service of *By Recommendation Only*.

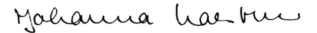

PREFACE

The idea for this series of guides came to me upon hearing friends complain about the immense task of planning a wedding. Having daughters about to be married, they were totally overwhelmed by the choices in the phone book's yellow pages and were looking for help and advice from friends. So I set out to write guides to event and wedding resources. I visited recommended vendors, observed events, and called references. I also talked to clients and peers in order to present a well-rounded view of each.

During the seven years that I worked on the guide, I witnessed the progress and development of each vendor. When seeing their work years ago, I remember wondering, "How can anyone top this?" However, they "topped" themselves, which is evidence that they truly love their work.

I learned about the existence of each vendor either through a recommendation or by encountering the vendor at an event. When I approached them, I never pretended to be a potential client. I clearly stated my reason for requesting an interview, which was to determine whether or not they met my criteria. I arrived with a previous edition in hand so that they could appreciate the quality of my work and evaluate the benefit of their association with me. Sometimes, word of the book led companies to call me, asking to be considered as candidates for my pages.

My research was thorough. My interview with the business owner or contact person was followed up by phone interviews with several references and a review of the company's work at an event. I looked at floral decorations in churches and reception locations; I tasted caterers' food in their kitchens; I listened to musicians at events or enjoyed a "private concert," and I browsed through photographers' portfolios. In short, I did all the things a careful party or wedding planner would do.

I met wonderful people during my research and made new friends. I also learned that art can be expressed in so many ways, even in cooking and food presentation. Many "outsiders" started their own businesses in order to express their creativity. Nurses, teachers, and housewives flourished in their second careers as florists, bakers, and caterers.

One of the interesting insights I gained was learning that there are clusters of professionals who work together. For example, caterers recommend only a few bakers, florists, or musicians to their clients. Most of them prefer not to experiment with new vendors once they have put a good team together. The best resources for "business to business" recommendations are caterers, musicians and photographers. Since they are present throughout the event, they're in the best position to see everything, from pre-event activities to dance time.

I've also noticed some changes over the years. Some of the bands have changed their appearance, from being "wild" when I first met them to looking now more like members of the establishment. Another change is in the use of electronic communications. When I began the first edition of the guide, very few businesses had fax machines. Now, those without them are the minority. And e-mail communication is on the rise.

Some businesses that you may be famliar with do not appear in this guide simply because I did not learn about their existence through recommendations. So I urge you, my readers, to use the form at the back of the guide to recommend to me your favorite event professionals, and also include a review of your experiences with your recommendation. Since companies change and people move on, I would also appreciate learning if a vendor should be removed from the guide. The purpose of this guide is to ensure client satisfaction with each and every vendor. Your feedback will help me realize this goal.

As you read the pages, keep in mind that the information presented there is my attempt to simply give you a feel for the company to help you with your selection process. Contact them for more specific information, get to know them, and, most important, determine if you can fully place your faith and trust in them to execute your ideas. I've learned that it is better to hire someone you can trust than to save a few dollars.

Have fun planning your next event!

WEDDING PLANNER

12 Months Before The Wedding

☐ Meet with wedding consultant to discuss budget, vendors, and wedding theme

☐ Set wedding date and time

☐ Decide on wedding theme and style

☐ Choose color scheme

☐ Determine number of guests

☐ Discuss expenses, financial responsibilities, and set budget

☐ Reserve ceremony site

☐ Reserve reception site

☐ Hire caterer, if not provided by reception site

☐ Begin compiling guest list

☐ Select bride's and groom's attendants

☐ Hire professional photographer

☐ Hire professional videographer

☐ Hire musicians and/or disc jockey

☐ Shop for wedding dress, veil, and accessories

☐ Announce engagement to family and friends

☐ Announce engagement in local newspaper

☐ Send "Save the Date" cards to out-of-town guests

6 Months Before The Wedding

- ❑ Meet with wedding consultant to review contracts and update budget
- ❑ Make sure all bridal attire, veil, and accessories have been ordered
- ❑ Select bridesmaids' dresses
- ❑ Have family members select and coordinate their dresses and accessories
- ❑ Select flower girl's attire
- ❑ Hire florist and plan floral arrangements
- ❑ Register with bridal gift registry local to each family
- ❑ Record engagement gifts received and send thank-you notes promptly
- ❑ Complete master list of guest names and addresses
- ❑ Order invitations, stationery, programs, napkins, etc.
- ❑ Select men's wedding attire and reserve sizes
- ❑ Arrange for limousine or other transportation to ceremony and reception sites
- ❑ Arrange transportation for wedding party
- ❑ Plan music for reception
- ❑ Plan honeymoon and arrange accommodations
- ❑ Reserve honeymoon suite for wedding night
- ❑ Order wedding rings, including engraving
- ❑ Visit doctor for complete physical exam and update immunizations

4 Months Before The Wedding

- ❑ Meet with wedding consultant to review wedding plans and discuss ideas

- ❑ Make arrangements for out-of-town guests

- ❑ Photocopy information about guest accommodations and mail to out-of-town guests

- ❑ Finalize honeymoon plans with travel agent

- ❑ Finalize living arrangements and shop for home furnishings

- ❑ Provide picture of wedding dress and fabric swatches to florist

- ❑ Arrange for rental equipment

- ❑ Order wedding cake and specialty breads

- ❑ Purchase accessories

- ❑ Finalize master guest list

- ❑ Contact calligrapher for addressing invitations, envelopes, place cards, etc.

- ❑ Check postage requirements for sealed invitations

- ❑ Inquire about marriage license

WEDDING PLANNER

2 Months Before The Wedding

- ❑ Meet with wedding consultant to review schedule of events

- ❑ Have wedding dress fitted

- ❑ Have bridesmaids' dresses fitted

- ❑ Provide wedding day event schedule to vendors and wedding party

- ❑ Confirm menu and all details with caterer

- ❑ Plan floral arrangements and finalize all details with florist

- ❑ Provide list of "must take" photos and finalize details with photographer

- ❑ Provide names of bridal party and family members to be announced and finalize details with musicians

- ❑ Finish addressing invitations and announcements

- ❑ Mail wedding invitations

- ❑ Confirm details with reception site coordinator, including rental equipment

- ❑ Arrange parking for ceremony and reception sites

- ❑ Finalize ceremony and rehearsal details with officiant

- ❑ Send invitations for rehearsal and dinner

- ❑ Plan bridesmaids' luncheon or party

- ❑ Make your wedding favors

- ❑ Choose going-away outfits

- ❑ Record gifts received and send thank-you notes

- ❑ Make appointment with hairdresser and makeup artist for a preview look

- ❑ Have engagement portrait taken

WEDDING PLANNER

---

1 Month Before The Wedding

- ☐ Meet on site with wedding consultant to review floor plans and finalize details
- ☐ Have final fitting and alterations of wedding dress
- ☐ Bridesmaids have final fitting of dresses
- ☐ Pick up sized wedding rings
- ☐ Make sure you have all of your accessories
- ☐ Purchase items for honeymoon
- ☐ Keep gift list current and write thank-you notes promptly
- ☐ Keep track of guests' response cards and special requirements
- ☐ Complete floor plans, seating arrangements, and place cards
- ☐ Arrange for someone to help you dress and run errands
- ☐ Arrange for someone to deliver luggage and airplane tickets to hotel on wedding day
- ☐ Give caterer a reliable estimate of number of guests
- ☐ Select gift for spouse, if gifts are exchanged
- ☐ Send invitations for rehearsal and dinner
- ☐ Select thank-you gifts for attendants and parents
- ☐ Finish wedding favors
- ☐ Confirm reserved sizes and pickup dates and times with formal wear shop
- ☐ Finalize moving arrangements
- ☐ Obtain marriage license

WEDDING PLANNER

1 to 2 Weeks Before The Wedding

- ❑ Send all vendors schedule of wedding day events and confirm services

- ❑ Confirm accommodations and transportation for out-of-town guests

- ❑ Create welcome baskets for out-of-town guests with special message, if desired

- ❑ If moving, give change of address to post office

- ❑ Move belongings into new home

- ❑ Finish addressing announcements and mail day before wedding

- ❑ Send wedding announcement to newspaper

- ❑ Contact guests who have not responded

- ❑ Review place cards for head table and assigned seating

- ❑ Confirm honeymoon plans and wedding night hotel reservations

- ❑ Pack suitcase for honeymoon

- ❑ Confirm song selections with vocalist and musicians

- ❑ Present gifts to attendants at rehearsal

- ❑ Give copies of special readings to assigned readers

- ❑ Assign someone to transport gifts, guest books, and personal belongings from reception site

- ❑ Rehearse with all participants, provide them with wedding day event schedule, and review their responsibilities

- ❑ Inform ushers of seating arrangements for ceremony

- ❑ Have manicure, pedicure, and massage 1 or 2 days before wedding

- ❑ Prepare emergency wedding basket with sewing items, aspirin, etc.

WEDDING PLANNER

Your Wedding Day

- ❏ Take a nice, warm bath

- ❏ Make sure you eat something; it's going to be a long day

- ❏ Check into hotel or confirm late registration

- ❏ Have suitcases and airplane tickets delivered to hotel suite

- ❏ Mail wedding announcements

- ❏ Allow plenty of time for hair, manicure, and makeup

- ❏ Bride and attendants should be dressed 2 hours before wedding

- ❏ Photographer will take photos about 2 hours before ceremony

- ❏ Flowers will arrive about 2 hours before ceremony

- ❏ Give wedding rings to best man and maid of honor

- ❏ Bring marriage license to ceremony

- ❏ Groom gives best man tip envelopes for officiant and other personnel

- ❏ Bring telegrams and special wedding day wishes to reception for best man to read

Relax! Your wedding consultant will attend to all the details as planned, so sit back and enjoy! Don't let anyone or anything spoil the first day of the rest of your life together. Take a few minutes during the reception to look at the beautiful setup, and relish the entire day.

INTRODUCTION

A main concern of a party planner is the cost of the event. In general, you will find that the old saying still holds: "You get what you pay for." Of course, there are many ways to stretch a budget, such as hosting an event in a public park or ordering simple food from a caterer. Sometimes scheduling is important: if you don't have to celebrate on a Saturday, you can cut costs substantially. For example, many musicians offer lower rates for Fridays and Sundays.

The following explanations clarify the type of information that appears on each page.

The **service area** describes the geographical area that the vendor prefers to service.

The **pricing** information is presented in dollar amounts. While it is easy to state the rental price of a hall, it is more difficult to be accurate in every other category. Therefore, other prices are presented as either a range or the minimum amount that a vendor will charge. Adding expensive flowers or food items naturally raises the price. Don't hesitate to discuss your budget with the vendor; it will save you time and disappointment. Most businesses will work with you to meet your budget, especially during harder economic times. Many companies will charge the prices quoted upon booking the service even though their prices may change by the time of your event.

The costs specific to each type of business are explained in the introduction to each section.

Extra charges are costs not included in the price noted on the page. They are incurred for additional services or special arrangements. Most extra charges are specific to the type of business and are noted in each introductory section. However, extra charges that may be relevant to all businesses are travel beyond specific areas, long distance phone calls, parking fees, and bridge tolls.

Since tax is charged by all vendors, it is not included as an extra charge. Some vendors include tax in their quoted price, which is noted on the page. Otherwise, you should always assume that it's extra.

Payment terms are specific to private events. Corporate functions are often subject to different payment terms and conditions. Inquire about these terms when you call.

A **deposit** must be paid at booking time and reserves the date for you. It is often non-refundable ("non-ref.") and can be regarded as payment for the initial consultation. Refundable deposits sometimes carry restrictions: they may be only partially refundable, or may become non-refundable when a cancellation occurs too close to the date of an event. Some companies will make a refund conditional upon booking another client for the canceled date.

Credit cards are accepted by many vendors. The phrase "major credit cards" translates to Visa, MasterCard, and American Express. Otherwise, either the specific credit cards mentioned or all credit cards are accepted.

Lead time is presented as a range. The **minimum** is the shortest time period in which a business can accommodate you if it isn't booked. The **maximum** is the advance notice a company requires during its busiest season. Of course, you can call even earlier if you are a long-term planner. Conversely, don't hesitate to call if your event is tomorrow; cancellations do occur, and some dates may be available on short notice. A wide range for lead time means that popular seasons (spring or summer for weddings, or Christmas and Valentine's Day) require earlier reservations.

One way to check out a business is to browse through its **portfolio**, a collection of samples of the vendor's work. Most professional caterers, florists, balloonists, photographers, and videographers can make one available to you. Another way to check out a vendor is to visit its store, studio, or restaurant. You should always call ahead to make an appointment for a consultation.

Do not hesitate to ask for **references**. You might have specific questions not answered in this guide, and a satisfied customer will be able to help you. Many brides and brides' mothers are very willing to share their experiences with you. Men, too, are eager to help. Also ask the prospective vendor for the names of other professionals with whom they work to also serve as references.

Ask to see a copy of the **business license, certificate of insurance,** and **health permit** (if the business deals with food). If you bring service people into your home, make sure the company pays **workman's compensation**; otherwise, you will be responsible for any injuries that may occur. The term **bonded** means that the company is licensed by the Labor Commission and has to put up a bond of $10,000 as extra insurance for the client if something goes wrong.

*Always check the **dates** of your contracts.* This will avoid disappointment and possible embarrassment.

Finally, ask as many questions as you can about a business and clarify every little detail. Minor issues, which you may consider unimportant, can become major irritations. *Never* assume that things will be done exactly as expected. Be very precise about the details, requirements, and refund clauses written into your signed contract. And make sure you get a copy. Also make sure that you record the name of the person in charge of your party or wedding. Meet with this person, make it clear that you will not accept substitutions or changes without your written approval, and add this as an addendum to the contract. Upon rare occasions, even respected companies have been known to send poorly trained, substitute personnel, thus ruining a once-in-a-lifetime event.

Note

Due to recent area code changes, please verify the listed telephone numbers with your local directory assistance if you encounter difficulties contacting a vendor.

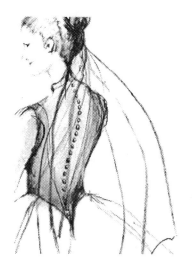

ATTIRE

NOTES

. . . .

. . . .

. . . .

. . . .

. . . .

. . . .

. . . .

. . . .

. . . .

. . . .

. . . .

. . . .

. . . .

. . . .

. . . .

. . . .

. . . .

INTRODUCTION

Y ou want to look your best on the very first day of the rest of your life. You also want to feel comfortable as you float through your wedding day. So finding the perfect dress that is "you" is naturally of utmost importance.

Where to start? First, set your wedding date, time, and location. Your dress should both reflect your personality and complement the theme of the day. Next, browse through wedding magazines to familiarize yourself with current trends and styles. And determine a budget to narrow down what can be an overwhelming selection. Dresses range from less than $400 to thousands of dollars. You may find that the ideal dress is out of your price range, but most salons can show you similar styles and silhouettes that fit your budget.

Before embarking on your shopping spree, find out the price ranges of dresses carried by a salon. Fully investigate the shop; even call the Better Business Bureau. Prices at bargain and discount houses are not always best; some discount places sell you copies of designer gowns. If you like a particular manufacturer's line, shop only at stores that can show you these gowns.

As you browse through bridal magazines, don't tear out the pages! Useful information, such as stores that carry a manufacturer's line, may be found elsewhere in the magazine. You can save time by calling a store to see if they carry a particular dress listed on a page of a specific issue of the publication.

Make an appointment with the salon's bridal consultant, allowing 1 to 1½ hours for your visit. Sample gowns are usually stocked in size 8 or 10 and usually run about a size smaller than retail sizing. Don't be discouraged; your bridal consultant can pin or hold the sample gowns up to you so that you can envision them in your size.

For more personalized service without feeling rushed, avoid evening or Saturday appointments at the salon. Bring along someone you trust, but don't confuse the issue with more than two people. Read store policy and contracts before signing. Get everything in writing: color, size, price, and any changes that need to be made. Most salons require 50% down at the time the order is placed with a no-refund or exchange policy.

Recommended Styles for Specific Body Types

- Small bust: a jewel neckline or boat neckline; horizontal pattern or ornamentation on upper bodice creates the illusion of a fuller bust line. Pleating or a sash waist also adds dimension.
- Big bust: sweetheart, princess (a line or seams, not a neckline), or portrait necklines minimize a large chest.
- Hourglass: a fuller skirt or a Basque waist will show off a slim waist and minimize hips.
- Thick waist: select a fabric that flows. An empire waist or a true waist; off the shoulders with an A-line skirt is usually the most flattering.

- Short waist: select an asymmetrical waistline, higher in the front than the back, which will lengthen torso, or a princess line to create a long silhouette.
- Pear-shape: avoid straight-across waistlines. Draw the eye up by selecting a style with lace, beads, or pattern on the bodice. Off-the-shoulder broadens shoulders and balances out hips.
- Full figure: select a V-neckline or sweetheart neckline and dropped waist; long tapered sleeves; veil with some height.
- Petite: simple, princess lines, sheath or A-lines with little ornamentation. Avoid drop or Basque waistlines. Add a veil with some volume.

Money Matters

Shop early! You'll have a greater chance of finding something within your price range. Also, keep in mind that you are shopping for your veil and accessories, and you'll need time for alterations which should be scheduled 6 to 8 weeks before the wedding. Special order gowns can take from 4 to 6 months to get. Informal dresses are often less expensive and take approximately 2 to 3 months to order. If your wedding is less than 4 months away, bridal salons may be able to place a rush order, usually at an additional 10% of the price of the dress.

Money Saving Tips

- Consider purchasing a sample or discontinued gown at a considerably reduced cost. Sample gowns can look like new once they are professionally dry-cleaned.
- Informal dresses are often less pricey and take approximately 2 to 3 months to order.

Bridal Galleria

(415) 346-6160
FAX: (415) 346-7523
bridal-1@pacbell.net
www.bridalgalleria.com

One Daniel Burnham Court (Van Ness at Post)
San Francisco, CA 94109

Contact: Grace Young

Service Area: Greater Bay Area and International

Specialties: Complete wedding center with the broadest selection of wedding lines, styles, and price ranges

Price Range: wedding gowns, $700 - $5,000
Extra Charges: shipping, alterations

Payment Terms: 50% deposit, balance due at first fitting	**Alterations:** on-site
	Bridesmaids: yes
Credit Cards: all credit cards	**Tuxedos:** yes
Lead Time: 4 - 6 months (rush orders can be accommodated)	**Accessories**: yes
	Headpieces: yes
Appointments: preferred	**Special Occasion:** yes

Thirteen years ago, business majors Grace and Alan ventured out to open a business that met the demands of brides. By pre-shopping the market and hand-selecting every gown, they maintain a clear vision of trends, style, tradition, and price range. Their good business sense keeps them one step ahead. As Grace says, "We keep reinventing ourselves each year." With their forward thinking, this progressive salon works closely with different designers and manufacturers to provide the latest in fashion and flexibility. The breadth of their inventory includes couture lines such as Lazaro, Christos, Alvina Valenta, and Yumi Katsura. Throughout the year, they host several trunk shows, showcasing the designer and the entire line of gowns – rare opportunities to meet the designer and try on gowns seen only in magazines.

This warm and inviting salon has large, fully mirrored private rooms for brides and a comfortable area for family and friends who wish to be a part of this bridal experience. Available for viewing are picture books of sample gowns and professional fashion show videos direct from the New York showrooms. For the bashful bride, they have satin changing robes in every room. They even have a complete tuxedo department with labels such as Donna Karan, Valentino, and Hugo Boss, among others. The bridesmaids' section has a full range of dresses as well as an open dressing area for large parties. Besides their team of highly experienced seamstresses, they have an on-site milliner to customize your headpiece. Bridal Galleria is also a good source for shoes and accessories, making them a specialty store in every look.

One of the late Herb Caen's columns mentions a bride's experience when she hung her gown on a sprinkler in her hotel room 2 hours before the wedding, causing the sprinkler to go off and damage the dress beyond repair. Bridal Galleria saved the day with a new gown, only minutes late for the ceremony. "We will turn things inside out to make a bride's day special!"

Clarissa's

(925) 930-0214
FAX: (925) 935-0630

1821 Mt. Diablo Boulevard
Walnut Creek, CA 94596

Contact: Despina or Elizabeth

Service Area: Greater Bay Area

Specialties: Selection of traditional and couture gowns with an emphasis on quality, silk and natural fabrics

Price Range: $700 - $4,000
Extra Charges: alterations, shipping

Payment Terms: 50% deposit, balance due at first fitting	**Alterations**: yes
	Bridesmaids: yes
Credit Cards: all credit cards	**Tuxedos:** no
Lead Time: 4 - 6 months (rush orders can be accommodated)	**Accessories:** yes
	Headpieces: yes
Appointments: preferred	**Special Occasion:** no

Mother and daughter relationships are very meaningful to Clarissa's bridal staff. Denise and Kathy, along with their mother Mary Ann, opened Clarissa's in 1983. The store's romantic name honored Mary Ann's mother, who inspired the wonderful relationship they share as mothers and daughters.

Respecting the bride's privacy, individual consultations are done in their large, 10' x 10' dressing rooms. The consultants pinpoint the bride's dreams and concerns, and help them through the "trying on" process. They are aware that brides often want to reflect the different sides of their personality during that walk down the aisle. The brides are shown gowns with different elements, combining fabric, necklines, and treatments, to reflect their individual style. Knowing that selecting the ideal gown is of utmost importance, the consultants strive to assist with this decision during every appointment. Many brides feel connected with Clarissa's longtime staff and stay in touch long after they have families of their own.

Clarissa's is proud to carry some of the best and brightest designers in the bridal industry. Amsale, Amalia, Carrera, Diamond, Galina, and Manale are a few of the elegant and creative designers found at Clarissa's. Denise, Kathy, and Mary Ann's commitment is not only to find the perfect gown but also to have a truly happy bride.

Happily Ever After
Custom Bridal Veils
(by appointment)
San Jose, CA

(408) 559-4979

Contact: Stacie Tamaki

Service Area: Greater Bay Area and beyond

Specialties: Exquisite custom headpieces, tiaras, elegant veils and treatments; origami cranes

Price Range: Average custom veil designs, $200 - $350; 1,000 origami cranes, from $1,500
Extra Charges: shipping, rush charges may apply

Payment Terms: 50% deposit, balance due at pickup
Credit Cards: no
Lead Time: 45 days
Appointments: yes

Bridesmaids: hair treatments
Tuxedos: no
Accessories: yes
Headpieces: yes
Special Occasion: hair treatments

Stacie stumbled into her true calling. After making a headpiece and veil for herself and her sister, she was commissioned a few years later to create six headpieces for a bridal fashion show. From there, the news of her veils was spread by word of mouth. The craftsmanship and quality finish in every headpiece is unbelievable. Stacie's collection of custom-designed headpieces ranges from delicate hand-beaded silk flowers or lace to complement the bride's wedding gown, to whimsical theme designs. Meticulously designed tiaras, many with an old-world feel, are sure to become heirlooms. They are finely detailed and delicate without being overpowering. "Accent pieces," describes Stacie.

Stacie pays the same attention to the veil treatment. Always keeping the bride in mind, Stacie consults on the different treatments and their effects. She may use a straight stitch on a satin edge for a finished look or use a zigzag stitch on a different color ribbon trim for a more playful look. My favorite is her fountain of tulle veils – a truly classic look. She uses a variety of tulles from shimmer to matte, and from white or ivory to diamond white to match the gown's color. She selects the appropriate comb and incorporates bobby-pin loops at various points to accommodate many different hair textures and styles. I particularly like the "fashion accessories" – individual pearls, crystals or beads on delicate branches of wire to be pinned in the hair as accents, perfect for any social occasion, for the unconventional bride, or to bring sparkle to a bridesmaid's hairstyle. The ring pillows and flower-girl baskets are original and scaled for the tiniest hands.

Her precise workmanship carries over to her origami cranes. In Japan, the crane symbolizes good health and long life. In America, the thousand cranes have become a symbol of good luck. Stacie uses a variety of papers and folds from 3" to a tiny ½". For impact, she strings them on gold thread and hangs them on parasols or wisteria wreaths. "The effect is magical."

Lily Dong Couture Bridal

(408) 255-8850
(415) 706-0266
FAX: (408) 777-8850
Lily@LilyDongCouture.com
www.LilyDongCouture.com

(by appointment)
Cupertino, CA

Contact: Lily Dong

Service Area: Greater Bay Area

Specialties: Exceptional custom wedding gowns to reflect your individual taste and vision

Price Range: consultations, $50 (applied to purchase); custom wedding gowns, from $2,000
Extra Charges: beadwork

Payment Terms: 1/3 of total labor, material, tax; 1/3 after muslin fitting, 1/3 at pickup
Bridesmaids: no
Credit Cards: no
Lead Time: from 3 months
Appointments: yes

Alterations: custom
Tuxedos: no
Accessories: made to match
Headpieces: made to match
Special Occasion: yes, including traditional Chinese "cheong sam" gowns

Much like a wedding ring, a wedding gown design should reflect the individual who wears it, as well as fit her perfectly. Lily Dong's artistry is prevalent in her exceptional couture gowns. Her elegant designs are created using a variety of silk fabrics, sometimes adding accent colors, and often capped with delicate hand beading. All of her creations start with a concept drawing of the "gown-to-be," and end with beautiful hand work.

Lily inherited her artistic ability from her father, a painter, and her skillfulness from her mother, a dressmaker, and fine-tuned it with a BFA. She began specializing in wedding gowns in 1991, with the goal to reinterpret the traditional wedding gown. At the beginning of every gown, Lily gets together with the bride for the initial consultation, after which the gown is designed and sketched out. She actively listens to the bride's description of her "dream" gown and takes into account her body proportions and personality, as well as the wedding style and location. "It's all about the bride," explains Lily. As the creator and editor, she is honest and helpful in translating a bride's verbal wishes into reality.

From the sketch, Lily creates a muslin test garment so the bride can conceptualize her one-of-a-kind gown. Lily shapes the muslin to the body regardless of proportion: petite, large busted, or any other shape that may be difficult to fit. "She is an expert at visual illusions and a master at accentuating the positives."

Many designs incorporate accessories into the look. Customized handbags, veils and shawls complete the ensemble. For brides with ties to the Far East, Lily also designs modernized chi-pao or cheong-sam. With a couture designer's aid, your choices are unlimited.

Marina Morrison Ltd.
Bridal Salon
30 Maiden Lane
San Francisco, CA 94108

(415) 984-9360
FAX: (415) 984-9370
MMLtdSalon@aol.com

Contact: Karen Metz

Service Area: International

Specialties: Well-defined collection of designer wedding gowns: modern, classic, well-made, understated

Price Range: from $1,800
Extra Charges: alterations, shipping

Payment Terms: 50% deposit, balance due at first fitting
Credit Cards: major credit cards
Lead Time: 3 - 9 months (rush orders by special arrangement)
Appointments: preferred

Alterations: yes
Bridesmaids: yes
Tuxedos: no
Accessories: yes
Headpieces: yes
Special Occasion: limited

Nestled in the midst of prestigious downtown San Francisco you will find the notable Maiden Lane. This tiny historic street is lined with independent stores with visions similar to Marina Morrison's: understated and elegant. Located in the Gump's building, this bridal salon is as ultra-chic as the gowns it stocks. Their defined tastes are consistent with the salon's location.

After many years with Priscilla of Boston, Karen Metz relocated to San Francisco in 1991, purchased Marina Morrison Ltd. on Sutter Street, and continued the reputation of fine wedding gown specialists. In 1997, she expanded the "gallery of wedding gowns" to an ultramodern studio in the Gump's building. Their gallery studio is crisp, clean and refined, reflective of the lines they carry. Emphasis is on careful placement of the waiting room mirrors, the largest of which is the backdrop to their runway stage. This mirror is positioned for the bride to see how the gown will flow when she is walking down the aisle. The other mirrors reflect how guests will see the bride on that special day.

Respecting individual approach to tradition and thoughtful follow-through is distinctive – their formula for success. They are selective about the lines they carry and are particular about selecting manufacturers who are different and special rather than all over the marketplace. Their distinctive hair jewelry, tiaras, bracelet bags and bridesmaid attire will surely set you aside from the ordinary bride.

The simple lines of the couture gowns are refined by the elegant fabrics and tailored construction. "The dress is really the frame for the person. When the bride walks out and hears that audible gasp from family and friends, it reassures the bride that she has made the right decision," explains Karen. Their gowns are simply exquisite!

Miss D's of San Carlos

(650) 593-2323
(650) 593-2769
FAX: (650) 593-2411
missds@prodigy.net

1179 San Carlos Avenue
San Carlos, CA 94070

Contact: Heidi Baldauf

Service Area: Greater Bay Area, International

Specialties: Extensive collection of well-edited and defined bridal gowns and private custom collection

Price Range: gowns, $900 - $5,000
Extra Charges: alterations, shipping

Payment Terms: 50% deposit, balance due at first fitting
Credit Cards: Visa, MasterCard
Lead Time: 4 - 6 months (rush orders accommodated)
Appointments: preferred

Alterations: on-site
Bridesmaids: yes
Tuxedos: no
Accessories: yes
Headpieces: yes
Special Occasion: yes

Established in 1939, Miss D's of San Carlos served as a specialty party and bridal store for *Peninsula Living.* Just as bridal was falling out of the department stores and into a specialty, Miss D's had the foresight to expand their bridal department. In 1970, Miss Dorinson ("Miss D") sold the business to Heidi's father, a place where Heidi grew up and worked while going to school. In 1980, Heidi worked full-time, bringing designs and sketches to life by creating her own Heidi line.

Heidi's designer eye captures individual bridal styles. A design that dazzled my traditional sense was one of Heidi's conceptual designs, trimmed in a customized Alencon beaded lace with rich beads instead of sequins for a traditional, yet stylish look. Her designs are for the bride with a clear vision of what she wants but is unable to find. They stock sizes for any bride, petite or full-figure, from $1,200 to $2,500. The bride gets to try on "the fit" and can then have the fabric, neckline, and skirt customized to make it her own. One satisfied bride joyfully remarked, "Miss D's combined the top of one dress with the skirt of another, added roses made of organza and silk to match the bodice, and created a dress sure to be used for several family weddings."

Miss D's inventory of bridge lines, "well-defined and fashion-edited styles you are comfortable wearing" and toned-down couture styles, "molded-to-wear fashions" offer brides a distinct look in a comfortable price range. They have great styles at great prices. "We are on the forefront of fashion without going overboard," says Heidi.

Trudys Brides

(408) 377-1987
FAX: (408) 371-0425
www.trudysbrides.com

1875 S. Bascom Avenue, Suite 134
Campbell, CA 95008

Contact: Trudy or Steven Blechman

Service Area: Greater Bay Area

Specialties: Enormous collection of bridal gowns; extensive selection of keepsakes, gifts and accessories, including tiaras

Price Range: $400 - $2,500
Extra Charges: alterations, shipping

Payment Terms: 50% deposit, balance due at pickup
Credit Cards: major credit cards
Lead Time: 3 - 6 months (rush orders available)
Appointments: preferred

Alterations: yes
Bridesmaids: yes
Tuxedos: no
Accessories: large selection
Headpieces: yes
Special Occasion: special order only

"Creating memories for 25 years." Trudys has based their reputation on providing a comfortable, welcoming environment for brides, their families, and friends. A family-owned and operated business, Trudys opened its doors in 1974 as a special occasion store in the Pruneyard Shopping Center in Campbell. In 1978, by popular demand, Trudys expanded their bridal department to 50% of their inventory. In 1980, Trudys Brides relocated to another site in the center, specializing in bridal wear with tremendous success.

Their enormous collection of fine bridal gifts and accessories is only surpassed by the volume of gowns sold at great values. They have one of the largest inventories of the latest wedding gowns on display for brides to see and touch, including samples for the larger bride. For optimum, personalized customer service, Trudys works by appointment. With the constant influx of new gowns, Trudys is always reducing the prices of their other samples. Brides can purchase their ideal gown off the rack at tremendous savings or special order it from the latest designer selections.

"It's very festive. People bring their family and friends. A social gathering," sums up Steven. They have a separate area with personal consultants versed in measurements to service bridesmaids. "They are our future brides. We treat them like gold," says Trudy. Letters of appreciation attest to their quality of service. They pride themselves on their organized system of quality assurance and control over tracking shipments, inspecting incoming orders, and following up with their brides. "Trudys offers value without compromise."

Unique Bride

(650) 347-7001
FAX: (650) 342-4515
www.uniquebride.com

1209 Howard Avenue
Burlingame, CA 94010

Contact: Peggy Andrews

Service Area: Greater Bay Area and International

Specialties: Understated, elegant collection of sophisticated bridal gowns in a remarkably friendly atmosphere

Price Range: wedding gowns from $1,000
Extra Charges: alterations

Payment Terms: 50% deposit, balance due upon dress arrival
Credit Cards: Visa, MasterCard
Lead Time: 3 - 6 months (rush by special arrangement)
Appointments: preferred

Alterations: on-site
Bridesmaids: yes
Tuxedos: no
Accessories: yes
Headpieces: yes
Special Occasion: yes

Since their opening in 1983, the Unique Bride has built their reputation as an upscale, customer service bridal salon in the heart of Burlingame. With their stock of refined wedding gowns, the Unique Bride caters to the savvy bride with discriminating taste. From the initial consultation to the final pickup, the Unique Bride prides itself on customer service. Their knowledgeable and spirited staff gives the designer interior a warm and friendly atmosphere. They are passionate about their gowns and go the extra mile to serve their clients. Their veteran seamstresses are all trained in altering, pressing and customizing couture gowns. "I couldn't have done it without my staff," comments Peggy.

After shopping for her out-of-town sisters' wedding dresses, Peggy Andrews, a nurse practitioner for 8 years, saw a great void in the market for alternative wedding dresses. "Something less traditional," Peggy recalls. In 1983, Peggy opened an 800-square-foot store on Howard Avenue. With the guidance and direction of bridal industry consultant Rhio Esterline, Peggy developed her niche in the bridal industry, expanding to a 1,600-square-foot space next door a few years later. In 1988, Peggy purchased the building across the street, giving the Unique Bride 5,000 square feet of retail space. Peggy, who grew up in Millbrae, is very active in the community, participating in fashion shows for the local churches and temples.

The selection of gowns ranges from elegantly traditional to uniquely on the cutting edge of fashion. Their reputation for sophisticated elegance and their understanding of fashions, many with traditional undertones, attracts the discriminating bride with a sense of style. Their unique look carries over to their large debutante business. Clients consistently comment about the sales staff's friendly and pleasantly honest opinions. "They have the nicest staff anywhere." "Great advice and ideas." The Unique Bride for the unique individual with discriminating taste.

National Gown Cleaners and Archival Products

(by appointment)
San Jose, CA

(800) 700-GOWN
(408) 241-3490
(650) 962-1997
FAX: (408) 241-3499
christine@nationalgown.com
www.nationalgown.com

Contact: Christine Morrissey

Service Area: International

Specialties: Hard-to-clean gowns, restorations, and products for conservation and preservation

Pricing: from $175
Extra Charges: alterations, pickup, delivery, shipping

Payment Terms: 50% deposit, balance due on pickup or delivery
Credit Cards: Visa, MasterCard
Alterations: yes
Gown Preservation: yes

Lead Time: 2 - 8 weeks
Rental: no
Samples sold: no
Consignment: no

From preserving an heirloom gown to cleaning and restoring a treasured keepsake, National Gown Cleaners brings museum preservation methods and products to the public. Christine is a private textile conservator and dry-cleaning consultant. The company began as a family business, providing cleaning, preservation, conservation, and restoration supplies to the museum and private textile conservation industries. In 1978, Christine, the company's president, incorporated a way of bringing to the public the fine art of preservation and conservation. Since the 1980's, National Gown Cleaners, headquartered in San Jose, has been nationally known for their expertise in cleaning, preserving, and restoring treasured, hard-to-clean attire. Their international sales offices are located in Switzerland and Japan.

National Gown Cleaners' and Christine's business philosophy is integrity and honesty. Both are recommended by many garment manufacturers and bridal salons, and have been featured in many magazines and newspapers, including *Elegant Bride*, *Western Cleaner and Launderer*, *California Bride*, and *The Wedding Sourcebook*. Their customers rave: "I still can't believe the magic you did on my gown." "Thank you for taking on the job to restore my grandmother's Chinese robe." "What can I possibly say that would measure my gratitude for the beautiful job you did in restoring my mother's gown for my daughter's wedding?"

Christine's goal is to educate the consumer. While not inexpensive, clients value the detailed process of preserving a gown. Even when working with celebrity, royalty, and priceless attire, Christine notes that all gowns have sentimental value. They use a Stoddard solvent, usually used for fur and leather. They carefully cover beads and protect delicate, hand-painted garments (such as kimonos) with muslin. These cautions restrict the agitation normally associated with cleaning. For gowns already cleaned, the company offers a variety of archival products.

BEVERAGES

NOTES

. . . .
. . . .
. . . .
. . . .
. . . .
. . . .
. . . .
. . . .
. . . .
. . . .
. . . .
. . . .
. . . .
. . . .
. . . .
. . . .
. . . .

INTRODUCTION

Traditionally, alcoholic beverages were considered a "must" for a good party, and there is seldom a wedding toast without champagne. As non-alcoholic beverages have become more and more popular, beverage companies now offer a wide variety.

Beverage services operate like caterers. A bar or beverage table is set up, and alcoholic and non-alcoholic drinks are poured for the guests. These services bring everything they need, clean up afterwards, and take back all closed bottles. Consumption planning is included in the service. Experienced companies have well-trained personnel, a liquor license, and carry at least $1,000,000 insurance. To be on the safe side, ask to see the license and proof of insurance.

It often happens that when the champagne is already poured for the toast, several glasses may go untouched, which results in both wastefulness and unnecessary expense. Ask the waiters to pour only for those who request it. Sparkling cider is a good substitute for people who don't drink alcohol.

Be creative about the beverages you serve. How about **espresso** or **cappuccino** with dessert instead of plain coffee?

The distinction between **host bar** and **no-host bar** is in who pays. At a "no-host bar," the guest pays the server directly for each order, as in a public bar. At a "host bar," the host makes payment arrangements with the beverage service beforehand. Applied charges can vary: per consumption, per person, or per person per hour.

Money Matters

Prices depend on the quality of the beverage. The cost is higher for premium beverages and specialty labels.

Extra Charges: While plastic cups are always included in the price, glassware is often an extra charge. A significant amount of ice may also incur an extra charge.

Money Saving Tips

- Ask the bartender to pour champagne only for those who request it.
- Offer champagne only at cocktails.
- Serve only a soft bar: beer wine, champagne, soft drinks, mineral waters.
- Have guests toast with the beverage they are served during dinner.

Bartenders Unlimited

(888) 411-4BAR
(415) 454-3731
FAX: (415) 454-6464
bars4you@bartnder.batnet.com
www.batnet.com/bartnder

1281 Andersen Drive, Suites I & J
San Rafael, CA 94901

Contact: Ward Thomas

Service Area: California

Specialties: California's oldest and largest complete beverage caterers

Pricing: $550 min.; prices based on number of people and style of service
Extra Charges: travel beyond Greater Bay Area may apply

Payment Terms: 75% deposit, balance due 25 days prior to event	**Delivery/Pickup:** n/a
	Bar Equipment: complete
Credit Cards: no	**Bartender:** yes
Lead Time: 24 hrs. to 2 years	

Established in 1979, Bartenders Unlimited is not only California's oldest and largest complete beverage caterer, but also a very distinguished and trusted company. Besides their liquor license, they carry $2 million of insurance, including personal and liquor liability, and property damage. Their elegantly hand-crafted wood bars with various accents include sponge-painted champagne bars with black granite tops, black faux marble bars and polished oak bars, all beautifully maintained and appropriate for any setting. Their large stock of glassware, equipment, and supplies allows them to provide complete service within 24 hours notice.

From intimate events of 10 to catered events of 30,000 plus, such as Super Bowl XXXIII, Bartenders Unlimited's goal is to provide the best possible service. Owner Thomas Ward's approach is hands-on: he works or visits over 60% of the 700 events they do annually. I complimented Thomas on his endless energy, to which he replied, "I thrive off this stuff. I love being at the events, visiting with clients and our staff. The staff makes Bartenders Unlimited stand out. They're fantastic and incredibly talented – the nucleus of the company." All the events I have had the pleasure of attending are always more than adequately staffed with knowledgeable and courteous bartenders who are always well groomed and formally dressed.

True to their name, the range of beverage services is unlimited: Top Shelf Hosted Full Bar; Premium Hosted Full Bar; Moderate Hosted Full Bar; Beer, Wine and Soda Bar; Picnic Service; No-Host Full Bar; Non-Alcoholic Service; Service and Equipment or Staff Only; Liqueur Package; Blender Drinks; Coffee Drinks; Espresso/Cappuccino and Coffee Service; Micro Draft Beer Service; Martini and Cigar Service; even a Sake Bar Service. Complete consultation is part of their service; full tuxedo or special costuming is optional. Bartenders Unlimited doesn't merely provide and dispense beverages, they create a menu and package designed to enhance your event.

CAKES - DESSERTS

NOTES

. . . .

. . . .

. . . .

. . . .

. . . .

. . . .

. . . .

. . . .

. . . .

. . . .

. . . .

. . . .

. . . .

. . . .

. . . .

. . . .

. . . .

INTRODUCTION

A cake is always a great dessert for a party and is nearly always a "must" for a wedding—a perfect conclusion to a festive day. During the last ten years I've noticed a trend towards more lavishly decorated cakes. Hand-crafted chocolate flowers, ribbons and pearls, colorful gum-paste flowers, or pulled sugar art enhance today's cakes. If you are planning to use live flower decoration, talk to your baker about coordinating the flowers with your florist. To alleviate concern about the presence of systemic insecticides, some bakers take extra precautions to wrap the stem and flower parts that come into contact with the cake. Alternatives are to decorate with silk flowers or fresh fruit.

Check the **serving size** with the baker. If the cake's tiers vary in flavor, you might want to order a bit more of each as your guests may want to taste each one. Multi-tiered and more complicated wedding cakes require **support pieces**. Bakers request a deposit for these pieces and usually ask that they be returned. On the other hand, more and more bakers use non-returnable items. Bakers often carry a selection of figurines for **cake top decoration**. **Cake knives** are generally not supplied by bakers but are available from caterers and sometimes florists.

Wedding coordinators often view the wedding cake as a focal point and feel they should be beautifully decorated. I've seen "cake table-scapes" with specialty linen, tulle, ribbons, bows, fruit and flowers. For less elaborate decoration, the bridesmaids' bouquets draped around the cake make for a simple, yet attractive table.

Money Matters

Cake prices vary quite a bit and depend mainly on the ingredients and the amount of work required for the decoration with frosting and flowers. Wedding cakes require delivery and setup fees which are most often charged separately. Some bakers prefer to let the florist handle the live flower decoration; others decorate with the flowers provided by the florist. Sometimes the decoration is included in the cake price, sometimes not, so check pricing carefully. A low, initial price might well turn out to be quite high when all the extra charges are added.

The difference in prices depends not only on the ingredients but also on the decoration, which is very time-consuming.

Money Saving Tips

- Supplement a smaller decorated wedding cake with sheet cakes.
- Remember that children don't eat as much as you think!
- Coordinate the serving size with the caterer and baker.

Aki's Bakery
The Cake Specialist
355 Meridian Avenue
San Jose, CA 95126

(408) 287-5404
FAX: (408) 287-0660

Contact: Penny Tom

Service Area: Greater South Bay

Specialties: Decorated cakes and tiered wedding cakes; dessert buffets

Price (per serving): $1.85 - $3.75
Extra Charges: delivery

Payment Terms: payment in full 2 weeks prior to event
Credit Cards: Visa, MasterCard, Discover
Lead Time: 2 weeks to 3 months

Tasting: yes, Wednesday and Saturday
Return of Cake Support: within 1 week
Fresh Flower Decoration: supplied by florist

"The cake was very moist," and "I got lots of compliments," are typical comments that I heard from brides who had ordered their wedding cakes from Aki's Bakery. Established in 1963, the bakery became famous for wedding and special occasion cakes. Large display boxes are filled with baked goods with wonderful aromas. Principal cake flavors are vanilla, chocolate, poppy seed, carrot, and almond, with fillings of lemon, custard, raspberry, tiramisu, and chocolate truffle. Icings are buttercream, vanilla fluff, and chocolate ganache. Aki bakes all the cakes himself. He is also famous for his large selection of cakes for birthdays, anniversaries, and showers.

Penny Tom, Aki's daughter, is a trained wedding consultant and can help with cake selection. She also experiments with new cake flavors and designs. The newest addition is their white- and dark-chocolate-wrapped, special occasion cake. Penny is also open to new ideas. She showed me a picture of a sophisticated-looking wedding cake, on which sat a cello made of sugar. I also saw one of Aki's beautifully decorated cakes, with peach and white garlands and adorned with pearls and tulle.

Available for rent is large selection of cake ornaments, fountains, unique cake stands, and staircases. Fresh or silk flowers are not included in the price.

Cake tasting is held on Wednesdays and Saturdays.

Amandine
Confiserie Suisse & Tea Room
898 Santa Cruz Avenue
Menlo Park, CA 94025

(650) 325-4776
(Phone & FAX)
www.tales.com/CA/Amandine

Contact: Ernst or Annegret Wiedmer

Service Area: Greater Bay Area

Specialties: Wedding and birthday cakes; dessert buffets; chocolate candies; petits fours; savory appetizers

Price (per serving): $1.50 - $3.50
Extra Charges: delivery, glass pedestals

Payment Terms: $100 deposit; balance due 2 weeks prior to event
Credit Cards: Visa, MasterCard
Lead Time: 1 month

Tasting: by appointment
Return of Cake Support: when convenient
Fresh Flower Decoration: supplied by florist

Ernst Wiedmer and his wife, Annegret, came to Menlo Park in 1982 and opened Andre's, their bakery and teahouse on Santa Cruz Avenue. Although the name was changed to Amandine in 1994, the owners and their great-tasting products remained the same. In honor of their homeland, their baked goods are made with the freshest ingredients of authentic Swiss recipes. Ernst believes that quality and his many years of experience contribute to the high value of his products, which are well worth the prices.

Today, more and more customers are enjoying his tarts, filled with mocha rum, chocolate-raspberry, or whipped cream. For weddings and parties, Ernst offers two types of his well-known Tuxedo Torte. One is a buttercream torte with mocha, rum, lemon, chocolate, chocolate-raspberry, pistachio, or carrot. The other torte is made with strawberry, kirsch, or whipped cream. Both are topped with shavings of white or dark chocolate. His new Scroll Torte is designed for Bar/Bat Mitzvahs. In the shape of a Torah scroll, it is decorated with dark chocolate and marzipan. Other cakes are available on request and can be frosted with buttercream and embellished with marzipan roses or sugar flowers. Ernst leaves the live flower decoration to your florist.

I tasted one of his cakes at a friend's wedding. It looked so appetizing, tasted so delicious, and received many compliments. Ernst's delicacies, including authentic chocolate truffles, candies, petits fours, and savory appetizers are available in his tearoom in Menlo Park.

Bakers Caro & Kano

(415) 552-8922
(415) 552-8988

2161 Third Street
San Francisco, CA 94107

Contact: Joseph Caro

Service Area: Greater Bay Area

Specialties: Gourmet, custom-designed wedding cakes

Price (per serving): from $4.50
Extra Charges: delivery and setup beyond San Francisco; deposit for equipment
                    and cake support, linen rental

Payment Terms: 20% deposit, balance   **Tasting:** yes
                    due 2 weeks prior to event   **Return of Cake Support:** 2 weeks
Credit Cards: major credit cards   **Fresh Flower Decoration:** yes
Lead Time: 2 months

These bakers are San Francisco's latest success story. They began their business in 1992 and, after only three years were featured on the cover of *Cooking Light* magazine and in a newspaper article, and were invited to the Gump's and Macy's wedding shows. They are on most of the lists of major upscale wedding facilities in the city.

With so much publicity you would think their prices were sky-high. Not true. They are true experts in the art of providing the bride with the cake she has always dreamed of while working within her budget. Many ideas also come from their elaborate portfolio, in which you can view beautiful cake designs for inspiration. Decorations of fresh or delicate gum paste flowers, pearls and ribbons speak to their limitless creativity. My favorite design is a fondant cake which they designed for the opening of the new Gump's department store. They sculpted a rose pattern "in reverse" into the fondant, then lightly dusted it with a shimmering gold leaf. Joseph has a background in art and developed his baking and decorating skills as an apprentice to his father at The Waldorf Astoria in New York. Joseph's partner David often draws upon his many years as an engineer to help with the structural design of a wedding cake.

I've had firsthand experience with one of their creations. After the tasting, we agreed on the Belgian Chocolate Torte, wrapped in marzipan, with layers of chocolate mousse and fresh raspberries. The cake, decorated to coordinate with the party theme, looked so elegant. "Happy Birthday" was written very tastefully in gold on a red ribbon. Everyone loved the cake, and some friends even told me later that, although they usually don't eat cake, this one was so delicious that they couldn't resist.

Cake Express
Specializing in Tiered Bridal Cakes
2480 Almaden Expressway
San Jose, CA 95125

(408) 267-9777
(Phone & FAX)

Contact: Cero Anthony

Service Area: Greater Bay Area

Specialties: Wedding and anniversary cakes, sculptured cakes, white chocolate wrap and gum paste flowers; matching corporate logos

Price (per serving): $2.20 - $3.00
Extra Charges: nominal delivery charge

Payment Terms: 10% deposit, balance due 2 weeks prior to event
Credit Cards: no
Lead Time: to 2 months

Tasting: yes
Return of Cake Support: within 30 days
Fresh Flower Decoration: supplied by florist

After taking courses in professional baking and cake decoration, including classes at the California Culinary Academy, Cero Anthony was hooked and opened his bakery in 1980. He exhibits his cake creations and personally hosts free cake-tastings for prospective clients in a showroom adjacent to the kitchen from which wonderful aromas emanate. I know how good they are from personal experience.

Cero's specialties are his fancy decorations, such as his Royal English Crown cake. Its special, ornate sugar icing is very complex. His other frostings are made of butter cream, vanilla mousse, and fondant. He can create basket weave and lattice work effects, and can add bridges, staircases, and fountains. He comes up with at least one new design every year. His 1994 cake decoration was a pleated design. His 1995 creation was a double-burnt almond wedding cake, with a caramelized custard filling and decorated with toasted almond slivers, white chocolate curls and a ribbon matching the color scheme of the wedding. White-chocolate-wrapped cakes and gum paste flowers are two of his newest specialties. My favorite is an elegant three-tiered wedding cake with ivory and white rolled fondant. Lacy ribbons and calla lilies cascaded from the top. Cero's most popular cakes are white, marble, chocolate, chocolate chip, poppy seed, carrot, banana nut, and strawberry cream. Fillings are vanilla, chocolate, mocha, fudge, cream cheese, liqueurs, and fresh fruit.

Free cake-tasting is usually held on Tuesday afternoons and evenings. If you want the cake decoration to include fresh flowers, Cero will work with the florist to create the design.

Cakework
Custom Wedding and Party Cakes
613 York Street
San Francisco, CA 94110

(415) 821-1333
FAX: (415) 821-0200
C@cakework.com
www.cakework.com

Contact: Cecile Gady

Service Area: Greater Bay Area and beyond

Specialties: Beautiful custom-designed cakes in unusual designs for weddings and other occasions; wedding favors

Price (per serving): $4.50 - $10
Extra Charges: delivery, refundable deposit for cake support

Payment Terms: 50% deposit, balance due prior to event
Credit Cards: no
Lead Time: 1 - 6 months

Tasting: yes
Return of Cake Support: within 1 month
Fresh Flower Decoration: supplied by florist

Cecile, another artist who turned to food, is one of the most often recommended bakers in the area. As a former sculptor with a passion for baking, these two talents came together naturally. While others offer sheet cakes decorated with pumpkins, Cecile makes cakes that look like real pumpkins. For a rock collector, she created river rocks and displayed them on a piece of slate. On my last visit, she was working on a sculpture of the Roman Forum, with its crumbling walls and exposed masonry for an awards dinner. It was carried in on a litter covered with dark red velvet cloth and gold tassels. Her new kitchen is filled with wonderful aromas and displays an exquisite wall design. My favorite is her tangy orange cake with dark chocolate custard and bittersweet chocolate mousse. My friend, who is a former baker, could not stop raving about her cakes, tasting so much "like Grandma used to make."

Cecile's Hawaiian white chocolate cakes, decorated with colorful chocolate plumeria flowers, are fun to look at, and the white chocolate-pleated cakes, with chocolate roses and ribbons spilling down the tiers, are just breathtaking. Her prices are not inexpensive for such work-intensive cakes, but she tries hard to accommodate her customers. Prospective customers can schedule cake tastings and a browse through her portfolio.

Cakework has become quite famous over the past few years. *Town & Country* magazine recently featured Cecile's banana truffle cake in its wedding section. She has appeared on television, was featured in *San Francisco Focus* magazine, and some of her cakes can be seen in Williams-Sonoma's wedding planner.

Elegant Cheese Cakes™
Wedding Cakes & Other Fine Delectables
103-2 Harvard Avenue
Half Moon Bay, CA 94019

(650) 728-2248
FAX: (650) 728-2911
www.elegantcheesecakes.com

Contact: Susan Morgan

Service Area: Greater Bay Area and beyond;
select items can be shipped all over U.S.

Specialties: Original, chocolate, sculpted wedding and celebration cakes, done in cheesecake
and traditional cake flavors; chocolate favors, place cards, and centerpieces

Price (per serving): from $6.50
Extra Charges: delivery and setup or shipping

Payment Terms: $100 non-ref. deposit,
balance due 10 days prior to event
Credit Cards: no
Lead Time: 2 days to 9 months

Tasting: yes, by appointment
Return of Cake Support: within a week
Fresh Flower Decoration: provided by florist

I first interviewed Susan shortly after she started in business. Now, 10 years later, she is known throughout the Bay Area for her fabulous wedding and special occasion cakes. Since 1995, some of her individual items, such as truffle box cakes, place cards, and favors, have been available by order year round from the Horchow and Neiman Marcus catalog and shipped from coast to coast. Susan and her cakes have been featured more recently in *Bon Appetit, Bridal Guide, Modern Bride, Bargain Weddings* and *Victoria Magazine.* Clients describe her work as "outstanding" and "unbelievable."

I have tasted Susan's wonderful cakes several times, and was particularly impressed by two of her most fabulous creations. One was a centerpiece done in a Wine Country theme for an event coordinators' conference: an open picnic basket from which spilled all kinds of picnic items. It looked so real that everyone was in awe. For a BRO party, Susan made one of the most opulent cakes I've ever seen: the 4-tiered, white chocolate cake was decorated with irregular chocolate pleats, large and medium size garden roses touched with opalescent dust for a dewy look, draped ribbons and bows edged with gold, and a string of pearls cascading from the top. Next to this stood her signature cake, the miniature "day-after" cake she delivers to every bride and groom. Pictures in her portfolio show cakes in the shapes of billiard sets and tennis rackets used as centerpieces for Bar Mitzvahs. She made a carousel wedding cake for a wedding at the Carousel Museum.

Susan is very conscious of quality. She will not make more than 3 wedding cakes per weekend to ensure freshness. She schedules tastings and appointments (Thursdays through Saturdays) so that "my clients get to taste the fresh product they will get on their wedding day."

Have Your Cake

(650) 873-8488

Distinctive & Delicious

www.ByRecOnly.com/haveyourcake

308 Alida Way
So. San Francisco, CA 94080

Contact: Maralyn Tabatsky

Service Area: Greater Bay Area

Specialties: Wedding and custom-designed celebration cakes; dessert buffets;
sugar and chocolate artistry; Kosher kitchen

Price (per serving): $4.00 - $8.00
Extra Charges: delivery, fresh flowers

Payment Terms: 50% part. ref. deposit,
balance due 10 days prior to event
Credit Cards: no
Lead Time: 1 week to 6 months

Tasting: yes
Return of Cake Support: within 1 week
Fresh Flower Decoration: yes

One of Maralyn's signature cakes, a buttercream cake, was pictured on the cover of the previous edition of the guide. Her rolled fondant creations, embellished with custom-crafted sugar flowers, wrapped with real lace; her Australian-style embroidery work interwoven with ribbons, and her cakes with quilting and art deco designs certainly added a new dimension to my cake experience. Decorated with real, chocolate, or sugar flowers, her work is always so tasteful and elegant. As I browsed through her extensive portfolio with all her wonderful desserts, I had a hard time deciding which one I liked best. Among the pictures is a haunted castle for a Halloween wedding and a re-creation of a Buddhist temple in Nepal where the couple met. Another cake looked like a chocolate Chagall painting whose theme was also used for the invitations.

In September 1995, after more than nine years in business, Maralyn moved to her new Kosher kitchen where she bakes under rabbinical supervision. A few months later, she hosted an open house where I and many other event professionals indulged in her delicacies. Chocolate truffle, Italian cream and almond cakes seemed to be the favorites, along with her cheesecakes, a variety of petits fours, fruit tartlets, swan profiteroles, cookies, and chocolate-dipped strawberries.

Maralyn inherited her passion for baking from her mother. She bakes every cake from scratch and is happy to use a family recipe or to look for a special one. Supplementary sheet cake is offered for larger parties to keep within the budget. She believes in a very thorough consultation and works closely with the bride and groom, doing her best to coordinate the cake with the wedding theme. Her clients commented: "The best I've ever had, and I got so many compliments from my friends," and "Maralyn is so accommodating." She is also highly respected by other event professionals.

Marjolaine French Pastries

(408) 867-2226
FAX: (408) 379-7210

14441 Big Basin Way
Saratoga, CA 95070

Contact: Margaret Novak or Lynne Morrison

Service Area: Greater Bay Area

Specialties: Party and wedding cakes; fresh French pastries
(croissants, eclairs, petits fours); breads

Price (per serving): $3 - $5
Extra Charges: delivery, fresh flower decoration

Payment Terms: $100 non-ref. deposit,
balance due 2 weeks prior to event
Credit Cards: Visa, MasterCard
Lead Time: 1 - 3 months

Tasting: yes
Return of Cake Support: within 1 week
Fresh Flower Decoration: yes

When Margaret returned from France, she had such a hard time finding decent croissants in the area that she decided to open her own French bakery. Marjolaine French Pastries in downtown Saratoga has been in business since 1983, and now Margaret leaves the business of running the bakery to her husband Joe. She manages her wedding flower business and loves to custom-design the wedding cakes to coordinate with the wedding florals. She remains available for consultations and handling complicated designs. Marjolaine was recommended by another well-known baker who considers the bakery to be among the finest in the Bay Area. A French teacher at the Alliance Française takes her classes to Marjolaine because she considers it quite authentically French.

Marjolaine offers a wide variety of fine cakes: chocolate, almond, vanilla genoise, carrot, hazelnut, Devil's food, and spice, as well as cheese and pound cakes. The fillings are white and dark chocolate, berries, lemon and espresso mousses, Grand Marnier whipped cream with fresh strawberries, and almond frasier with apricot preserves or fresh strawberries. Icings include buttercream, whipped cream, white and dark chocolate ganache, rolled fondant, chocolate curls, and marzipan. Their latest creation, tiramisu, is very popular. Only the best ingredients are used, such as pure butter and fresh eggs, and many are imported from Europe. Marjolaine's portfolios display all kinds of cake shapes and decorations. One of their specialties is petits fours, a small cake dessert, which is a wonderful treat for an elegant party. Make sure to get some of their delicious French pastries, the aroma from which tantalizes you on your approach. Sample tasting (5 cakes) is held on Saturdays by appointment only!

Their other retail location is at 134 Main Street in Los Altos (650/949-2226). They also have a production kitchen in Campbell.

Montclair Baking
Wedding and Special Occasion Cakes
2220 Mountain Blvd., Suite 140
Oakland, CA 94611

(510) 530-8052
FAX: (510) 530-5771

Contact: Cheryl Lew

Service Area: Greater Bay Area

Specialties: Quality handcrafted baked goods and wedding cakes; petits fours, pies; dessert buffets

Price (per serving): $3.00 - $8.00
Extra Charges: delivery; fresh flowers; hand-molded, pulled sugar and gold leaf

Payment Terms: 25% deposit, balance due 10 days prior to event
Credit Cards: Visa, MasterCard
Lead Time: 1 month to 1 year

Tasting: yes
Return of Cake Support: within 1 month
Fresh Flower Decoration: yes

Chef, owner and operator of Montclair Baking, Cheryl Lew is a self-taught baker with a BA in Asian-American Studies. She and her dedicated staff pride themselves on their "quality handcrafted baked goods made with great care and joy." Anyone who visits Cheryl's quaint Oakland neighborhood bakery, with its fashionable, custom wedding cakes and award-studded wall, will surely agree.

Using only the freshest seasonal and organic fruits for her fillings from local farmers' markets, Cheryl's integrity is never compromised. To ensure quality, she limits production to between five and ten cakes per weekend. She meets personally with each client, devoting an abundance of time and expert advice. Up to 20 sample choices are offered, all lusciously light and each numbered with their descriptive flavor. She recommends taking them home to share with family.

Cheryl finishes her cakes with chocolate, marzipan, buttercream and fondant, handcrafted beautifully with sculpted bows, ruffles, laces, and flowers for various themes. She is one of the few Bay Area bakers who decorates with pulled sugar. Her talent at incorporating the client's visions into the design was evident in an orchid cake for an artist and poet that utilized their orchid haiku as the overall, symbolic wedding theme.

One of my favorite designs is the "Fred and Ginger" cake, minutely detailed, including a top hat, veil, and scarf of fondant. This cake was among those that earned Cheryl national recognition at the Domaine Carneros Ultimate Wedding Cake Contest (1994,1996). In 1994, the *San Francisco Chronicle* featured the bakery as one of its "Bakers Dozen" best bakeries in the Greater Bay Area. In 1995, Cheryl was recognized as one of the Bay Area's noted wedding cake designers by the same publication, and was featured on the cover of *Bay Food* as one of the Bay Area's best pastry chefs.

Nancy's Fancies
Fine Natural Baking
765A Old County Road
San Carlos, CA 94070

(650) 591-8867

Contact: Nancy Kux

Service Area: Greater Bay Area

Specialties: Customized cakes and desserts, elaborately decorated;
individual attention to each client

Price (per serving): $3.25 - $8.00
Extra Charges: travel beyond 30 miles, $50 ref. deposit for cake supports

Payment Terms: $50 deposit, balance
due 1 week prior to event
Credit Cards: no
Lead Time: 3 - 6 months

Tasting: yes
Return of Cake Support: within 1 week
Fresh Flower Decoration: supplied by florist

Like so many great bakers, Nancy started baking when she was 12 years old. After a detour to elementary school teaching, she decided to start her own baking business and is now one of the highly recommended bakers in the area. She uses only the best ingredients: real eggs, fresh, unsalted butter, and cream cheese. She is well known for her extensive use of fresh fruit toppings.

We sit in her kitchen and talk. As she shows me her latest work, I am surrounded by the faint noises of her helpers and the smell of butter and sugar. Cakes are stacked like packages. An art deco cake is done with 18-karat gold, white and dark chocolate curls, designs in European buttercream, differently colored fondant, and marzipan frosting. The handmade flower decoration is made with piped buttercream, fondant and marzipan flowers. Nancy's specialty is custom-designed cakes. She will copy family recipes and even incorporate wedding dress designs into the frosting. I fell in love with a castle-shaped cake with golden turrets. Her fresh flower decoration complements the cake, and she will even go so far as to recommend the right tablecloth for the cake table. All of these details are learned from a thorough consultation with her clients, during which they are offered a cake tasting.

I've seen Nancy's creations quite often over the years, and they always look wonderful. Instead of providing a groom's cake for one wedding, Nancy baked a cake in the shape of a cartoon figure for the bride's son. Her success results from her selection of good employees, her recipes, and colorful, detailed decoration. Her clients and peers love and respect her and her work, and recommend her highly.

For larger parties, Nancy is glad to provide a sheet cake to keep the cost within your budget.

Not Just Cheesecakes

Los Gatos (408) 395-6091
Campbell (408) 871-2707

653 E. Campbell Avenue, #1
Campbell, CA 95008

Contact: Debbie Caracciolo-Smith

Service Area: Greater Bay Area and West Coast

Specialties: Custom-designed cakes and cheesecakes; birthday, anniversary, theme cakes, and 23-karat gold leaf

Price (per serving): cakes, from $3.00; cheesecakes, from $3.50
Extra Charges: delivery, setup, fresh flower decoration, refundable deposit for cake support

Payment Terms: 50% deposit, balance due 7 days prior to event
Credit Cards: no
Lead Time: 1 - 4 months

Tasting: by appointment
Return of Cake Support: within 1 month
Fresh Flower Decoration: yes

When you talk to Debbie you immediately notice her bubbling Italian temperament and understand how much she enjoys her job, meeting her customers, helping them get exactly what they want, and welcoming the challenge. For instance, with the aid of another artist, she created a tie-dyed wedding cake, air-brushed with food coloring, for 300 guests. For a Renaissance wedding in Woodside, Debbie created not only the opulent cake but also the voluptuous cake table with an heirloom tablecloth, colorful garden roses, hydrangeas, pomegranates, and champagne grapes. For a beach wedding, she formed seashells and coral out of white chocolate to decorate the base of a hand-sculpted lighthouse, complete with a working beacon. Debbie likes to create new cake designs to suit unique requests. She has re-created many Martha Stewart designs, especially those in current *Wedding* issues. It's no surprise that she is well known for her specialty cakes, and I have heard customers praise her work many times. Her beautiful cake table designs show another facet of her many talents.

While most of us are still asleep, Debbie is up baking to make sure her customers get the freshest muffins. For almost 20 years she has been known around Los Gatos as the "Muffin Lady." With the same concern for freshness, Debbie bakes each cake from scratch and uses only the best ingredients. She even offered me a peek into her refrigerator to prove it. Some of her cake flavors are white cake with semi-sweet chocolate chunks, tiramisu, toasted almond, apricot, buttercream, and chocolate espresso. A few cheescake flavors are triple chocolate, white chocolate raspberry, tiramisu, and praline. Her creations can be covered with white or dark chocolate wrap, fondant, marzipan, buttercream, or white chocolate buttercream. Lace work, string work, basketweave, chocolate wrap and hand-painted cakes are Debbie's specialties.

Her showroom displays her cakes, seasonal wedding designs, and provides a comfortable consultation area.

Katrina Rozelle

Pastries and Desserts

215-B Alamo Plaza
Alamo, CA 94507

(925) 837-6337
FAX: (925) 837-0694

Contact: Katrina Topp (Owner) or Sonya Roth (Office Manager)

Service Area: Greater Bay Area, including Carmel

Specialties: Wedding cakes; celebration cakes for every occasion

Price (per serving): $3.25 - $20.00
Extra Charges: delivery charge based on distance, fresh flower work, handmade extras

Payment Terms: 25% deposit, balance due 10 days prior to event
Credit Cards: Visa, MasterCard
Lead Time: 2 months

Tasting: yes
Return of Cake Support: within 60 days
Fresh Flower Decoration: yes

Katrina's fame is not restricted to the East Bay. In fact, her work has been featured in *Perfect Weddings*, *Bride's Magazine*, *In Style Magazine*, and in several Bay Area publications. *Town and Country Magazine* has also recognized her as one of the country's best wedding cake providers. During my research I saw many of her cakes all over the Bay Area. Whether they are simple designs or sophisticated creations, Katrina's cakes look just wonderful. They are meticulously done, elegant, and the most perfect I have seen – and taste as good. Not only did *San Francisco Focus* vote her pastries and desserts "Best in the Bay Area" but I also found them great when I sampled them during a cake tasting. Her devil's food, genoise, pound, and chiffon cakes can be filled with a variety of chocolate mousses, Bavarians, fresh fruit, and much more. Each one is customized to the client's specifications.

Covered with marzipan, rolled fondant, chocolate glazes or buttercreams, Katrina's cakes can be embellished with fresh flowers or handmade flowers of marzipan, chocolate, or gum paste. She will sometimes use very thin 23-karat gold for ribbons and decorations. What makes her cakes so special is the balance between the cake and the decoration – always perfect. In addition to her cakes, Katrina now offers a line of her own handmade Belgian-style chocolates.

It would seem that Katrina inherited her love for food from her grandmother, a chef to the Royal Family of Sweden. While attending the Culinary Academy in San Francisco, she was selected to study under the head pastry chef. After graduating, she became a pastry chef for the famous Narsai David before she opened her own shop in 1987. In addition to her business, she is frequently asked to make special appearances and give demonstrations throughout the Bay Area.

Katrina's second location is 5931 College Avenue, Oakland, CA 94618 (510) 655-3209

Candace Weekly
Elegant Wedding Cakes & Specialty Desserts
(by appointment)
San Francisco, CA

(415) 563-4099
FAX: (415) 680-2473

Contact: Candace Weekly

Service Area: Greater Bay Area

Specialties: Elegant wedding and specialty desserts; allergy-free recipes

Price (per serving): $4.50 - $8.00 (includes all decorations)
Extra Charges: delivery beyond San Francisco city limits

Payment Terms: 20% deposit, balance due 2 weeks prior to event
Credit Cards: no
Lead Time: 3 months

Tasting: by appointment
Return of Cake Support: no
Fresh Flower Decoration: yes

A cup of freshly brewed tea and four of her most popular desserts were waiting for me when I arrived for my meeting with Candace. There was a tiramisu, a chocolate raspberry decadence, lemon chiffon, and a vanilla Bavarian cream with strawberries. Each dessert was wrapped in either white chocolate or white fondant, and decorated with a chocolate bow and a beautiful chocolate rose, reminding me of 18th century Rococo roses. The desserts were "phenomenal," a word borrowed from one client's description of Candace's work. The chiffon cake melted in my mouth, but before it did, I was able to tell that she had used only the purest ingredients.

Candace, a Bay Area native, has always enjoyed baking. She studied with Karen Shapiro, a famous local baker, and graduated from the California Culinary Academy. Candace takes the taste and appearance of her cakes quite seriously. She bakes and hand-decorates them right before the event. This is why she won't accept more than 4 wedding cake orders per weekend. For brides who prefer fresh flowers, Candace personally selects them and decorates according to the client's specifications. All handmade or fresh flower decorations are included in her price per serving. Always placing an emphasis on personalized service, Candace has developed recipes for egg or wheat/gluten allergy sufferers and is currently developing recipes for people who prefer not to eat refined white sugar. Just think – clients won't have to resort to finding a specialty cake mix or a flourless chocolate torte!

One event coordinator of a hotel told me that she has been working with Candace ever since she met her. One bride and her mother, who had very definite ideas about wanting something out of the ordinary and made with only pure ingredients, were extremely pleased with their cake.

CATERERS

NOTES

. . . .

. . . .

. . . .

. . . .

. . . .

. . . .

. . . .

. . . .

. . . .

. . . .

. . . .

. . . .

. . . .

. . . .

. . . .

. . . .

INTRODUCTION

The caterer is one of the pillars of a party's success. The taste and presentation of the food and the service provided will be remembered for a long time. For best results, chef and crew will usually prepare the food in their commercial kitchen and add the finishing touches at the event site.

During my research, I observed every caterer's food and presentation at least once at an actual event, from extravagant functions to casual affairs. The important aspect for me was not the size of the event, but rather the way the food was prepared, how it tasted, and how it was presented. I usually arrived to see it just before the event began, when everything was ready to go. I would often hang around in the kitchen, watching the preparation and sampling the food.

Most caterers do not have a **liquor license**, but they will either serve what you provide or subcontract with a licensed bar service. Regardless of whether or not they have a liquor license, they will usually help you with beverage planning and also do the ordering. Please note that the liability for serving alcohol rests with the party providing it; caterers carry insurance if they do. Some caterers have a license to serve only beer, wine and champagne.

In addition to providing the food, most caterers offer **event planning and coordination**. Some will do this for free, while others will charge a coordination fee. To make sure there are no surprises, ask if they will be present at the event. The caterer is responsible for buffet table decoration. A few caterers also prefer to do the other table decorations as well in order to ensure an aesthetically coordinated effect.

Some caterers service only one event per day, while others do ten simultaneously. Both can be equally good in service and quality. If you choose one of the larger catering establishments, get the name of the person who will be in charge of your event. Record that person's name in the contract and get to know him or her, making sure that your requirements are clearly understood. It's most important to have someone in charge whom you trust to handle an event as important as your wedding.

Take the time to carefully review every little detail with the caterer in order to avoid disappointments and unpleasant surprises. At one party I attended, the caterers served only decaffeinated coffee – their choice, not the client's. They also refused to provide food for the band until the guests had finished eating, which was approximately the same time the band should have been getting the party started.

When you hire a caterer, you might also need to **rent** tables, chairs, linens, glasses, dishes, and/or silverware. Ask your caterer to outline what he or she provides as part of the service. Renting items through the caterer will often be more costly due to their time and effort. But this can save you the headache of managing the pickup, delivery, setup, breakdown, and liability for the equipment.

The caterer will need to know a close approximation of the **number of guests** in order to determine the quantity of food and service personnel. Caterers usually bring along 10% more food than required, as running out of food is a nightmare for them. Leftover food is sometimes left with you, and sometimes taken back. Caterers may prefer to keep the excess food since they consider it food you have not paid for. They also want to make sure you don't eat spoiled leftovers. If the food has been on display for several hours on a hot day, the caterer will dispose of it. Regardless of the reason, the caterer determines how the leftovers are to be dispensed with.

Money Matters

The **base price** is the absolute minimum price per person that the caterer will charge for lunch or dinner. As you know, prices vary widely depending on food selection. The price of a sit-down dinner is usually more expensive because it requires more staff.

Extra charges are costs that are additional to the food. They can be incurred for staff (service charge), rentals, production costs, corkage fees, or cake-cutting fees. **Rentals** include tables, chairs, dishes, and linen. **Production costs** are charges indirectly related to the event. More and more caterers are providing their own floral and other decorations at an extra cost. If caterers charge a corkage fee, they either have their own liquor license or use the fee to hire additional staff. To discourage you from bringing your own wine, the **corkage fee** might be as high as $15 per bottle. Similarly, a **cake-cutting fee** might be charged if the caterer can provide the wedding cake. Beverages, including coffee and punch, are usually extra.

Though **gratuities** are usually optional, several caterers itemize service gratuities separately. A gratuity or service charge is a mandatory "tip," which is taxable.

It is quite difficult to **compare pricing** among caterers without considering everything that's involved. Some caterers charge only for the food, others include dishes, while still others have inclusive prices. Be sure to ask about all the extra and hidden charges, and calculate carefully. If gratuity is not listed as an extra charges, it is optional; otherwise, it will appear on the bill. Since tax is always charged, it is not included under "Extra charges." Very few caterers include tax in the quoted prices.

Money Saving Tips

- Consider an afternoon tea or cocktail and hors d'oeuvres for your wedding reception.
- Serve more vegetables than meat, or offer an entree other than meat.
- Reduce the number of service personnel, but keep in mind that someone needs to rearrange the half-empty plates on the buffet table!
- Find out if the caterer offers children's menus, which are usually less expensive.

Beets
Fine Catering
170 Lindbergh Avenue
Livermore, CA 94550

(925) 294-8667
FAX: (925) 294-8666
beets@beetscater.com
www.beetscater.com

Contact: Read Philips

Service Area: Greater Bay Area

Specialties: Seasonal, fresh, customized comfort food

Base Prices: lunch, from $12; dinner, from $15; includes china and linen
Extra Charges: service charge

Payment Terms: $300 deposit, 50% 2 months prior, balance due day of event
Credit Cards: major credit cards

Lead Time: 48 hrs. to 9 months
No. of Guests (min/max): 30 / no max
Liquor License: yes

I've known Read for several years. This petite, easygoing and energetic woman is a graduate of the Culinary Institute in New York and also has a BA in economics. She has worked in the food business since 1979, including spending two years in Italy just outside of Florence. What better background to run a successful catering company! Read believes in continuing education; when I last met with her, she had just returned from attending a renowned catering seminar and was full of new ideas. Her flexibility, her willingness to work within a budget, and her dedication and that of her staff make every event special. I experienced Read's versatility firsthand during an open house at Shrine Event Center, where she is the in-house caterer. The food stations displayed picnic food, a salad bar, and Cajun and Arabian ethnic food. The roast beef was very tender, and the barbecued lamb was one of the best I've ever tasted. Beets also hosted a paella station at the 1996 BRO Party. Dressed in starched, white jackets, Read and her chef added freshly sautéed jumbo prawns to the delicious dish. They and a florist had created a fabulous authentic look to their display, including a harbor view in the background.

Read believes in using fresh, seasonal, local produce and other foods from the valley. She and her staff like to create new menu items; her pumpkin ravioli was an instant hit. She invites prospective customers for a food tasting twice a year at Shrine Event Center, when she usually introduces her new food creations.

Read's excellent work and reasonable prices have led her to many recommended caterer lists all over the Bay Area.

Betty Zlatchin Catering

(415) 641-8599
FAX: (415) 641-5563

1177 Indiana Street
San Francisco, CA 94107

Contact: Betty Zlatchin

Service Area: Greater Bay Area

Specialties: Fresh Mediterranean and California cuisine

Base Prices (food only): lunch, from $17; dinner, from $38
Extra Charges: staff, rental, production

Payment Terms: 10% non-ref. deposit,
  70% 3 weeks prior to event, balance is billed
Credit Cards: no

Lead Time: 3 days to 1 year
No. of Guests (min/max): no min / 2,000
Liquor License: no

Betty traces her love of hospitality back to her Southern upbringing, her experience as a flight attendant, and her travels to Southern France and Italy. She impresses me as one of the warmest and friendliest people in the industry. The first party she catered earned her a bottle of Chateau Lafitte. Many years later I visited her and her fully licensed catering business at their new premises on Indiana Street. The large kitchen and the light, airy offices were designed to be both practical and a nice atmosphere for the longtime staff of whom she is very proud. She has recently acquired two fabulous, large metal platters and a heavy brocade cloth to make her lush, bountiful buffets even more stunning. We browsed together through pictures of her latest works: a gay, authentic Tuscan dinner in the Wine Country and an architect's sit-down dinner. For the latter, she used blueprints as place mats and decorated the tables with duct tape and various metal objects.

I observed Betty's preparations for a large private party. The Mexican station was almost finished and looked very pretty, with a large, authentic Mexican serape, sombreros, and rustic serving platters filled with freshly prepared salsa and guacamole. Across the courtyard at the seafood station, a server was opening the fresh oysters and displaying them on ice. Beer-steamed jumbo prawns were served in a bowl of ice, with flowers and ivy frozen into the bowl. On the large Italian buffet in the dining room, done in a black & white color scheme, sat marble slabs and large white platters on different levels, waiting for the food just getting final touches.

Betty has no planned menus; she creates them according to her clients' requests. Clients can't say enough about her delicious food and its lush presentation, and comment on the great help they received from her in coordinating the entire event.

Blue Heron Catering
Personal Attention to Your Event
(by appointment)
Oakland, CA

(510) 836-0303
FAX: (510) 836-4676
BHCatering@aol.com

Contact: Karen A. Lucas or Lisa Wilson

Service Area: Greater Bay Area

Specialties: Fresh, innovative California, Mediterranean, and Pacific Rim cuisine; customized ethnic and vegetarian menus; full event coordination

Base Prices (food only): lunch, from $18; dinner, from $24; min. $800
Extra Charges: staff, rentals

Payment Terms: 50% deposit, balance due at event
Credit Cards: no

Lead Time: 1 week to 1 year
No. of Guests (min/max): 50 / 800
Liquor License: no, but will serve

While Karen prepared for an upcoming event, I chatted with Lisa on the other side of the large prep area in their commercial kitchen in Oakland. Both caterers have impressive backgrounds from their many years in the food industry. After graduation, Karen traveled abroad and worked as an apprentice in Asia, the Middle East, France, and Italy. Back in the U.S., she eventually became head chef of several famous restaurants in the area. At the Broadway Terrace Cafe she met Lisa, who had graduated from the California Culinary Academy and had worked with such renowned celebrities as Carlo Middione of Vivande and Narsai David.

In 1988, Karen and Lisa founded the Blue Heron and wrote their cookbook, *Antipasto Feasts*. Their commitment to quality is evidenced by their accepting only two large jobs at the same time, allowing either one of them to be on-site. They enjoy creating and coordinating the entire event. In collaboration with their clients, they can create and build props related to the party theme. They are also open to including a client's recipe on the menu.

Karen was in charge of the wedding I observed. Out of the kitchen drifted the wonderful smell of baking marinated chicken breasts. The fruit display on marble platters cascaded down at the center of the buffet table surrounded by large, white platters of food, decorated with herbs and kale.

During the last few years, I've come across many Blue Heron clients who rave about their work. Customers love how easy it is to work with them, their attention to detail, and their wonderful food and presentation. Blue Heron Catering has received the Oakland Chamber of Commerce's "Mayor's Outstanding Achievement Award" as Small Business of the Year, and was also named one of the top three caterers in the Bay Area by *Bay Foods* readers' awards.

Bonne Bouche Catering

(831) 479-9637
FAX: (831) 479-9641
BBouche@aol.com

P.O. Box 1573
Capitola, CA 95010

Contact: Aimée Murphy or Karen Aulbach

Service Area: Greater Bay Area, Napa to Monterey

Specialties: Seasonal, locally-produced organic foods; customized menus; theme menus

Base Prices (food only): lunch, from $15; dinner, from $20
Extra Charges: service, rentals, gratuity

Payment Terms: 30% non-ref. deposit to reserve date, balance due day of event
Credit Cards: no

Lead Time: 1 week to 1 year
No. of Guests (min/max): no min / no max
Liquor License: no, but will serve

"Cool, calm, and collected, especially on such a hot day" was one thought I had about Aimée and Karen as I left a winery's tiny kitchen where they were setting out hors d'oeuvres for the wedding guests in the garden below. They were as attentive to me as they were to attractively arranging the chicken, basil and pecan salad in puff-pastry; vine-ripened tomato and basil bruschetta, and spinach lavosh pinwheels of smoked turkey with red onion and roasted red pepper cream. They prepared a plate of these for me and insisted that, before I left, I also try the lavender poached salmon with caper-dill crème fraîche and the chicken provençale with a sauce of capers, garlic and kalamata olives. I couldn't resist and found everything absolutely delicious. Aimée, Karen, and sous-chef Jenny were so relaxed and pleasant that I thought I was chatting with long-time friends; I *knew* I was chatting with an extraordinarily professional team.

Aimée (event coordinator) and Karen (executive chef) met while working at Willow Street Woodfired Pizza. Karen, who has been "cooking for 20 years" as executive chef in many Bay Area restaurants, and Aimée, who worked in several restaurants and as floor manager of Restaurant Lulu in San Francisco, founded Bonne Bouche in 1996 as an "opportunity to exceed clients' expectations." And, from all reports, they have, and continue to do so. Their goal is to make everyone involved in the planning feel important, and they spend lots of time with clients to personalize the event, down to the last creative detail. All of their offerings, including their wonderful focaccia, are house-made, and while they have a wide variety of dinnerware, linens, and props for any theme, they are always on the lookout for new items. This dynamic duo enjoys the business because, as Aimée says, "It's a chance to be 100% creative and let our imaginations run wild."

Bonne Bouche was the exclusive caterer for the National Steinbeck Center's pre-opening events in the summer of '98 and has been featured in *Victoria Magazine*. Their take-out service, called No Reservations, offers a menu as varied and creative as their Bonne Bouche fare.

The Catering Caravan
Personalized Catering
3952 Nelson Court
Palo Alto, CA 94306

(650) 493-2486
FAX: (650) 858-1420

Contact: Jo Kadis

Service Area: Greater Bay Area

Specialties: Customized ethnic food, personalized service, and event coordination for weddings, Bar/Bat Mitzvahs, and private parties

Base Prices (food only): lunch, from $7.95; dinner, from $12
Extra Charges: staff, rentals, paper products; coordination fee may be applied

Payment Terms: 25% to reserve date, 25% due 2 weeks prior, balance is billed
Credit Cards: no

Lead Time: 1 week to 6 months
No. of Guests (min/max): 2 / 350
Liquor License: no, but will serve

Jo Kadis, owner of The Catering Caravan, loves to cook. Her vast collection of recipes (over 2,000 in her computer alone) includes old favorites, contemporary California cuisine, and national and international dishes. Several of Jo's recipes have earned the honor of appearing in an article in *Sunset Magazine*. She believes that food should be presented beautifully and served in appetite-satisfying portions that taste even better. The Catering Caravan can even accommodate special dietary restrictions, including vegetarian requests, with dishes to satisfy any guest. Not only does Jo love to cook, but she also enjoys consulting extensively with her clients, inviting them to mix and match dishes from several sample menus, and then coordinating their entire event.

For Jo, perfection is of utmost importance. She once replaced tablecloths at the last minute because the color of the original ones was not quite right. I observed an international buffet that Jo had prepared for an elegant wedding at Holbrook Palmer Park. The delicate dolmas stuffed with rice, assorted quiche squares, hot German potato salad, and tortellini with pesto sauce tasted wonderful, were beautifully presented, and even labeled. For a Korean wedding, she prepared Asian dishes, which blended well with the authentic Korean food brought by the relatives. Jo also plans events around different ethnic cuisines and has received rave reviews for The Catering Caravan's famous Moroccan Nights theme. You can whisk your guests off to North Africa after Jo and her staff transform your living room with exotic tenting, traditional Moroccan decorations and serving pieces, floor seating, and even belly dancers.

Flexibility is a very important aspect of Jo's business, as seen by her willingness to include clients' recipes and to provide food only or full-service catering. She will also provide services to a hostess who prepares her own food. She is also flexible when it comes to budgets. Her clients love her "terrific job" and "scrumptious feast," and recommend her "every chance I get."

CaterMarin
Glorious Food - Pure & Abundant
1750 Bridgeway
Sausalito, CA 94965

(415) 331-8655
(415) 892-2777
FAX: (415) 331-8669

Contact: Terry Eberle or Cynthia Bussing

Service Area: Greater Bay Area

Specialties: Fresh California cuisine incorporating your individual ideas; vegetarian menus available

Base Prices (food only): lunch, from $12; dinner, from $18
Extra Charges: staff, rental

Payment Terms: $250 non-ref. deposit, 85% due 3 weeks prior to event, balance is billed
Credit Cards: Visa, MasterCard

Lead Time: 2 weeks to 1 year
No. of Guests (min/max): 10 / no max
Liquor License: licensed service available

"We'll do the worrying for you" is the motto of Terry Eberle, owner of CaterMarin which was established in 1982. Understanding the client's vision and offering hand-holding throughout the planning stages are her specialties. Terry often gives clients her home number in case they come up with concerns over the weekend.

CaterMarin, a complete catering company, uses fresh ingredients in their cuisine. Their abundant collection of attractive props, marble slabs, baskets and serving platters add to their already beautiful presentations. My favorite is their international food stations. At a CaterMarin event I attended, the Asian Station, decorated with large palm leaves, a wooden barrel and bamboo umbrella, was dramatically complemented with their olive and black specialty linens. The chef was stir-frying fresh vegetables, pork and chicken to be served over wonton crisps and tangy sauces. The Italian Station had a selection of Fusili and Penne Pasta prepared-to-order, with a choice of fresh tomato with basil and garlic or Gorgonzola cream sauce with button mushrooms, fresh peas, topped with thyme and lemon juice. The Beef Station, complete with carving chef, was beautifully displayed in front of a dramatic view of the sun setting over the Golden Gate Bridge. The Caviar Tasting Station was complemented with champagne, giving this event a stylistic edge. The caviars included Sevruga with the traditional accompaniments and "specialty caviars" such as Passion Fruit Caviar served with mascarpone and ginger snaps, and Wasabi Tobikko, a dazzling, neon green caviar. The Dessert Buffet presented a dazzling assortment of Hazelnut Daquoise, Linzer cookies, chocolate earthquake cookies, and fresh raspberry chocolate hearts.

Whether you prefer a sit-down or buffet dinner, CaterMarin works with you to design a menu, keeping your budget in mind.

Cheese Please
Gourmet Shop - Full Catering Service
299 California Drive
Burlingame, CA 94010

(650) 696-3963
FAX: (650) 696-3964

Contact: John Linderman or Susan Walter

Service Area: Greater Bay Area and beyond

Specialties: Custom-designed menus of California, French, Italian and Pacific Rim cuisines

Base Prices (food only): lunch, from $12.50; dinner, from $22.50
Extra Charges: staff, rentals, service charge, coordination

Payment Terms: 50% deposit, balance
                  due day of event
Credit Cards: Visa, MasterCard

Lead Time: 2 days to 2 months
No. of Guests (min/max): no min / no max
Liquor License: beer, wine, champagne

Many things have changed since I last visited with John: he moved his catering business to a larger facility, and, more important, Susan Walter, his dear friend, became his partner. As owner of the 4-star Ecco restaurant and author of four cookbooks, Susan is no stranger to the San Francisco food scene. I also learned that she had been assisting John at the parties I reviewed for my first edition. John is just a delightful person, a real Californian, who has a contagious laugh and likes to travel. His gourmet shop, in existence now for 20 years, has evolved into a successful catering business. These combined business components allow a high degree of flexibility. They can do everything, from delivering a cheese or smoked salmon platter, to creating an elegant buffet for 2,000. In addition to enjoying their delicious food, I admire their attention to detail. The two partners contribute their expertise to creating the most wonderful food, using only fresh local products. While Susan is in charge of the kitchen, John serves as Maître d'. They pay close attention to their clients' desires and offer expert advice. John and Susan's main concern is pleasing their clients. In return, they receive high praise for making their events so successful.

The previous time I saw John's work, I admired the several Mediterranean food stations he had so lovingly decorated. He incorporated such props as an olive oil can, a straw hat, and bunches of country flowers into the presentation. I still remember the wonderful foccacia bread and the delicious ratatouille. This time I observed an elegant sit-down dinner at a mansion. The delicious appetizers were served on silver platters decorated with flowers. The cream cheese in the tiny red potato halves was so well seasoned that I couldn't discern the different ingredients. Susan had used a Swedish-style marinade for the salmon appetizer and served it with cucumbers, dill garnish and crisp rye toast cut into hearts. Then came a wonderful flower petal salad, followed by the entree, Poussin Français (whole baby chickens) with wild mushrooms, herb Yukon Gold mashed potatoes, and grilled asparagus with lemon sabayon.

Classic Catering

Diablo View Plaza
2653A Pleasant Hill Road
Pleasant Hill, CA 94523

(925) 939-9224
FAX: (925) 975-0677

Contact: Jacqueline Putkey

Service Area: Greater Bay Area

Specialties: Freshly prepared seasonal, California and Mediterranean cuisines; desserts

Base Prices (food only): lunch, from $20; dinner, from $30
Extra Charges: serviceware, rental, linens, staff

Payment Terms: $300 non-ref. deposit, 50% due 2 months prior, balance due day of event
Credit Cards: no

Lead Time: 1 month to 1 year
No. of Guests (min/max): 30 / 1,000
Liquor License: no, but will serve

This highly organized, professionally trained culinary staff is led by owners Jacqueline Putkey and Thomas McKillop, executive chef. Since 1989, Classic Catering has been providing full-service catering, from brunches, boxed or served lunches, to cocktail parties, hors d'oeuvre stations, and elegant sit-down events.

Classic Catering freshly prepares their menus to reflect the season. Their decorative buffet displays, created exclusively with seasonal fruits, vegetables, and herbs, reflect their artistic style. Their event specialists can customize your menus and coordinate other components, such as rentals, locations, flowers and cakes. They offer consultations and tastings to customize and personalize menus for their clients.

On one occasion, I was able to sample their delicious artichoke and smoked cheddar frittata; stuffed garlic mushrooms with herbs; corn crab cakes with green chile crème fraîche; and pasta sauté with pesto cream, asparagus and pine nuts. The buffet was artistically presented with assorted dishes to reflect the season and event. Large ripe strawberries were layered with edible flowers, adding color and beauty. The centerpiece was creatively arranged with artichokes, asparagus, and garlic – a preview of their freshly prepared menu. The draping of material on the buffet table, matching the theme of the party, reflects their attention to detail.

One comment from an impressed mother of the bride was, "The food was perfect, [of] the same quality I would expect while dining at a good restaurant. Thank you for making our event so extraordinary."

Connoisseur Catering

(650) 365-0548
FAX: (650) 365-0578

959 Woodside Road
Redwood City, CA 94061

Contact: Joni Walker

Service Area: South Bay, Peninsula, San Francisco

Specialties: Freshly prepared regional American cuisine, with emphasis on Pacific Rim;
International cuisine

Base Prices (food only): lunch, from $10.95; dinner, from $16.95
Extra Charges: staff, gratuity, rentals, punch, coffee

Payment Terms: 40% deposit, balance due day of event

Credit Cards: no

Lead Time: 1 week to 6 months
No. of Guests (min/max): no min / 1,500
Liquor License: no, but available

"Her buffets are absolutely gorgeous!" was one client's rave about Joni's food and service. During the Christmas season I met her unexpectedly at Filoli where she was preparing one of her lush dinners for a fund-raising event. Every time I've come across her work, the food was absolutely delicious and attractively displayed. Appetizers are often served on antique mirrors, decorated with flowers, and the serving platters are always the latest in design. Tablecloths are draped, or scalloped and tied together with ribbons or ropes with tassels, and the buffets are decorated with flowers and many props. Joni's goal of perfection inspires her to even scout out attractive black jumpers and white blouses for the female servers.

I observed two of Joni's dinner setups. One adhered to a tighter budget and consisted primarily of vegetables. The other was quite the opposite. The bridegroom loved the meat and sausages that were freshly barbecued outside. I loved how the light wood meat platters were decorated: what looked like a large chrysanthemum in a bed of rosemary was actually a slightly browned onion. A medley of colorful, roasted vegetables was served on a huge, cobalt blue platter. Large leaves of Romaine lettuce, filled with Caesar salad, were arranged in a circle and easily handled by the guests. Red and green pasta dishes, and freshly baked foccacia bread and herb muffins were offered at another station.

Joni offers everything from custom-designed menus to neatly printed food suggestions for breakfast, lunch and dinner. Food for those with special dietary needs can also be ordered. Joni has done many fund-raising parties at beautiful Filoli and also catered an event for Martha Stewart in the East Bay.

Continental Catering
Too Caterers

425 El Camino Real
Menlo Park, CA 94025

(CC) (650) 322-4189
(TC) (650) 473-6439
(CC) FAX: (650) 322-1023
(TC) FAX: (650) 473-6539
wendyk@mediacity.com

Contact: Paul Alexander or Wendy Kleckner

Service Area: Greater Bay Area

Specialties: Customized menus, California and ethnic cuisine; Kosher cuisine under strict Orthodox supervision

Base Prices: lunch, from $18.50; dinner, from $21; includes china, silver, and glassware
Extra Charges: staff, gratuity, rentals

Payment Terms: 25% deposit 10 days prior, balance due day of event
Credit Cards: no

Lead Time: 1 week to 1 year
No. of Guests (min/max): 40 / no max
Liquor License: no

Continental Caterers is continuing its 60-year tradition as one of the five largest catering companies in the Bay Area. Now under the able leadership of owner Paul Alexander, a Stanford graduate, the company emphasizes freshness and quality of ingredients. Menus are contemporary and creative, reflecting California's full bounty. The innovative food presentation showcases seasonal ingredients and pays attention to the health conscious.

Paul has put a lot of energy into training his staff, who are both courteous and knowledgable. Assisting Paul with menu development and event coordination is Wendy Kleckner, known for her imaginative menus, ebullient manner, and attention to detail. Continental's menus are customized to client needs and budget.

I saw Continental's work at an auction at the Stanford Pavilion, a more casual affair. The Italian, traditional Mexican and Oriental food stations were colorfully decorated accordingly. In contrast, a sit-down dinner for a wedding at Villa Montalvo was done very elegantly, with silver chargers and crystal on cream-colored satin tablecloths.

Affiliated with Continental but housed in a separate warehouse is the strictly kosher Too Caterers, managed and operated by Wendy. All dishes, glasses and silverware are stored in cupboards and are opened only by a rabbi for an Orthodox Jewish event. I observed the kitchen activities at Kohl Mansion. The kitchen was covered in foil and cloth, and the sink with aluminum foil and tape, as the rabbi supervised the preparations. Wendy has been catering Kosher weddings for 18 years and is the authority for Kosher events in the Bay Area. She supervises Kosher events at the Westin St. Francis.

Delicious! Inc.
Personalized Catering Since 1975
26 Medway Road, #7
San Rafael, CA 94901

(415) 453-3710
FAX: (415) 453-1299
www.deliciouscatering.com

Contact: Jan Goldberg or Mary Jo Odishoo

Service Area: Greater Bay Area

Specialties: Contemporarily designed menus personalized to appeal
to a variety of tastes; Kosher-style available

Base Prices (food only): lunch, from $16; dinner, from $20; gourmet lunch boxes, from $7.25
Extra Charges: rentals, staff, service, beverages, delivery

Payment Terms: 10% with contract, 75%
2 weeks prior, balance net 15 days
Credit Cards: Visa, MasterCard

Lead Time: 48 hrs. to 1 year
No. of Guests (min/max): 20 / 600
Liquor License: wine & beer

"Catering is a service, not just cooking," sums up Jan Goldberg, owner of Delicious! Inc. This is Jan's motto, which is deeply rooted in her dedicated staff and one of the many reasons the company has been successful for 23 years. I have always admired their quality of service and have found the friendly staff to be flexible, well organized, easy to work with, and extremely responsive to peoples' needs. They even exceed clients' expectations by assigning an extra staff member to attend to guests' particular dietary needs or handicaps. "Taking care of special needs on a special day," is the key to their style of service, opening the door to a variety of menus they plan following current Bay Area food trends.

From graciously served dinners to creative food stations, Delicious! is always sensitive and attentive to the dynamics of the event. For one event that involved a large number of children, Delicious! served the adults an elegant sit-down dinner while the children were intrigued by the fun food stations offering their nutritious favorites. Special arrangements were made with the DJ to keep the children entertained while the adults enjoyed their meal. "...one [child] was heard to say that is was 'the best Bar Mitzvah food I've ever had.' Kudos! Service and food perfectly balanced and well orchestrated!"

This is one of the many ways Delicious!'s trained event planners work closely with clients to create personalized and memorable events. They plan menus, lay out the floor plan, coordinate the colors, and help with the timeline. They can even assist you in arranging for entertainment, flowers, décor, invitations, and other aspects to bring the event together.

"...thanks and appreciation for one more event...as smooth and as clear as glass." "Fantastic party...rave reviews on food, both flavor and presentation; portions generous; fine service. You started our year with an almost impossible standard to equal," rave clients.

Divine Catering

A Complete Food Service Company
(by appointment)
Atherton, CA

(650) 473-4036
(408) 295-3570

Contact: Gregg Shriner

Service Area: Greater Bay Area

Specialties: Food creations for parties and weddings; event coordination

Base Prices (food only): lunch, from $6; dinner, from $7
Extra Charges: staff, rentals, coffee, punch

Payment Terms: 50% deposit 1 week prior to event, balance is billed
Credit Cards: no

Lead Time: 1 day to 18 months
No. of Guests (min/max): 10 / no max
Liquor License: no

With more than 30 years in business, Gregg Shriner is one of the most experienced caterers in the area. He has worked as a cook and chef in hotels and restaurants all over the country. The company's name comes from their work with Catholic schools. Gregg provides the food for Sacred Heart School in Atherton. His business is based at Sacred Heart Prep. and other schools throughout the area.

Gregg is very easy to work with. He can provide either catering only or plan and coordinate the whole event. His quoted prices are all-inclusive; however, he is glad to show you a breakdown of his charges, including his profit margin. When budgeting is a concern, Gregg is willing to work out a payment schedule past the date of your event.

I observed Gregg's work at my friend's wedding and became one of his many admirers, who all say the same thing: "It was an outstanding job, even more so when you consider his reasonable prices." The food was very well presented and tasted wonderful. I also noted the efficiency with which he and his staff worked in the background, rearranging the buffet, helping with the cake, and clearing the tables – true masters of their profession!

Gregg also loves challenges. He invited me to a wedding at a location with neither water nor power. Cheerfully standing behind the hot barbecue on a hot summer afternoon, he prepared Hoisin chicken skewers and artichoke chicken in sherry pepper sauce. I also saw the wonderfully presented meat and spinach Béchamel lasagna (made from scratch), the herb-roasted red potatoes and the different salads. The bride and groom came up to me to rave about Gregg's work. Just the other day a friend of mine told me about a great caterer with such reasonable prices – the same Divine Catering.

Englund's Catering Service
Discover the Difference
4061 Port Chicago Hwy., Suite J
Concord, CA 94520

(925) 609-5989
FAX: (925) 609-5950
englunds@earthlink.net
www.englundscatering.com

Contact: Derry Englund

Service Area: Greater Bay Area

Specialties: American and California cuisines with emphasis on quality meats

Base Prices: lunch, from $13.95; dinner, from $15.95; service included
Extra Charges: rentals

Payment Terms: $200 non-ref. deposit, 60% due 10 days prior, balance due day of event
Credit Cards: major credit cards

Lead Time: 1 week to 1 year
No. of Guests (min/max): 50 / 2,000
Liquor License: no, but will serve

Growing up behind the counter of his father's well-known butcher shop made Derry an expert on fine meats. After his father retired, Derry and his brother continued to run the business. In 1988, Derry branched out into full-time catering and, as a pro, does all of the meat preparation. He is very nice and accommodating. During our first meeting he taught me the difference between USDA choice and other meats.

I sampled the food Derry prepared for a wedding on a hot summer day. The menu included fresh vegetables with dips; a garden salad; white and wild rice pilaf with garden vegetables, herbs, and mushrooms; broccoli with hollandaise sauce, barbecued chicken and steak; and his creation of strawberries with a sweet dip. The exceptionally tender steaks with an herb crust were among the most delicious I've ever tasted. The juicy chicken with a crunchy crust was also done to perfection.

About every two months, Derry invites all of his prospective brides to an open house at the Centre Concord. Here you can sample his food and see its presentation, including the different table settings and linen. The guests are not obligated to sign the contract after the meal, however, his guests are so impressed that he has a 90% booking rate. Reasonable prices and easy-to-read menus make the company a favorite for fund-raising dinners. To ensure high-quality work, Derry will not book more than three events per day. Each event is staffed with an experienced coordinator. Derry and his company are on many preferred caterer lists around the Bay Area and are highly respected by colleagues and customers alike. Complete menus and price lists are available upon request.

Event of the Season
Caterers
148 Stetson Avenue
Corte Madera, CA 94925

(415) 927-4721

Contact: Vernon Jacobs

Service Area: Greater Bay Area and Wine Country

Specialties: An eclectic and inspired fusion of Mediterranean, Asian, and California cuisines

Base Prices (food only): lunch, from $15.50; dinner, from $16.50
Extra Charges: staff, gratuity, rentals

Payment Terms: $250 part. ref. deposit, 50% due 4 weeks prior, balance due after event
Credit Cards: no

Lead Time: 3 days to 1 year
No. of Guests (min/max): 60 / 400
Liquor License: no

After working for other caterers, Vernon started his own catering company over 10 years ago. He specializes in imaginative, full-flavored food with fewer calories, made only from the freshest ingredients. He consults extensively with his clients and translates their wishes into food and design. He is also well acquainted with many event locations in the Bay Area and can create magical menus no matter what kind of kitchen facilities the site may have.

Besides catering weddings throughout the Bay Area, the company does numerous corporate events, including breakfasts and luncheons, as well as special parties. One such party which I attended was a food and wine pairing. The appetizers accompanying the champagne were petite pastry puffs filled with crab Thermidor. They tasted delicious and were so small you could eat them in one bite. The white wines were matched with dolmas with a fresh mint and yogurt sauce, cheese quesadillas, Norwegian smoked salmon with cream cheese, thinly sliced cucumbers, onions and capers, grilled spicy Thai prawns, and a tropical fruit platter. Accompanying the red wines were cheese tortellini with delicious low-caloric sauces; triangles of focaccia with tomatoes, basil, French chèvre and mozzarella cheeses; Brie baked in phyllo; petite open sandwiches with chateaubriand and sauce Bearnaise and assorted grilled Sonoma sausages with different mustards. Strawberries dipped in dark chocolate topped off the feast.

One of the wine experts knew Vernon from other wine and food dinners and raved about his extraordinary menus and organizational skills.

Executive...Catering for
Special Gatherings and Events

(415) 552-8932
FAX: (415) 552-8988

2161 Third Street
San Francisco, CA 94107

Contact: Joseph Caro

Service Area: Greater Bay Area

Specialties: Regional, international sophisticated buffets to elegant sit-down dining with classic French technique

Base Prices (food only): lunch, from $9.95; dinner, $35 - $110; $500 min.
Extra Charges: staff, rentals

Payment Terms: 25% deposit at contract signing
Credit Cards: major credit cards

Lead Time: 10 days to 1 year
No. of Guests (min/max): 20 / no max
Liquor License: licensed service available

Joseph Caro, with eight years of premier wedding cake designs, took the great opportunity to merge with a commercial facility designed for fine catering to become Executive...Catering for Special Gatherings and Events. To ensure the finest in dining experience, the staff is expert at providing a variety of service styles from formal French to casual bistro and festive buffets. "It is so interesting and fun," says Joseph, "to design a menu with a client and then adapt a style of service to that menu."

Joseph's executive chef, with over 20 years of experience in the San Francisco area, has an incredible approach to food and its preparation. He draws from a broad palette of international food styles, including Pacific Rim, Classic French, and Mediterranean. The chef conducts a menu consultation with the clients to help shape the menu based on the season, budget and overall style of the event. Executive...Catering is proud of their skills to blend food styles and wines with the client's personal tastes as well as the specific requirements of the venue.

In their proposals, Executive...Catering itemizes all the various components of the client's event. The client can clearly see all of the costs, such as food, labor, décor, and rentals, thus outlining their value to dollar spent.

Industry professionals and clients rave: "The best way to describe Joseph and his service is 'professional'." "Trustworthy, personable, confident, and accommodating – everything you would look for in a caterer."

85

Four Seasons Catering

(650) 968-9308
(650) 968-9320
(evenings & weekends)
FAX: (650) 968-0126

2580C Wyandotte Avenue
Mountain View, CA 94043

Contact: Alfred or Frank Schumann

Service Area: Greater Bay Area

Specialties: Continental, California, and Mediterranean cuisines; Kosher catering

Base Prices: lunch, from $10; dinner, from $15; includes china, glassware, white linen, cutlery
Extra Charges: staff, gratuity, extra rentals

Payment Terms: 25% deposit; 50% 1 week prior, balance due day of event
Credit Cards: no

Lead Time: 1 week to 1 year
No. of Guests (min/max): 30 / 2,000
Liquor License: full liquor license

Alfred and Frank Schumann started Four Seasons Catering in 1981. If you include their involvement in their father's catering business and owning a restaurant, their experience dates back to 1960. They are all-around caterers who gladly service fund-raising dinners where their good ideas help save money for the sponsors. They also offer early morning breakfasts. Alfred and Frank are easygoing, very flexible, and tailor the menus strictly to the customer's preference.

Specialties are theme parties with different stations. When I met with Alfred in their office, I browsed through several portfolios of pictures he has collected over the years. I was able to trace how the styles have changed to the elegant buffets and sit-down dinners for today's weddings. I also saw pictures of colorful theme parties and rustic company picnics.

I observed their work at a wedding at Ralston Hall. The appetizers were served outside during the toast while the delicious entrees were set up on four beautifully decorated stations among an abundance of flowers. A decorated poached salmon, grilled swordfish, and sautéed jumbo prawns were the main attractions at the seafood station. There were also a carving station offering roast beef, stuffed chicken breast, and roasted potatoes; a pasta station with Caesar, spinach and ambrosia salads; and a fruit and cheese station. As I was leaving, the event coordinator made a point of telling me about the consistently great performance of this catering company. They service many repeat customers who have been hiring them for years, always finding something new and tempting.

The Orthodox Jewish catering division has been run by Sally Fanberg since 1993. Alfred showed me the separate work space, oven, refrigerator, sink and the locked cupboards filled with dishes and utensils for Bar/Bat Mitzvahs and Jewish weddings.

La Bocca Fina
Picnic Pleasures to Opulent Feasts
2416 Radley Court, #1
Hayward, CA 94545

(510) 264-0276
FAX: (510) 264-0277

Contact: Teri A. Menchini

Service Area: Greater Bay Area and beyond

Specialties: Highlighting local California food products incorporated into American, Mediterranean, Pacific Rim, or South-of-the-Border cuisines

Base Prices (food only): lunch, from $20; dinner, from $25
Extra Charges: service personnel, wide variety of linens, china, glassware, flatware patterns

Payment Terms: $500 deposit plus 25%, 50% due 30 days prior, balance due day of event
Credit Cards: no

Lead Time: 1 week to 18 months
No. of Guests (min/max): no min / no max
Liquor License: licensed service available

The more I got to know Teri, the more I respected this creative, hard-working caterer and wonderful person. I had the opportunity to work with her when she assumed the role of principal organizer for the 1996 BRO Party. She coordinated and oversaw the 8 caterers, their food stations, and the 12 dessert displays; assigned florists to decorate each station, and organized the linen and rental items. I saw how she took care of every little detail, sending faxes to the participants, following up by phone calls, and pulling everything together. Working with her, I felt assured that the party was in excellent hands.

When you visit Teri in her attractive office with its Mediterranean flair, you learn that she not only emphasizes good food for "La Bocca Fina" ("the finicky eater"), but also has a fine hand at beautiful decoration. I enjoyed watching her create a wonderful, early autumn buffet with bouquets of crabapple branches and fruit, and other colorful branches with berries, accented with gray eucalyptus. The food, fruit and plant display formed a perfect union. Even more spectacular was a Hawaiian buffet, decorated with lush tropical flowers and palms. The shucked oysters had such delicious toppings that my friends still rave about them.

Teri is a chef, a graduate of the California Culinary Academy. She has owned her company since 1982. Seasonal menus are always encouraged, and all menu components are cooked on-site to guarantee freshness and taste. The company focuses on detailed event design and impeccable coordination, personalized menus, and stunning visual presentations. Special emphasis is placed on personal contact, listening to the client's visions, and reflecting the client's individual style. Extensive consultations are conducted in their office, during which all of the specifics are discussed. Clients are assisted with menu planning, and event design and coordination, thus creating a memorable event while adhering to the budget. The complete staff of chef, bar, and waiter personnel work together to ensure complete client satisfaction.

Paula LeDuc
Fine Catering and Event Planning
1350 Park Avenue
Emeryville, CA 94608

(510) 547-7825
FAX: (510) 547-2076
paula_leduc_inc@email.msn.com

Contact: Paula LeDuc

Service Area: Coast to Coast

Specialties: Personalized in-season menus using the highest quality fresh ingredients provided by local farmers and growers; complete event planning services

Base Prices (food only): lunch, from $25; dinner, from $40; min. $500
Extra Charges: staff, rentals, coordination

Payment Terms: 25% to 50% deposit, balance is billed
Credit Cards: no

Lead Time: 1 week to 1 year
No. of Guests (min/max): no min / no max
Liquor License: licensed service available

Paula's fame and the reputation of her great catering company are well deserved. Each time she walks with me through one of her fabulous events, she notices every little speck on the floor and every irregularity at a buffet setup. She reached her goal a long time ago: to provide the same fine food enjoyed in a gourmet restaurant. Her hors d'oeuvres are the smallest, yet most work-intensive I have ever seen. Just recently at an event for the Pacific Stock Exchange, I tasted a delicious tiny beggar's purse, made of thin crêpe filled with crème fraîche and caviar, and tied up with a piece of chive. The tables for this corporate event were simply, yet elegantly set with gold and dark red striped tablecloths and large glass bowls overflowing with fragrant red garden roses. The wedding setup I observed that same evening was fantastic – very lush with vibrant colors and beautiful lighting.

Paula was one of three caterers selected by Martha Stewart to cater a wedding menu for her first *Weddings* issue of *Martha Stewart Living*. Paula's catered events include two private dinners for President Clinton during this past year, the 25th anniversary event for *The Godfather*, the Disney premier of *The Rock* on Alcatraz and *Jack*, and an 800-guest gala dinner at Neibaum-Coppola celebrating the re-release of Coppola's *Napoleon*. She also provides catering services for Giorgio Armani, and her food has been enjoyed by Black & White Ball patrons (1993, 1995, and 1997), as well as by those in attendance at the San Francisco Ballet's opening night galas for the past five years. Paula has been featured in several national publications and was most recently cited "San Francisco's Best Caterer" by *Town and Country Magazine's* wedding issue (Feb. '97).

Paula thrives on challenge, never appears nervous, and can enjoy a joke at the same time food is about to be served to 500 guests. Clients love the company's work and often give them carte blanche to organize their event.

Melon's
Full Service Catering and Event Planning
100 Ebbtide
Sausalito, CA 94965

(415) 331-0888
FAX: (415) 331-9504
melons@pacbell.net

Contact: Ann Lyons

Service Area: Coast to Coast

Specialties: Regional American and global cuisine, freshly prepared and served by a friendly, professional staff

Base Prices (food only): lunch, from $15; dinner, from $25; drop-off food, min. $50
Extra Charges: staff, rentals, service charge

Payment Terms: 10% deposit, 40% 2 weeks prior to event, balance is billed
Credit Cards: no

Lead Time: 2 days to 1 year
No. of Guests (min/max): no min / no max
Liquor License: yes

I could not have picked a better day to meet with Ann at the Ebbtide quarters. I came just at the right time to participate in the birthday feast and champagne toast for a kitchen employee. Ann was highly recommended to me when I worked on my first guide. No matter where I saw her work, at a wedding in a mansion or, more recently, at the Maritime Museum, the buffets were always a symphony of colorful food, presented on fashionable platters and in baskets and glass containers. Accompanying the food were fresh fruit, vegetables, and bread baked in-house. A summer flower bouquet enhanced the setup for the wedding, and the turquoise tablecloth reflected the color of the sky.

Ann, who owns Melon's, is recognized as one of the Bay Area's acclaimed wedding caterers and is also known for her creative theme parties. She and her staff are skilled at designing every aspect of an event, pulling from their resources to bring together the finest seasonal foods, entertainment, florals, decor, lighting, rentals, and locations. For over 20 years, Ann has been providing the highest quality food and professional service, and has garnered client praise for her company's diverse cooking styles and creative presentations. At one event she was presented with an "Academy Award" for her appetizers by *San Francisco Examiner* food editor, Jim Wood.

Ann will consult extensively with her clients and will go to great lengths to satisfy everyone's taste. A full-time pastry chef prepares beautiful wedding cakes in Melon's kitchen. To ensure high quality and freshness, the food is usually prepared on-site.

Now We're Cooking!
Catering, Event Planning, Decor
2150 Third Street
San Francisco, CA 94107

(415) 255-6355
FAX: (415) 255-6377
lw@nowcook.com
www.nowcook.com

Contact: Laurence Whiting

Service Area: Throughout California

Specialties: Innovative, seasonal, California cuisine with Mediterranean influence; classic style with contemporary flair

Base Prices (food only): lunch, from $20; dinner, from $25; min. $1,000
Extra Charges: staff, rentals, design, service charge

Payment Terms: 50% deposit, balance due day of event
Credit Cards: Visa, MasterCard

Lead Time: 1 week to 2 years
No. of Guests (min/max): no min / no max
Liquor License: yes

It is no surprise to see Now We're Cooking! on the preferred caterers list of many San Francisco-and-beyond venues, including many elegant mansions, the Wattis Room of San Francisco's Davies Symphony Hall, as well as their new restaurant, Disegno!, at the San Francisco Design Center. Their service is always superb. As establishing rapport is important to Laurence, he always matches the client with his professional planners, Kathleen Kirkpatrick, Clara Lester, or Charlotte Moore. Their presence and Laurence's involvement throughout gives clients a comforting and familiar feeling as they arrive at their reception.

Originally from Los Angeles, Laurence branched out from his artistic family into a world of finance and accounting for 8 years. Deep down, he craved more creativity and found the answer when he acquired an accounting position at "Along Came Mary," a prestigious Hollywood premier catering company. For 3 ½ years, Laurence learned about working at a high-quality establishment. In 1989, Laurence took this knowledge and experience to a natural next step – opening his own catering business. He moved to San Francisco and established Now We're Cooking! with goals of creating fine, upscale catering. With a staff of 25 full-time employees, Laurence prides himself in providing incredible service from the first contact until the final sweep of the broom at the end of the party.

Their signature cuisine is California classic with Mediterranean and Italian influence, but they enjoy working with adventurous clients who want something unusual or exotic. Chef Regina Medoro goes to great lengths to research recipes and culture. One of the functions I attended offered an authentic Persian menu at the James Leary Flood Mansion. Chef Medoro and Laurence went as far as dining at the bride's recommended Persian restaurant to get the full vision of what she wanted for her reception. The mouth-watering, tiny morsels of rock-salt-roasted prawns, grilled eggplant rotellini, and Caspian skewers of swordfish and sturgeon jumping with flavor, were served on antique framed mirrors. Just one of their many special touches!

Panache Catering
Simply Beautiful Food
3261 Ash Street
Palo Alto, CA 94306

(650) 327-2075
FAX: (650) 327-7105
panache1@msn.com

Contact: Carole Christian

Service Area: Greater Bay Area

Specialties: New California cuisine; elegant buffets and dinners; fingerfood for all occasions; picnics for private and corporate events

Base Prices (food only): lunch, from $15; dinner, from $28
Extra Charges: staff, rentals, coffee, punch, paper products

Payment Terms: $300 deposit, 50% first installment, balance due prior to event
Credit Cards: no

Lead Time: 5 days to 9 months
No. of Guests (min/max): 8 / 400
Liquor License: bar service available

Panache was the first catering company I interviewed when I began my research for the first edition of the guide. They provided me with the first recommendations for the many highly valued businesses which set the tone and title for the series. Panache began operating in 1986, and since 1991 Carole has been managing the company on her own. Her creative cooking style is based on new California cuisine. She has many innovative ideas for unique menus and buffets, and loves to create new delicacies. The food is usually presented in baskets, art deco dishes, or on heirloom silver plates, and garnished with herbs and flowers from Carole's garden. All barbecued fare is cooked on-site over a mesquite grill.

The last time I attended a Panache event was at a beautiful May wedding. The lawn area was tented to protect against the cold weather. Flower beds and blooming vines, seen through the opaque tent walls, added to the decoration. The floral design of the linen, glass bowls filled with spring flowers, and elegant china and silverware looked festive. The attractive buffet was set up in the front right side of the house. The menu matched the elegant ambience. After several trays of hors d'oeuvres were passed around, the meal began with two entrees: salmon wrapped in puff pastry and grilled tenderloin of beef with Sauce Bernaise. There was also a delicious salad of baby greens, orange sections, walnuts and goat cheese; roasted vegetables, crab and shrimp salad on artichoke bottoms, and wild rice pilaf with pecans and scallions.

My neighbor who had hired her for a picnic in the park commented on the excellent food and service. I also tasted Carole's delicious food at this neighbor's recent open house. Other clients also rave about the food, service, and Carole's consulting skills. Panache can accommodate any type of event, whether classy, casual, or elegant.

Parsley Sage Rosemary & Thyme
Catering & Event Professionals
(by appointment)
San Jose, CA

(800) 798-8388
(650) 988-6570
FAX: (800) 952-0212
Debbie@psrt.com
www.psrt.com

Contact: Debbie Blackwell or Vince Guasch

Service Area: Greater Bay Area

Specialties: California fresh to sushi, barbecues to ethnic cuisines

Base Prices (food only): lunch, from $15; dinner, from $30
Extra Charges: staff, rentals, corkage fee, gratuity

Payment Terms: 50% deposit, balance due 1 week prior to event
Credit Cards: no

Lead Time: 1 week to 1 year
No. of Guests (min/max): 100 / 5,000
Liquor License: no, but will serve

The location was the American Musical Theatre and the theme was "Hollywood Nights." Parsley Sage Rosemary & Thyme (PSRT) brought all the components of a Hollywood production into place for one of Silicon Valley's major computer companies, from DJ and Karaoke to Casino slot machines and roulette wheels. But nothing beat the taste of their fresh and hot hors d'oeuvres.

Most of the guests thought Tinseltown Music and gambling would comprise the entertainment, but the biggest production turned out to be the up-to-the-minute fresh food that was being prepared in the PSRT portable gourmet kitchen. I was amazed to see the kitchen's setup, stations staffed by different cooks preparing grilled quesadilla, deep-fried popcorn shrimp, bacon-rolled scallops, and rolled sushi. Their fleet of trucks varied from the complete mobile kitchen and refrigeration trucks to a catch-all truck for any emergency that may arise.

Each morsel of food and the desserts I tasted were delicious. Thousands of flavors were dancing in my mouth. Hot hors d'oeuvres seldom remain hot in a buffet service for 700 guests, but PSRT managed to keep the food piping hot and the Bananas Foster from melting.

Both corporate and social client reviews were nothing less than magnificent: "We were totally blown away." "Debbie and Vince 'feel their work'." "200% goes into every presentation and food." "Consistently great ideas and food." "Very easy to work with." "They were above and beyond our expectations." "Their services are presented as a package." "The kitchen was left spotless." "They take care of everything."

The Party Helpers

(408) 435-7337
FAX: (408) 435-7454
www.thepartyhelpers.com

780 Montague Expressway, Suite 706
San Jose, CA 95131

Contact: Kristin Dickens or Kevin Zarzeczny

Service Area: Greater Bay Area

Specialties: Elegant, casual Continental or California cuisine

Base Prices (food only): lunch, from $13; dinner, from $18
Extra Charges: staff, gratuity, rentals, coffee, punch

Payment Terms: 10% deposit, 40% 3 months prior, balance due prior to event
Credit Cards: no

Lead Time: 1 week to 1 year
No. of Guests (min/max): 8 / 1,000
Liquor License: no

The Party Helpers is among the more established catering companies in the South Bay. Owner Kristin Dickens has had many years of experience catering elegant weddings, as well as corporate parties and picnics. Her current chef, Barbara Prado, is an accomplished creative chef with over seven years of experience. She recently prepared a grilled lobster dinner for a wedding in Woodside without a formal kitchen.

The food prepared for an October wedding at a winery was very delicious. I tried the different gourmet cheeses, the home-made dips with fresh vegetables, and the Italian sausage with peppers, onions, and Mendocino mustard. The chicken crêpes were neatly stacked waiting to be heated. Kristin had used her own tablecloths with overlays for the dinner tables. The buffet was done in the same design. To enhance the setup, they used ribbons with the same color and ivy. The chafing dishes were hidden in lattice boxes.

Kristin offers a menu tasting before every large event. When I interviewed her, she was planning a large Indian wedding on short notice. She had to find authentic recipes and actually met three times with the wedding party to ensure the right taste.

A frequent customer loves the variety in her comprehensive menus and the emphasis she puts on decoration and display.

Something Special Catering, Inc.
Quality Food at Reasonable Prices
532 N. Santa Cruz Avenue, Unit C
Los Gatos, CA 95030

(408) 395-4276
FAX: (408) 395-4808

Contact: Debbie Finet

Service Area: Greater Bay Area

Specialties: California, vegetarian, and health food cuisines (no cholesterol)

Base Prices (food only): lunch, from $12; dinner, from $25
Extra Charges: staff, rentals, punch

Payment Terms: $500 deposit, balance due 1 day prior to event
Credit Cards: no

Lead Time: 1 day to 1 year
No. of Guests (min/max): 2 / 1,000
Liquor License: no, but will serve

Debbie's love of food dates back to her teenage years when she earned extra money working at restaurants. She also managed a cafeteria on a German army base, and later co-owned a deli in Washington State. In 1991 she moved to California, bought Something Special Catering, and, in just a few years, turned it into one of the leading catering companies in the South Bay. Her business volume tripled in 1994, and she now has three full-time chefs (one cooks only vegetarian) and over fifty other employees. In May 1995, she opened a cafe for lunch in Palo Alto on Page Mill Road, and in 1996 became the exclusive caterer for Villa Montalvo. Even with all this success, Debbie is still as nice and personable as she was when we first met. Attending to her growing company does not allow her time to browse through *Gourmet* magazines, but she encourages her chefs to do so and is open to innovative ideas. She also believes in buying the freshest produce and meats, all of which are cooked at the safest temperatures.

One of Debbie's specialties is weddings, for which she offers a complete consultation. Her clients like her personality, her attention to detail, and her work ethics.

I saw her elegant buffet table with a colorful tablecloth, decorated with grape leaves, ivy, fresh grapes and strawberries at Byington Winery. Baked brie with brown sugar and walnuts, crinkle hair pasta salad with tomatoes, capers and fresh basil, a mixed garden salad, green beans sautéed in olive oil and garlic, and wonderfully aromatic stuffed chicken breast were the main items on the menu. Since then I have tasted her food on many occasions, which is always high quality and always includes "something special."

Sous City
Custom-Designed Catering
(by appointment)
Santa Cruz, CA

(831) 475-7864
FAX: (831) 724-0181

Contact: Sue Slater

Service Area: South Bay, Monterey Bay, Santa Cruz County

Specialties: California cuisine with French accent

Base Prices: lunch, from $18; dinner, from $25; includes labor and flatware; min. $500
Extra Charges: gratuity, rentals, beverages

Payment Terms: $350 non-ref. deposit, balance due 1 week prior to event
Credit Cards: no

Lead Time: 1 week to 9 months
No. of Guests (min/max): 2 / 1,100
Liquor License: no

Sue Slater, owner of Sous City, has an impressive background. After earning an Associate Degree in food service technology, she went to Paris to learn the secrets of fine French cuisine. She spent a year studying at the cooking school of the famous Cordon Bleu in Paris. After some time as an apprentice in a Paris restaurant, she returned to the Bay Area and worked in various places before opening her own catering company. Her experience and her love of food has earned her several prizes in culinary salons. Besides being Sous City's chef, she also teaches at Cabrillo College.

Sue uses only the freshest ingredients. The chicken is cut just before it is prepared, and the pesto and dressings are homemade. Most of the food is cooked on-site to guarantee the best taste and flavor. Fresh herbs and edible flowers are used to enhance both taste and appearance.

I can confirm everything Sue told me. At a wedding in Santa Cruz, I saw the pretty buffet table and tasted some of her delicious food. I tasted all the appetizers: asagio soufflé on tiny red baked potatoes, triopetas wrapped in phyllo dough, and oven-dried tomatoes with brie and pesto. A large decorated platter held a variety of freshly sautéed vegetables. Shark kabobs with fresh pineapple salsa were the main course, waiting to be barbecued. I was sorry I had to leave and not indulge more in all these delicacies.

Clients give Sue glowing recommendations, describing her unique food, her lovely presentation, and her nice personality. Sous City was voted best caterer in Santa Cruz County for 1996 by *Good Times Magazine* readers poll. Exclusive sites are available through Sous City.

Taste
Catering - Event Planning
3450 Third Street, 4D
San Francisco, CA 94124

(415) 550-6464
FAX: (415) 550-1858
www.tastecatering.com

Contact: Catherine Jirik, Susana Muñoz, or Wayne Davis

Service Area: West Coast

Specialties: Taste in the art of entertaining: superb cuisine, gracious service, elegant presentation and event planning

Base Prices (food only): lunch, from $15; dinner, from $25
Extra Charges: staff, rentals

Payment Terms: 50% deposit, balance due day of event
Credit Cards: no

Lead Time: 1 week to 1 year
No. of Guests (min/max): 10 / 15,000
Liquor License: yes

"Taste was actually the catering company in the area whose founder, Timothy Maxsoni, took catering to a much higher level, and, in the late '70s, started bringing gourmet food to his discriminating customers." So I was told. Long before I began publishing my guides, I had read about their wonderful food and presentation at the Black & White Ball and at other social and political events. In 1992, Edible Art, another high-class company, merged with Taste, and MeMe Pederson became the new president, keeping to the tradition of excellence.

The company is known for its variety of excellent food and sophisticated and innovative presentation. Colors, textures and shapes are combined to delight the eye. The chef will often create a dish to coordinate with the theme of an event. Dedicated, attentive staff and elegant equipment are also part of their service. No wonder that Taste is there when famous visitors are in town. The company has catered events for each U.S. president from Carter to Clinton. At a fund-raising dinner for President Clinton, a guest had fallen into the swimming pool. MeMe came to the rescue and had his shirt and suit dried and ironed before Mr. Clinton arrived.

The San Francisco Opera's 75th Anniversary Gala Dinner, a Ralph Lauren party, and a Moroccan palace theme, complete with caftans for the guests and a live camel brought in from Los Angeles, are just samples of the varied events Taste handles on a regular basis. I have seen their excellent work for events, such as the opening of a De Young Museum exhibit where the food and decoration followed the natural approach of Albert Bierstadt; a corporate sit-down dinner, at which the sample plates prepared for each course resembled works of art; an elegant wedding, where each tablecloth was ironed right before it was put on the table, and a fun casino night.

Trumpetvine
Catering and Event Planning
2533 Seventh Street
Berkeley, CA 94710

(510) 848-7268
FAX: (510) 848-7302
trumpetvin@aol.com
www.ByRecOnly.com/trumpetvine

Contact: Deborah Bowen Lyons or Fernando Ciurlizza

Service Area: Greater Bay Area

Specialties: Freshly cooked, upscale California-style cuisine; fabulous service and food with emphasis on elegance and abundance; reasonable prices

Prices (food only): lunch, from $15; dinner, from $25; min. $500 for take-out; staffed event, $1,000
Extra Charges: rental, staff

Payment Terms: 10% deposit, 75% 10 days prior to event, balance is billed
Credit Cards: Visa, MasterCard

Lead Time: 1 day to 1 year
No. of Guests (min/max): 15 / no max
Liquor License: beer, wine, champagne

Deborah Bowen Lyons, one of the company's founders and current president, brings a good deal of experience to her job. She started out in the food business as a catering manager for Narsai David which eventually led to the positions of catering sous chef for the Caravansary, restaurant food writer for the *Sausalito Review*, and instructor for Tante Marie's Cooking School. Her magic team of chef Michelle Burns and manager Fernando Ciurlizza brings unusual food and interest to Trumpetvine. One of Fernando's Peruvian specialties is Ocapa, an unbelievable potato mint sauce. Their dramatic style places emphasis on abundance and elegance without being too fussy.

Ever since opening in 1979, they pride themselves on preparing impeccably fresh, organic produce, cooked from scratch and with only the finest ingredients. Their events range from "big zany events" for companies on the cutting edge to events that bring families together. They often replicate authentic recipes and suggest incorporating family serving pieces in their presentation. They work closely with clients to personalize menus that fit the mood and theme of the party.

I attended an open house held at their Berkeley kitchen. Their open kitchen was set up for an intimate tasting of their California-style dishes. Platters of fresh, roasted vegetables, asparagus-filled pork and tangerine-trimmed salmon were elegantly displayed on various marble and glass platforms. The look is stunning; each bite had a deliciously unique taste.

"Deborah added many unexpected extras," boasted one of their repeat customers. "The vegetable sculpture was the talk of the party – as fresh and tasty as it was attractive."

Yank Sing

(415) 362-4799
FAX: (415) 362-3688
yanksing@yanksing.com
www.yanksing.com

427 Battery (at Clay)
San Francisco, CA 94111

Contact: George Ong

Service Area: Greater Bay Area

Specialties: Deem Sum (fresh, handmade Chinese fingerfood)

Base Prices (food only): lunch, from $25; buffet, from $35, sit-down dinner, from $55
Extra Charges: severs, rentals

Payment Terms: 50% deposit, balance due 2 weeks prior to event
Credit Cards: major credit cards

Lead Time: 1 month to 1 year
No. of Guests (min/max): 50 / 2,000
Liquor License: yes

Tantalizing, bite-sized Chinese delectables made of Peking duck, fresh fish, fowl, beef, pork, vegetables, exotic spices, and rice will make your mouth water. Yank Sing creates daily over 100 types of freshly steamed, fried, baked, and roasted Deem Sum. Several chefs are at hand in order to create their various fresh, up-to-the-minute delicacies. From fluffy barbecued pork buns and goldfish-shaped shrimp dumplings to mouth-watering prawns dipped in a light tempura-like batter, you can't eat just one.

Deem Sum, literally translated to "touch the heart," does just that in every event Yank Sing caters. With over 14 years of experience with both corporate and social events, the company is on many preferred and recommended caterers' lists, including the Asian Art Museum, the California Academy of Sciences, the James Leary Flood Mansion, and many major hotels. From full catering services for significant events, such as Super Bowl XXXI and the opening reception of Chao Shao to an exhibit for food suppliers of the Moscone Convention Center and San Francisco International Airport, Yank Sing delivers an appetizing feast.

From preparation to presentation and service, Yank Sing can completely plan your celebration. At every event at which I encountered them, they always outshone the competition. Crowds always form around their food stations whenever they cater a party. Customers and professional references rave. "They do whatever needs to be done." "You can feel confident, you can count on them." "Every aspect – flowers, trees, lighting, chairs, tables, and displays – was coordinated. Service was great; food was even better."

EVENT COORDINATORS

NOTES

INTRODUCTION

Coordinators come and go! Many remember the fun they had planning their own wedding and feel they are experienced enough to try their hand at wedding consulting and coordinating. However, it's a very difficult and demanding job. Nervous brides and mothers need everything, from a family counselor to someone who is patient, considerate, experienced, cheerful, very thorough, and available 24 hours a day!

Many industry professionals such as caterers, locations, disc jockeys, and musicians offer wedding coordination services as part of the package. While their services are valuable, they might be more limited in scope compared to an independent professional wedding coordinator who has only your interests in mind. Coordinators can thoroughly review all of your contracts, negotiate prices, find unique venues, and pre-qualify other industry professionals bearing in mind your budget and style. I heard a story the other day about a catering manager of a large hotel who wanted to charge more for the menu than was initially stated. The event coordinator checked his notes and made the manager honor the original price.

It's also most pleasant to leave the organization to someone else on your special day so that you and your family are not pulled away to answer questions. All you do is enjoy. The coordinator usually brings along an "emergency kit" containing everything one might ever need.

All of the wedding coordinators reviewed in the guide have been in business for several years. Many have even attended extensive seminars on wedding coordination and are highly respected in the industry. It's so important to choose one whose personality clicks with yours since you will be working very closely together.

Wedding coordinators can often get you better prices from vendors than you can get on your own. If the coordinator enjoys working with a vendor, he or she will return with future business, and thus might be offered lower prices.

Money Matters

Prices depend on the extent of the coordinator's service. You can request "mini" consultations for simply helping with the budget, advising on etiquette, or finding a location. Or you can request your coordinator to assist with all of the planning, including being there on your special day.

Most coordinators charge by either: 1) hourly rate, itemizing and billing for service on a regular basis; 2) flat rate, usually a cost savings based on an estimated number of hours of service required; 3) percentage, based on the overall budget, or 4) a combination of these. Fees average about $50 per hour; complete wedding service can run into several thousand dollars (approximately 10-15% of your wedding budget).

A Bride's Best Friend
Wedding Consultant/Organizer
330-D Sir Francis Drake Blvd.
San Anselmo, CA 94960

(415) 453-1662
FAX: (415) 453-1799
abrides.best.friend@lycosmail.com
www.abridesbestfriend.net

Contact: Elizabeth Betsy Ayers or Marty Rosenblum

Service Area: San Francisco, Marin, Wine Country, East Bay

Specialties: Wedding and event consulting and coordination; invitations, favors, calligraphy; specializing in Jewish weddings and mixed marriages

Pricing: customized packages, from $100 to full production
Extra Charges: travel beyond 1 hour

Payment Terms: 50% deposit, balance due prior to event; hourly rate is billed
Credit Cards: no

Lead Time: 1 week to 1 year
Portfolio: yes

I first met Betsy when she and her husband, Marty, ran Marty's Parties catering company. Marty was the chef while Betsy organized events and took charge of their fabulous buffets. In 1995, the couple decided to slow down a bit, and Betsy began helping friends organize their offices and setting up systems for helping caterers coordinate parties.

Then, one week last October, two brides who wanted to book the catering company asked Betsy to help them coordinate their weddings. She took these requests as an omen to start her own business, though she was certainly not new to the event planning business. Before working with her husband, she worked for quite a few caterers and spent several years with a Bay Area event company. I met Betsy in her new, attractive office with the beautiful view in the newly renovated, historic Tamalpais theater building. Her brochure clearly spells out her services that encompass all aspects of planning and coordinating events, from helping to choose the right vendors and sites through arranging for wedding cake tiers, rentals, and accommodations for out-of-town guests – anything to make the day easier and more enjoyable for the bride and her family.

Betsy, a "people person," had always enjoyed helping brides make their event as memorable and as successful as possible. She chose the name "A Bride's Best Friend" to offer the kind of help a friend would, someone you could call about anything at anytime. She even comes up with good suggestions when the budget is too limited for her services. She always brings along an emergency bag and a small picnic basket with a snack or energy drink to be consumed before the wedding.

They have been in the event business for over 20 years and have a select group of vendors who work with them. They are extremely professional and personable, and are a pleasure to work with.

A Joyous Occasion
Certified Wedding Consultant
(by appointment)
San Jose, CA

(408) 267-0773
FAX: (408) 267-0785
www.weddings-online.com/con/AJoyousOccasion

Contact: Marcia Coleman-Joyner (Certified by Ann Nola's Association of Certified Professional Wedding Consultants)
Service Area: Greater Bay Area and beyond

Specialties: Full-service wedding consultant, wedding day coordinator, event planner

Pricing: à la carte: $65/hr., commission or flat fee, depending on services
Extra Charges: travel and toll calls beyond Santa Clara County

Payment Terms: $350 non-ref. deposit, balance due 1 week prior to event
Credit Cards: no

Lead Time: 2 weeks to 1 year
Portfolio: yes

Marcia and her sister Gretchen started their business in 1989 and soon became known as "GreMar." Since Gretchen relocated to Boston, Marcia has been running the business, with an average of 38 to 45 weddings per year. She also coordinates events for corporate clients.

Marcia begins with a free, no-obligation consultation, the most extensive one I've come across. She learns about the couple's desires, personalities, and life-styles, and also includes budget preparation. She knows how to cut corners for smaller budgets. For a full-service wedding, Marcia charges a combination of 1) a percentage of the vendor's fee (for only those vendors she is requested to procure); 2) an hourly rate for on-site consultations; and 3) a flat fee to coordinate the day. If she is merely to coordinate the day, an hourly rate for on-site consultations and a flat fee for 8 hours of coordination apply, including the rehearsal. On occasion, Marcia has provided guidance only on an hourly basis. She has also been requested to only provide a list of proven wedding professionals within the couples' budget, for which she charges a nominal flat fee. The à la carte pricing allows couples to pick and choose only the services they need and to stay within their budget. No wedding is too big or too small. Marcia will also work with a service already contracted by the couple. Given her experience and knowledge, she can assist in all areas; however, the final decisions are always left to the client.

I know Marcia to be a highly respected, very professional and warm person. During her many years in business, she has organized weddings for couples across the country, has taught classes for wedding consultants, and once stepped in as wedding coordinator 48 hours before the wedding. References think she is easy to work with, very experienced, professional, and, on the wedding day, indispensable. The owner of a winery said, "When Marcia coordinates the wedding, it's like a vacation. We can all sit back and relax."

Always r.s.v.p.*

(650) 854-6399
FAX: (650) 854-6395
rsvpyes@aol.com

3570 Alameda de las Pulgas
Menlo Park, CA 94025

Contact: Suzy Somers

Service Area: Greater Bay Area and International

Specialties: *Remarkable, sensational, versatile parties… and papers

Pricing: event design, $70/hr.
Extra Charges: none

Payment Terms: 50% due day of proposal,
balance due day of event
Credit Cards: no

Lead Time: 1 week to 1 year
Delivery/Pickup: yes
Portfolio: yes, beautiful ones

As soon as I entered the small store, I could feel the positive energy and friendly, easygoing air about the place. Laughter was emanating from the invitation area where Suzy's assistant was consulting on a party invitation. A former client was stopping by to say hello. It's obvious how much people enjoy dropping in to do business or chat. That's because Suzy enjoys people so much, and you can't help but enjoy her. Once a year she donates her time to organizing a fund-raiser.

Suzy had always liked throwing parties or helping her friends with theirs. She later turned from teaching to event planning, a natural choice. After 13 years of working from her home, she found this adorable shop, where she and her long-time employees have been meeting with clients to plan their events for the past three years. At the start of our interview, Suzy made it very clear that she only charges by the hour. There are no hidden costs, nor is money added to the vendor's bill. All savings are passed on to the client. Suzy works with everybody who can best meet your requests and is proud of the incredible relationship she has developed with her crew, vendors, and clients. A trademark of her party planning is her well-trained staff, who greet the guests and bid them farewell. There is no shortage of ideas. Invitations can be created for each event; one creative idea was to send out invitations packaged in a bottle.

Browsing through Suzy's portfolio gave me a good sense of her creativity and flexibility. She had chosen striped and polka dot tablecloths for a black & white, contemporary wedding. Since the bride's favorite flowers, Casablanca lilies, were rather expensive that particular weekend, they were mixed with other flowers to cut down on cost. The simple, yet striking centerpieces were tall, thin, black metal sculptures, some filled with dendrobium orchids and others with Casablanca lilies and magnolia leaves. The napkins were tied with black licorice, a rather whimsical twist.

Bridal Network

(by appointment)
Oakland, CA

(510) 339-3370
(415) 362-0199
FAX: (510) 339-0652

Contact: Connie Olson Kearns

Service Area: Greater Bay Area and Napa Valley

Specialties: Wedding consulting and coordination

Pricing: from $2,500
Extra Charges: none

Payment Terms: by installments
Credit Cards: none

Lead Time: 4 - 18 months
Portfolio: yes

Whenever I observe one of the more beautiful and elaborate weddings, I can be sure to find Connie working in the background as the event coordinator. I can also expect to find something special I have never seen before: a lawn transformed by lighting into a gorgeous tapestry, or a dance floor painted with the interwoven initials of the couple in Botticelli style. To fulfill the dreams of her customers, Connie often takes their ideas a step further, doing something they had never thought of, such as re-create the interior of a pavilion inside a ballroom with the help of other excellent event professionals, or change the Venetian Room at the Fairmont into a Shakespearian forest, even bring in chefs from ethnic restaurants to create authentic cuisines.

This highly respected company has been in business since 1980. Connie believes that her experience in catering and event planning while working for large hotels and elegant clubs was essential for her successful career. I would add that her thorough knowledge of the essentials of a wedding, down to the smallest detail, and her understanding of human nature (particularly of brides and their mothers), as well as the importance of a positive relationship with vendors and personnel make her company special.

Discreet and with impeccable taste, Connie has had many customers who are prominent society figures. Her classy, elegant Northern Californian weddings are also sought after by celebrities from the Los Angeles area. I am not the only one who admires her class and her style; many recommendations and repeat customers quickly book up her calendar. Over the years she has been invited to give public speeches about her work and experience throughout the country. The last time we talked, she was just about to fly down to Los Angeles where she was invited by the Caterers Association of America to speak about the anatomy of a perfect wedding.

The Carefree Bride
Complete Wedding Arrangements
(by appointment)
San Rafael, CA

(415) 492-0430
(Phone & FAX)
(415) 454-5896
FAX: (415) 454-2013
bride4444@aol.com

Contact: Carolyn Kinnaird or Janet Ellinwood

Service Area: Greater Bay Area and International

Specialties: Wedding and event planning

Pricing: Complete service, $900 - $2,500; hourly consultation available
Extra Charges: none

Payment Terms: 50% deposit, balance due 45 days after contract signing
Credit Cards: Visa, MasterCard

Lead Time: 3 weeks to 1 year
Portfolio: many

When I first met Janet in her home, our interview was interrupted from time to time by her children who would come in from playing outside and ask her questions. Watching her respond to them, I could just imagine her dealing with different vendors or a crisis – never flustered and having everything under control in a warm, caring way. She started her company in 1982 and since then has organized over 580 weddings.

Carolyn has been working with Janet for several years. She had previously worked at her real estate company where she learned all about contracts and what to point out when touring mansions with her clients. She learned about coordinating events while serving on the board of the Marin Ballet for eight years. The first interview, during which Carolyn learns about the client's ideas, is free of charge and takes place in the living room of her sprawling, contemporary home in Lucas Valley. Tea is served as you look out the windows onto an atrium garden.

A large portfolio documents their work. Their service ranges from as little as the hour-long consultation, to helping with the invitations or finding a location, to complete organization of the entire wedding. They emphasize the individuality of each wedding, and they work with their clients to achieve exactly what they want. Both Janet and Carolyn are good listeners, caring and warm. They are willing to work with vendors they have never dealt with before, and like to involve the groom and mother in the planning. They come up with a thorough schedule for each wedding and stick to it. Carolyn deals with the day to day business with brides, while Janet handles the contracts and communications. Both women are present at the wedding so that one can help with the final bridal preparations while the other is available to attend to other logistics.

I know several vendors who enjoy working with Janet and Carolyn. Their clients agree that they do an excellent job, are very competent and helpful, and well worth the fee.

Custom Celebrations
Classic Elegance in Wedding Coordination
878 Muender Avenue
Sunnyvale, CA 94086

(408) 732-7499
FAX: (408) 774-9110

Contact: Sarah Rondeau
(Certified Professional Wedding Consultant & Accredited Wedding Consultant)
Service Area: Greater Bay Area

Specialties: Wedding and event consulting; classes in wedding etiquette and afternoon tea

Pricing: flat fee based on services, from $375
Extra Charges: none

Payment Terms: 50% deposit, balance due
2 weeks prior to event
Credit Cards: no

Lead Time: 3 weeks to 1 year
Portfolio: yes

Sarah has an impressive background in coordinating weddings and other events. With her creativity and breadth of experience, she can help you plan the perfect event, from an informal, afternoon bridal tea to an extravagant wedding. The client and personal service come first, and style and budget are considered when finding the right professionals. Sarah's friendly and accommodating way guides you through the seemingly overwhelming task of planning and coordinating your wedding. Her flat fee is determined by the services selected.

During the first meeting, which is free of charge, Sarah and her staff learn about the client's wants and needs. They will then propose a plan to meet the established budget. Their goal is for each customer to receive the best possible service, information, and guidance. Their extensive and beautiful library of video tapes, catalogues, photographs, and the like are helpful in presenting a variety of choices.

Sarah plans as many weddings for clients who may simply live out of town, out of state, or out of the country as she does for those who live in the Greater Bay Area. She has worked simultaneously with clients in Japan, France, Great Britain, and Argentina. Many of her clients are business professionals who look to Sarah to help accomplish the wedding planning while they are away from home. Whether attempting to locate a site, preparing time tables and schedules, or planning the entire event, the client chooses what best suits them.

Sarah is expert at the art of the invitation. She has an extensive selection that includes custom designs in paper, lettering styles, and calligraphy. She can guide you in your selection, determining the best wording and design from the most classic to contemporary invitations and social stationery. Sarah's goal is to make the planning of the wedding as enjoyable as the wedding itself.

Events of Distinction
Full Service Event Planning
41 Heather Avenue
San Francisco, CA 94118

(415) 751-0211
(Phone & FAX)
evntdist@jps.net
www.jps.net/evntdist

Contact: Joyce Scardina Becker
Certified Wedding Consultant and Certified Meeting Planner

Service Area: U.S. and international

Specialties: Event planner, wedding specialist; designer of custom floral arrangements;
table favors; invitations and other printed materials

Pricing: Flat fee or $65/hr. for consulting services
Extra Charges: long distance calls, travel beyond Bay Area

Payment Terms: monthly installments, last installment due 2 weeks prior to event
Credit Cards: no

Lead Time: 2 weeks to 2 years
Portfolio: yes

Everything in Joyce's background points to being an accomplished event planner: she learned patience as a teacher, arranged numerous fund-raising and social events for various non-profit organizations, completed a certified floral program at City College, and graduated from San Francisco State with a degree in hospitality management. Joyce started her own event company in 1995 and became a certified wedding consultant and meeting planner. In addition to her event planning activities, Joyce serves on the faculty of San Francisco State University, teaching a Wedding Consultant Certification Program which she developed. This is the only program of its kind in the nation, providing a comprehensive education for students who wish to pursue a professional career in wedding planning. Joyce also has been quoted in numerous bridal books and magazines, and she has written several articles for national magazines on various subjects pertaining to weddings and special events. A recent issue of *Northern California Wedding* magazine had a feature article about "The Wedding of the Century" that Joyce helped to plan.

Joyce holds an initial complimentary consultation with her clients to better understand their needs, then works to ensure that every aspect of the wedding fulfills those needs. She is an expert at budgeting, site and vendor selection, and contract negotiations, as well as coordination of wedding day activities. To keep everything organized, all contracts and details are gathered in a 3-ring binder and presented to the client.

One client was pleased with Joyce's event creation for a holiday party and commented on how well her suggestions worked. Another client was impressed with Joyce's professionalism and knowledge about the event business. She told me that Joyce was terrific to work with, paid close attention to every detail, and had great ideas.

109

Glorious Weddings
Affordable Elegance
P.O. Box 563
Larkspur, CA 94977

(415) 453-8896
FAX: (415) 453-8834

Contact: Carol Rothman

Service Area: Greater Bay Area and beyond

Specialties: Wedding and event consulting

Pricing: $75/hr. or flat fee for customized service
Extra Charges: none

Payment Terms: in full at booking
Credit Cards: no

Lead Time: 1 week to 1 year
Portfolio: yes

Carol started her wedding and event consulting business in 1991 and, with her wealth of experience, her professionalism, and her warm and friendly demeanor, has become one of the leading wedding coordinators in the area. Clients rave about her invaluable assistance, which includes her calm approach, great suggestions, creativity, and good taste, as well as her role as diplomatic mediator in difficult family situations.

Carol will do as much or as little as you want, from finding a place or helping with invitations to planning the entire event. She takes care of all the paperwork, keeping records and paying bills. She will accompany clients on visits to all the vendors and will negotiate the best prices. Carol's emphasis is on teamwork to make the wedding a success. In an elegant portfolio you can see samples of work from the different vendors she likes to work with, not only because they do a great job, but also because they love what they're doing and are very nice to deal with.

Multicultural weddings are a favorite of hers. She is always interested in learning something new and incorporating different customs and traditions. She certainly had the opportunity to do so for a very traditional Korean wedding that she coordinated for an arranged marriage. In addition to the logistics involved in planning a wedding for 600 guests, some of the communication between her and her clients required the assistance of an interpreter.

A week before the event, Carol will send out a detailed schedule to everyone involved. Vendors will receive maps with directions to the site and are contacted by phone two days prior to the event. Her custom-designed weddings are priced according to the service provided and not based on a fixed percentage of the budget. Her first meeting is free of charge, and she prides herself on adhering to the initial budget.

"I Do" Weddings and Events

(408) 265-2223
FAX: (408) 265-0633
michelle@idowed.com
www.idowed.com

5638 Waltrip Lane
San Jose, CA 95118

Contact: Michelle Hodges (Certified Wedding Consultant)

Service Area: Greater Bay Area

Specialties: Weddings and special events (planning, coordinating, consulting); invitations, accessories, rental items

Pricing: from $55/hr. to full production, $850 - $3,200
Extra Charges: shipping, delivery

Payment Terms: $150 - $300 deposit, 50% 90 days prior, balance due 30 days prior to event
Credit Cards: no

Lead Time: 1 week to 1 year
Portfolio: yes

Over the many years I have known Michelle, meeting her at professional conferences or workshops, I have continued to think of her as the perfect event coordinator: always friendly, very organized, and well dressed. After pursuing a BA in biology, she worked as a legal and medical secretary. However, her dream was to run her own business. She took classes in floriculture, but soon discovered that her strength was her organizational abilities. "I was drawn to the industry by fate," she told me. Her thoroughness led her to enroll in the best classes. Michelle is certified by June Wedding, Inc., and the Association of Certified Professional Wedding Consultants (ACPWC) whose classes she regularly attends. Since 1997, Michelle has been the on-site coordinator for United Artists at the San Jose Pavilion Theater, organizing their corporate events and business functions.

Michelle's main goal is to both create the couple's dream wedding and eliminate tension during the planning and on the day itself. She makes sure that family and friends are at ease and enjoy the wedding day. She has worked at many locations, but also loves to do home weddings, which are more personal, intimate, and touching.

During a free introductory meeting, clients discuss the services they want. Michelle can either help with the smaller tasks, such as budget creation and assistance with contracts and schedules, or organize the entire wedding. Peers consider her great to work with, very efficient and organized, while clients rave about her services. One mother described how much Michelle helped her daughter create the exact wedding she wanted, and how the bride and groom were able to spend so much time with their guests. The mother will hire her again for her other daughters' weddings.

Instead of You
Personalized Event Services
(by appointment)
Berkeley, CA

(800) 446-7832
FAX: (510) 548-2463
maxine@instead-of-you.com
www.instead-of-you.com
www.ByRecOnly.com/insteadofyou

Contact: Maxine Andrew

Service Area: United States and International

Specialties: Full service wedding and event coordination, event styling; honeymoon planning

Pricing: $80/hour or flat rate
Extra Charges: event-related expenses; overnight accommodations

Payment Terms: 50% deposit, balance due in monthly installments
Credit Cards: no

Lead Time: 2 weeks to 1½ years
Portfolio: yes

Maxine Andrew started Instead of You in 1989 while completing her degree at UC Berkeley. Her company immediately received exposure on an ABC-TV segment about personalized services designed to make people's lives easier and less hectic. Maxine's services extend from supervising home renovations and moves, to full-service coordination of corporate functions, beautiful weddings, and special events. For one couple, she planned a honeymoon, consolidated two homes, put one home on the market, and hired movers to relocate the couple to their new home while the couple was on their 2½-week honeymoon. The couple returned to find all of their furniture beautifully arranged and their possessions carefully put away.

Maxine's weddings are just as extraordinary. Her events can range from elegant and traditional to exotic and multicultural. For an Islamic/Indian wedding for 650 guests, she made arrangements for the groom to arrive on a beautiful white horse. For a Jewish/Native-American wedding, she set the ceremony under an incredible chuppah, complete with sage smoke scenting the air and accompanied by tribal drummers and a dozen violinists. Maxine can do anything "instead of you."

Event professionals comment, "Maxine always balances the interest of both her clients and vendors." (Maxine calls it "creating a seamless network of vendors to support a client.") "Innovative and creative" and "fun and calming" are comments from her clients. I say, Maxine never leaves a detail unattended. Her knowledge and resources seem endless.

In July 1996, Maxine appeared on the Phil Donahue Show as a panelist discussing "Making Life Easier in the '90s" and received recognition as "Bay Area's Best Event Coordinator" during KRON's Wedding Week in April 1996. Her web site and services were featured on CNET's *The Web* in 1998, and pictures of events coordinated and styled by Maxine are often seen in local and national magazines.

Just Married Productions®
Surprisingly Affordable
131 Magnolia Avenue
Larkspur, CA 94939

(415) 924-3563

FAX: (415) 924-2434
justmarried@earthlink.com
www.weddingtips.com/enos/consulting.html

Contact: Dolores Enos, JWIC
Award-winning Consultant
Service Area: Greater Bay Area

Specialties: Weddings: from helping with various parts to complete wedding consultation and coordination

Pricing: $60 - $3,000
Extra Charges: travel, invitations

Payment Terms: initial deposit and progressive payments
Credit Cards: no

Lead Time: 2 weeks to 1 year
Portfolio: yes

You might have a hard time finding someone who is more experienced than Dolores in all the different aspects of the wedding industry. She helped her husband set up his wedding photography business and would accompany him to the event to coach the bride and groom, help with makeup, and fluff up the dresses. She soon learned all of the other aspects involved with weddings and began to offer consulting and coordination services, at no charge, to clients who hired her husband. To become more expert in this field, she took a course sponsored by June Wedding, Inc. in 1990 and is now a certified event professional. In 1991, she was awarded "Wedding Consultant of the Year" and founded the wedding trade show, "Just Married Productions," that is now well known beyond Marin. She became acquainted with a wide variety of event professionals, whose personalities and style matched her brides. I always look forward to meeting Dolores at national conferences for which she has organized several continuing education seminars. This is where I learned how beautifully she can set up a room and what a perfectionist she is.

Over the years, Dolores found herself enjoying the consulting and coordination aspects so much that she now has her own company. "You always do best what you love doing," she said, thus striving to become even better. She particularly enjoys the creative aspects: helping design an elegant ambiance for a room, with damask tablecloths, golden chargers, elegant china candelabra, beautiful flowers, and harp music; or leaving her mark on a fun New Year's wedding. Due to her excellent work, Dolores has been chosen to represent United Artist Satellite Theaters as the North Bay Satellite Coordinator. She also has an advice web site, "Ask Auntie Dee" (www.weddingtips.com/wtask.html).

"What a great event, thanks to her impeccable work!" "She took the pressure off me by taking care of negotiations and problems." "She handled every difficulty and challenge with diplomacy and grace." These were comments I heard from Dolores' clients. *Please call for an appointment.*

L'Affaire Du Temps
Have the affair of all time
698 Ann Place
Milpitas, CA 95035

(408) 946-7758
FAX: (408) 946-7688
laffaire@msn.com
www.laffairedutemps.com

Contact: Patricia Bruneau

Service Area: Greater Bay Area

Specialties: Weddings, specializing in the renewal of vows;
service-oriented consulting and coordination

Pricing: full service, from $3,500; day only, from $2,000
Extra Charges: overnight accommodations

Payment Terms: $750 non-ref. deposit,
last installment due 2 weeks prior to event
Credit Cards: no

Lead Time: 1 week to 2 years
Portfolio: yes

Patricia was highly recommended to me by several vendors long before I met her. Her background is in marketing and sales in the electronics industry. Before she began her own business in 1992, she met the requirements for earning the title of "Professional Wedding Consultant" through the Association of Certified Professional Wedding Consultants (ACPWC). She is also a "Certified Wedding Consultant" through June Wedding, Inc., and is now the Northern California Regional Director of this organization. Both organizations emphasize high-quality, continuing education. Patricia has been quoted in many times in *Modern Bride Magazine*, *Bride's Magazine*, and in the books *The Complete Idiot's Guide to the Perfect Wedding* and *The Wedding Sourcebook*. She has also appeared on "The Caryl and Marilyn Show" on ABC television.

Patricia's goal is to execute her client's wishes for their special event. If you hire her for a full-service wedding, she will schedule times with you to visit facilities and vendors. Patricia considers her service unique because of the time she commits to each couple. She makes sure that every phone call is returned within 24 hours. Two weeks before the wedding, she will send each vendor a package with all the information about the wedding, including a map, a floor plan for the setup, and schedule. She will book only one wedding a day and participates in all rehearsals.

Vendors and clients alike find her very professional and comment on how she masters each situation. A bride told me how wonderful Patricia was. "Pat provided the ultimate customer service: she was on top of everything, very organized, never distracted, and made us feel we were the most important people in her life."

Tie The Knot
Weddings & Special Events
(by appointment)
Palo Alto/San Francisco, CA

(650) 968-2564
(408) 746-0881
FAX: (408) 746-2830
TTKnot@aol.com

Contact: Annena Sorenson
(Nationally Certified Professional Wedding Consultant)
Service Area: Greater Bay Area, Wine Country and International

Specialties: Wedding consulting, coordination, design, long-distance planning

Pricing: flat fee based on services; custom packages from $1,500
Extra Charges: out-of-state calls, some travel expenses

Payment Terms: 2 - 3 installments
Credit Cards: no

Lead Time: 4 weeks to 18 months
Portfolio: several

I've known Annena since she had her own successful catering business, calling on her art background for her spectacular buffet designs. She organized one of the best wedding shows I've attended. Calm and collected, extremely well organized, never fazed, even in the trickiest of situations, a wonderful speaker, and very friendly are thoughts that come to mind about Annena.

She has planned international conferences for the wedding and event industry, working with the editors of *Bride's Magazine and Modern Bride*. At one of the conferences held in San Francisco, Annena coordinated the elegant luncheon with the theme "Designing a Room." She worked with designers, florists, and lighting technicians to create a stunning effect based on five tabletop themes: Wine Country, Romantic Garden, Enchantment, European, and Art Deco. Everyone was in awe of the room's design, with its trellises, columns, live plants, flowers, and spectacular lighting. Annena later told me that no one ever knew that most of the vendors had arrived two hours late.

"What really drives me is that I want to surpass the expectations of my clients," says Annena. A bride's mother wrote to Annena after the wedding: "There simply isn't a way to appropriately thank you for so many months of always being there, always caring, always having the perfect solution, always being available, always making us believe we were your most important concern. After almost 30 years of professional life, in several different arenas, I want you to know that there aren't many like you out there."

Annena has become one of the most highly respected event coordinators in the area during her 12 years in business.

...to the Last Detail

(650) 938-0553
(Phone & FAX)
celebrate@LastDetail.com
www.lastdetail.com

(by appointment)
Mountain View, CA

Contact: Mickey Farrance

Service Area: Silicon Valley

Specialties: Weddings and celebrations planning, management, and logistics
for professional and executive brides

Pricing: customized services from $600; $55/hr.
Extra Charges: none

Payment Terms: 50% deposit, balance due 24 hours prior to event
Credit Cards: no

Lead Time: 2 - 18 months
Portfolio: yes

A former rocket scientist, Mickey Farrance creates events that are "out of this world." A mechanical engineer in the aerospace industry for 18 years, Mickey handles her clients' events as meticulously as she did her NASA space projects.

Mickey opened ...to the Last Detail in 1994 after years of managing company picnics, seminars, team-building events, product launches, and milestone events. This petite bundle of energy is hard to miss. Wearing a delightful hat at every wedding or party is Mickey's way of "establishing a presence."

Mickey begins with an initial consultation to determine where the client is in the planning process and creates a proposal based on the client's individual needs. She can recommend wedding service vendors who meet the requirements specified by the client and can handle details ranging from addressing invitations to coordinating the seemingly infinite activities on the day of the event. What I find refreshing is Mickey's code of ethics: an outline of fair, upright, and ethical behavior that she both follows and looks for in the vendors she works with.

Her to-do-lists and timelines are personalized for each client, and budgets are detailed for even the busiest career bride to follow. Her customized services are based on the client's specific needs and are priced accordingly. Clients and corporations alike consistently praise Mickey's flexibility and keen mind for details. "It's now my mission to help people slow down and celebrate life," sums up Mickey. Being a coordinator myself, I can honestly say that Mickey has it all covered.

Tosca Productions
Wedding Coordination & Event Design
(by appointment)
Daly City, CA

(650) 992-1211
FAX: (650) 757-7284
tosca@toscaproductions.com
www.toscaproductions.com

Contact: Tosca J. Clark (Certified Professional Wedding Consultant)

Service Area: Greater Bay Area

Specialties: Specializing in elegant, multi-cultural, and theme weddings; event design; custom maps and programs; invitations and accessories

Pricing: customized flat rate packages or $75/hr.
Extra Charges: international calls

Payment Terms: 1/3 deposit, 1/3 halfway, balance due 2 weeks prior to event
Credit Cards: no

Lead Time: 6 weeks to 18 months
Portfolio: yes

"When I met Tosca I knew at once she was the one. I was not disappointed. Tosca helped with everything: the contracts, the flowers, the tablecloths. In fact, she saved us $2,000 by renegotiating the contract with the florist; arranged demo tapes for the bands and found out where we could listen to them; organized accommodations for the overnight guests, and returned all calls promptly. My husband and I had such a good time at our wedding." This and many similar quotes come from brides and industry professionals who adore her. Just the other day she received a thank-you letter 3 pages long.

Since starting out in 1988, Tosca has perfected her style. She loves challenges and keeps her cool, even when rerouting a bride's limo so that the bride would arrive in time. Every detail is recorded on her computer; copies of contracts, floor plans, checklists, and meticulously thought-out event schedules are presented to the couple in a personalized binder. With her endless energy and enthusiasm, she seamlessly produces elegant, traditional, and theme weddings to perfection. One challenge was to execute a groom's desire to spoil his bride and her bridesmaids the day before their surprise wedding. He wanted her to be completely swept off her feet. After consulting with the groom about what the bride liked to do, Tosca planned the day. Then, armed with contingency plans for every possible scenario, she secretly followed the party to make sure everything went flawlessly. Fourteen various flowers were secretly stashed at different spots all over the city for the bride to find during her adventures. Later she would discover that the first letter of each flower's name together spelled the magical question, "Will you marry me?" "Building on the couple's ideas and making them a reality is what it's all about!" exclaims Tosca.

I got to know Tosca well while working together on a BRO party and admired her organizational skills and creativity. As she is so highly respected by her professional peers, I asked her to assume authorship of this edition of *By Recommendation Only*. I know from my own experience with her that every couple will be in the best of hands with Tosca as their wedding coordinator.

The Wedding Resource

(415) 928-8621

Full Service Event Planning
(by appointment)
San Francisco, CA

Contact: Diane Breivis or Kathryn Kenna

Service Area: Greater Bay Area and Wine Country

Specialties: Wedding coordination, event design, graphic design

Pricing: $75/hr. or flat fee based on services
Extra Charges: graphic design services

Payment Terms: periodic installments
Credit Cards: no

Lead Time: 1 - 18 months
Portfolio: yes

"Thank you so much for your wonderful calming assistance..." reads a client's thank-you note to Diane and Kathryn. Behind their warm and assuring personalities one finds hard workers who are very organized and on top of every aspect of the business. Vendors love to work with them and comment on their professionalism and attention to details.

Diane and Kathryn offer a complimentary interview to discuss general questions clients may have about working with a consultant. At that time, they decide on a payment plan based on the services required, which is generally a flat fee. The first working meeting usually lasts a couple of hours and includes budget work as well as site and vendor referrals. They will make suggestions regarding the ceremony, advise on etiquette, and help with decision-making. They welcome working with vendors with whom they have had no previous experience and are happy to share information and photos from weddings they have done. Portfolios from photographers, bakers, and florists, and tapes and videos from musicians are available in their office. Diane and Kathryn feel strongly about only hiring someone you feel comfortable with, and they never request referral fees or commissions from vendors you select.

Kathryn brings her years of experience as an interior decorator to the business. She understands the gathering of elements to create beauty, comfort and charm. Diane is quite knowledgeable about wedding customs and rituals of different ethnic groups. Together they help clients create a celebration that reflects who they are, capturing the spirit of their history as well as their plans for a future together.

Zest Productions
Weddings, Events, Entertainment
(by appointment)
Los Altos Hills, CA

(650) 948-2827
FAX: (650) 948-5546
cay@zestproductions.com

Contact: Cay Lemon

Service Area: Greater Bay Area

Specialties: Wedding and event planning and coordination; entertainment for all occasions

Pricing: $100/hr.
Extra Charges: travel, phone calls out of state

Payment Terms: 50% deposit, balance due day of event
Credit Cards: no

Lead Time: 1 week to 1 year
Portfolio: yes

This redheaded, spunky woman with a great sense of humor and professional demeanor has the perfect background for her profession. Cay, a musician, traveled the world before settling down and working for an event production company in the Bay Area for over five years. During that time she was highly praised and respected by her peers and customers alike.

Cay has been on her own since 1993. She is well qualified to handle every aspect of an event with her limitless access to resources. She will find the right music, coordinate the wedding day only, or help you plan and coordinate the entire event. The purpose of her first client meeting, which is free of charge, is to establish rapport and learn about preferences and tastes. Cay stresses the personal nature of each wedding which should be specially designed, taking into consideration the budget and preferences of the couple. "A good party," she says, "works on all senses," incorporating the smell of summer flowers or the scents of cinnamon and cloves during the holiday season. Although she has many ideas, her open-mindedness allows her to create what the client wants. She showed me the extensive checklists she uses during the planning stages. A precise schedule for the day of the occasion, distributed to all the participating vendors, helps to ensure a flawless event.

Clients commented about how much she adds to a wedding, and they love her great ideas, her organizational skills, and her good sense of timing, all moving with the flow. The greatest compliment I heard was, "You know, she just puts her heart into it."

FLOWERS

NOTES

INTRODUCTION

Flowers are a necessity for any elegant event. A well-done floral decoration or rented plants can change an unattractive hall into a charming garden or fairy tale castle. However, you don't need a large budget; even small bouquets on the tables can give a room a festive atmosphere.

Flower handling is very time-consuming work, so don't be surprised by high prices. Many florists get their flowers from the San Francisco Flower Market, which opens around 2 a.m. Florists must arrive early to get the best selection. The flowers are conditioned in the shop: some are placed in cold water, some in warm water, and others in a special solution until they are used.

Traditionally, bouquets were made by "wiring and taping." This method involves cutting off the stems, inserting a little wet cotton ball into the base of the flowers to keep them fresh, and affixing wire in place of the stems. Green tape is then wound around the wire. The florist can more easily adjust the position of each flower, the bouquet becomes much lighter, and not one hanging flower head is seen.

Many florists use moist floral foam, called an oasis, as a water base for the flower's stem. This saves quite a bit of work since the stems are simply pushed into the foam, keeping the flowers nice and fresh. Heavy blossoms, though, require wire support. An oasis can be fitted into special handles for carried bouquets. Keep in mind that large bouquets are basically water containers that can become quite heavy and uncomfortable. If you plan to **throw your bouquet**, ask your florist for an extra one since a bouquet with a handle might prove too dangerous. Over the past few years, hand-tied bouquets have become very popular because of their natural appearance. However, one florist pointed out that they are not practical during hot summer days. One photographer mentioned that the flowers came out of the cooler only for the ceremony and photography session.

If you want to **preserve your bouquet**, you can have it freeze-dried and stored in a shadow box. Freeze-drying is a rather expensive and lengthy process. Single, wilted flowers can be replaced with fresh ones.

Fresh bouquets with garlands and wreaths look wonderful and are very decorative on gazebos and arches, but their construction is very time-consuming. To keep the flowers moist, the florist can use water picks or cages made of chicken wire to hold oases.

Weddings with smaller budgets don't have to forego table decorations. A simple, cost-saving approach is to fill baskets with blooming plants (using four to six 3"x4" containers) and to cover the tops of the pots with moss. Bouquets used at the ceremony site can be brought to the reception. The money you save can be spent on personal flowers or on a beautiful cake table (see introduction to CAKES - DESSERTS).

Often overlooked is the importance of **coordinating the flower decorations** provided by the florist and caterer. A coordinated look is more aesthetically pleasing than the contrast between a caterer's tropical flowers on the buffet table and the florist's English garden flowers as table decoration.

The delicate scent of flowers adds to a festive atmosphere. Be aware, though, that some flowers emit very strong scents and may cause discomfort for some. As an alternative, I saw an attractive arrangement of greenery with bows and ribbons. Silk or dried flowers are other alternatives.

Money Matters

As with caterers, the final **price** is difficult to predict. Even though some florists quote a base price of $100, most of them will do whatever you want as long as it's tasteful. Rather than use carnations, many prefer to incorporate more fashionable and expensive garden roses and lilies. Florists who quote a minimum price let you decide how to spend it between personal flowers and decoration.

Money Saving Tips

- Use flowers in season.
- Substitute expensive flowers with less expensive ones.
- Include your favorite expensive flowers in only half of your centerpieces.
- Include your bouquet as part of the head-table decoration.
- Include the bridesmaids' bouquets as part of the cake table decoration.
- Use the flowers from the ceremony to decorate the entry or guestbook table.
- Use your own creativity to decorate toasting flutes and cake knives.
- Don't schedule your wedding around Mother's Day or Valentine's Day since flowers are twice as expensive at those times.

Belle Fleur
(formerly Big Basin Floral)
(by appointment)
Campbell, CA

(408) 379-2226
FAX: (408) 379-7210
pasionflr@aol.com

Contact: Margaret Novak

Service Area: Greater Bay Area

Specialties: Custom-designed, natural creations for weddings and special events

Base Price: bridal bouquet, $75; centerpiece, $20; altar piece, $100
Extra Charges: delivery, rentals

Payment Terms: $100 non-ref. deposit,
          balance due 2 weeks prior to event
Credit Cards: Visa, MasterCard

Lead Time: 1 day to 12 months
Bouquet Preservation: can recommend

"Almost anything is possible. It's like threads to pull through the whole event to create ambience," is Margaret's characteristic style. One fine example of her creativity was connecting the bridesmaids' bouquets to line the head table, tapering the ends with the pew decorations and placing the bride's bouquet as the cascading centerpiece.

Margaret builds on her client's ideas to create the mood of the day. For a dramatic look, she sprayed fan palms gold and transformed the site with sensational centerpieces created from the palm-lined aisles. She designed a curly willow tripod and added gardenia centers for fragrance. No one knew they were the same pieces used during the ceremony.

As co-owner of Marjolaine French Pastries, Margaret left Big Basin Floral for a couple of years to assist her husband, Joe, in opening a second Marjolaine location in Los Altos. With weddings and events as Margaret's main focus, she relocated to Campbell in 1998 and changed the name of Big Basin Floral to Belle Fleur. While I was visiting Margaret, one client gave her a big hug, exclaiming, "We've missed your touch. The flowers have not been the same since you've been gone."

With a BA in Fine Arts from UC Berkeley, Margaret has an eye for design. Portfolios are filled with samples of traditional, classic, romantic, tropical, and dramatic bouquets and arrangements, created with the help of her in-house floral designers. She loves to combine unusual color and texture to create a mood. She buys directly from the growers where she searches for new flowers with unusual colors, such as the creamy peach Sahara rose, a true ivory Vendella rose, or discovering the Leonidas, a brown-colored rose with a terra cotta center and a creamy exterior for an autumn wedding. She finds it "thrilling on the day of the event to see everything come together."

Personalized consultations are by appointment only.

Blossoms by Jylene

(650) 780-0111

Flower Shop (formerly of Stanford Shopping Cntr.) FAX: (650) 780-0130

1757 E. Bayshore Road, Suite 16

www.ByRecOnly.com/blossoms

Redwood City, CA 94063

Contact: Jill Slater

Service Area: Greater Bay Area

Specialties: Floral designs for weddings, parties, and Bar/Bat Mitzvahs

Base Price: bridal bouquet, $65; boutonniere, $6.50; corsage, $15; centerpiece, $30;
Extra Charges: delivery, setup

Payment Terms: 20% deposit, balance due prior to event
Credit Cards: major credit cards

Lead Time: 1 month
Bouquet Preservation: referrals available

The same family, whose daughter's wedding I had described in a previous edition, hired Jill again for their son's wedding. His affair was done quite differently but was just as beautiful. Azaleas were planted next to the gazebo, which was entwined with flower garlands of hydrangeas, garden roses, stock and dendrobium orchids. Generous, white-washed clay pots, planted with ivy, azaleas and hydrangeas, lined the aisle. Baskets made of ivy and filled with white tulips, sweet peas, gerbera daisies, garden roses and bouvardia were designed for the tables. Ivy topiaries dotted with luscious garden roses added to the buffet decoration. Rented panels of podocarpus, enhanced with fresh hydrangeas and fragrant garden roses, hid the caterer's work area. The petite, pretty bride carried a round nosegay bouquet of white and champagne roses and lilies of the valley.

Jill's portfolio exhibits a large variety of bouquets, decorated arches, chuppas, centerpieces, altar arrangements, and creative flowers for the hair. She first consults with her customers and then designs the décor. She is very service-oriented and helps wherever she can, for example, by pinning corsages. She also creates decorations for many Bar/Bat Mitzvahs, and can handle events of any size. Her new, larger location in Redwood City is now even better equipped to cater to the bride and other special event needs and artistry.

Jill's access to custom-made props lets her decorate with more than just flowers. She owns a large variety of vases, baskets and arches, and has access to many other props, from aisle runners to horse and carriage. Her customers praise her imagination and talent, which are obvious when you peruse her extensive portfolio. Jill is spokeswoman for the San Francisco Flower Mart and the California Cut Flower Commission. She is often seen on local television, inspiring her audience about flowers.

Branch Out
Event Floral Design
(by appointment)
San Francisco, CA

(415) 648-1887
FAX: (415) 648-8391
www.ByRecOnly.com/branchout

Contact: Leighsa Spiegler

Service Area: Wine Country to Carmel

Specialties: Event floral designs in European garden and Japanese-inspired styles,
integrating unusual combinations of texture and color with visually interesting details

Base Price: bridal bouquet, $125; centerpiece, $35; altar piece, $125
Extra Charges: delivery, installation, rentals

Payment Terms: 50% deposit, balance due
3 weeks prior to event
Credit Cards: Visa, MasterCard

Lead Time: 1 week to 1 year
Bouquet Preservation: yes

In the dictionary, "to branch out" is defined as "to expand." Leighsa further defines it "to enlarge the scope of one's imagination. Diverse, unlike." Vendors and clients alike describe Leighsa's artistry as "over the top," "flower art," and "gifted."

Leighsa immerses herself in her floral designs and becomes chameleon-like. She begins with the client's creative style, then branches out to blend and reflect the overall mood and environment. She doesn't stop at the flowers but combines elements such as lighting, linens, and other treatments to set the tone. For a stately party, she took into account the art pieces and china to bring out the colorful, rich tones of the home. With sugared fruits, gardenias, candles, organza treatments, and overlays, the room was breathtaking. What made people turn their heads was the design created for Neptune's statue. Not one corner of the estate was missed. "I immerse myself in the flower arrangement; I just become part of it," exclaims Leighsa.

With a formal education in floriculture and numerous design awards in 1996, Leighsa was inducted into the American Institute of Floral Designers. In 1993, she started her own floral events company, Branch Out. Her style is a mixture of Western, Japanesque and European styles, blending a series of elements that only a vivid imagination could combine. From sugared fruits, berries, nuts, and golden wheat to painted aisle runners, vine chuppahs, topiaries, and props, Branch Out's imagination is beyond reach. Leighsa's secret: "I hear music (melodic harmonies) in my head when I am designing. This helps me to see the proper placement for the flowers." For a BRO party she transformed the octagonal walls and lower staircase of the Kohl Mansion into an enchanted rain forest. Bamboo trunks, banded with bear grass and raffia, were held delicately with quince branches. Black and colored river rocks were strewn along the base of the design. Foliage and horsetail lined the foyer. You could just feel the harmony.

Design with Flowers

(650) 254-1810
www.designwithflowers.com

897 Independence Avenue, #2F
Mountain View, CA 94043

Contact: Carol Ralles

Service Area: South Bay, San Francisco, Peninsula

Specialties: Charm, individual style, and elegance

Base Price: bridal bouquet, $125; centerpiece, $35; altar piece, $150
Extra Charges: delivery, setup, rentals

Payment Terms: $100 non-ref. deposit,
              balance due 2 weeks prior to event
Credit Cards: no

Lead Time: 2 weeks to 6 months
Bouquet Preservation: no

Whether the bride loves sunflowers or rare orchids, garden roses or masses of peonies, Carol uses flowers to create the scene, be it formal, casual, romantic, or whimsical. She has an extraordinary range and flair, and an eye for the elements of surprise and dramatic detail.

I have seen Carol's work quite often. At one wedding I saw her elegant table decoration of European-style glass bowls filled with phalaeonopsis orchids, champagne roses and tendrils of creeping fig. The linen on the cake table was gathered and tied into rosettes with satin ribbons. For another occasion, she had decorated a large buffet table with birch branches, cherry blossoms, springeri and red ginger, making an impact and creating drama in the large room.

Four years ago, Carol established her own design studio as an outgrowth of her successful experiences working as a floral designer. After extensive training with the leading Bay Area European and Asian designers, Carol now trains younger designers in the fine art of flower arranging for weddings.

"Stunning and elegant." "The details make the difference." These were comments I heard from her clients.

Designs by Peggy
Certified Florist and Wedding Coordinator
(by appointment)
Sunnyvale, CA

(408) 730-8379
Peggy.Lehman@juno.com

Contact: Peggy Lehman

Service Area: Greater Bay Area

Specialties: A bride's dream come true at a realistic price

Base Price: bridal bouquet, $60; centerpiece, $18; altar piece, $70
Extra Charges: delivery beyond 5 miles, rentals, breakdown

Payment Terms: 1/3 deposit, balance due 10 days prior to event
Credit Cards: no

Lead Time: 10 days to 1 year
Bouquet Preservation: no

Peggy was the very first florist I interviewed. She taught me all the basics of handling and conditioning flowers. Her goal is to fulfill the bride's dreams while staying within the budget. During the first appointment, which is free of charge, you get a good overview of her work from her extensive portfolio. She learns her client's preferences and makes suggestions accordingly. Sometimes she'll include the bride's and groom's hobbies in the decoration, such as sea shells or sports items. She can also suggest appropriate styles for petite or tall brides. For vintage styles, she'll come up with a floral design reflecting the era. Peggy is also good at using money-saving ideas, such as using streamer ribbons to enlarge the bouquet's appearance. If she underestimates the cost, she will honor the original price proposal.

She has accumulated many props, baskets and containers over the years. One specialty item is her heart-shaped, white metal arch. Decorated beneath with silk greenery and on top with fresh flowers, it looks absolutely gorgeous, yet is still affordable. Intriguing also are her custom-made holders for pew decoration. Enhanced with flowers and ribbons, they take on a different look each time. I saw her pew decoration at the Capital Club in San Jose, where she followed the bride's white and gold color scheme. The centerpieces were white dendrobium orchids, white Lady Liberty roses, freesias, stock, and ferns in gold bowls that were decorated with white and gold ribbons. For a more daring bride, she arranged blue irises to resemble a French braid in the middle of the bouquet. Irises and ferns were placed inside a translucent balloon in the centerpieces.

Fleurs de France

Flowers For Weddings And Special Occasions

(by appointment)

Sebastopol/Berkeley, CA

(510) 649-1009

(707) 824-8158

FAX: (707) 824-9058

fleursfrance@earthlink.net

www.fleursfrance.com

Contact: Jessica Switala

Service Area: Greater Bay Area and beyond

Specialties: Refreshing, abundant, natural and romantic garden look

Base Price: bridal bouquet, $100; centerpiece, $40; altar piece, $125
Extra Charges: delivery, rentals

Payment Terms: 50% deposit, balance
                  due 1 week prior to event
Credit Cards: no

Lead Time: 2 weeks to 1 year
Bouquet Preservation: no

Flowers have always been Jessica's love. She owned a flower stand in Berkeley several years ago and found she had a natural gift with flowers. For the past 18 years she has been creating bouquets and floral arrangements exclusively for weddings and special events. She lived in France for several years, and her flower selections and designs remind me of the French countryside.

Jessica often works events with her brother, photographer Andrew Partos, and has one of the best and varied florist's portfolios I have seen. A wide variety of beautiful bouquets, arrangements, and decorations make it easy for customers to find something that reflects their own taste or come up with ideas for their event.

Jessica loves the challenge of creating something exquisite and beautiful for the special day. She believes that every event is individual and unique, and spends a lot of time with the client in consultation and follows up until the event so that the details are carefully planned, including getting swatches to take shopping for flowers. An event coordinator who is very familiar with her work thinks her flower designs are exquisite and likes the thoughtful way she consults with clients. Another client admired how well the bouquets complemented the dresses, the quality of the flowers, and the design of the hand-tied bridal bouquet.

Jessica's unique style is prevalent in the events she designs. For a mother of the bride, she designed a delicate floral bracelet complementing the mother's gown. For a dazzling effect, she used an abundant amount of fresh, tiny champagne grapes cascading from every layer of the wedding cake. It is quite evident in her work that Jessica doesn't merely use flowers to accent, but beautifully arranges them to become an integral element in each of her events. Always complimentary to the subject and as fresh as possible, her designs are picture perfect.

Floramor Studios
Florist
569 Seventh Street
San Francisco, CA 94103

(415) 864-0145
(415) 781-3317
FAX: (415) 864-3455
sffloramor@aol.com

Contact: Laura Little or Stephen O'Connell

Service Area: U.S.

Specialties: Walking through a magic English garden;
creating the total visual look: tablecloths, settings, and flowers

Base Price: bridal bouquet, $125; centerpiece, $45; altar piece, $150
Extra Charges: depending on size of order and distance

Payment Terms: 50% deposit of estimated total, balance due 4 days prior to event
Credit Cards: major credit cards

Lead Time: 3 days to 18 months
Bouquet Preservation: no

Upon arriving on the West Coast over 15 years ago, Laura got her first job in a flower shop. She enjoyed her job so much that she and her partner, Stephen (now her husband), opened their own design studio. Laura's strong background in art contributes to their wonderful work and great service; they have become one of the leading florists in San Francisco. The rapid growth of their business required yet a second move to larger facilities, allowing for a much larger inventory of props as their service extends beyond floral design to the creation of a total visual look. Their warehouse is filled with hard-to-find items such as the finest Dupioni silk and moiré table linens; gold charger plates, and a wide variety of specialty props. They also have a location at the Fairmont Hotel in San Francisco. For the last spectacular wedding setup I saw, Laura ordered 3½-foot French-style iron candelabra with crystal chimneys.

This particular wedding was not only a work of art but was also work-intensive. A heat wave and a parade happening by the hotel made working conditions more difficult than usual. After only three hours of sleep and near exhaustion, Laura still took the time to describe the setup to me. A wave of greenery with thousands of garden roses and over a hundred lilies and gardenias at the altar faced the couple and the guests. Lush pew decorations and the pink rose lighting pattern on the ceiling transformed the ceremony site into an intimate garden setting. Each of the 50 tables at the reception was decked out as if set up for a luxurious, private dinner party. The rose patterned, damask tablecloths were created to coordinate with the theme and colors of the room. The candelabra were loosely decorated with a variety of garden roses, dendrobium orchids, eremurus and birch. All of the flowers looked, as always, beautiful and immaculate.

Even though they usually work on more elaborate weddings, one coordinator told me that she also recommends Floramor to clients with less extensive budgets because even their least expensive designs are beautiful.

The Flower Garden
Wedding Florist
(by appointment)
Santa Cruz, CA

(831) 425-4833
electric@cruzio.com

Contact: Liz Chamberlin

Service Area: South Peninsula, Santa Cruz, Monterey Bay

Specialties: Unique flowers with natural, free-flowing design; Italian-French country look

Base Price: bridal bouquet, $100; centerpiece, $40; altar piece, $125
Extra Charges: none

Payment Terms: $100 non-ref. deposit, balance due 1 month prior to event
Credit Cards: no

Lead Time: 2 weeks to 1 year
Bouquet Preservation: yes

Liz is as much an artist as she is a florist. She expresses her artistry through her many varieties of floral creations and through her consideration of the overall look. Important to Liz are the fashion and color of the bride's dress for which she designs a bouquet to accent rather than overwhelm. Scale is equally important: she will use larger flowers that will be viewed from a distance, such as gazebo or altar decoration, then select smaller flowers of the same family in the pieces that will be viewed up close, as in the bouquets, centerpieces, and ground garlands.

I chatted with Liz as she carefully placed peach roses, lavender, freesia, bells-of-Ireland, tuberoses, lisianthus, lacy candytuft and maidenhair fern on a simple, yet elegant wedding cake. They blended beautifully with the icing, while here and there she included a sprig of sparkling blue forget-me-not. Contrasting to the pastel colors of this wedding are photos of bolder color creations. Regardless of theme or color preference, all of her flowers are naturally placed as if they were meant to be next to each other. Liz's attention to detail is also seen in the photos of a '20s wedding for which she researched the style and design of that decade. She also has new ideas about how to create a memento of the bridal bouquet. Her Italian pillar vases, bamboo pedestals, Greek columns, and terra cotta vases compliment her creations.

Liz visits several growers for the freshest flowers. She enlivens her arrangements with colorful "wild" flowers from her own garden, such as viscaria, clarkia, jasmine, baby dianthus, and fairy roses. This friendly, warm and easygoing florist is also very accommodating. One bride's mother was insistent about an overabundance of flowers for an altar decoration. Upon seeing this photo, I noticed this to be true but was still impressed by the tasteful and attractive design. A bride who initially may not have a clear idea of what she wants will be gently guided along with significant questions as Liz gets to know her. Clients and other professionals comment on Liz's creativity and unusual presentations, as well as her professionalism and reliability.

Flowers by Julie
Specializing in Weddings and Parties
(by appointment)
Belmont, CA

(650) 592-3699
FAX: (650) 654-0674

Contact: Julie Zanoni

Service Area: Greater Bay Area (except Wine Country in summer)

Specialties: Natural garden look and contemporary design

Base Price: bridal bouquet, $75; centerpiece, $14; altar piece, $50
Extra Charges: none

Payment Terms: $200 deposit, balance due
7 days prior to event
Credit Cards: no

Lead Time: 1 week to 9 months
Bouquet Preservation: no

Julie spent 6 years in the same flower shop where so many other great florists learned the art of the trade. Her reputation and her business have grown since she started soon after the birth of her daughter 13 years ago. Julie is very service-oriented and will do consultations in the client's home. Even though she wires and tapes most of her personal flowers, she is still quite affordable. Keeping up with demand, she is constantly adding new props: chuppahs, archways, white lattices for backdrops, and standing wicker baskets. Glass vases from Italy standing 26 inches tall are her latest acquisitions.

Julie's large portfolio displays her work by category. You can browse through collections of bride's and bridesmaid's bouquets, boutonnieres, corsages, aisle and church decorations, and centerpieces. It's fun to look at Julie's pictures as she is also a good photographer. Her style is simple elegance. I especially loved her delicate bridal bouquet consisting of lilies of the valley, accented with just a few gardenias and stephanotis. Another favorite is a lush garland adorning the edge of a lace tablecloth at a head table. Her great sense of color is obvious from how well the colors in her creations match the dresses and tablecloths.

I saw Julie's work at a garden wedding. Entry to the backyard was through an arch that Julie had generously decorated. The chuppah, built by her husband, had a covering of lace, and tulle and flowers decorated the poles. The colorful flowers of the large pool float, also built by her husband, consisted of roses, freesias, belladonna, and alstromeria, which were the same flowers used for the table decoration. All of the flowers looked wonderful. Julie's clients commented about both her beautiful flowers and how easy it was to work with her. One reference told me that everyone wanted to take home the centerpiece, and that five friends had asked for the florist's name because the flowers were so lovely.

Flowers by Linda

(650) 969-7695

Flowers for All Occasions

FAX: (650) 969-1554

162 East Dana Avenue
Mountain View, CA 94041

Contact: Linda Rapposelli

Service Area: Peninsula, East Bay, South Bay

Specialties: Romantic garden look for weddings; corporate accounts;
theme parties, rental items

Base Price: bridal bouquet, from $60; centerpiece, from $15; altar piece, from $50
Extra Charges: delivery, rentals

Payment Terms: 25% part.-ref. deposit,
balance due 1 week prior to event
Credit Cards: all credit cards

Lead Time: 2 weeks to 6 months
Bouquet Preservation: no

Linda was already working in a flower shop at the age of 14, first on the East Coast and then in Los Altos where her parents had moved. After high school she worked there for several years before going out on her own. Her business grew steadily and really took off in 1990. Forty percent of her business is weddings; the rest is corporate accounts, weekly deliveries to clubs and hotels, and theme parties. She told me about a Louisiana theme for which she had created little swamps for table decorations. They consisted of a soft green painted glass bowl with river rocks at the bottom, reeds and bear grass, and even fish swimming around.

Wedding flowers at the Decathlon Club were just wonderful. They were white, pink, and red in color, contrasting beautifully with a black tablecloth. For the centerpieces, she filled her own elegant silver bowls with an airy floral design of red roses, white freesias, starburst mums, ivy, ferns, and two white candles. The head table had a similar but larger design with additional snapdragons, large tulips and sweet peas. Candelabra decorated with flowers stood on either side. For a smaller outdoor wedding she created floral centerpieces around a hurricane lamp. The head table was enhanced with a garland of plumosa and white ribbons. All of her flowers looked not only festive but also very fresh.

Linda first learns what the client wants and then contributes her ideas. Her clients love her work. Ivy topiary plants and tall glass vases are favorites among her extensive inventory of rental items from centerpiece containers to arches and columns.

Dawn from the Decathlon Club remarked, "Linda includes fragrances with flower design."

You can reach Linda's Pleasanton workshop by calling (925) 248-0319.

Shawna Futagaki
Floral Designer
1054 Brockhampton Court
San Jose, CA 95136

(408) 265-3543
FAX: (408) 287-7182
sfuta@aol.com

Contact: Shawna Futagaki

Service Area: Greater Bay Area and Monterey Bay

Specialties: All styles, from contemporary to garden look for weddings, banquets, and parties

Base Price: bridal bouquet, $75; centerpiece, $20; altar piece, $75
Extra Charges: delivery, rentals

Payment Terms: $100 non-ref. deposit,
     balance due 2 weeks prior to event
Credit Cards: no

Lead Time: 1 week to 1 year
Bouquet Preservation: yes

"She put all her energy, her heart, and her soul into this wedding…it exceeded our expectations." "Her professionalism and her creativity made our wedding extra special." These were comments I heard from Shawna's clients. She also came highly recommended to me.

Shawna's life has now come full circle. Her family owned a flower shop in San Jose where she would help as a child. She never liked being forced to do anything, but working with flowers came very naturally to her. She thought the flower business was much too easy to consider as a profession, so she decided to pursue a degree in clothing design. While working in other fields, she continued working with flowers on the side. Finally, with the encouragement of a friend and an offer from a floral wholesaler to work with him, she returned to working with flowers on a full-time basis. Shawna has direct access to the freshest imported flowers from abroad or directly shipped by local growers. Large walk-in refrigerators store the flowers which are delivered in refrigerated trucks. As personalized as Shawna's designs are, so is her service. She will consult with you in your home at no extra charge. Her sparkling personality and her artistic ideas make her a great person to work with.

Gardenias, stephanotis, white roses, and white miniature orchids, enhanced with pearl spray, made up a bride's bouquet. Two beautiful flower girl baskets consisted of stargazer lilies, dendrobium orchids, hot pink roses, bear grass, ferns, and ribbons. All the wedding flowers, carefully packed for transportation, were immaculate. I have also seen Shawna's larger arrangements in which each flower looks perfect. Her flowers are always tastefully chosen, and she so obviously has a great eye for color. One larger creation, consisting of stargazer lilies, orchids, roses, tulips, and stock, and accented with blue and purple anemones and heather, greeted guests at a church entrance.

Gloria's
Floral Designs
2579 Heatherstone Drive
San Rafael, CA 94903

(415) 492-9567
FAX: (415) 492-8250
gkaga@earthlink.net
www.jps.net/wtcal/glorias

Contact: Gloria Kaga

Service Area: Greater Bay Area and beyond

Specialties: Creations of all styles by multifaceted floral designer

Base Price: bridal bouquet, $85; centerpiece, $25; altar piece, $85
Extra Charges: 10% service and installation fee

Payment Terms: 20% deposit, 50% due 1 month prior, balance due 1 month prior to event
Credit Cards: major credit cards

Lead Time: 1 week to 18 months
Bouquet Preservation: no

Gloria's warmth and dedication bring her many great reviews from her clients. "As wonderful as the floral arrangements were, they were almost overshadowed by your high level of service. You delivered on everything you promised and more!" "…your natural enthusiasm and genuine interest in my wedding day meant so much to me and made the process of choosing my flowers so enjoyable." "Thank you for being a true professional." The praises go on.

Gloria has owned her floral design business at the same location for over 22 years. Her variety of styles – traditional, contemporary, romantic and a modified ikebana style (the Japanese art of arranging flowers) – can be seen in her extensive portfolios. Gloria tunes in to what her clients want, defines the style, and helps them with ideas. Her designs enhance the setting, reflect the season, and complement the wedding dresses.

Since Gloria's studio is air-conditioned with walk-in refrigeration, the hot summer months do not present a problem. The studio stores her many props, including two chuppahs. One elegant chuppah is covered with tulle or Battenberg lace; another with poles made from oak saplings provides a more natural look. Other props include arches, trellises, pedestals, stands for aisle decoration, topiary trees, tall blown-glass vases, and many containers. Gloria also has one of the largest selections of wedding invitations in the area, which she offers at a discounted price.

Gloria is well known in her community and is referred by many restaurants, hotels and country clubs. Her thoroughness, dependability and dedication limit her and her staff to only two weddings per day, so book early.

Gwendolyn Valiente Design Studio

(408) 629-9747

Floral Designs and Party Planning

FAX: (408) 363-8003

6030 Allen Avenue
San Jose, CA 95123

Contact: Gwendolyn Valiente

Service Area: Greater Bay Area, Napa to Carmel

Specialties: European floral design in personalized style and taste; event planning

Base Price: bridal bouquet, $100; centerpiece, $35; altar piece, $85
Extra Charges: event planning, props and linen

Payment Terms: $500 non-ref. deposit, balance due 2 weeks prior to event
Credit Cards: major credit cards

Lead Time: 1 day to 1 year
Bouquet Preservation: yes

I observed how Gwendolyn's beautiful floral decorations adorned the dinner tables at a wedding. Centerpieces with 18-inch candles consisted of lilies, roses, lisianthus, bouvardia, tuberose, snapdragons, and stock. Flowers cascaded down the cake to the table, which was covered with silk organza and sprinkled with rose petals. She had also provided the favors for this event: gourmet truffles in gold boxes tied with organza ribbons. Gwendolyn is known for achieving a total look. She began including consultations as part of her business so that everyone she recommends will do their best to create the event of your dreams. I have seen Gwendolyn's work at many events. She can create very romantic weddings or a fun party look with her different containers, fabric, ribbons and tassels. She is constantly adding to her already large inventory of props since she likes everything to blend together perfectly. For one event she went to estate sales to find antique coffee and tea pots that would serve as containers. For a BRO party, Gwendolyn brought one of her newest, attractive props – a 10-foot metal arbor with chandelier, artfully decorated with flowers.

When you first meet with Gwendolyn, she will show you her portfolios to help you decide what you want. After learning about your taste and budget, she will help you create an enjoyable event. To ensure the quality of the flowers, she visits the growers herself, even venturing out into the fields, to find the best flowers and the right colors. She likes to include herbs, such as lamb's ear, salvia, rosemary, and lavender, and enhances seasonal designs with grapes, pears, and pumpkins.

Gwendolyn has been working with flowers for over 14 years. She has a large floral refrigerator in her studio, and her refrigerated van can transport her designs all over the Bay Area. Almost all of her business comes through word of mouth.

In Any Event, Inc.

(650) 851-3520
FAX: (650) 851-3521

3036 Woodside Road
Woodside, CA 94062

Contact: Rob Eckert (weddings) or Rick Davis

Service Area: Greater Bay Area and beyond

Specialties: Natural garden look for parties and weddings; gifts

Base Price: bridal bouquet, $65; centerpiece, $35; altar piece, $85
Extra Charges: delivery and setup, rentals

Payment Terms: credit cards for deposit, balance is billed
Credit Cards: Visa, MasterCard, Discover

Lead Time: 1 week to 1 year
Bouquet Preservation: no

Each time I visit Rick in his attractive store I find lots of things I'd love to own: iron candelabra, dishes, vases, beautiful table linen, and flowers. There is also a selection of tasteful gifts for the bridal party. The picture-perfect Rubrum lilies I bought lasted for over two weeks. Rick has a horticultural degree and used to be a landscape designer. In 1983 he opened his shop in Woodside. He favors a natural garden look rather than highly stylized tropical arrangements, and likes to work with seasonal flowers and fruits. Over the years Rick has added to his elegant line of rentals: boxwood hedges, 19th century columns, balustrades, and a 10' x 10' iron gazebo. His clients come from much farther away than Woodside and highly praise both his work and his personality. Some of their comments are: "His arrangements are always terrific, fresh, and never skimpy." "He is totally reliable." "Wonderful to work with." "I would never hire anybody else!"

As his business grew, Rick needed more help. Rob Eckert joined Rick's staff in 1991 and handles most of the wedding work. Rob is also very nice and fun to be with. I observed a beautiful wedding in Atherton where he not only provided the flowers but also did the wedding coordination. The tennis court was covered with a large, lined tent that opened to the garden area. The large dance floor inside was surrounded by beige carpeting and live plants that produced a wonderful garden-like effect. The round dining tables were covered with very attractive Jacquard tablecloths. Bouquets in various designs decorated each table. Some centerpieces stood on tall candelabra, while others sat on short glass vases. The roses, lisianthus, and bella donna looked like they had just been picked from flower beds. Flowers were placed around the appetizer tables on the lawn, and garlands were wound around the umbrella poles. Several flower floats bobbed in the pool, and large bouquets were waiting in the shade before being placed on the large buffet.

In Full Bloom
Floral Design Studio
(by appointment)
Menlo Park, CA

(650) 364-1858
FAX: (650) 364-2186

Contact: Susan Groves

Service Area: Greater Bay Area

Specialties: English garden grandeur to understated elegance

Base Price: bridal bouquet, $100; centerpiece, $50; altar piece, $100
Extra Charges: design setup and delivery

Payment Terms: $500 non-ref. deposit,
        balance due 2 weeks prior to event
Credit Cards: no

Lead Time: 1 month to 1 year
Bouquet Preservation: no

"We were not just satisfied with her work, but were enriched by it." "...received more compliments than we could keep track of." "The care she took to understand our tastes and needs..." "...did even more than she promised!" Such were the comments from Susan's customers.

Susan set up her floral design studio in 1988. Her work is that of a perfectionist. She conditions every single flower and wires it, if necessary. She uses tulle or ribbons quite effectively in her creations. Theme props, such as ceramic angels embedded in moss with flowers and soft ferns, create a mini-garden. I have seen Susan's work many times over the years at meetings of event professionals, at my annual parties, and in portfolios. Her many different interesting designs, done with high-quality flowers, always earn her much applause.

Susan's church decoration is still among my favorites. I compared it to a painting by the French impressionist Monet. A back ledge, about 30 feet long, supported a large wooden cross. The ledge was covered with decorative foliage, spray roses and Longiflorum lilies, which expanded into a larger arrangement at the base of the cross. Large white flowers, including white larkspur and delphinium, dominated the design, with colored flowers scattered in between. Similar but smaller bouquets were placed on the narrower ledges in front of the pulpit. Other extraordinary, much more contemporary creations were the bridesmaids' bouquets I saw in a photographer's album. Long, hand-tied bouquets of tulips in shades of deep fuschia looked just stunning with the black dresses.

Susan's work is published in *Floral Style*, now in bookstores nationwide. She is also on numerous preferred lists of Bay Area venues.

Laurie Chestnutt Florals

(650) 325-9926
(Phone & FAX)

(by appointment)
Palo Alto, CA

Contact: Laurie Chestnutt

Service Area: Greater Bay Area

Specialties: Creating an emotional and visual experience for the discerning bride

Base Price: bridal bouquet, $90; centerpiece, $45; altar piece, $100
Extra Charges: delivery, setup, rentals

Payment Terms: $200 non-ref. deposit, balance
due within 1 week of event
Credit Cards: all credit cards

Lead Time: 1 week to 1 year
Bouquet Preservation: no

Laurie's contribution to a BRO party was a garland that draped the bannister leading to the second floor of the Kohl Mansion. Made of magnolia leaves, gardenias, and gold-painted grapes, it was the most magnificent one I've ever seen. Her wedding work was just as impressive, with top-grade Ecuadorian roses, lilies of the valley, hyacinths, lilac, sweet peas and trailing pink jasmine that made up the white and cream bridal bouquet. The smaller bridesmaids' bouquets included some of the same flowers but added the soft colors of ranunculus, tulips, lisianthus, and lilac. Even more colorful was the extraordinary, custom-made candelabra-like two-tiered stand with five 24" candles, covered with a symphony of colorful spring flowers, including peonies, tulips and roses. The creations were perfectly in tune with the clear blue spring day. The flower-loving bride had also ordered a veil sprinkled with flowers, flower shoe clips and bustle flowers.

After receiving a degree in ornamental horticulture, Laurie worked for two prominent florists in San Francisco and San Mateo for eight years and has now owned her own business for over 17 years. She wires and tapes flowers for bouquets or uses floral foam holders, as requested by the client or required by design. Laurie presents her floral art with a natural look and welcomes challenges. During the last few years Laurie has added many props to her collection, such as a willow arch and a willow chuppah. You can admire them in her portfolio, decorated with dogwood, Casablanca lilies, peonies, and clusters of blackberries.

Every client I talked to praised her creativity, her personalized service, and her calm and pleasant manner. Laurie is on the preferred list of the Garden Court Hotel, Stanford Park Hotel, Thomas Fogarty Winery, and Stanford Memorial Church.

Majestic Celebrations
Floral Design
(by appointment)
Union City, CA

(510) 471-4648
FAX: (510) 471-4477
minal@majestic-celebrations.com
www.majestic-celebrations.com

Contact: Minal Patel

Service Area: Greater Bay Area and beyond

Specialties: Contemporary and traditional custom florals designed around theme, color and style; exquisite chupphas, canopies and mundups; free delivery within Bay Area

Base Price: bridal bouquet, $95; centerpiece, $35; altar piece, $125
Extra Charges: rentals, custom mundup (Indian wedding canopy)

Payment Terms: $250 deposit, 50% due 3 months prior, balance due 3 weeks prior to event
Credit Cards: no

Lead Time: to 18 months
Bouquet Preservation: can recommend

Personal attention and dedication are Majestic Celebration's mission in every client they service. From the time you meet with Minal Patel, owner and floral designer, you get a real sense of security. Since special events are all they do, they give the client a tremendous amount of time and attention in planning the overall floral design, exceeding everyone's expectations.

Their classic to contemporary styles reflective of their client's theme and color are beautifully carried through every floral aspect. From providing elaborately detailed ceremony arches and canopies to creative centerpieces and "delicate floral tapestry" on the cake, Minal is present to ensure the perfect ambiance.

They always buy their flowers in bulk, distributing any extra flowers to enhance the overall look. All of their high-quality arrangements are prepared the night before using the freshest of flowers. Even on a restrictive budget, their dedication to quality is never a compromise. "Our goal is to create a memorable event for life's greatest occasions," comments Minal.

Some of my favorite floral arrangements were creatively thought out. One was a regal nosegay of red roses, cleverly wired, with gold grapes interspersed to look like gold pearls, and stems wrapped with a gold rope tassel. Another was a fabulous centerpiece, reaching the ceiling and set in a tall glass vase of whole lemons to give a dramatic yet unobstructed view. Their exquisite custom-made wedding canopies, chuppahs and mundups are delicately layered with sheer fabrics, or elaborately detailed and embellished to reflect multicultural weddings.

Clients and professionals alike consistently praise Minal's abundant use of florals and her flexible, accommodating manner.

Manisse Designs
A Tradition in Beautiful Flowers & Linen
519 Marine View Avenue, Suite C
Belmont, CA 94002

(650) 591-8332
FAX: (650) 413-1522
manisse@pacbell.net

Contact: Manisse Newell

Service Area: Greater Bay Area

Specialties: Party planning with emphasis on design and floral artistry in Flemish, French and English country tradition; distinctive linen rental

Base Price: bridal bouquet, $150; centerpiece, $65; altar piece, $95
Extra Charges: delivery, setup

Payment Terms: $800 deposit to hold date, 50% due upon proposal acceptance, balance due 6 weeks prior to event
Credit Cards: Visa, MasterCard

Lead Time: 2 weeks to 1 year
Bouquet Preservation: no

The floral decoration for a garden wedding in Atherton looked just gorgeous. The garland around the entrance door was designed with garden roses, hydrangeas, rhubrum lilies, and stock on top, and tapered to clusters and then single blossoms of the same flowers among the greens toward the bottom. To keep them fresh in the summer afternoon sun, the flowers were kept in hidden oases and water picks. Two wreaths enhanced the lamps next to the entrance. The canopy for the ceremony was decorated with flower designs similar to those on the door. Manisse had complemented the centerpieces, consisting of glass bowls filled with garden roses, with her rose-patterned linens. The napkins tied together with ivy runners were another nice accent.

This famous designer is a very modest person with a great sense of humor. I only learned from an information sheet that she had created receptions for several queens and princes, for Presidents Reagan and Ford and their wives, as well as for the famous tenor Luciano Pavarotti. Manisse was twice in charge of all the decor and floral designs for the San Francisco Opera Ball on opening night. She was invited by AT&T, along with the 18 best arrangers in the U.S., to exhibit at the Philadelphia Flower Show. She lectures and does demos for groups around the country and has participated in *Bouquets to Art* as exhibitor and lecturer throughout its existence.

You can admire photos of her work in her large portfolio. There is no limit to her creativity, like bellowing draped silk hung from the ceiling of a tent to break up space. Manisse has many props; linens; brass, silver, glass and crystal containers; and ideas to make your event special.

Michael Daigian Design

(415) 821-7710
FAX: (415) 821-3227

3450 Third Street, #3D
San Francisco, CA 94124

Contact: Michael Daigian

Service Area: Greater Bay Area

Specialties: Seasonal and tropical flowers in a variety of styles; architectural designs

Base Price: bridal bouquet, $125; centerpiece, $50; altar piece, $100
Extra Charges: delivery, setup, and breakdown

Payment Terms: $150 deposit, 50% 3 weeks prior to event, balance due upon delivery
Credit Cards: major credit cards

Lead Time: 1 week to 3 months
Bouquet Preservation: no

Michael Daigian is the heart and soul of this well-known flower design studio in San Francisco. He presents his craft not only in flowers but also in decorations that create wonderful themes, of which I've seen several. For the Albert Bierstadt exhibit at the de Young Museum, Michael created a floral display reflecting the artist's paintings. For a Bar Mitzvah, fun centerpieces were made of twinkling acrylic poles and imitation rollerblades. Michael also loves to do weddings. His large portfolio is filled with beautiful bridal bouquets, decorated chuppahs, topiaries, and table decorations with fruit and flowers. One of his tabletop designs, with tablecloth, china and flatware, was chosen best of the show for "Special Event 10." You can also see his work in the *Tiffany Wedding Book* and in the movie "Sister Act." He has exhibited his work at every *Bouquets to Art* celebration and has also served as a panelist for the event. An article by Pat Steger in the *San Francisco Chronicle* mentioned Michael's beautiful floral designs that were seen at a fund-raiser for President Clinton.

Michael's grandfather owned one of San Francisco's landmark flower stands. After pursuing a degree in marine biology and a job as a welder, Michael recognized that flowers were a necessity in his life, as were more contemporary designs. His designs are usually natural rather than contrived, but he also enjoys bending the rules: instead of using the flowers as they naturally exist, his creations can be unusual or whimsical. He is a creative artist and excellent craftsman with a modest and charming personality, whose designs add elegance and warmth to any occasion.

He is currently under contract with Tiffany & Co., Restaurant Lulu, the Donatello Hotel, and other hotels and restaurants throughout the Bay Area.

Patricia Gibbons Floral Designer

(510) 527-3197
FAX: (510) 527-8310

(by appointment)
El Cerrito, CA

Contact: Pat Gibbons

Service Area: Greater Bay Area and Napa

Specialties: High-quality — lush, abundant garden-style floral design
with emphasis on color and texture

Base Price: bridal bouquet, $95; centerpiece, $35; altar piece, $95
Extra Charges: setup, rentals

Payment Terms: 50% deposit, balance due 2
weeks before event; or flexible payment plan
Credit Cards: no

Lead Time: 3 weeks to 1 year
Bouquet Preservation: no

"It's the play of color and texture," is how Pat describes her lush garden-style designs. That statement could not be truer. Growing up in the country, with flowers as her picture window and the family business of fabric design, Pat has always had an appreciation for beauty. As a painter and gardener, Pat moved from the East Coast to the East Bay, finding her creative niche in floral design. It's about 20 years later, and her business has grown through the many referrals of her clients and associates.

As part of her commitment to excellence, Pat gives a great deal of time and attention to each client. She dedicates herself and her experienced staff to only one wedding per day, and the results are inspiring and beautiful. Her clients' satisfaction and her fine selection of only the highest quality flowers is evident in countless thank-you letters.

I find Pat to be an expert at creating harmonious effects, from the lush bouquets with matching boutonnieres to the handmade flower girl baskets and floral ring pillows. Just as important, she ties in all the elements of the wedding to blend with the landscape and surroundings. For one wedding, she designed a clever and spectacular floral backdrop. Resembling a section of the garden, it beautifully framed the bride and groom. Later, this large arrangement separated into multiple smaller ones for reuse at the reception. Pat does this quite often to make the presentations look aesthetically pleasing, while making the best use of the client's money.

Pat's large assortment of pedestals, wrought iron candelabra, urns, and birch or tulle chuppahs are amazingly transformed and tailored to the style of each event. My favorite are her custom topiaries, abundant with flowers, yet still having an air of lightness and delicacy. Her friendly manner, creative ideas, and versatile sense of color, texture and design make her a pro at sculpting any event.

Perfect Petals
Floral Design
908 Clinton Road
Los Altos, CA 94024

(650) 964-6295
perfpetals@aol.com

Contact: Melinda Reed

Service Area: South Bay and Peninsula

Specialties: Personalized floral designs; theme parties; costumes

Base Price: bridal bouquet (small nosegay), $50; centerpiece, $15; altar piece, $60
Extra Charges: delivery, setup, rentals

Payment Terms: $100 non-ref. deposit,
balance due 1 week prior to event
Credit Cards: no

Lead Time: 1 week to 1 year
Bouquet Preservation: no

One bride had always dreamed of walking through candlelight to the altar, but the church didn't allow open flames. So Melinda set out to find an alternative to fulfill the bride's wish and finally found battery-lit candles that very closely resembled real ones. The candles sat on top of a post that was decorated with a smilax garland that ended in a large white bow of tulle and silk ribbon enhanced with lemon branches and gold berries. Melinda also came up with a way of securing the decoration since neither tacks nor glue were allowed on the dark wood of the pews. The bouquets for the reception again reflected her business' name. Softly scented Casablanca lilies, gardenia, white tulips, and stock with bear grass and golden ting ting carried out the bride's white and gold color scheme.

Melinda's experience with flowers goes back to her own wedding for which she did some of the flowers. She then worked many years for well-known designers. She is particularly selective and uses only top quality flowers which she orders primarily from the local growers. Her first consultation with you takes place over a cup of tea in her cozy living room. She will first listen to what you have in mind and then come up with ideas, all custom-designed for the client. She loves to include heirloom pieces in her design and makes her own props.

Melinda transformed one client's home into a Renaissance castle. For another client, she planned the wedding flowers over the phone, shipped the flowers to Maryland, and located a wholesaler there with refrigeration who had space for her to work. Both clients commented on her fabulous work, her many ideas, her obvious love for her work, and her friendly and organized manner.

Plan Decor
Floral Design, Rentals
980 David Road, #E
Burlingame, CA 94010

(650) 652-9009
FAX: (650) 652-9007
plandecor@yahoo.com

Contact: Karen Baba

Service Area: Greater Bay Area

Specialties: Romantic European garden design with emphasis on colors and textures

Base Price: bridal bouquet, $90; centerpiece, $45; altar piece, $200
Extra Charges: service charge, take-down

Payment Terms: $100 deposit, balance due 2 weeks prior to event
Credit Cards: no

Lead Time: 1 week to 8 months
Bouquet Preservation: yes

Plan Decor is the dream business of Karen Baba who began her career as a horticulturist 20 years ago. She prefers a European garden and floral abundant look, and her creations are obviously designed with the setting in mind. I saw some of her work at a wedding in a Victorian-style home. Her mantelpiece creation of dogwood, lisianthus, lilac, apple blossoms, garden roses, larkspur and viburnum snowballs reflected beautifully in the mirror behind. I was also impressed by her sterling candelabra centerpieces, delicately decorated with lisianthus, garden roses, lilac and ivy tendrils. Two elegant arrangements stood on either side of the ceremony site at the bottom of a staircase, while garlands were gracefully woven around the banister.

Karen loves to create an awesome look with the wide variety of unique props, such as columns, Laura Lee stands, sweet cherubs, and an array of candelabra. The birch arch that was built in her studio is just perfect for a garden wedding. All accessories are included in the price and can be rented separately. In addition to working with fresh flowers, Karen's business also offers dried flowers. If you've ever ordered wreaths or other dried arrangements from Gardener's Eden or Smith & Hawken, you already may have purchased Karen's work.

Karen prides herself on her ability to work with a diversity of budgets and settings, with the goal of carrying out her clients' wishes to the very last detail. One bride was so pleased about how Karen had read her mind and "created exactly what I had envisioned. That day I walked into my dream." Other references commented on her fantastic work, her easygoing personality, and recommend her highly. Karen's displays can be seen in the *Bouquets to Art* exhibit at the Legion of Honor, Flowers at Filoli, and at Hillsborough's Kitchen Tour.

Podesta Baldocchi
Rediscover a San Francisco Tradition
508 Fourth Street
San Francisco, CA 94107

(415) 346-1300
FAX: (415) 543-1689

Contact: Michael Guelfi

Service Area: Coast to Coast

Specialties: Wedding, special events, and theme parties, with emphasis on complete, overall decor, including plant rental, props, lighting, linens, and chuppahs

Base Price: bridal bouquet, $100; centerpiece, $35; altar piece, $125
Extra Charges: delivery and setup

Payment Terms: 50% deposit, balance due 3 weeks prior to event
Credit Cards: major credit cards

Lead Time: 1 day to 1 year
Bouquet Preservation: no

A San Francisco tradition since 1871, Podesta Baldocchi has enriched many grand events with flowers and decor. Among such events were the opening of the Palace Hotel in 1875, the Panama Pacific Exposition in 1915, the World's Fair in 1939, the signing of the Japanese Peace Treaty in 1951, Macy's annual flower shows, the opening of the San Francisco Ballet in 1998, and the U.S. Open Golf Tournament at the Olympic Country Club in June 1998.

In keeping with quality, service and tradition, the Guelfi brothers' state-of-the-art design studio offers an abundance of design choices. Their retail store, with its fashionable interior design displays, offers an eclectic assortment of gifts, colorful dishes, silverware laced between orchid plants, green topiaries, and vivid floral bouquets and arrangements. From the cozy consultation rooms upstairs and downstairs you can view top floral designers creatively working their magic. The enormous warehouse is filled with fashionable urns, a large assortment of vases, candelabra, pedestals, columns, arches, chuppahs, decorative linens, and chair covers. This full-service flower shop employs 10 full-time designers, one full-time wedding designer, one full-time event designer, and a large support staff to produce the grandest of affairs. Their portfolios feature extensive varieties of bouquets and arrangements to spark your imagination. They offer free consultation and provide a detailed proposal outlining options to create the perfect look for your special occasion.

"The prevailing image, coupled with innovative designers and managers, has made Podesta Baldocchi a San Francisco tradition as well as a local trend-setter in quality, service and beauty."

Rosies & Posies
Complete Floral Services
1581 W. Campbell Avenue, #D
Campbell, CA 95008

(408) 378-4046
FAX: (408) 378-4811

Contact: Malak Nadejah

Service Area: South Bay to Santa Cruz

Specialties: Complete floral services; fresh, dried and silk flowers for weddings and other events

Base Price: bridal bouquet, $50; centerpiece, $10; altar piece, $50; wedding packages available
Extra Charges: delivery (depending on order and distance)

Payment Terms: 20% deposit, balance
            due 4 weeks prior to event
Credit Cards: all credit cards

Lead Time: 1 week to 1 year
Bouquet Preservation: no

The flower bouquets and personal flowers that Malak had prepared for a wedding at Ralston Hall were wonderful. She had created a large arrangement of fresh and subtly aromatic rubrum lilies, pink calla lilies, gladioli, white spidermums, chrysanthemums and alstromerias. Dark green, shiny leaves and ferns gave the design more depth, and the gold sprayed bear grass added an elegant twist. Hairpieces and baskets for the flower girls were especially cute. The bride's bouquet consisted of white gardenias, white and pink roses, a cascade of white dendrobium orchids, dark tea leaves, and gold bear grass. Malak's prices for the different items seemed quite low compared to other florists.

Malak has been working with flowers since 1985. She enjoyed the work so much that she bought her own business five years later. She offers fresh and silk flowers, and can provide everything from aisle runners and arches to many different containers and baskets. She offers three wedding packages, or can custom-design the whole event. She showed me her huge portfolio, consisting of several albums displaying her different styles.

Clients compliment her work and the freshness of the flowers.

Simply The Best

(408) 246-3180

Floral Design and Gifts
(by appointment)
Santa Clara, CA

Contact: Ginger Mathis

Service Area: South Bay and Peninsula

Specialties: Custom wedding designs; party arrangements for all occasions

Base Price: bridal bouquet, $50; centerpiece, $20; altar piece, $65
Extra Charges: delivery, setup, rentals

Payment Terms: $100 non-ref. deposit,
          balance due 2 weeks prior to event
Credit Cards: no

Lead Time: 3 weeks to 1 year
Bouquet Preservation: no

Ginger prides herself on her personalized florist service. She conducts a thorough, initial consultation at no charge and makes every effort to work within the customer's budget. Instead of offering wedding packages, she custom designs everything. She accepts only one event per weekend so that she can concentrate her efforts on each event.

I watched Ginger apply the finishing touches to arrangements for a May wedding at the Saratoga Country Club. The fresh-looking flowers were a symphony of white and pink. The bride's graceful bouquet, custom-designed for her petite stature, was created with white phalaenopsis orchids and soft pink roses accented with delicate sprigs of lily of the valley. The flowers for the centerpieces consisted of white and pink tulips, roses, stock, and alstromaeria arranged in a stunning hurricane lamp for the evening wedding reception.

Ginger prefers to deliver the wedding flowers herself. At one wedding, a very young flower girl accidentally sat on her bouquet. Her tears changed to smiles when she saw how quickly Ginger repaired the damaged bouquet.

Over the 12 years that Ginger has been in business, which began as a hobby, she has accumulated a respectably large portfolio. Her clients are impressed with the high quality of flowers and how expertly she interprets their wishes. They comment on her creativity, dependability, and attention to detail; and admire her ability to coordinate all aspects while staying within the budget.

Except for appearing in this guide, Ginger's business comes from word of mouth. She has been associated with this guide since its first edition in 1990.

Sunshine Flowers

(925) 228-6123
FAX: (925) 228-2183

(by appointment)
Martinez, CA

Contact: Constance Day

Service Area: Greater Bay Area, Wine Country

Specialties: From traditional garden look to contemporary flower design, using fresh or freeze-dried flowers to create the mood of the entire event

Base Price: bridal bouquet, $100; centerpiece, $30; altar piece, $100
Extra Charges: delivery, event planning, wedding coordination

Payment Terms: $100 deposit, balance due 2 weeks prior to event
Credit Cards: Visa, MasterCard

Lead Time: 1 week to 18 months
Bouquet Preservation: yes

"Absolutely gorgeous!" "You are true artists!" "You are not only a fabulous florist but a help in every other way." These are some of the rave reviews about Constance, who creates stunning floral designs for weddings and special events. Her large, hilltop studio is equipped with walk-in and reach-in refrigeration, a large selection of ribbons and other materials, baskets, containers, and props. In the adjacent greenhouses sit the many potted topiaries, plants, and flowers that she includes in her designs. She also incorporates freeze-dried flowers which, although more expensive, last much longer. Constance tries to accommodate her clients in every way. She designs bridesmaids' bouquets to also serve as table decorations and centerpieces, many of which can be given away as gifts. She encourages prospective customers to visit her studio and look through portfolios and actual examples of design work. Her consultations are complimentary.

For an elaborate wedding at a private club, Constance used small topiaries, enhanced with roses, anemones, and Queen Anne's lace, for the table decorations. The head table was adorned with garlands, and on both sides were large bouquets of larkspur, roses, anemones, snapdragons, Queen Anne's lace, and ivy placed on white columns draped with tulle. The tulle, roses, and anemones were repeated in the cake table decoration, all with the freshest of flowers.

With a degree in agriculture from UC Berkeley and floral design training by American and European teachers, Constance's style incorporates a traditional and contemporary look. However, it was her background that contributed more to her endeavor. She grew up in the midst of New England's garden club atmosphere and was influenced by her grandmother (a landscape architect), her father (an avid gardener), and her mother (an artist).

Tapestry
Bridal & Special Event Flowers
(by appointment)
San Francisco, CA

(415) 550-1015
FAX: (415) 550-8206
karen@tapestryflowers.com
www.tapestryflowers.com

Contact: Karen Axel AIFD

Service Area: Greater Bay Area

Specialties: Natural, hand-crafted creations with sensuous colors and textures

Base Price: bridal bouquet, $125; centerpiece, $45; altar piece, $125
Extra Charges: delivery, setup, rentals

Payment Terms: 25% deposit, balance due 2 weeks prior to event
Credit Cards: Visa, MasterCard

Lead Time: 1 month to 1 year
Bouquet Preservation: can recommend

For Karen, the word "tapestry" evoked feelings of rich and opulent, textured flower work, so it became the perfect name to describe her style and her business. As in a tapestry, Karen feels that every aspect of decoration must work together: tablecloths, napkins, flowers, props and lighting – items that she provides to achieve the ultimate look. "I gave Karen just a few suggestions, and she came up with an amazing, full concept and exquisite design," raved one client.

In 1994, Karen was inducted into the American Institute of Floral Designers (AIFD), of which only a few Bay Area florists are members. She limits her events from one to three per weekend so she can devote time to designing and personalizing every event. Her detailed and prompt proposals are reflective of her professional integrity.

"I enjoy adding that special touch – something more emotional," comments Karen. It shows in her designs. She also works up 'til the last minute to ensure that her decorations look as fresh as possible. For one event, limes were so recently cut that they were still glistening on the tables between the candles and lavish flowers. For a wedding in a redwood grove, Karen led the way by laying a carpet runner of crimson, golden, coral and magenta rose petals. Simply breathtaking! In working with Karen, it would surprise me not to hear audible awe when guests enter the room.

Karen is a wonderful artist. Her bouquets and arrangements range from light and flowing, opulent and romantic, to whimsical and detailed. Her large selections of custom-made candelabra, vases and props are stunning. Her theme centerpieces of a bed of roses, an arrangement of flowers in a wire teapot, and a shoe made of gardenias have to be some of my favorites. "If Karen is the florist, I know I don't have to worry," commented another client. She took the words right out of my mouth.

Wedding Flowers
Designed Especially For You
6682 Danridge Drive
San Jose, CA 95129

(408) 253-0527
(Phone & FAX)

Contact: Ruth Gliever

Service Area: South Bay and Peninsula

Specialties: Wedding and party flowers in versatile styles; international weddings

Base Price: bridal bouquet, $40; centerpiece, $20; altar piece, $50
Extra Charges: delivery beyond 15 miles

Payment Terms: payment due upon delivery
Credit Cards: no

Lead Time: 1 week to 6 months
Bouquet Preservation: no

What Ruth Gliever likes to do most is work with flowers. She used to manage a flower shop and design flower decorations. Now she owns her own business, specializing in wedding flowers. She bends over backwards for her brides and does everything she can for them. Her motto is, "You are only as good as your last work." Since she does all the work herself, she accepts only two weddings per weekend. Except for her wedding arch, all props, vases and baskets are included in her price. Her willingness to accommodate everyone has led her to do several international weddings; she recently did the flowers for an Indian bride and a Persian bride.

The wedding decorations were ready for delivery when I arrived to visit Ruth. They were for a large wedding, with floral arrangements for both the church and the reception hall. Fresh irises, roses, heather, baby's breath, ferns, and leaves were placed in altar baskets. The bride's bouquet, a cascade, was made of white flowers: roses, stephanotis, and baby's breath. The bridesmaids had smaller bouquets of the same flowers in red.

Her clients love her fresh, beautiful, and detail-oriented, yet moderately priced floral arrangements. They also comment on her patience, even with the fussiest bride. Ruth is a very sweet person and very helpful in selecting the right flowers with you.

The Wild Geranium

(408) 354-5171

Beautiful Flowers For All Occasions
244 Loma Alta Avenue
Los Gatos, CA 95030

Contact: Lindsay Catterton

Service Area: Greater Bay Area

Specialties: English garden look and design with unusual flowers

Base Price: bridal bouquet, $100; centerpiece, $20; altar piece, $75
Extra Charges: delivery, setup

Payment Terms: 10% deposit, balance due 2 weeks prior to event
Credit Cards: no

Lead Time: 1 week to 9 months
Bouquet Preservation: no

My most recent experience with this florist's work was at a beautiful all-white wedding. A large bouquet of Casablanca lilies decorated the top of the white lace chuppah, and eucalyptus and vines of passion flower and ivy flowed down the tulle-covered poles. The bride's bouquet was a cascade of dendrobium orchids, gardenias, stephanotis and lilies of the valley. When Lindsay showed it to me, I quickly caught its wonderful scent. The two-tiered centerpieces consisted of Casablanca lilies, white tulips, sweet peas, larkspur, and Queen Anne's lace. Instead of greenery, small inexpensive mums were used as filler, providing an opulent and expensive impression. All of the flowers, carefully wrapped and placed in boxes, looked immaculate.

Unusual arrangements, like the one with a garden look on one side and a contemporary look on the other side, and the tropical decoration pieces are seen in Lindsay's portfolio. Since 1989, Lindsay has been invited to display interpretations of art through flowers at the University of Santa Clara's de Saisset Museum, an honor she is very proud of.

Lindsay turned her lifelong love affair with flowers into a business in 1983. She shops at wholesalers and growers, and her delivered arrangements often consist of flowers cut only the day before. Floral foam holds the water supply, and she wires the heavier blossoms. She has professional refrigeration and delivery. Lindsay's work, including her fabulous centerpieces, is her signature and her advertisement, bringing new business all the time. "The best flowers I have ever seen," and "Gorgeous, very fresh flowers," were comments from her customers.

Laurel Ann Winzler
Floral and Interior Design
(by appointment)
San Francisco, CA

(415) 386-8360
FAX: (415) 750-0485
flaurel1@aol.com

Contact: Laurel Ann Winzler

Service Area: Greater Bay Area

Specialties: Floral work with emphasis on European-style arrangements; hairpieces, chuppahs

Base Price: bridal bouquet, $100; centerpiece, $50; altar piece, $120
Extra Charges: delivery

Payment Terms: $500 non-ref. deposit, 50% 3 months prior, balance due day of event
Credit Cards: no

Lead Time: 3 days to 1 year
Bouquet Preservation: no

Culture, music, art, and literature have always been highly regarded and instilled in Laurel's upbringing. Her Italian grandmother inspired her sense of style and vision, which can be seen in Laurel's distinctive style in dress and living. Her flair for drama and color is obvious in many of her arrangements and variety of chuppahs. In 1988, with encouragement from her colleagues and other professionals, Laurel left a position at a law firm to feed her artistic soul. With the San Francisco Symphony as her first client, it was a natural transition.

From the time Laurel meets with her clients, there is a real sense of caring. Laurel's ability to channel clients' ideas, hopes and feelings, and bring them to life is her form of artistic expression. Extremely knowledgeable, with years of exposure to top-level craftsmanship in theatrical production and opera performances, Laurel has developed a sixth sense. She can step into a room and easily assess where the client's budget can be most effectively spent. Her artistic ability is complemented and balanced by her well-organized and professional nature.

In working with Laurel, I find that quality is never compromised. At the market, she purchases all her own flowers and never leaves without making sure the best flowers have been selected. Her arrangements are always fresh, carefully placed, and molded to achieve her client's vision.

I witnessed Laurel's resourcefulness during one wedding on which we worked together. She was waiting for roses to be shipped from the bride's uncle in Ecuador. When she learned that the roses were accidentally shipped to another state, Laurel, with approval, remedied the situation. Off to the market, she saved the day by purchasing a beautiful assortment of comparable flowers. Though the shipment finally did arrive, the roses were unsalvageable. As a special touch for the bride's mother, Laurel scattered the Ecuadorian rose petals throughout the room adding a bit of sentimentality to the decor.

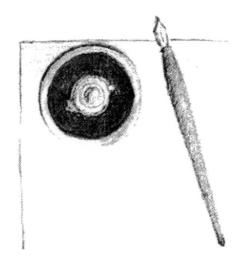

INVITATIONS

NOTES

INTRODUCTION

Invitations set the tone, style and formality for every event. While the Crane Company is still thought of as the premier wedding invitation supplier, other companies produce equally elegant designs and quality products. Today, there seems to be no end to the creativity, design, and papers that make up wonderful invitations. Add to these different styles of calligraphy and unique presentation. I've seen invitations designed around a theme and others that are so unique. Some arrive in bottles; others are like puzzles that the guests put together.

All of the invitation companies and calligraphers reviewed in the guide are experienced in guiding you with proper wording, as well as addressing and printing techniques. Their expertise will save you time in selecting or customizing something truly unique. The added advantage of these personalized services is that they can assist you with all of your stationery needs. Place cards, menus, announcements, guest accommodation cards, maps, programs, and save-the-date cards can all have a consistent and complimentary look.

Invitations should be ordered no later than three months prior to your event. Always order additional envelopes to handle name or address errors. Remember to weigh a completely assembled invitation for proper postage. Hand-cancel each invitation to avoid ugly post office marks on your beautifully calligraphed invitations.

Invitations should be mailed four to six weeks before the wedding and eight weeks before for out-of-town guests.

The pages in this section present such a wide variety of invitation ideas that I'm sure you'll come across one that appeals to you.

Money Matters

Prices vary from about $1.50 to more than $20 per invitation. You can save money by assembling the invitations by yourself.

By Invitation Only

Distinctive Invitations and Announcements
626 Walnut Street, Suite 206
San Carlos, CA 94070

(650) 594-1126
FAX: (650) 594-0134

Contact: Pamela Smith or Tina Ficher

Service Area: Greater Bay Area and beyond

Specialties: Extensive collection of elegant and custom-designed invitations; custom calligraphy

Pricing: an average of $500 for 100 invitations, including response cards and envelopes
Extra Charges: none

Payment Terms: 50% non-ref. deposit,
balance due at pickup
Credit Cards: Visa, MasterCard
Lead Time: 3 - 4 months

Delivery/Pickup: yes
Portfolio: many

With Pamela's degree in tourism and Tina's business management degree, this mother and daughter certainly make a wonderful team. When I first met them, they were both wedding and event planners. With such backgrounds, they can give you a good idea about what goes into planning a wedding, besides consulting about the invitations. During an extensive interview, they get to know the client's preferences, theme, colors, and ambience, all of which determine the type of invitation and the appropriate wording. The next step is selecting the calligraphy style, which they also provide. Pamela and Tina offer their advice and assistance with the goal of pleasing the client and are happy to help with other questions about the event.

I love visiting them in their cozy, elegantly decorated suite and browsing through their large collection of albums displaying the newest invitations purchased at the famous New York National Stationery Show. I fell in love with a handmade paper invitation, created with different flower petals or confetti, velum overlays, and enhanced with different ribbons. I also admired the unique, custom-designed invitations by artists local to this area.

The selection of distinctive invitations, announcements, place cards, menus, and seasonal announcements has steadily grown over the eight years Pamela and Tina have been in business. They are highly respected among their peers and clients for their knowledge and friendly, soft approach.

Please call to schedule an appointment.

Cuyahoga
Calligraphy and Graphics
(by appointment)
San Francisco, CA

(415) 474-5027
(Phone & FAX)

Contact: Joan Leavitt

Service Area: Coast to Coast

Specialties: Hand-designed invitations from handmade papers

Pricing: 100 invitations and response cards, from $350
Extra Charges: shipping, stuffing, addressing envelopes, rush orders

Payment Terms: 30% non-ref. deposit,
                     balance COD
Credit Cards: no

Lead Time: 3 weeks to 4 months
Delivery/Pickup: yes
Portfolio: sample books

Joan's business is named for the river that flows through Cleveland, her childhood home. She has loved letterforms and paper since she was a child. After moving to San Francisco, she studied graphic design, calligraphy, both English and Hebrew, and joined the Friends of Calligraphy. During her first years, she focused on developing her 10 hands of English style and 5 of Hebrew calligraphy, and now offers others depending on her client's needs. Her love for beautiful papers led her to integrate her calligraphy with the production of unique invitations.

You can get a good overview of her work from her portfolio. Joan's three primary methods used for the invitations are: 1) offset lithography; 2) letter press, which involves making a plate from a negative and pressing each invitation to provide an old style, textured look; and 3) foil stamp embossed printing, with a plate also made from a negative. Her invitations often are square, and her response cards are usually postcards, a very hot item with brides. The invitations often include a gilded leaf from her neighborhood park's eucalyptus tree. Different colored French, gold or copper mesh ribbons can enhance the invitation. The paper for the inner envelope can be selected from several sample books of handmade Oriental paper, cut to size and closed with sealing wax. Joan feels that a custom-designed invitation is much more than just design and choice of paper. It is the expression of who the couple is and sets the tone for their event. This can be accomplished by including the wedding band inscription or a favorite symbol in a corner.

Place cards matching the style of the invitation are available, as are hand-crafted guest scrolls. Joan also offers Jewish and American wedding contracts, church and temple programs, menu cards, etc. She can provide handmade guest books by another local artist. Joan donates 10% of each order to your favorite charity.

Giorgi's of Walnut Creek

Gifts - Accessories - Invitations

1509 Locust Street
Walnut Creek, CA 94596

(925) 945-0424

FAX: (925) 939-2450

giorgi@gte.net

www.weddinglinks.com/mem/giorgi's.htm

Contact: Georgette or Chuck O'Brien

Service Area: Greater Bay Area

Specialties: The ultimate in wedding accessories, customized headpieces, cake tops, and favors; invitations, ribbon printing, calligraphy, and engraving

Pricing: depending on item
Extra Charges: favor assembly, shipping may apply

Payment Terms: invitations or special orders: 50% deposit, balance due at pickup	**Lead Time:** depends on item
	Delivery/Pickup: yes
Credit Cards: Visa, MasterCard	**Portfolio:** many sample books and accessories

Located in the heart of downtown Walnut Creek, Giorgi's has been open since 1986. Every inch of the store is filled with high-quality gifts, accessories, and invitations to complete any wedding. Georgette and Chuck bring a warmth and familiarity to this quaint neighborhood.

What makes Giorgi's special compared to other gift stores is their personalized service and custom accessories. "We shop the world for unique and custom-made items found nowhere else," says Georgette. Chuck resculpts porcelain cake tops to fit a theme or ethnic background. He can change a figurine to match the couple's hair and skin tone or restyle their outfits. I was particularly amazed at the transformation of a groom's tuxedo into a Scottish kilt ensemble. Georgette is equally talented in customizing ring pillows, wedding favors, and headpieces. She was even commissioned to design 1900's authentic hats, bouquets, and garters for various EuroDisney's stores on Main Street, making news in *Diablo Magazine*. Georgette designs headpieces for style and wearability, sometimes incorporating 3 or 4 looks for different parts of the day. Many of her wedding favors incorporate what she calls the "playful part of the wedding." They work one-on-one with their clients, offering a range of items from elegant truffle boxes with theme or seasonal flavors to selections of wedding invitations.

They pride themselves on educating the client about paper quality, printing techniques, etiquette guidance, and the extreme importance of properly addressing invitations and envelopes. They exercise extreme caution in counting and proofing their invitations for errors. "We play the devil's advocate." In addition to offering hand calligraphy, they have an on-site inscriber machine to address special occasion invitations in beautiful calligraphic styles.

Giorgi's of Walnut Creek is the all-inclusive boutique for quality wedding accessories.

in Print

(650) 948-1040
FAX: (650) 948-2784
inprintla@aol.com

(by appointment)
Los Altos, CA

Contact: Elli Bernacchi

Service Area: Greater Bay Area

Specialties: Unique, custom-designed invitations, personalized announcements, imported papers and ribbons, graphic design, stationery, calligraphy, guest & photo albums, gifts, favors

Pricing: each invitation, from $1; custom invitation, from $3; hand calligraphy, $1.50; computer calligraphy, $.75
Extra Charges: none

Payment Terms: 50% deposit, balance due upon delivery
Credit Cards: major credit cards

Lead Time: 1 week to 2 months
Delivery/Pickup: all orders can be shipped
Portfolio: thousands of invitations

"There is an invitation waiting to be designed just for you, better than you imagine it could be!" This just about says it all. Elli Bernacchi and her staff offer the finest in personalized service and individualized attention for creating your perfect invitation.

Though she began a custom stationery and imprintable business in 1991, Elli realized there was a great void in the invitation industry for unique, customized invitations. With a passion for specialty paper and calligraphy, Elli sought out importers of unique handmade papers, romantic ribbons, and unusual type styles. Her company is built on the idea that clients should be able to feel and touch the actual invitation. Pulling samples together, Elli spends a tremendous amount of time and energy bringing her client's vision to reality. While working with Elli on several weddings, I could feel her excitement in creating a sample before one's very eyes. "Assembling an actual piece brings an abstract idea to life for the brides," exclaims Elli.

Her studio is filled with an uncountable amount of handmade, imported, specialty papers; ribbons, one-of-a-kind or traditional invitations; programs, maps, and exquisite favors. Her line of guest books and photo albums ranges from beautiful, natural flower-embedded covers to elegant silks and brocades. Most of her national and international treasures come from her visits to the annual National Stationery Show in New York, the largest show in the country. She can take a traditional invitation, embellish it with unique paper and ribbon, and create a happy medium between traditional and custom styles. Budget-minded clients can help with production, thereby cutting costs dramatically.

With her enormous selection, there is an invitation complete for any special occasion and season. After all, the invitation does set the tone of your event. A selection of her invitations is available at Flora in Allied Arts, Menlo Park.

Inviting Ideas
Invitations and Announcements
840 E. Campbell Avenue
Campbell, CA 95008

(408) 371-7787
FAX: (408) 371-7791

Contact: Ruth Pupkin or Barbara Silverman

Service Area: Greater Bay Area

Specialties: Invitations and announcements, stationery, in-house printing on blank stock and envelope addressing for private and corporate events

Pricing: budget and up
Extra Charges: shipping

Payment Terms: 60% deposit, balance due at pickup
Credit Cards: major credit cards

Lead Time: 4 months
Delivery/Pickup: no
Portfolio: many invitation books

You can't help but fall in love with Ruth and Barbara's store across the street from the Pruneyard Shopping Center. They meet with their clients in a cozy little house, built in the 1920s, with an art deco fireplace and comfortable white wicker furniture. The shelves on the walls are filled with business stationery and sample books of invitations for weddings and Bar/Bat Mitzvahs. The attractive cards they found at the famous New York Stationery Show are also exhibited on the walls. My favorites were those with floral backgrounds, overlaid with vellum and tied together with colorful bows. Barbara and Ruth showed me the famous Crane invitation with its timeless beauty and the very popular William Arthur invitation, as I learned about engraved lettering done with a copper plate and the less expensive thermography process. Their printer can produce a variety of different print styles in hundreds of colors on blank stock. An artist is on hand for custom artwork, as well as two in-house printers for rush orders. Ketubbahs (Jewish wedding contracts) and wedding programs are also available.

Since buying the business in June of 1989, they have doubled their inventory of invitation books and now have more than 80. There is something for everybody, and the budget-minded bride receives the same attention as the bride ordering the most expensive paper. Consulting is done strictly on an individual basis. You can get help with the proper wording when creating the text for the invitation. A busy person can fax the order rather than make a trip to Campbell. Their store hours are Monday through Saturday from 10 a.m. to 5 p.m. Evening appointments can be scheduled, but please call first!

Janèl Claire Design

(formerly Petite Pomme Design)
1025 Carleton Street, Studio 14
Berkeley, CA 94710

(510) 883-1870
FAX: (510) 883-1871
janelclaire@earthlink.net

Contact: Janèl Claire

Service Area: Greater Bay Area and beyond

Specialties: Custom invitations for weddings and special events; optional letter press and calligraphy

Pricing: $10 - $20
Extra Charges: none

Payment Terms: 50% deposit, balance COD
Credit Cards: no
Lead Time: 6 - 12 weeks

Delivery/Pickup: no
Portfolio: yes

From personalized Christmas cards and invitations to creative packages, Janèl has always customized gifts and cards to reflect the personality of the recipient. What began as a customized wedding invitation for a friend turned into a successful word-of-mouth business.

As a graphic designer for 10 years, Janèl brings innovative ideas to her completely customized invitation business. In viewing her wide selection of invitations, one aspect remains constant: Janèl's way of incorporating a customized symbol or logo to identify the client's personality, culture, or theme. One bride commented, "Janèl designed my package based on my culture, background and color scheme." She doesn't merely create an invitation but a complete packet to outline and set the tone of the event. For a weekend-long event, Janèl designed a crafted, bound booklet of all the activities and information needed for the out-of-town guests. From golfing and tourist attractions to rehearsal and wedding schedules, she incorporated humor and fun into this beautiful keepsake.

By consulting with her clients, Janèl envisions the overall design and customizes every piece of printed material, from the invitation and envelopes to the place cards and menu cards. For a Japanese/American couple, she designed a plum blossom, a symbol of good fortune, and incorporated it throughout, including the flap of the return envelopes. The circular response card provided enough room for the guests to write their special wishes to the couple – a great keepsake for years to come.

Janèl finds creative ways to bring elegance to even limited budgets. On a single-color, traditional, printed invitation, she added a personal touch by hand-coloring each flower and detail. Grateful clients commented: "I was able to watch my designs in progress as Janèl created them on her computer." "She showed true interest in our occasion."

jerdon

Fine Wedding and Social Stationery and Gifts

(by appointment)
Sunnyvale, CA

(408) 245-5594
FAX: (408) 736-1277
dreate@aol.com
www.jerdon.com

Contact: Denise Reate

Service Area: Greater Bay Area

Specialties: All-inclusive source for all your printed needs; fine gifts and accessories

Pricing: custom invitations, from $3; addressing invitations (inner & outer), $2.25; maps, from $1.25
Extra Charges: assembly, shipping

Payment Terms: payment in full at placement of order
Credit Cards: no

Lead Time: 2 - 7 days
Delivery/Pickup: yes
Portfolio: many samples

The tremendous amount of care in providing only the finest gifts and invitations are evident immediately upon entering jerdon's studio. jerdon resulted from Denise's own frustration of finding an all-inclusive source for her invitation and accessory needs. Her extensive experience in career counseling combined with her business sense gives her an intuitive talent for identifying her client's needs. Her enthusiasm to create and tie together all elements of a wedding seems to come naturally. As Denise plainly put it, "We start with a blank product and they leave with a complete product. They don't have to think about a thing."

A wide assortment of fine invitations and custom envelopments, beautiful accessories, elegant favors, table cards, save-the-date cards, place cards, menu cards, and escort cards are matched, combined, and packaged for each individual. Envelopes can be hand- or computer-generated calligraphy to perfectly match the invitation letter styles. Programs are customized, designed and typeset. For your out-of-town guests, maps and accommodation cards are coordinated with the event motif and designed for ease of use. These can be assembled for clients who have little time on their hands.

Clients praise Denise for her personal care and attention to wording. As a coordinator, I find jerdon to be the wise choice for anyone with distinct tastes, limited time, and a need for personalized attention.

Adrienne D. Keats
Calligraphy & Design
(by appointment)
San Francisco & New York

(415) 759-5678
FAX: (415) 661-5249
(212) 794-3511
FAX: (212) 794-1819

Contact: Adrienne D. Keats

Service Area: United States

Specialties: Hand-calligraphed wedding invitations in English and Hebrew; announcements, addressed envelopes, place cards, menus, programs, etc.

Pricing: custom invitation; envelopes, $2.25 per 3-line address
Extra Charges: delivery and shipping fees, travel

Payment Terms: 50% deposit, balance due upon delivery
Credit Cards: no

Lead Time: 1 week to 3 months
Delivery/Pickup: yes, extra
Portfolio: yes

"It is a professional business, not just a hobby." "Always consistent." "Fast turn around." These are just a few comments about Adrienne. With 22 years of experience, Adrienne has attended innumerable workshops and classes all over the country on different styles, design, layout and techniques. Having been involved in art throughout her life, Adrienne found the perfect way of expressing herself – through her calligraphy.

Adrienne loves to interact with clients and is always mindful of their tastes. Her aim is customer satisfaction, and she always follows the client's lead.

Adrienne personalizes every informational packet she sends out. The address is hand-calligraphed with the recipient's name in brush script across the top. It is much too beautiful to toss so I find myself collecting every correspondence envelope I receive from her.

All of her work is done by hand. Each envelope is addressed by hand, not computer. Custom invitations are one of her specialties. Adrienne creates an original invitation and submits it to the client for approval. The client is then provided with a camera-ready invitation and specifications to bring to the printer. What you would think could only be done perfectly by a computer, Adrienne does by her amazingly steady hand. Her type styles vary from an elegant, stately Copperplate to whimsical Trajan. One particular promotional piece captured my attention. The names of various zoo animals were creatively calligraphed into the characteristics of each animal. The shapes and colors all showed the animal's movement. What talent!

166

Papineau Calligraphy

(510) 339-2301
FAX: (510) 339-6759

5772 Thornhill Drive
Oakland, CA 94611

Contact: Michele Papineau

Service Area: Coast to Coast

Specialties: Fine hand-lettering for invitations, vows, envelopes, monograms, place cards, table seating, programs, menus, family trees, etc.

Pricing: Invitation, RSVP, reception card design: from $200; inner & outer envelopes, from $2.50 (black ink); single envelope, from $1.50 (black ink); place cards, $1.25 (black ink)
Extra Charges: stuffing, shipping, long distance phone calls

Payment Terms: COD
Credit Cards: no

Lead Time: 2 weeks to 2 years
Delivery/Pickup: available
Portfolio: yes

Michele says she inherited her patience from her father (whose hobbies were calligraphy and sign painting) and her professionalism from 12 years in the corporate world. Her hand is so steady that clients often comment, "Did you really do it by hand?" In business for 19 years, Michele receives much of her work through referrals and repeat clientele. In 1981, she started Papineau Calligraphy by subletting a corner of a print shop in the lovely Montclair District of Oakland, and since 1989 has occupied the entire space.

Her studio walls display her clients' beautifully framed pieces and samples of her talented hand. One particular art piece that captured my heart was "A toast to Grandmother's 90th birthday," containing a beautifully framed collection of five grandchildren's fondest memories of their grandmother dedicated to her on her 90th birthday and calligraphed in Michele's amazing hand. I am sure there was not a dry eye at the celebration.

Michele also has many other items on display. One sample that caught my attention was one for which she had hand-lettered 70 original wedding invitations and envelopes in copper ink on beautiful Italian-made paper. She has many invitations on display for which she creates the original artwork that is then sent to the printer or engraver for reproduction. From birthdays to Bar Mitzvahs, if there is an occasion, Michele can be a part of it.

Michele also displays what she calls her "famous" collection. This includes pieces she has done for famous people, including one titled "An Honorable Profession," commissioned as a gift for President Clinton. Christmas cards that she has created over the years share a special place on her studio walls. My favorite was "The Legend of Santa Claus." Each fold outlined various legends from Asia to Europe. Michele adds a touch of elegance to anything that can be hand-lettered. Please call for an appointment before visiting her studio.

Pleasant Thoughts
A Paper and Gift Store
510 Sycamore Valley Road W.
Danville, CA 94526

(925) 837-0706
FAX: (925) 820-6417
www.pleasantthoughts.com

Contact: Deborah Boot-Bini (Manager)

Service Area: Greater Bay Area

Specialties: Premier destination for innovative invitations, classic engraving; guest books, gifts and accessories for weddings and special celebrations

Pricing: from $300 for invitation sets of 100
Extra Charges: shipping

Payment Terms: 50% deposit, balance due at pickup
Credit Cards: major credit cards

Lead Time: 1 - 6 weeks
Delivery/Pickup: yes
Portfolio: many sample invitation books

"They are the 'Miss Manners' of weddings. Between Marilyn and Deborah, they know everything there is to know about wedding etiquette," raved a repeat customer. "A solid, dependable and talented service," confirmed another customer. When I asked what made their store so unique, Marilyn responded that their longtime veteran staff is an attribute to their dedicated clientele.

Much more than just a gift store, Pleasant Thoughts is a specialty store, located in the Danville Livery Shopping Center since 1989. Marilyn and her husband Roger started their specialty paper and gift business in 1979. They have an extensive selection of invitations to fit any budget and occasion, including do-it-yourself supplies for the crafty consumer who wants to add a personal touch. I couldn't tear myself away from the beautiful displays of handmade and archival papers, beautifully embellished wedding albums, organizers, guest books, cards, frames, and gifts.

Two comfortable, semi-private booths separating the retail counter are specially designed so that you can view invitations at your own pace and are close enough if you need assistance. I viewed several of their specialty albums, including an interactive wedding invitation book in which you can lift and paste different type styles, papers, and treatments for a personal touch. When I asked for a specific theme, such as shells or cityscape, Deborah, without a blink, pulled all the invitation books relating to the themes I had in mind. Talk about knowing your inventory! With the overwhelming selection of invitations, type styles, various printing choices (engraving, hot stamping, thermography, letterpress, etc.), it is easy to see why someone would come to Pleasant Thoughts for wedding and special occasion needs.

Polly Rose Stationers & Freeze Dried Flowers

Distinctive Invitations/Bouquet Preservation
198 Castro Street
Mountain View, CA 94041

(650) 964-5522
FAX: (650) 964-2715
ruth@best.com
www.pollyrose.com

Contact: Ruth Lee

Service Area: Greater Bay Area

Specialties: Exceptional selection of invitations, imprintables, distinctive cards and gifts;
bridal bouquet preservation

Pricing: budget and up
Extra Charges: delivery

Payment Terms: 50% deposit, balance due at pickup
Credit Cards: Visa, MasterCard

Lead Time: 1 - 10 days
Delivery/Pickup: locally only, when available
Portfolio: many sample albums

Walking into Polly Rose Stationers & Freeze Dried Flowers quaint corner store in downtown Mountain View, you can't help but be spellbound by the delightful selection of gifts, cards and invitations. "You must enjoy shopping," I said to Ruth, owner and floral preserver. "It's Christmas every day," she replied.

In the back of the store, two beautiful, overstuffed floral sofas welcome you into a cozy area to browse through the extensive selection of distinctive wedding invitations. They feature fine social stationery, announcements and invitations, such as Regency, William Arthur, and Chase, to the more contemporary Love Knots from Checkerboard and a large selection of imprintables, thus providing invitations for every taste and budget. They even provide 24-hour turnaround for in-house imprinting on their imprintables, invitations perfect for customizing. To ensure 100% satisfaction they also provide, at no extra charge, a proof of all invitation orders for the customer's approval. They personally assist with the proper wording and layout for any occasion. Florists and clients alike enjoy the "at home" atmosphere and personal attention.

What's even more unique about this stationer is their flower preservation from any sentimental occasion. From the bridal bouquets and floral cake tops to centerpieces and arrangements, Ruth creates a treasured keepsake. Bridal bouquets, whole or in part, can be preserved in "under dome" frames for hanging or display. Ruth's wide selection of finished frames range from Victorian to contemporary, available in a variety of shapes and sizes. Many of my favorite freeze-dried keepsakes were arranged in wreaths, swags, and wire-mesh theme centerpieces. The possibilities are limited only by your imagination.

Ruth offers a discount on bouquet preservation when included with an invitation order.

Printed Affair
Invitations and Announcements
460 Boulevard Way
Oakland, CA 94610

(510) 654-9903
FAX: (510) 654-9916

Contact: Leslie Bond or Marcia Redford

Service Area: Greater Bay Area

Specialties: Distinctive invitations and creative papers for entertaining, special occasions, and correspondence

Pricing: depending on item
Extra Charges: shipping, addressing, assembly

Payment Terms: 50% deposit, balance due at pickup
Credit Cards: Visa, MasterCard

Lead Time: 3 weeks/weddings; 3 days for many other invitations
Delivery/Pickup: yes
Portfolio: many books and papers

"Service, Service, Service – ideas – time, and lots of TLC," is how Leslie and Marcia set themselves apart. Their warm and inviting nature set me right at ease when I visited them in their quiet, neighborhood studio office on the Oakland/Piedmont border. Friends for many years, Leslie and Marcia conceived Printed Affair in June 1994 and opened their doors in October that same year. Oddly enough, they were highly recommended to me by their competition.

The assortment of printed papers for weddings, showers, rehearsals, Bar/Bat Mitzvahs, anniversaries, and every social occasion complement their large stock of invitation lines, from theme-oriented designs to a full line of traditional Crane's invitations. Leslie and Marcia enjoy finding the right invitation. "It's like pieces to a puzzle," explains Leslie.

They are open Tuesday through Saturday from 10 a.m. to 4 p.m. and accommodate other scheduled appointments. Their doors are open for anyone to browse for ideas, and they welcome the opportunity to create an invitation to fit the individual style and event.

I enjoyed browsing through some of their customized invitations. They have a good sense of design and thoroughly enjoy working with their customers. "It's our cup of tea," adds Marcia.

They enjoy a steady stream of repeat customers. During my visit, an exhausted woman stopped by after an endless search for odd size envelopes for her daughter's birth announcements. Every place she visited either did not have the unique size or did not want to sell envelopes without an invitation order. After she showed Leslie and Marcia the invitation, not only were they able to find her envelopes for the announcements, but they actually stocked the entire matching set. This very satisfied customer was thrilled to find a new source for her invitation needs.

Script and Sparkle

(by appointment)
Millbrae, CA

(650) 952-5869
(650) 952-4145
FAX: (650) 589-9976

Contact: Susan or Carolyne

Service Area: Coast to Coast and International

Specialties: Personal service with 20% discount for invitations and stationery

Pricing: 100 wedding invitations, from $100
Extra Charges: shipping, rush orders

Payment Terms: 50% deposit, balance COD
Credit Cards: no
Lead Time: 3 - 6 months for weddings; 1 week for rush orders

Delivery/Pickup: yes
Portfolio: thousands of invitations

Susan and Carolyne grew up in the Bay Area and had been friends for many years when they came up with the idea to open a business. They decided to sell invitations at a discount and also offer personalized service. That was seven years ago on April 1st.

Their business has grown mostly from referrals, and many wedding clients have returned to them for other stationery needs. Susan and Carolyne pride themselves on their personalized service and on one of the largest and newest selections of invitation books. They set up a one-to-one two-hour consultation, so clients need only one appointment to take care of their stationery needs. Susan and Carolyne work closely with their clients on wording, type style, and color scheme. For a complete service, Script and Sparkle's calligrapher can address envelopes and personalize place cards. They offer invitations for all occasions, birth announcements, personal and professional stationery, and business cards. As a convenience, they can accommodate just about any printed need, from favor boxes, napkins, coasters, and matches to accessories and gifts for the wedding party, all at 20% off.

To keep up on the latest trends, they attend the National Stationery Show in New York every spring and are always updating their selections with the newest books.

They love working with their clients, and it shows. Clients comment about their personalized services. One client commented, "Over 100 envelopes were addressed before realizing they were the wrong ones. Script and Sparkle ordered correct envelopes and addressed all of them at no charge." Now that's service. As Susan and Carolyne say, " We have been having fun for seven years."

Wedding RSVP

(888) WED-RSVP
(804) 293-7787

100 West South Street, Suite 2A
Charlottesville, VA 22902

FAX: (804) 293-3393
AButler@WeddingRSVP.com
www.WeddingRSVP.com

Contact: Adam Butler

Service Area: International

Specialties: Customized web site and toll-free number for guests to RSVP for your wedding

Pricing: from $440
Extra Charges: none

Payment Terms: payment in full at contract signing
Credit Cards: major credit cards

Lead Time: 4 days to 1 year
Portfolio: see web site

"Wedding RSVP heals the information gap between hosts and guests by serving as a personalized information source for your wedding." It's a great story: Two brothers, Adam and Rawls, met in Kentucky to attend a wedding. One dressed in a suit without a gift and one dressed in a tuxedo bearing a gift, both set off to find the ceremony site with only an address at hand. After an extensive search for the church on Main Street, they finally found someone in this small, quiet town to ask for directions. They came to discover that the church was located two streets off of Main, consequently missing the entire ceremony. Amazed and exhausted, Adam and Rawls spent the rest of the evening wondering how this breakdown of communication could have been prevented. From their somewhat humorous adventure stemmed the perfect solution – Wedding RSVP. A 24-hour, human-operated, easy-to-remember toll free number allows guests to call and get directions on the spot.

Wedding RSVP's purpose is twofold: to provide guests with essential information and give wedding couples an accurate, up-to-date guest count. The customized web site or toll-free number offers guests an easy way to RSVP, and provides detailed ceremony and reception times and locations, maps, suggested attire, gift registry, accommodations, menu selections, and information about any planned activities during their stay. Brides and grooms eliminate the cost of response cards and postage while saving time and avoiding the headaches associated with tracking an accurate guest count. Just think! You won't have to pay for any miscounted guest, and will avoid the embarrassment of missing someone in your seating arrangements. I love the fact that guests can relay special wishes to you.

Clients and vendors alike have been waiting for such a convenient way to respond. "I feel so [part of the] '90s, being up with the times and technology." "What an innovative way of tracking the actual number of guests." These comments are just a hint of what clients and guests are saying.

LOCATIONS

NOTES

INTRODUCTION

There are many locations in the area for parties or receptions, and more and more locations are offering sites for ceremonies as well. Also, many private clubs rent their premises to the public. Many communities often rent out large rooms, halls, or even mansions at fairly moderate prices.

Make sure you find out if the **rental price** *includes all tables and chairs or if you have to rent them separately.* The location's rental price might not be such a bargain after all.

Many locations require a certificate of insurance which relieves the site of liability for any mishaps. A certificate of insurance is often available through your home owners or renter's insurance policy. Some insurance companies will not provide it when alcohol is served. When applicable, this is noted under "Extra charges."

I found a wide variety of what locations consider changing rooms. A changing room can be an elaborate suite or simply the ladies room.

The term **dance floor** refers to a dedicated area for dancing that is available in a variety of surfaces depending on the location. If you specifically want a hardwood floor, you might have to rent it.

The term **parking** can be defined as a parking lot, the street, or a garage. Some locations require valet parking in difficult parking situations.

Whether or not a location permits **amplified music** is a consideration, as many event sites are located in residential neighborhoods. If you want to hire a live band, an enclosed room would be a wise choice.

Under **restrictions, no rice, etc.** refers to anything you can shower on the bride and groom. Throwing rice or bird seed is no longer allowed at most locations. Insurance companies consider this dangerous and charge high-risk premiums. Smoking indoors is unlawful in California, which is why I didn't mention this under "Restrictions."

Locations with Catering

Hosting your event at a location with catering takes a major burden off your shoulders. Once you have selected the location, everything else more or less falls into place. A party or wedding planning consultant is usually on staff at these locations.

Normal event time for catered locations is four to five hours. Hotels often have busy schedules, particularly on weekends. A florist told me of one instance where there was only one hour between events, barely enough time for setting up and no time for any cleaning whatsoever. Events with overlapping times can create a privacy or noise issue, for example, if the band at the party nextdoor is loud. Therefore, you should ask about the events scheduled prior to your party or wedding.

Money Matters

Pricing: The charge for renting a location with catering may not appear very high because the charge is included in the costs of the food and alcoholic beverage. One reference complained to me that she saw a bottle of the champagne that was served at her party for $10 less at a local food store. There is often a minimum for the bar.

Even though a location is listed with an in-house caterer, it might be possible to bring in your own. This could result in a buy-out fee paid to the in-house caterer for which the client is responsible.

Extra Charges: To discourage you from bringing your own wine and liquor, a **corkage fee**, which can be as high as $15, is charged for each bottle. Similarly, if a location works with a particular baker, you are encouraged to order your cake from them; otherwise, a **cake-cutting fee** applies. Your bill will also include a **gratuity** (up to 19%) which is routinely added for parties of more than six people.

Locations without Catering

The locations listed in this section either do not have a catering service or let you choose to use theirs or bring in your own. Most of these locations have an event coordinator on staff who can help you with the planning. They usually have a list of those businesses they prefer to work with. A location without in-house catering gives you more freedom to select the vendors who can more closely express your ideas, but is often more costly.

When you reserve a location, keep in mind that there is a **setup** time of one to two hours and **cleanup** time of at least one hour. Thus, for a four-hour reception you might actually need a room for six or seven hours.

Wineries

Each of the wineries I visited had its own special ambience. Some are very elegant, while others are more rustic. It's wonderful to dine next to the growing vine, and it is something special to sit next to large oak barrels of aging wine.

Most wineries allow only their wine to be served. Check the prices in the tasting room and find out if the winery will offer you a discount.

Money Matters

Prices vary according to the day of the week and the season. Saturday is the most expensive day of the week, while Sunday is often somewhat less. Friday evenings are substantially lower during non-holiday times of the year. The month of December and New Year's Eve are always the most expensive dates. However, you can sometimes use the site's Christmas decorations at no extra charge.

More and more locations are offering sites for ceremonies. Prices vary widely, ranging from a setup fee at $1 per chair to $800 for a special site. The charge for the ceremony can also be considered an hour of overtime.

Money Saving Tips

- Don't schedule your event during the month of December.
- Check for special sales at wineries.
- If your caterer charges extra for finding a location, try to find one on your own.
- Negotiate before signing the contract.

A Catered Affair
Banquet Facilities
3255 Scott Blvd., Building 4
Santa Clara, CA 95054

(408) 727-6480
FAX: (408) 727-2525
www.acateredaffair.com

Contact: Bob Changras (Owner); Kelly Bromiley or Judy Mirassou (Event Coordinators)

Specialties: Banquet facilities for weddings and corporate events

Food: California and International cuisines for corporate functions, theme parties, open houses; wedding buffets (wedding packages from $26.95)
No. of Guests: sit-down, to 250; cocktails, to 350

Price (location): none
Extra Charges: 18% gratuity, rentals

Payment Terms: $500 deposit, 50% 1 month prior, balance due 1 week prior to event
Credit Cards: major credit cards
Lead Time: 3 months
Rental Time: 5 hrs.
Wheelchair Access: yes

Changing Room: yes
Dance Floor: yes
Parking: ample
Music: amplified permitted
Restrictions: no rice, etc.

After working as catering manager for A Catered Affair for the past 13 years, Bob Changras has assumed ownership of the company. Located in the heart of Silicon Valley, the restaurant is open for lunch during the week, and during evenings and on weekends it is available for any type of catered affair. This nice, roomy place, with its wallpaper, black & white checkerboard floor, English antiques, and many plants, is quite special and versatile. I've seen the restaurant look very festive for a wedding, with elegant table settings and a gorgeous buffet. For a company party, it can be transformed into a more rustic setting to host, for example, a Munich Oktoberfest. For a BRO party, they hosted the carving station with delicious, tender meats.

Bob and his staff offer a very reasonable wedding package: hot and cold buffets, unlimited champagne, wine, beer, punch, coffee, a three-tiered wedding cake, and use of the restaurant and service personnel.

Bob is also a highly respected and experienced caterer. He places much emphasis on the quality of his food and its presentation. Everything except breads and cakes are prepared in-house. Their buffet tables, with an abundance of colorful vegetables and fruit combined with ivy and flowers, have earned several prizes at wedding shows. Theme parties are one of their specialties. To celebrate a company's connection with Hollywood, they created a glitzy feast, with large golden Oscars as focal points. Their Polynesian parties are well known for the authentic look and taste. Customers like the wonderful food and great personalities of the creative and highly organized staff.

Arboleda

(831) 623-1066
FAX: (831) 623-2066
arboleda@hollinet.com
www.arboleda.com

3600 San Juan Canyon Road, P.O. Box 138
San Juan Bautista, CA 95045

Contact: Kim Kmetovic Cox

Specialties: Secluded Mediterranean-style home in a beautiful country setting
reminiscent of Provence

No. of Guests: May - October: to 250; November - April: to 50

Pricing: May - October: $3,000 for 75 guests; $5,000 for 250 guests; November - April: $2,700 for
50 guest max. (pricing includes weekend accommodations with breakfast for 15 guests)
Extra Charges: rentals

Payment Terms: $1,000 non-ref. deposit, 50% due 90 days prior, balance due 2 weeks prior	**Changing Room:** yes
	Dance Floor: small indoors, outdoors arranged
Credit Cards: Visa, MasterCard	**Parking:** ample
Lead Time: 1 - 12 months	**Music:** amplified permitted
Rental Time: entire weekend or negotiable	**Restrictions:** no rice, etc.; smoking
Wheelchair Access: yes	outdoors only

"Don't just do something, sit there" appears on the living room wall of this charming Mediterranean-style country home, just an hour south of San Jose and 4 miles from the quaint town of San Juan Bautista. The quote is an invitation from owner Kim Cox to her guests to bask in the serenity and beauty of her architectural creation that integrates the masculine and feminine, the old with the new, all the while taking every advantage of the natural environment. "Arboleda" means "grove of trees," named for the sycamores and willows that twist and bend, serving as wonderful backdrops to the various ceremony sites for formal as well as alternative style weddings – a photographer's dream.

The approach to Kim's 5 acres meanders past gardens, braying donkeys and a whimsical, rustic pump house. Past the home is a large pond of water hyacinthus that serves as a water source for the creek running through an arbor of trees to the front of the home, which is ideal for a bride's entrance. Beyond the creek is a large grassy area, perfect for larger weddings. To the left, a large earthenware urn punctuates the lawn. Cleverly engineered underground conduits run from the pond to irrigate the organic vegetable garden that provides fare for weekend guests. There is always something blooming in the many flower gardens of Arboleda.

Kim, ever the gracious hostess, pays as much attention to crafting the experience of her guests as she does to Arboleda itself. Her artistic background is evident everywhere in the eclectically and tastefully appointed home with high beamed ceilings, providing an airy, open feeling. Up to 15 guests can be accommodated in 5 bedrooms, each done in a unique style combining the antique with the modern. The commercial kitchen provides ample workspace. Brides commented on how easy and great Kim is to work with, and how she's "up for anything." The intimacy of Arboleda magnified the personal meaning of their special day.

Byington
Winery and Vineyard
21850 Bear Creek Road
Los Gatos, CA 95030

(408) 354-1111
FAX: (408) 354-2782
event@Byington.com
www.Byington.com

Contact: Sheryl Byington-Brissenden

Specialties: Italian-style chateau winery with elegant rooms for parties and weddings; tiled terrace for outdoor use; ceremony site with gazebo

No. of Guests: weddings, to 250; corporate events, to 500

Pricing: $750 - $4,300, depending on day and time of year; ceremony, $750
Extra Charges: security deposit, dance floor

Payment Terms: 50% non-ref. deposit, balance due 6 months prior to event
Credit Cards: major credit cards
Lead Time: 3 months to 1 year
Rental Time: 8 hrs.; ceremony only, 3 hrs.
Wheelchair Access: yes

Changing Room: yes
Dance Floor: can be rented
Parking: ample
Music: amplified permitted
Restrictions: no bird seed, no beer, no hard liquor

One of the most beautiful and elegant wineries in the area is Byington Winery, located on the western side of the Santa Cruz Mountains overlooking the redwood slopes down to the Monterey Bay. The winery celebrated its eighth anniversary in June 1998. Like aging wine, this winery gets better and better. With grapes growing on vines that surround the sprawling building, the wisteria climbing up the walls to the balcony of the second floor, and the tables in front on the manicured lawn, the winery is inviting for a picnic. A white gazebo on the knoll behind the main building is a beautiful spot for a ceremony.

The wine tasting room, wine cellar, and offices are downstairs. On the upper level is a large room, seating 150, where all festivities take place. It has a huge fireplace, hardwood floor, and is surrounded by a tiled verandah. A private, very elegant suite for the bride is adjacent to the kitchen with its professional 8-burner stove. To the right is another large room that opens to the wine cellar with its attractive oak barrels. The rooms are trimmed with Honduran mahogany by a master craftsman and are furnished with treasured antiques. Everything about the place reflects high quality and good taste.

The fee for using the winery includes event coordinators; tables, chairs, and glassware; and the use of the private suite. You can choose to have only your ceremony, both the ceremony and reception, or just the reception at the winery. Corporate meetings and receptions can be arranged by the event staff.

The winery is available for weddings on Friday, Saturday and Sunday.

California Academy of Sciences
Aquarium, Planetarium and Museum
Golden Gate Park
San Francisco, CA 94118

(415) 750-7219
FAX: (415) 750-7346
arianda@calacademy.org

Contact: Anne Rianda

Specialties: Many possibilities for cocktail parties and sit-down dinners
in the Aquarium, the Natural History Museum, and the Planetarium

No. of Guests: sit-down, to 500; cocktails, to 2,000

Pricing: $2,000 - $10,000
Extra Charges: $500 security deposit, certificate of insurance

Payment Terms: 30% non-ref. deposit, balance
due 3 weeks prior to event (except December)
Credit Cards: no
Lead Time: to 1 year
Rental Time: 5½ - 6½ hrs. depending on season
Wheelchair Access: yes

Changing Room: yes
Dance Floor: no
Parking: ample
Music: amplified permitted
Restrictions: no rice, etc.; no wall decoration,
no amplified music in Aquarium

Dining to the sight and sound of California sea lions, or next to an African water hole with a gi-raffe looking over your shoulder, or in the dim light of a deep sea aquarium surrounded by sharks – these are just a few of the many options offered by the California Academy of Sciences. The facility also houses a planetarium for a star or laser show, as well as an auditorium for other use. One of their experienced event coordinators gave me a tour through the museum and pointed out the many different ways to set up an event. For example, gray screens can block off hallways or passageways. You can request a packet of detailed information about the facility that includes maps; a price list for the rooms; rental, decoration and setup guidelines; and even a plan for emergency procedures. It also includes colored pictures of previous stunning events so that you get a very good idea of what you can do with this extraordinary space. I was invited to observe their own annual fund-raising event. Spotlit tables covered with shimmering sequined tablecloths seemed to float in space. Each hall was done in a different color with flower decorations in different designs.

One party planner told me that she loves doing parties in the museum and mentioned that the staff is very accommodating. She also suggested arranging for plenty of help since you have to walk a fair way to reach your party's location. There is no kitchen, and only limited food preparation areas. Due to the changing exhibits, there is always a new, exciting theme which encourages many clients to return to host other events.The Academy of Sciences accommodates only one event per evening. In summer, the rental time is 7 p.m. to 12:30 a.m. to allow for the museum's extended hours. During the rest of the year, the rental time is 6 p.m. to 12:30 a.m. Audio/visual and electronic equipment are available; call for rates.

Captain Walsh House
Gracious Gothic Charm
235 East L Street
Benicia, CA 94510

(707) 747-5653
FAX: (707) 747-6265

Contact: Reed or Steve Robbins

Specialties: Restored historical landmark specializing in elegant garden weddings

Food: California French Fusion cuisine (menus from $22)

No. of Guests: sit-down: indoors, 60; outdoors, 175

Price (location): $1,250 for first 50 guests; $250 for each additional 50
Extra Charges: gratuity, $10 per person for rentals, staff, linens, gold band china

Payment Terms: 50% non-ref. deposit at reservation; balance due 2 weeks prior to event
Credit Cards: major credit cards
Lead Time: 12 - 24 months
Rental Time: 1 event per day
Wheelchair Access: yes

Changing Room: yes
Dance Floor: yes, outside under tent
Parking: street and city parking lot
Music: amplified permitted until 8 pm
Restrictions: no rice, etc.

Across the street from historic Benecia's City Hall is Captain Walsh House. This Gothic revival mansion was commissioned by M.G. Vallejo for his daughter Epiphania in 1849. Architect Andrew Jackson Downing designed and built the house in Boston. It was then dismantled, shipped around Cape Horn to Benicia, and re-assembled. A few years later, Captain Walsh and his wife bought the property. Reed Robbins, an architectural designer, fell in love with the house, neglected since the '60s, on a business trip to Benicia. She and her husband Steve eventually bought it and painstakingly restored it beyond its original beauty. Hand-painted walls with faux finishes and beautiful antique furniture make the place a real jewel. The five guest rooms have the same Gothic charm in their varied and distinctive decor. Their efforts paid off as they have been recognized by Better Homes & Gardens' *Bedroom & Bath* as one of the three best decorated bed & breakfast inns in the U.S. It is also the only 3-star establishment in Solano County, according to *Northern California Best Places*. The inn has also been featured in *Modern Bride, Sunset Magazine*, and on Frommer's guide's cover, as well as on the Home & Garden TV program "Awesome Interiors."

The west garden and entire ground floor are available for weddings and other special events. The wedding ceremony is held in front of the wedding arch. A lighted tent over the reception area is decorated with the same attention to detail. The parlor and dining room have seasonal decorations. A graduate of the S.F. Culinary Academy creates the food after Reed assists you with the menu design. Reed will coordinate the entire event as well as apply her artistic talent to flower decorations and bridal bouquets. In keeping with their high standards, they will schedule only one event per day.

Chaminade at Santa Cruz

(831) 475-5600
(800) 283-6569
FAX: (831) 476-4798
www.chaminade.com

One Chaminade Lane
Santa Cruz, CA 95065

Contact: Catering Manager

Specialties: Mediterranean-style resort atop forested hills with panoramic view of Monterey Bay

Food: California cuisine; high-quality gourmet food; sit-down and buffet
(estimates per person: luncheon, $60 - $70; dinner, $70 - $90)
No. of Guests: 25 - 270

Price (location): $550 - $950; ceremony, $550 - $950
Extra Charges: none

Payment Terms: $500 - $6,000 deposit, balance due day of event	**Changing Room:** complimentary with ceremony
Credit Cards: major credit cards	**Dance Floor:** yes
Lead Time: up to 1 year	**Parking:** complimentary valet
Rental Time: 2 time slots on Saturdays (see text)	**Music:** amplified; some restricted areas
Wheelchair Access: yes	**Restrictions:** all beverages supplied by Chaminade

Chaminade is a beautiful resort hotel, located on 280 acres of forest land. Once a Marianist academy, the fully renovated facility offers a public restaurant, the Santa Cruz Ballroom, and nine banquet/meeting rooms. Blooming flower beds surround the buildings, and hidden gardens are inviting for a rest. The sprawling facility has 152 guest rooms, tennis courts, a swimming pool, executive fitness center, and miles of hiking trails.

Wedding ceremonies are held on a lawn-covered bluff with a beautiful view of the bay and the Monterey Peninsula as a backdrop. Two large events can be scheduled on Saturdays, with time periods of 11 a.m. to 4:30 p.m. and 5 p.m. to midnight. The Greenhouse and Sunset Patio offer ocean-view dining for lunch on Saturdays for groups of up to 150 people. One DJ loves working at Chaminade so much that he doesn't charge travel time.

My family attended a Christmas brunch at Chaminade. The elegant ambience and the wide variety of delicious and abundant food were enjoyed by all. Waiters and cooks were continuously busy rearranging and refilling the buffet to maintain its attractive appearance, and the food was always hot.

Buffet breakfast, lunch and dinner in California-cuisine style are served to the public in the Sunset Dining Room seven days a week. Please make reservations. Guests of all catered events receive discounted room rates year round.

Chateau La Cresta
at the Historic Mountain Winery
14831 Pierce Road
Saratoga, CA 95070

(408) 741-0763
FAX: (408) 741-0733
events@chateaulacresta.com
www.chateaulacresta.com

Contact: Mark Karakas (Proprietor)

Specialties: Historic winery with indoor and outdoor facilities

Food: Regional American and International gourmet cuisine; vegetarian (hors d'oeuvres,
            breakfast, breaks, lunch ($15.50), desserts, deli, buffet ($26.50), brunch, and dinner ($18)
No. of Guests: Chateau, to 100 seated; Winery, to 250 (incl. dance floor); outdoors, to 1,500

Price (location): $400 - $4,500
Extra Charges: gratuity, dance floor, PA system, heaters, shuttle

Payment Terms: 50% non-ref. deposit,
            balance due 1 week prior to event
Credit Cards: major credit cards
Lead Time: 3 days to 1 year
Rental Time: 7 - 8 hrs. (2 time slots available)
Wheelchair Access: restricted access

Changing Room: yes
Dance Floor: yes
Parking: ample
Music: amplified permitted
Restrictions: rose petals only

Situated on a dramatic crest of the Santa Cruz mountains is the 580-acre Chateau La Cresta at the Mountain Winery. Constructed in 1905 by Paul Masson in a French country style, it is listed on the *National Registry of Historic Places*. With breathtaking views of the entire South Bay, this is a dramatic setting for spectacular events, from Renaissance theme parties in winter, to elegant weddings in spring, to concert series in summer. The old-world ambiance with stone masonry lends itself to an endless range of theme possibilities. The ever-changing fun environment at the Mountain Winery is an "Adult's Disneyland," and proprietor Mark Karakas and award-winning, 4-star chef Kevin Gilday make it happen.

Their philosophy, "Make this feel like an extension of our living room," is clearly visible from the events they coordinate. Mark and Kevin believe it takes a good staff to orchestrate any production and compensate them accordingly. Their seasoned, long-term staff are equally dedicated to providing top-notch events. Clients are comforted to see the same friendly personnel in place on the day of their event.

Since this is a non-producing winery, an assortment of wines and beers is available. What also sets them apart is their genuine concern about producing a successful event. At the outdoor wedding I attended, I noticed Mark glancing out the window to see that the wind was picking up. He waited only seconds before alerting the staff to prepare cake and coffee service indoors. Anticipating every moment to ensure of his guests' comfort is Mark's hospitable way. The excitement he exudes when describing their events is contagious. While viewing the Winery room, he spoke of a Renaissance event scheduled that evening. His description of the setting aroused my excitement. Their events are complete, and their winery is truly a "vineyard in the sky."

The City Club
of San Francisco
155 Sansome Street, 10th Floor
San Francisco, CA 94104

(415) 362-2480
FAX: (415) 362-0965

Contact: Catering Director

Specialties: Sophisticated, exclusive, art deco club with a museum ambience

Food: Elegant Continental and California cuisines (menus from $18)

No. of Guests: meeting rooms, 6 - 40 seated; main dining room, to 220 seated; cocktails, to 600

Price (location): $300 to $1,250; food and beverage minimum, $7,500 (weekends)
Extra Charges: service charge, beverages, rental chairs (for over 180); cake-cutting, corkage

Payment Terms: 25% non-ref. deposit,
    balance due 1 week prior to event
Credit Cards: Visa, MasterCard
Lead Time: 1 week to 1 year
Rental Time: 4 hrs., overtime available
Wheelchair Access: yes

Changing Room: yes
Dance Floor: yes
Parking: on street and in public garages
Music: amplified permitted
Restrictions: no rice, etc.; no wall decoration,

The 10th and 11th floors of the Stock Exchange Tower accommodate not only the elegant City Club, but also just about enough art to fill a small museum. The Mexican Museum offers monthly tours there. The elevator doors, through which you enter the club, are creations of copper, silver, bronze, and brass, executed by Harry Dixon from photos by Michael Goodman. Most famous is the 30-foot high fresco of Diego Rivera's "Riches of California." The City Club has two large, elegant rooms with lots of atmosphere. The Cafe lounge is lighter in color, while the walls of the main dining room are done in clear, lacquered ash and adorned with decorative panels. Both rooms have gold-leaf ceilings in different designs and large working fireplaces. They are most often used together, one for cocktails and hors d'oeuvres and the other for dinner. Five smaller private dining rooms are also available. All of the rooms have large windows overlooking the Financial District. A fresh flower decoration is ever present.

My last visit included an invitation to lunch so I could experience the club's excellent food and outstanding service. The catering director informed me that the club trains all of its service personnel. You can make selections from an extensive menu or have your menu custom-designed, and you are assured of its attractive presentation. Flexibility is one strength the staff is very proud of. During weekly catering staff meetings, held well in advance of an event, they discuss each detail and also review their performance at past events. During my tour through this beautiful event site, the catering manager pointed out their latest improvements: new wall coverings and new, even more comfortable armchairs.

Compass Rose
Yacht Charters
1070 Marina Village Parkway, Suite 106
Alameda, CA 94501

(510) 523-9500
FAX: (510) 523-9200
cmpsrse@best.com
www.compassrosecharters.com

Contact: Bradford H. Agler

Specialties: Private, intimate, elegant charters

Food: California cuisine with French influence, ethnic cuisine (menus from $10)

No. of Guests: sit-down, 8; buffet, 48

Price (location): weekdays, $325/hr., Friday evenings and weekends, $400/hr.
Extra Charges: food and beverages

Payment Terms: 50% deposit, balance due 5 days prior to event	**Changing Room:** yes
	Dance Floor: yes
Credit Cards: major credit cards	**Parking:** parking lot
Lead Time: 2 days to 1 year	**Music:** amplified permitted
Rental Time: 3 hrs. min.	**Restrictions:** no rice, etc.
Wheelchair Access: no	

When I first visited Bradford, owner of Compass Rose Yacht Charters, the Camelot had been decorated for a wedding. I immediately fell in love with this comfortable luxury yacht. Bradford bought the vessel in 1989 and named it Camelot, symbolic of a haven of independence and freedom. This 65-foot, elegantly furnished motor yacht comes with complete customized service for whatever you have in mind: weddings, rehearsal dinners, receptions, private parties. The ship's route is determined by the client.

The yacht is certified with the Coast Guard. It has a large salon with a built-in bar and a formal dining room, each with rich mahogany paneling and elegantly furnished. Music is heard through a built-in, state-of-the-art sound system. The captain can perform ceremonies, and a highly trained, tuxedo-attired staff offer their services. Customized menus and bar service reflect the high standards of this company. A gourmet sit-down dinner for eight can be served on the finest china, crystal and silverware. Passed hors d'oeuvres and a buffet are recommended for larger groups. An experienced event coordinator can help you with every aspect of your party, book hotel accommodations, and will provide a larger yacht if your guest list exceeds 48.

Crow Canyon Country Club

(925) 735-5700
FAX: (925) 735-6516

711 Silver Lake Drive
Danville, CA 94526

Contact: Private Party Department

Specialties: Elegant, sprawling, newly remodeled country club with indoor facilities for large and small functions

Food: Continental cuisine for luncheons and dinners (sit-down, buffets and stations) (menus from $15)
No. of Guests: sit-down, to 300; cocktails, to 500

Price (location): large dining room, $800
Extra Charges: service charge, cake-cutting fee, corkage fee

Payment Terms: $1,000 deposit, full payment due 2 weeks prior to event
Credit Cards: no
Lead Time: 1 - 18 months
Rental Time: 5 hrs.
Wheelchair Access: yes

Dance Floor: large, built-in dance floor
Parking: ample
Music: amplified permitted
Restrictions: no rice, etc.; no picture-taking on golf course

The Crow Canyon Country Club, built in 1977, is among the more elegant country clubs in the Contra Costa area. Impressive and extraordinary carved wooden doors give entry to a spacious lobby that is always decorated with fresh floral bouquets. The lobby leads to the large, elegant dining room, lit by sparkling chandeliers. The club was completely remodeled in 1995. Attractive wallpaper, curtains, and newly upholstered chairs make the club even more beautiful and seemingly more spacious. A large comfortable bar adjacent to the ballroom is also available. The terrace provides a spectacular view of the golf course, with Mount Diablo in the background, just perfect for pictures. The built-in dance floor is square in shape. The dining room can be partitioned for both large and small groups, with enough space for a ceremony and reception. Three additional rooms, accommodating 10 to 80 people, offer clients several choices.

Event planning assistance is provided by the experienced Private Party staff, which will coordinate the entire event to make everything as easy as possible. The Private Party director and her staff are very flexible and willing to work with everyone, which could explain the club's popularity. During my last visit on a weekday, I was surprised to learn the number of people who were attending meetings, as well as business and private luncheons that day.

Two time slots for weddings are available on Saturdays and one on Sundays. Various time slots are available for weekday business.

Decathlon Club

(408) 736-3237

FAX: (408) 738-0320
www.Decathlon-Club.com

3250 Central Expressway
Santa Clara, CA 95051

Contact: Catering Department

Specialties: Exclusive private club with garden-like setting; indoor and outdoor facilities; available to members and non-members

Food: Gourmet California cuisine

No. of Guests: sit-down indoors, to 600; cocktails, 25 - 1,000; two meeting rooms, to 20 each

Price (location/food): $1,250 - $1,500 room rental; menus from $24 per person
Extra Charges: gratuity, beverage package, ceremony ($500)

Payment Terms: $1,250 non-ref. deposit, 75%
  45 days prior, balance due 3 days prior to event
Credit Cards: major credit cards
Lead Time: 3 - 18 months
Rental Time: Saturday, 11-4, 6-11; Sunday, 6 hrs.
Wheelchair Access: yes

Changing Room: yes
Dance Floor: 2 (included in price)
Parking: 3 parking lots
Music: amplified permitted
Restrictions: no rice, etc.

The soothing sounds of waterfalls, a tranquil, rock-filled creek surrounded by lush tropical plants, and ficus trees separate the club from its spacious banquet facilities. The large skylights, redwood accents, and rippling creek around the multi-level dance floors add to the feeling of being in a natural surrounding.

The Main Dining Room, with its chandeliers, gold Chiavari chairs, and wall of windows, is ideal for a wedding reception or large party. It overlooks the Tennis Deck, a perfect setting for an outdoor hors d'oeuvres reception. The indoor Terrace, overlooking the creek bed, can form part of the reception area or be used for a garden-like ceremony. The light posts and twinkling tree lights add a warm finishing touch. Two conference rooms can be used for rehearsal dinners or as changing rooms for the wedding party.

I visited the Decathlon Club while they were setting up for a wedding reception for two sisters. Every inch was cleverly and attractively utilized. The sign-in table was set up at the guest entrance, the gift table securely, yet conveniently placed, and the cake table for the two brides could be viewed from all angles. The lower dance-floor deck staged the romantic serenading Mariachi, while the upper deck was secured for the 11- piece band.

The Decathlon Club can arrange all the details including the decorations, entertainment, and various elements to facilitate an event. Their extensive menus and beverage packages are accommodating to individual needs, styles and tastes.

Discovery Yacht Charters
Schooner Ka'iulani
P.O. Box 1145
Sausalito, CA 94966

(415) 331-1333
FAX: (415) 789-9273
charter@sfyacht.com
www.sfyacht.com

Contact: Captain Rob Michaan

Specialties: Luxury sailing adventures for weddings, special events, corporate events; romantic sunsets; sail training

Food: beverage menus, from $15; food menus, from $20 (20 person min.)

No. of Guests: Licensed for 49 guests

Price (location): $425/hr. (see minimal rental times); remote pickups: San Francisco and Berkeley
Extra Charges: entertainment, 15% gratuity

Payment Terms: 50% deposit at reservation, balance due 2 weeks prior to sailing	**Changing Room:** yes
	Dance Floor: no
Credit Cards: Visa, MasterCard	**Parking:** yes
Lead Time: 1 week to 1 year	**Music:** yes
Rental Time: 3 hr. min; weddings: 4 hr. min.	**Restrictions:** no rice, glitter, confetti, high heels or red wine
Wheelchair Access: no	

Ka'iulani, named after Princess Victoria Ka'iulani, last heir to the Hawaiian throne, is Discovery Yacht Charters' gorgeous, 86-foot classic cold-molded wooden schooner. This 49-passenger, authentic replica of an 1850's coastal trading ship is a sight to behold. Extensively upgraded to offer safe and comfortable luxury sailing, Ka'iulani features traditional rigging, hardware and meticulously maintained varnish and bronze. The luxurious interior salon, with skylights, modern nautical equipment, and bronze-trimmed potbelly stove, is spacious and comfortable.

As she made her way out of the Sausalito harbor to the Golden Gate, we enjoyed the breathtaking views from the comfortable teak decks. Once outside the Golden Gate, she turned towards San Francisco, raising her sails, cutting the engine and gallantly blowing along the spectacular cityscape, circumnavigating the bay at what seemed just an arm's length from shore. At Pier 39, she headed north past Alcatraz, Angel Island, through Raccoon Straight, then back to Sausalito. An attentive, friendly crew, led by mighty Captain Rob, navigated this 3-hour adventure.

The Ka'iulani is available for private luxury sailing adventures, special events, tours, marine science programs, sail training (grades 4 to 12), and team-building programs. For weddings, Captain Rob will gladly find a calm, quiet cove where he will officiate a romantic, nautical ceremony. They work with a variety of professional caterers to provide the finest quality of food, from tantalizing hors d'oeuvres to lavish buffets, wines and spirits for all budgets. They can recommend or arrange for professional musicians, photographers, videographers. They even provide you with a high quality "masthead skycam" to record your sailing excursion. As one adventurous romantic put it, "There is just something about seeing the city from aboard a yacht. Your cares just seem to blow away." So splash on some lotion, zip up your jackets, and hop aboard the Ka'iulani for the adventure of a lifetime.

Dunn Mehler Gallery

(650) 726-7667
FAX: (650) 726-5977
dayle@dunnmehler.com
www.dunnmehler.com

337 Mirada Road
Half Moon Bay, CA 94019

Contact: Dayle Dunn

Specialties: Contemporary art gallery on Miramar Beach

No. of Guests: sit-down, to 60; cocktails, to 80

Pricing: events: gallery and second floor, $1,250 - $3,500; second floor only, $600
Extra Charges: certificate of insurance, $100 for photos in private quarters

Payment Terms: 25% non-ref. deposit,
            balance due 30 days prior to event
Credit Cards: all credit cards
Lead Time: 1 week to 9 months
Rental Time: 4 - 10 hrs.
Wheelchair Access: yes

Changing Room: yes
Dance Floor: tiled
Parking: street
Music: controlled amplified permitted
Restrictions: no rice, etc.

Their gallery was a dream come true for Dayle Dunn and Carl Mehler. The two art lovers found an empty space next to Miramar Beach on which Carl, an architect, designed a contemporary structure from wood and stone to be a place for art, work, and festivities. Artists are scouted out in shows around the country. You can enjoy viewing or buying their creations: sculptures, pottery, weavings, woodwork, jewelry, and photography. From time to time, art classes and story-telling sessions are held for children and adults. The gallery was not originally designed for private or corporate functions. However, when a couple visiting the gallery approached Dayle to see if they could have their wedding and reception there, a new venture was born.

The first two stories of the gallery are now available for events. The ceremony usually takes place in the gallery. The bride is guaranteed a dramatic entrance down the spiral staircase, and the area between the two tall windows in the front is perfect for minister, bride and groom. The open, second-story gallery is a great spot for the photographer. After toasts are made and appetizers are served, the reception takes place on the second floor. The gallery's sophisticated lighting system allows for dramatically spotlighted tables. The bride and one guest are allowed the use of the owners' private quarters above. Not only was I taken with the view, but the apartment and the furniture were exactly my taste. I didn't want to leave.

This quote said it all: "We picked our wedding date because we thought the weather would be beautiful. It poured. But it didn't matter. We thoroughly enjoyed ourselves because Dayle and Carl were wonderful, professional and caring, and it mattered to them that this was our special day."

The Elizabeth F. Gamble Garden Center

(650) 329-1356

FAX: (650) 329-1688

1431 Waverley Street
Palo Alto, CA 94301

Contact: Gabrielle Gross (Wedding Coordinator)

Specialties: Edwardian mansion in beautiful garden setting

No. of Guests: indoors: sit-down, to 50; cocktails, to 75; outdoors: sit-down, to 75; cocktails, to 75

Pricing: Saturday & Sunday, $950/8 hrs.; Tuesday - Thursday, $50/hr.; Friday, $75/hr.; 30 guests max.
Extra Charges: $500 ref. security deposit, rentals, certificate of insurance

Payment Terms: $475 deposit, balance due 120 days prior to event	**Changing Room:** yes
	Dance Floor: on brick terraces
Credit Cards: no	**Parking:** lot, street
Lead Time: 6 weeks to 18 months	**Music:** amplified not permitted
Rental Time: 8 hrs.	**Restrictions:** rose petals only
Wheelchair Access: yes	

This historic Georgian Revival-style home was built for Edwin Percy Gamble at the beginning of the century. Miss Gamble, the owner's daughter, gave the estate to the City of Palo Alto and, in 1985, it was leased to the Elizabeth F. Gamble Garden Center Foundation. The center has earned a place in the hearts of Palo Altans for its well-known garden-related activities, featuring classes in horticulture and landscaping. The beautiful gardens are often visited to get new ideas for backyards. We visited the center when we were looking to plant different varieties of climbing roses in our garden.

I have visited the garden center many times, at one time to attend one of the first weddings ever held there, and returned to observe the work of different vendors. Flowers are constantly in bloom from early spring till late fall. A favorite place for springtime ceremonies is the wisteria garden, while in the summer the fragrant rose garden is more desired. After the ceremony, champagne and hors d'oeuvres are usually served in front of the tea house, followed by a buffet lunch or dinner at the carriage house. There are other areas for guests to stroll that also offer great settings for the photographer: the woodland garden with its towering oak and magnolia trees, the cherry allée, the beautiful lawn areas around the house, and the demonstration gardens, to name a few.

The mansion can also be used during the winter months. The drawing room, library and dining room can accommodate up to 75 guests. In December, the mansion is beautifully decorated for Christmas. Gabrielle Gross, the wedding coordinator, is wonderful and very easy to work with, helping you to create a truly memorable event. The facility offers special rates for mid-week weddings for 30 or fewer.

The Faculty Club

(510) 540-5678
(510) 643-0834
FAX : (510) 540-6204

University of California
Berkeley, CA 94720

Contact: Janet Lukehart

Specialties: Faculty club built in California-craftsman style

Food: American and California cuisine (menus from $13)

No. of Guests: sit-down, to 250; cocktails, to 400

Price (location): Great Hall, $800; Heyns & Seaborg Rooms, $300
Extra Charges: ceremony setup, coat check, parking, use of fireplace

Payment Terms: $750 deposit, balance due 2 weeks prior to event	**Changing Room:** yes **Dance Floor:** yes
Credit Cards: no	**Parking:** parking lot
Lead Time: 2 weeks to 1 year	**Music:** amplified permitted up to 11 pm
Rental Time: 6 hrs.	**Restrictions:** no nails or staples on walls
Wheelchair Access: yes	

Situated on the eastern end of the Faculty Glade, this beautiful clubhouse is surrounded by lawns and oak trees. When you enter the Faculty Club, you know immediately that this almost century-old house is a meeting place for the learned. How many scientific discussions have been held here; how many solutions have been found?

The oldest part of the building, the Great Hall, was designed by the famous architect Bernard Maybeck. Its arched ceiling, redwood interior, and huge fireplace have been carefully preserved, and it still serves as the main dining room. During the years other dining areas, patios, and kitchen facilities were added. The second largest is the Heyns room, with an L-shaped brick patio outside. Also available is the Seaborg Room with its cozy fireplace and private deck. This room, which honors the university's Nobel laureates, overlooks Faculty Glade.

The heart and soul of the Faculty Club is Janet Lukehart. She began working there as a waitress 19 years ago and is now in charge of event coordination. She is open to new ideas, and has dealt with all kinds of situations, such as a large wedding attended by 70 or 80 people in wheelchairs or an Orthodox Jewish wedding with glatt Kosher fare. Additional services which make things easier are baby-sitting and help with the ever-difficult parking situation in Berkeley.

Guests can be accommodated in the on-site hotel.

Fremont Hills Country Club

(650) 948-1763
(650) 948-8261

FAX: (650) 948-3271
www.fremonthills.com

12889 Viscaino Place
Los Altos Hills, CA 94022

Contact: James Gardner

Specialties: Spacious, attractively remodeled clubhouse on country club grounds; conference room

No. of Guests: sit-down, to 200; conference room, 20

Pricing: $2,300 for non-members; holiday season, $2,500
Extra Charges: dance floor, refundable cleaning deposit, bartenders and gratuity

Payment Terms: $1,000 deposit, balance due 60 days prior to event
Credit Cards: no
Lead Time: 2 weeks to 1 year
Rental Time: 5 pm - midnight
Wheelchair Access: yes

Changing Room: yes
Dance Floor: 15' x 15'
Parking: ample
Music: amplified permitted
Restrictions: no rice, etc.; no open flames; all beverages supplied by country club

Almost five years passed from the initial planning stages to the completion of the remodeled clubhouse, but every hour of planning and all the expense was worth it. The clubhouse was just ready for events when I visited the facility. Nevertheless, I immediately fell in love with the old/new place. Its greatest feature is its versatility: you can imagine having the most elegant wedding there and, at the same time, you won't feel out of place in your tennis outfit.

The rooms on the upper floor of the clubhouse are available for rent. The large dining room seems quite spacious with its cathedral ceiling, light colored paint, and many doors and windows that open onto the surrounding deck. The wall-to-wall carpeting has a very pretty design that blends well with almost every color or theme. The club is available from 5 p.m. to midnight. The marble and wood of the permanent bar in the member's lounge is also color coordinated, and its large fireplace is most inviting. A folding partition can separate the dining room and lounge, and a small conference room is available for corporate meetings. The club will set up all tables, chairs, and dance floor.

A large professional kitchen can be used by licensed and insured caterers. All beverages must be purchased through the club.

Garden Court Hotel

520 Cowper Street
Palo Alto, CA 94301

(650) 323-1912
(800) 824-9028
FAX: (650) 322-3440
ahotel@gardencourt.com
www.ByRecOnly.com/gardencourt

Contact: Catering Manager

Specialties: Modern, elegant hotel for indoor events; outdoor patios

Food: Catering by Il Fornaio Cucina Italiana

No. of Guests: sit-down, to 230; cocktails, to 300

Price (location): Grove Ballroom and Courtyard Ballroom, $350 to $1,000 on weekends
Extra Charges: service charge, cake-cutting fee, corkage fee, coat check

Payment Terms: $1,500 non-ref. deposit, estimated balance due 10 days prior to event	**Changing Room:** no **Dance Floor:** yes
Credit Cards: major credit cards	**Parking:** valet
Lead Time: 3 months to 1 year	**Music:** amplified permitted
Rental Time: 5 hrs.	**Restrictions:** no rice, etc.
Wheelchair Access: yes	

The elegant Garden Court Hotel, built in 1988, has become a well-known landmark and meeting place in downtown Palo Alto. Its Mediterranean-style architecture, painted an ocher color with dark green trim, has vine-covered terraces and balconies that surround a courtyard full of flowers and greenery. With only 62 luxury guest rooms, the hotel can provide very personalized service.

The catering manager toured me through most of the hotel. The comfortable guest rooms are decorated in soft colors, and the large bathrooms are tiled from floor to ceiling. Special touches include fresh fruit, flowers, newspapers, cozy bathrobes, magazines, and small chocolate treats at bedtime.

The Grove Ballroom on the second floor has fabric-covered and faux marbled walls, with floor-to-ceiling arched windows and windowed doors that open to a large balcony. Also on this level is the smaller Terrace Room, perfect for rehearsal dinners or business meetings. Renting the Courtyard Ballroom on the ground floor includes the use of the patio. Each room is light and airy, and beautifully decorated. For receptions of 75 or more guests, the hotel offers a complimentary overnight wedding package that includes a guest room for bride and groom with Jacuzzi or fireplace, champagne, engraved flutes, continental breakfast, an extended checkout time, and complimentary valet parking. Hurricane lamps with a green copper ivy design for the dinner tables and a large floral bouquet for the buffet table are complimentary as well. The hotel has two time slots on Saturdays for parties and weddings. The food is provided by the award-winning Il Fornaio Cucina Italiana.

Gatewood-Keane Mansion

(415) 861-3287
(Phone & FAX)
craigo@backdoor.com

(by appointment)
San Francisco, CA

Contact: Craig Williams (Event Director)

Specialties: Exclusive 1875 Victorian Mansion

Food: Nouvelle California cuisine with Asian undertones (lunch, from $35; dinner, from $55)

No. of Guests: sit-down, 50; cocktails, 85 - 100

Price (location): $1,800 off-season (Feb. to Aug.); $2,500 high season (Sept. to Jan.)
Extra Charges: staff, rentals, services, gratuity

Payment Terms: 20% non-ref. deposit, 50% due 90 days prior, balance due 30 days prior to event	**Changing Room:** yes
	Dance Floor: can be provided
Credit Cards: no	**Parking:** valet
Lead Time: 1 - 6 months	**Music:** limited amplified music
Rental Time: 8 hrs. (incl. setup/clean up)	**Restrictions:** no smoking; no petals, rice,
Wheelchair Access: no	bubbles, etc.

From the moment you enter the Gatewood-Keane Mansion you get the sense of walking into an artist's private home. Walls are brushed and stencil painted much to look like a canvas. Crimson reds, jade green, gold leaf, and rich jewel tone walls complement the paintings and original artwork of the late William Gatewood.

The mansion was built in 1875 and sold in 1877 to Peter Difley, a successful builder and bricklayer. Prior to his retirement, Mr. Difley gave the mansion as a wedding gift to his daughter Mary on her marriage to Thomas Keane. The Keanes raised their eight children there, and, in 1905, divided the mansion into separate rental units. In 1982, William Gatewood purchased it and began ten years of restoration. Internationally known for his magnificent "modernistic" kimono canvas paintings, Gatewood's bequest to the mansion is the aura of an artist's work in progress.

Eclectic with Asian undertones, the Gatewood-Keane Mansion is one of San Francisco's best kept secrets. "It is an artist's canvas," describes Craig Williams, director of the Gatewood-Keane and owner of When Only The Best Will Do, an event planning and fine catering company. With over 20 years of experience in the industry and selected to represent many of the Victorians in San Francisco, Craig has been nicknamed the "Mr. Victorian." His full-event services are tailored to every client and event. His energy is contagious; his food is divine. Whether he is creating a dessert buffet in the Ladies Parlor, with mirrored gold leaf stenciled walls, an intimate sit-down dinner in the Gentleman's Parlor under the candlelit chandelier, or an afternoon tea in the Morning Room with its magnificent dropped "Tin Ceiling," Craig and his professional, friendly staff orchestrate a splashing and memorable affair.

Guglielmo Winery
Villa Emile
1480 E. Main Avenue
Morgan Hill, CA 95037

(408) 779-2145
FAX: (408) 779-3166

Contact: Event Coordinator

Specialties: Large lawn area with stage and dance floor, surrounded by vineyards

No. of Guests: sit-down, to 600; cocktails, to 1,000

Pricing: to 300 guests: $2,800 - $3,100 on Saturdays; $2,200 - $2,500 on Sundays
Extra Charges: wine, beer, gratuity, $600 refundable security deposit, certificate of insurance

Payment Terms: 50% deposit, balance
                due 1 month prior to event
Credit Cards: major credit cards
Lead Time: 1 week to 1 year
Rental Time: 7 hrs. (recept.); 8 hrs. (w/ceremony)
Wheelchair Access: yes

Changing Room: yes
Dance Floor: concrete
Parking: ample
Music: amplified permitted until 9 pm
Restrictions: no rice, etc.; wine from
                winery only

The Guglielmo Winery dates back to 1925 when Emilio and Emilia Guglielmo, Italian immigrants living in San Francisco, purchased their first 15 acres of vineyards in Morgan Hill. Delayed by the Prohibition, the first wine was hauled in barrels to their home in the city. It was bottled in the basement with the help of the whole family and was sold to restaurants and for private use. The wines were an immediate success, and, in the early 1940s, the family moved to Morgan Hill. Now the third generation of the Guglielmo family is running the winery, which has grown to 117 acres, producing estate bottled wines and offering an attractive place for private and corporate events.

Situated at the southern end of Santa Clara Valley, the winery is only about 20 minutes south of San Jose. The area used for events consists of a lawn area with a large stage and dance floor on one side. In front of the old Villa Emile is the bar where wine and champagne are served. A vine-covered trellis provides shade and, stretching along one side of the lawn area, is a perfect place to set up a buffet. The other two sides are enclosed by grapevines, with the oak-covered rolling hills as backdrop. On the far end of the lawn is a shrine of St. Francis, a site often used for ceremonies.

Included in the price are the use of the Victorian bridal suite; groom's room; wine bar server; 5-foot round tables with umbrellas, chairs and linen; banquet tables; a cake table with canopy, and setup and breakdown. For an additional fee, a 40' x 80' tent is available for shading or extreme weather. The event coordinator can offer assistance, and a wine specialist will recommend the right wine for your menu. A discount on wine is given to clients. All parties must end by 10 p.m.

Holbrook Palmer Park

(650) 688-6534

150 Watkins Avenue
Atherton, CA 94025

Contact: Jean Cardona

Specialties: Historic, remodeled summer residence with carriage house, water tower
and contemporary pavilion for weddings and events

No. of Guests: Pavilion: indoors, 150; indoors/outdoors, 200; main house, 50; carriage house, 80

Pricing: to 100 guests, $1,800 - $2,000; to 200 guests, $2,300 - $2,500
Extra Charges: piano, outdoor heaters, certificate of insurance

Payment Terms: $500 ref. security deposit,
    payment in full 1 month prior to event
Credit Cards: no
Lead Time: 2 - 18 months
Rental Time: 7 hrs.; 2 events on Saturdays
Wheelchair Access: yes

Changing Room: yes
Dance Floor: can be arranged
Parking: ample
Music: amplified permitted
Restrictions: bird seed outdoors only

Holbrook Palmer Park, between El Camino Real and Middlefield Road in Atherton, has 22 acres of lawn and open space with big old oak trees. Outdoor facilities include a children's playground and picnic tables. This beautiful park was the summer residence of the Palmer family until 1964 when it was given to the town.

When Jean Cardona became the facility's program director, she set out to gradually bring the charming buildings up to their old splendor. Cheerful peach and white walls and the green rugs complement each other beautifully and, together with the elegant drapes, make the larger drawing room a perfect place for smaller weddings, parties, meetings and classes. Also restored are the bathrooms, rooms for the bride and groom, and the kitchen. Wide back stairs, framed by planter boxes, lead down to the white gazebo, built especially for ceremonies.

The authentic carriage house, dating back to 1896, was the next one to be updated. It is used primarily for parties with western and Dickens Christmas themes, and for business functions. Its wooden floor lends itself to dancing. During my last visit, Jean showed me the Jennings Pavilion, with its large patio surrounded by gardens. The freshly painted interior makes it appear much larger, and the new English floral carpet adds to its elegance. I have seen the pavilion dressed up for a spectacular wedding, as well as for a '50s party, where props transformed the exterior into an authentic diner, and the patio was used for a street fair theme.

Jean and her staff are very flexible, helpful, open to suggestions, and will gladly answer all of your questions.

Hollins House at Pasatiempo
Restaurant
20 Clubhouse Road
Santa Cruz, CA 95060

(831) 459-9177
FAX: (831) 459-9198
www.hollinshouse.com

Contact: Banquet Coordinator

Specialties: Beautiful historic restaurant overlooking golf course and Monterey Bay

Food: Regional American cuisine (buffet, from $23.75)

No. of Guests: restaurant, to 150; outdoors, 250; Hollins Room, to 45

Price (location): $1,000 for up to 150 guests; $1,250 for over 150 guests; ceremony, $500
Extra Charges: gratuity, cake-cutting fee, corkage fee

Payment Terms: $750 deposit, balance due day of event
Credit Cards: major credit cards
Lead Time: 6 - 12 months
Rental Time: 5 hrs.
Wheelchair Access: yes

Changing Room: yes
Dance Floor: yes
Music: amplified permitted until 9 pm
Parking: ample
Restrictions: no rice, etc.

The Hollins House was named after champion golfer Marion Hollins. She opened the Pasatiempo golf course in 1929 and continued the development of a sports complex, which was completed in 1937. Today, only the golf course and the beautiful clubhouse remain.

Hollins House is an elegant restaurant, serving regional American cuisine. It offers a spectacular panoramic view over the golf course and Monterey Bay. The dining room is decorated in peach and teal, with crystal chandeliers and marble fireplaces. Curtains with a floral design frame the large windows. The nicely landscaped lawn and garden facilities are available in the summer. The white gazebo is perfect for a wedding ceremony, with the adjoining area large enough for 200 guests. The smaller Hollins Room can accommodate up to 45 guests and is available during restaurant hours. The facilities are available for Saturday weddings from 11 a.m. until 4 p.m., and for Sunday weddings from 4 p.m. until 9 p.m. The chef will customize delicious, healthful menus, and a professional event consultant can help with arrangements. Customers told me that they could not have been more pleased with the exceptional food and service. You can sample their food during a reasonably priced Sunday brunch or during dinner from Wednesday through Saturday.

During the day when the restaurant is closed, the Hollins House is a perfect place for conferences and meetings. The MacKenzie Clubhouse, 200 feet away, can be included for larger groups as well. Packages for daytime use depend on season and menu selection.

Kennolyn Conference Center
Hilltop Hacienda / Logging Town
8400 Glen Haven Road
Soquel, CA 95073

(831) 479-6700
FAX: (831) 479-6730
Kennolyncc@aol.com
www.kennolyn.com

Contact: Pam Caldwell

Specialties: Hilltop Hacienda facility overlooking the ocean;
                Logging Town facility available for weekend weddings

Food: Freshly prepared California cuisine; buffet or served (menus from $29.95)

No. of Guests: Hacienda: sit-down indoors, 150; sit-down indoors and outdoors, 300

Price (location): facilities, $1,000 - $2,500; ceremony (including arch and chairs), $500
Extra Charges: service charge, $500 ref. security deposit, additional rentals, insurance waiver

Payment Terms: 25% deposit, balance
            due 3 days prior to event
Credit Cards: Visa, MasterCard
Lead Time: 6 - 18 months
Rental Time: 5 hrs.
Wheelchair Access: most areas

Changing Room: yes
Dance Floor: outdoors or rented
Parking: ample
Music: amplified permitted until 10 pm
Restrictions: no rice, etc.

The Hilltop Hacienda facility is part of the 300-acre estate purchased by Max and Marion Caldwell in 1946. The Mexican-style hacienda, as the name says, is situated on top of a mountain, surrounded by a redwood forest and meadows, that overlooks the bay down to the Monterey Peninsula. Entry is through a spacious, tiled courtyard with a fountain in the middle and with vines covering part of the walls. The large terrace on the other side of the main building is partially covered by a large overhanging roof and offers the marvelous view. A large lawn area slopes down to the tennis courts. The interior of the building is decorated in Spanish motif. The rectangular-shaped room has a high ceiling and large windows and doors on the longer sides and a fireplace on one of the shorter walls.

About a mile away from the Hacienda across the main road is the Logging Town facility, available from September through mid-June for company retreats or weekend weddings for groups of 65+ people. The facilities surround a small, western-style town square, with swimming pool; tennis and basketball/volleyball courts, and game room. You can stay overnight in log cabins in the surrounding woodsy area.

In 1995, Pam Caldwell started Kennolyn Conference Center and opened the facilities for weddings. Pam received her MBA from Georgetown University after working for a very reputable East Bay catering company and for a large hotel in Sun Valley, Idaho. The chef hails from a catering company in the Santa Cruz area. The menu package offers everything from a gourmet sit-down dinner to an all-American picnic. Clients love the special attention, great food and service, and want to come back for more. *Please call for an appointment.*

Kohl Mansion

(650) 992-4668

FAX: (650) 342-1704
TheKohl@IBM.net
www.ByRecOnly.com/kohlmansion

2750 Adeline Drive
Burlingame, CA 94010

Contact: Linda Hylen (Director of Events)

Specialties: Ground floor and garden patio of Tudor mansion; swimming pool, tennis courts, rose garden

No. of Guests: sit-down, to 450; cocktails, to 1,000

Pricing: $2,800 - $6,500 on weekends, $400/hr. on weekdays; $4,000 to $8,500 during December; rates depend on date and number of guests

Extra Charges: certificate of insurance

Payment Terms: 50% plus $500 security deposit at booking, balance due 60 days prior to event	**Changing Room:** bride's & groom's
Credit Cards: no	**Dance Floor:** yes
Lead Time: 1 - 12 months	**Parking:** yes
Rental Time: 8 hrs., overtime available	**Music:** amplified permitted until 11 pm
Wheelchair Access: yes	**Restrictions:** none

This beautiful, Tudor-style mansion is one of the great houses on the Peninsula. It is situated on 40 secluded acres and is a perfect setting for every special event. It was built over a period of two years by Frederick Kohl and his wife, Elizabeth, who hosted its first party at Christmas in 1914. In 1931 the mansion was bought by the Sisters of Mercy and converted into a school which is still in operation today. On weekdays after 3 p.m. and on weekends, the mansion is available for weddings and corporate or private parties. The grounds, including tennis, basketball and volleyball courts and swimming pool, are available separately for picnics from May to November. The mansion is beautifully decorated during the Christmas season.

Several rooms flow into each other on the ground floor of the mansion, adding to the site's versatility. The elegant Library is often used for smaller receptions. The wood-paneled Great Hall, with its vaulted ceiling, huge fireplace and wall-to-wall windows, has fine acoustics and is perfect for receptions, chamber music and drama. In contrast to the paneled hall, the neighboring Dining Room and Morning Room are very light and airy. The entire ground floor of the mansion was the site of the 1996 BRO party. With the help of Linda Hylen and many BRO vendors, the mansion was transformed into a stunning site, with floral decorations, banners extending from the walls, and special lighting effects. The guests drifted from one room to the next, sampling the fare and listening to the entertainers. The more than 400 guests were in awe of the spectacular site.

Linda Hylen is an event coordinator with many years of experience. Her goal is to accommodate the guests as if they were at home. Under Linda's guidance, all the vendors are coached to treat guests with the utmost care.

Ladera Oaks
Swim and Tennis Club
3249 Alpine Road
Portola Valley, CA 94028

(650) 854-3101
FAX: (650) 854-5982
ladera@nanospace.com

Contact: Receptionist

Specialties: Remodeled clubhouse with covered patio and beautifully landscaped garden;
site for wedding ceremony

No. of Guests: indoors, to 175; indoors/outdoors, to 350

Pricing: $12 - $15 per guest, min. $600 - $3,000, depending on day and time of year
Extra Charges: piano, extra time, outdoor heaters

Payment Terms: $500 deposit, use fee
                  due 1 month prior to event
Credit Cards: no
Lead Time: 3 months to 1 year
Rental Time: 7 - 8 hrs.
Wheelchair Access: yes

Changing Room: yes
Dance Floor: yes
Parking: ample
Music: amplified permitted indoors only
Restrictions: none

The clubhouse of the Ladera Oaks Swim and Tennis Club is a pleasant site for a party or wedding. It has light hardwood floors and an open ceiling. One side of the hall has floor-to-ceiling windows and doors, opening to a vine-covered trellised patio. Adjacent to the main room is a large bar area, which is included in the rental price after 6 p.m. It also opens to the patio and the beautifully landscaped garden with a fountain in the center. The garden consists of lawn areas and flower beds with seasonal flowers and rose bushes. Rental of the hall includes use of the garden. The clubhouse looks immaculate and can be used for elegant events as well as less formal family get-togethers. The clubhouse took on a garden look with the floral tablecloths my friends had chosen for their reception. We all felt very comfortable and right at home.

An elevated brick platform is used for wedding ceremonies on the south side of the garden. Trellises with trumpet vines cover the back wall. Up to 250 guests can be comfortably seated on the grassy area next to the platform. The total rental time is divided into 2 hours for setup, 4 to 5 hours for the reception, and 1 hour for cleanup. An hourly rate is charged for additional time.

The club owns tables and chairs which are set up by club personnel at no extra charge. Amplified music is allowed inside only because of the club's neighborhood location.

The Lakeview Club

(510) 271-4115
(510) 271-4129
FAX: (510) 271-4127
www.lakeviewclub.com

300 Lakeside Drive, Suite 2800
Oakland, CA 94612

Contact: Robert Romero (Special Event Coordinator)

Specialties: Elegant private club overlooking Lake Merritt

Food: Continental and California gourmet cuisine with uncompromising service (menus from $15.95)

No. of Guests: sit-down, to 320; cocktails, 500

Price (location): $300 for non-members, $150 for ceremony room
Extra Charges: gratuity, garage (optional)

Payment Terms: $500 - $1,000 deposit,
   balance due for non-members prior to event
Credit Cards: major credit cards
Lead Time: 1 week to 18 months
Rental Time: 5 hrs.
Wheelchair Access: yes

Changing Room: yes
Dance Floor: marble
Parking: garage
Music: amplified permitted
Restrictions: no rice, etc.

Long before I visited the Lakeview Club, I had heard about it many times. The club is famous for its outstanding food and service, as well as for its spectacular location atop the Kaiser Center in Oakland overlooking Lake Merritt. A large lobby leads to the different rooms situated toward the outside of the building, each providing a beautiful view. The largest one is the Peralta Room, which has a large built-in marble dance floor and seats about 320. Clients are free to incorporate the ever-present fresh flowers with their own decoration. Half the size of the Peralta Room is the De Anza Room. Several other rooms used for meetings and classrooms are also available. Except on Sundays when an opening fee is charged, there is no extra charge for room rental. The Lakeview Club is affiliated with more than 200 exclusive private clubs around the world. The common trademark of the ones I know is their excellence, and their letters of praise confirm this.

Robert Romero, the special event coordinator, joined the Club. His extensive background in food and beverage service spans over 15 years. Working in various positions at the Club has made him an expert in all areas of operation. From consultation to executing the day's event, Robert has the confidence and expertise to create and deliver a most memorable and pleasant wedding or special event experience. The Lakeview Club is accommodating to all special requests concerning menu and dietary choices, as well as to special activities or needs to make your day perfect.

Clients comment about the highly professional staff, and about Robert: "Having you there to help us made all the difference in the world." "Your enthusiastic dedication to ensuring that the event was perfect to the last detail was a key factor in providing such a glorious event."

The Majestic

(415) 441-1100
(800) 869-8966
FAX: (415) 673-7331
hotelmaj@pacbell.net

1500 Sutter Street
San Francisco, CA 94109

Contact: William Day (Assistant General Manager)

Specialties: Pacific Heights mansion with unique ambience

Food: Light, flavorful, California cuisine with an Asian touch (menus from $20)

No. of Guests: restaurant: sit-down, to 125; suites, to 10

Price (location): $2,000
Extra Charges: gratuity, parking, cake-cutting fee, corkage fee, coffee

Payment Terms: 50% deposit, balance due day of event
Credit Cards: all credit cards
Lead Time: 1 week to 60 days
Rental Time: 6 hrs., overtime permitted
Wheelchair Access: yes

Changing Room: yes
Dance Floor: yes
Parking: valet
Music: amplified with restrictions
Restrictions: no rice, etc.; no smoking in hotel

You can't miss this brilliantly white, five-story building situated high enough on Pacific Heights to afford a good view of the city. The ornate Edwardian building dates back to 1902 and was designed to be one of the early grand hotels in the city. Today, it carries the "Certificate of Recognition for Architectural Preservation and Restoration" from the California Heritage Council. The restaurant, where most events take place, reminds me of the Belle Époque. The ornaments on walls and ceiling, and the dainty pilasters make the celadon and peach room light and elegant. The large mahogany bar is inviting for a chat and drink in the evening.

The hotel has undergone major changes recently. The new general manager hails from one of the most beautiful, smaller hotels in the city that is known for its intimate, elegant weddings. He brought with him a French Maître d' and a chef who graduated several years ago from the Culinary Institute in the city, having worked for a year in France and for several years in the U.S. I had the opportunity to talk to the chef; his descriptions of the delicacies, which are mostly created by him, actually made me hungry! He believes in a marriage of simple foods so that the flavors can mingle and create a wholesome dish. He has suggestions for menu creation, and for gourmets it's a "Mecca."

One event planner raved about the "lovely facility" and "excellent food and service," with particular praise for the "excellent, excellent staff." One bride told me, "It was my dream reception. Everything was exquisite. The food couldn't have been better, and the staff was very experienced and so easy to work with." Her guests commented positively on the "sophisticated event."

Manhattans of Saratoga

(408) 257-2131

FAX: (408) 257-5548

12378 Saratoga-Sunnyvale Road
Saratoga, CA 95070

www.manhattans-saratoga.com

Contact: Carrie Fujita (Executive Sales & Marketing Director)

Specialties: Spacious, romantic facility for any special occasion

Food: American and continental cuisines; customized beverage and menus for weddings, social, corporate, and holiday events (wedding packages, from $29.95; corporate packages, from $10.95)
No. of Guests: sit-down, 250 - 300; cocktails, to 450
Price (location): ceremony only, $400
Extra Charges: corkage fee, gratuity, digital baby grand piano

Payment Terms: 25% deposit, balance due 2 weeks prior to wedding	**Changing Room:** yes
Credit Cards: major credit cards	**Dance Floor:** yes
Lead Time: 1 day to 2 years	**Parking:** ample
Rental Time: 5 hrs., additional upon availability	**Music:** amplified permitted
Wheelchair Access: yes	**Restrictions:** no nails, tape; petals ok, rice in patio area only

Opened as a restaurant in 1994, Manhattans of Saratoga soon discovered their niche and converted to a banquet facility. The outdoor patio and back area can be used for ceremonies and cocktail receptions; the indoor facility can be configured to host ceremonies, dancing, buffets, and sit-down receptions. Manhattans romantic interior, with Greek and Roman statues, imagery and artwork, customized distressed faux marble floors, crystal chandeliers and track lighting, adds to this unique venue. What really stood out to me were the beautiful white brocade, high-back chairs, adding not only comfort, but also an elegant ambience to the dining experience. Their gold trim china, silver service, gold base hurricane lamps set on 16" round mirrors, beveled glass table tops, and distinctive linens are included in their various customized packages.

Their inclusive, special occasion menus are designed and customized to meet all price points and various food tastes for all occasions. An added value are the eight beverage/bar packages and off-day discounts. Every combination of drinks and number of hours you select for your event has a fixed price per person, making it easier to calculate your total drink costs. On off-days and hours, including Friday, Sunday, and from 11 a.m. to 4 p.m. on Saturday, Manhattans discounts their packages 10% to 15%. My clients always breathe a sigh of relief when they can budget their entire reception during the beginning stages of their planning.

It is rare to find great reviews on all aspects surveyed. Consistent praises are sung about Manhattans' incredible, attentive service and responsiveness, and their exceptional food. Manhattans is an all-in-one value.

The Martine Inn
Elegance in Accommodations
255 Oceanview Blvd.
Pacific Grove, CA 93950

(831) 373-3388
(800) 852-5588
FAX: (831) 373-3896
www.martineinn.com

Contact: Event Coordinator

Specialties: Elegant Victorian inn with beautiful views of Monterey Bay

Food: Menus designed as requested; specialty menus created from 1880's "White House" recipes reformulated to meet current tastes (5-course menus from $35); beer, wine, champagne
No. of Guests: sit-down, 70; buffet, 120

Price (location): $250 - $950, depending on number of guests
Extra Charges: cake-cutting and corkage fees if not provided by Inn

Payment Terms: non-ref. use fee at booking
Credit Cards: major credit cards
Lead Time: 1 week to 1 year
Rental Time: 1 pm - 5 pm; flexible if entire inn is rented (not available on holiday weekends)
Wheelchair Access: yes

Changing Room: yes
Dance Floor: hardwood floor
Parking: ample
Music: amplified permitted until 10 pm
Restrictions: no smoking

Charm and elegance await you as you step inside The Martine Inn, a restored bed & breakfast inn overlooking the Monterey Bay. Built in 1899, it became the home of the Parke family of pharmaceutical fame, whose descendants still visit the inn today. While the exterior is stuccoed, the interior is reminiscent of early 20th century, with its authentic, museum-quality antiques, mostly of American vintage. Owner Don Martine and wife Marion paid meticulous attention to detail as they remodeled the inn, considering the size and ambience of each room as they researched Victorian wall coverings and period colors. They celebrated their wedding at the grand opening in 1984.

Each of the 20 guest rooms, with private bath complete with claw-foot tub, is unique, with beautiful antique bedroom suites, including one originally owned by the legendary Edith Head. The private courtyard, with a pond, Oriental fountain, and lush Bougainvilleas, lends itself beautifully for the ceremony, buffets, or dancing. Buffets can also be set up in the conference room and library, the latter of which is also suitable for dancing. The dining room offers a magnificent view of the bay and was elegantly set for the wedding dinner. Don houses a few of his vintage MG's on the property.

The Inn specializes in authentic Victorian fare, with as many as 12 courses, served to you in front of a 40-piece place setting at a table laid with 1800's-style porcelain, Victorian and Old Sheffield silver tableware sets over lace tablecloths. The talented chef, who is happy to copy family recipes, also creates traditional wedding cakes. The friendly wedding coordinator can help you with all of your needs. She has a list of preferred vendors in the area and is pleased to make all the arrangements for you. Clients commented on the excellent planning and how the warm and friendly staff made everyone feel special.

Merchants Exchange Ballroom and Conference Center
465 California Street, 15th Floor
San Francisco, CA 94104

(415) 421-7730
FAX: (415) 421-6726
ken@clintonreilly.com
www.clintonreilly.com

Contact: Ken G. Deutsch (General Manager)

Specialties: Remodeled historic men's club for private and corporate functions

No. of Guests: sit-down, to 400, cocktail, to 1,000

Pricing: from $3,750 for ballroom, depending on day of week; smaller conference rooms available
Extra Charges: dance floor, tables and chairs

Payment Terms: 50% deposit, $500 ref. cleaning
   deposit, balance due 14 days prior to event
Credit Cards: no
Lead Time: 1 week to 1 year
Rental Time: flexible
Wheelchair Access: yes

Changing Room: yes
Dance Floor: yes
Parking: street & garages nearby
Music: amplified permitted
Restrictions: no rice, etc.

I first visited this spectacular site when it was home to the Commercial Club, which closed in 1994. Now, the 15th floor of this historic San Francisco landmark is open once again for its guests' enjoyment. Designed by Willis Polk in 1903, it was one of the first steel-framed high-rises in San Francisco and survived the 1906 earthquake. Designed by architect Julia Morgan, the Merchants Exchange, with its barrel-vaulted lobby and its Beaux Arts architectural style and decor, still reflects the grandeur of the early 20th century. The designers of the former Commercial Club retained much of the classic style. The large arched windows in the ballroom matched the mirrors across the room, and the pattern of the ornate ceiling was reflected in the carpet design.

The facility's new management replaced the carpeting and drapery with custom-designed fabrics of gold and rosy hues, but kept intact the old beauty of the club with its warm, mahogany paneled walls and coffered ceiling. The huge, sandstone working fireplace has carvings of a Phoenix, the insignia of the Commercial Club, and the four major insignias of the merchant trade. A 25-foot mahogany bar dominates the lounge. Walk through the lounge to the lobby with another working fireplace, a perfect spot for taking time out from the buzz of the party. Several smaller conference rooms can also be used as a changing room or to entertain guests. The large kitchen is available to properly licensed and insured caterers.

Ken Deutsch, a director of catering in the hospitality industry for over 22 years, brings his vast knowledge and experience to the Merchants Exchange. From working with him, I got to know a sincere and understanding professional whose goal is to fulfill everyone's needs, ensuring a pleasurable experience from the planning stages to the event.

Mill Rose Inn

(650) 726-8750
(800) 900-ROSE
FAX: (650) 726-3031
www. the@millroseinn.com

615 Mill Street
Half Moon Bay, CA 94019

Contact: Eve Baldwin (Wedding Consultant)

Specialties: Four Diamond Award English country inn with banquet room and lush, romantic gardens for wedding ceremonies and receptions

No. of Guests: to 150 (all seated)

Pricing: $3,900 on Saturdays and Sundays; smaller packages midweek, from $500
Extra Charges: certificate of insurance

Payment Terms: in full upon reservation
Credit Cards: all credit cards
Lead Time: 1 - 26 months
Rental Time: 8 hrs.
Wheelchair Access: yes

Changing Room: bride's & groom's
Dance Floor: yes
Parking: ample street parking
Music: amplified permitted
Restrictions: no rice, etc.

When I visited the inn in late April, the air was filled with the sweet fragrance of blooming rose bushes and hedges that surrounded the Mill Rose Inn, which made me realize how perfectly the name suited the place. The cozy Victorian inn is tucked away from Half Moon Bay's busy Main Street. It is well known for its lush, English country garden, where benches and chairs invite you for a rest. I know of no other inn in the area with such a beautiful garden. Over the years, Eve and Terry Baldwin, both horticulturists, have created a blooming oasis and keep it well maintained.

Two weeks after that visit, I returned to observe an elegant wedding. The ceremony took place behind the inn on the flagstone courtyard in the shade of a majestic maple tree. "Isn't it like a fairy tale?" the caterer exclaimed. Garlands and white ribbons decorated the balcony railing and the banisters leading down the stairs to the ceremony site. Baskets full of cascading impatiens and fuchsias, topiaries decorated with flowers, and large pots of hydrangeas looked like islands in bloom. Appetizers and champagne were offered in the lush front garden, while harp music floated through the air. The tables in the rear courtyard were being set for the elegant sit-down dinner.

Eve helps with wedding consultation and coordination, thus alleviating much of the day's pressure. She provides all of the flower decorations, except for personal flowers. Included in the rental fee are three large suites for the wedding day. Taped music can be heard through the built-in indoor and outdoor speakers. Tiny white lights glimmer at twilight, and heaters are included for cooler evenings. A tent is available for inclement weather. All tables, chairs and market umbrellas are provided. Photos in an extensive portfolio capture the beautiful flowers and garden that change with the seasons.

Mirassou Champagne Cellars

(408) 395-3790

FAX: (408) 395-5830
e-mail@mirassou.com

300 College Avenue
Los Gatos, CA 95030

Contact: Hospitality Coordinator

Specialties: Patio and wine cellar of historic winery

No. of Guests: Blanc de Noirs Room, 130; outdoors, to 150 seated; La Cave for ceremonies, to 75

Pricing: $10 - $20 per person (includes location and wine)
Extra Charges: food, extra rentals

Payment Terms: 50% non-ref. deposit,
    balance due 1 week prior to event
Credit Cards: major credit cards
Lead Time: 2 weeks to 6 months
Rental Time: 2 - 5 hrs., until 9:30 pm
Wheelchair Access: yes

Changing Room: yes
Dance Floor: outdoor and indoor
Parking: ample
Music: amplified permitted until 9 pm
Restrictions: no rice, etc.

While the Mirassou Winery is located in San Jose, Los Gatos is home to the Champagne Cellars on the grounds of the old Novitiate Winery. The cellars opened their doors at the new location in November 1989. The secluded area, above the valley and away from its hustle and bustle, is a perfect place for all kinds of events.

Outdoor events take place on the large patio, flanked by the winery building, trees and plants. A staircase on one side makes for a dramatic entrance for the bride. Two elevated decks can be used for the ceremony or music. Moveable trellises obscure the winery visitors from the patio, providing privacy during the day. The large changing rooms for the bridal party are attractively furnished. There is a separate parking area for special event guests.

The tasting room is accessed through La Cave, the long entrance hall with a vaulted ceiling. Its dim lighting makes it perfect for a candle lighting ceremony or a smaller party. On the other side of the tasting room is the Blanc de Noirs Room. Its redwood walls, columns with redwood casing, large barrel cask heads, and racks with wine bottles give it a rustic and comfortable feeling. This room can be used during the day for meetings or luncheons and after business hours (Wednesday through Sunday, 12 p.m. to 5 p.m.).

The rental price of the location includes wine and champagne, as well as two consultations with the event coordinator.

Mirassou Winery
America's Oldest Winemaking Family
3000 Aborn Road
San Jose, CA 95135

(408) 274-4000
FAX: (408) 270-5881
e-mail@mirassou.com

Contact: Hospitality Coordinator

Specialties: Indoor and outdoor events in America's oldest winery

Food: Multi-course sit-down gourmet lunches (from $29.75) and dinners (from $49.50)

No. of Guests: outdoor courtyard, to 125 seated; wine tasting room, to 65 seated; Heritage House (Mirassou family home), to 40 seated
Price (location): included in per person charge for event or meal
Extra Charges: gratuity

Payment Terms: small deposit, balance is billed
Credit Cards: major credit cards
Lead Time: 1 month to 1 year
Rental Time: 2 - 5 hrs.
Wheelchair Access: yes

Changing Room: yes
Dance Floor: no
Parking: ample
Music: amplified not permitted
Restrictions: none

Mirassou is the oldest winemaking family in the United States. In the early 1850s, Pierre Pellier planted the first cuttings he had brought over from France. He chose the eastern foothills of the Santa Clara Valley for his vineyard. His son-in-law, Pierre Huste Mirassou, joined him in the business, and today the family's fifth generation manages the winery.

Lunch and dinner are served inside in the attractive tasting room or outside on the lush Heritage House garden patio. Weddings can be held in the outdoor courtyard with its grapevine fountain. Mirassou's success with private and corporate events led the winery to hire its own chef. Candlelight dinners, which are open to the public, are so popular that they fill up as soon as the invitations are received. This certainly says a lot about the ambience and the food, usually served to the tones of soft music – a delight for the palate as well as the ear.

I spoke to the experienced chef who obviously loves what he does. Designing the multi-course menus to complement the body and character of Mirassou's fine wines is as important to him as shopping for the best produce available, smoking the meats, or preparing his fine reduction sauces.

The winery also has two smaller conference rooms that are available for meetings.

Montclair Women's Cultural Arts Club
An Historic Clubhouse
1650 Mountain Blvd.
Oakland, CA 94611

(510) 339-1832
FAX: (510) 339-1851

Contact: Barbara Price

Specialties: Historic and charming women's cultural club

No. of Guests: Salon: sit-down, 24; cocktails, 40; Gallery: sit-down, 24; cocktails, 60;
Courtyard: sit-down, 250; cocktails, 300; Ballroom: sit-down, 180; cocktails, 275
Pricing: (weekend & holiday rates) Entire club with Courtyard, $350/hr.; Ballroom only, $200/hr.;
Salon & Gallery, $150/hr.; Kitchen, $100 flat rate
Extra Charges: fireplace, sound system, console, piano, event coordination

Payment Terms: 50% non-ref. deposit, balance
due 45 prior to event; $500 ref. security deposit
Credit Cards: no
Lead Time: 1 - 18 months
Rental Time: 6 hrs. min.
Wheelchair Access: yes

Changing Room: yes
Dance Floor: yes
Parking: on street
Music: amplified permitted
Restrictions: no smoking, no mylar balloons,
no tape or tacks

Nestled in the Oakland hills in the quaint town of Montclair is the Montclair Women's Cultural Arts Club. This historic building, traditionally a women's club, has been renovated to a contemporary women's cultural club. Its art deco interior and playful, whimsical murals are as charming as its owner, Barbara Price. A producer of music, concerts, and special events, she has always been a supporter of services in women's cultural arts and music. A couple of years ago, she purchased this 1925 club, with its Mediterranean façade, to become a center dedicated to honoring women's arts. "I wanted an unusual property to create an identity," says Barbara. This is now the rehearsal home of Barbara's own Montclair Women's Big Band, the Women's Philharmonic, and the Linda Tillery & Cultural Heritage Choir.

From the time I walked into this hidden treasure, I was made to feel at home. Standing in the Salon, with its rich, vibrant, multi-colored, red sponged walls and surrounding murals of lush fruit trees, hidden fish, bees, and other beautiful creatures, I experienced a surreal feeling, as if I were part of a painting. Its mahogany bar, Mayan tiled fireplace, and antique accents add grace and beauty to this room. The Gallery, alone or extended with the Salon, is a warm setting for an intimate dinner or formal reception. The Ballroom, with hardwood floors and high beamed ceilings painted in blues and teals, has a large stage, oversized windows, and floor-to-ceiling drapes, swagged to add to the art deco feel of the room. The antique piano, a gift to the club, previously belonged to Antonia Brico, the country's first female conductor. The large double doorways lead to the courtyard, an ideal spot for ceremonies or outdoor receptions with its backdrop of trees. Several satisfied clients describe the club as charming, warm, and welcoming. "Makes you feel like you are entertaining in your own home."

Opera House
Banquet Facility
140 West Main Street
Los Gatos, CA 95030

(408) 354-1218
FAX: (408) 354-2759
www.operahousebanquets.com

Contact: Event Coordinators

Specialties: Refurbished historic opera house

No. of Guests: sit-down, to 450; cocktails, to 700

Pricing: $1,000 - $4,950
Extra Charges: ceremony, valet parking, beverage package, catering package,
certificate of insurance is recommended

Payment Terms: $1,000 - $2,000 non-ref.deposit,
50% 120 days prior, balance due 5 days prior
Credit Cards: no
Lead Time: 1 week to 18 months
Rental Time: any 5 hrs.; 1 event per day
Wheelchair Access: yes

Changing Room: yes
Dance Floor: yes
Parking: valet
Music: amplified permitted
Restrictions: no bird seed, smoking in
designated areas only

The Opera House was built in 1904 as a site for social and civic events for the Los Gatos area. About 10 years later it became a well-known department store, which eventually grew into a large emporium of antique wares. The extensive and careful remodeling after the 1906 earthquake left intact the unique pressed-metal walls and other artistic designs from the founder's era. The Bradbury wallpaper above the staircase certainly adds to the splendor. A specialist revived the old art of using up to 20 patterns of wallpaper to create an authentic Victorian design. Now, once again, the Opera House is a distinctive place for elegant events.

This banquet facility, over 8,000 square feet in size, is among the larger ones in the area. Its two levels, separated by approximately 10 steps, prevents smaller groups from feeling lost. On the lower level is a large, authentic cocktail bar with a removable dance floor. An elegant changing room is available for brides. Since large events would completely block downtown Los Gatos, valet parking is mandatory. You can have your ceremony at the Opera House for an additional $500 to set up a gazebo and chairs. An event coordinator will provide a preferred caterers list and will help you select the menu, flowers, music, and make other arrangements. During my recent visit to the Opera House, I noticed that it still looked as well kept as it was after opening six years ago: no spots on the floor, no fingerprints on the walls. An awning over the door offers protection from the rain, and a roomy elevator assists your ascent to the second level.

Pacific Athletic Club

(650) 593-1112
FAX: (650) 593-3106

200 Redwood Shores Parkway
Redwood City, CA 94065

Contact: Catering Department

Specialties: Indoor and outdoor facilities of sophisticated, elegant health club

Food: Customized menus of California gourmet cuisine (menus from $24.50)

No. of Guests: sit-down, to 240; corporate functions in pavilion, 300 - 600; boardroom, 12 - 20

Price (location): dining room, $1,100; lawn area, $700; ceremony, $400
Extra Charges: 18% gratuity, coat check, valet parking

Payment Terms: $1,500 deposit, 50% 2 month prior, balance due 10 days prior to event
Credit Cards: major credit cards up to $500
Lead Time: 1 day to 1 year
Rental Time: 4½ hrs.; overtime, $300/hr.
Wheelchair Access: yes

Changing Room: yes
Dance Floor: yes
Parking: ample, valet optional
Music: amplified permitted
Restrictions: no balloons, no bird seed, no confetti

The newest and largest health club reviewed in this guide was built in 1992. It was designed to cater to its health-conscious members as well as private and corporate clients. The sprawling club, with its indoor and outdoor facilities, reminds one of a resort. The lobby and dining room have beautiful skylights and are supported by pillars of huge Douglas firs from Oregon. The flagstone floor, the pillars, the exotic orchid plants, and the natural light create an open and airy atmosphere. The murals along the walls of the large, beautiful dining room can be spotlighted after dark. Computerized lighting creates many different effects. The adjoining reception area has a permanent dance floor with an alcove for a DJ or band.

The building, outside tennis courts and swimming pools are connected with lawns and wisteria-covered trellis areas, perfect for different size events. Some open areas can also be tented. The private courtyard was designed for a small wedding ceremony or an intimate luncheon or dinner. Larger wedding ceremonies or outdoor dining can take place on the lawn just in front of the dining room. Flexibility in working with clients is the forte of the catering staff. They also offer coat-check, a spa wedding package, and a reasonably priced valet service.

The area covering the three indoor tennis courts can be used for large corporate functions. Two meeting rooms are available for smaller functions. The facility has a large parking lot with optional valet parking. Since it is difficult to describe everything the club offers, visit it yourself and let the catering department's experienced staff help you with all your needs.

Palmdale Estates
House and Gardens
159 Washington Blvd.
Mission San Jose, CA 94539

(925) 462-1783
FAX: (925) 462-7522

Contact: Veena Roesler

Specialties: Ground floor and garden of elegant countryside estate; two separate garden areas

Food: Classic California cuisine with grilled specialties (menus from $20)

No. of Guests: indoors: sit-down, to 175; cocktails, to 250; outdoors, to 500

Pricing: $2,500 for 8 hrs.
Extra Charges: extra rentals

Payment Terms: $500 non-ref. deposit, balance due 6 months prior to event	**Changing Room:** yes
Credit Cards: no	**Dance Floor:** yes
Lead Time: 12 months	**Parking:** off property
Rental Time: 9 am - 5 pm or 3 pm - 11 pm	**Music:** low-level amplified outdoors
	Restrictions: no rice, etc.; no hard liquor

The Palmdale Estates, near Mission San Jose, got its name from the many large palms that grow on the property. The Best House, with its beautiful and large park-like gardens, seemingly offers peace and quiet. It is one of the few elegant, yet affordable locations for entertaining or for weddings in the Bay Area. The beautiful Tudor-style home was built by Irene Hansen for her mother and herself. After she married Clarence Best, it became the Best House. In 1949, the Sisters of the Holy Family acquired the estate and additional property to house an educational and spiritual center.

The ground floor of the Best House and the adjacent garden are ideal for elegant gatherings of all kinds. The house has a spacious foyer, ballroom, orchestra salon, formal dining room, and a marble-floored solarium. You can't help but notice how well it is maintained (the walls are touched up every week) and all the little details that make it so special. There are murals over the doors and the fireplace in the parlor, one in the changing room, and a large one in the solarium. Surrounding the house are blooming flower beds, and a rose garden next to the patio provides one of the many photo opportunities. The sunken garden, adjacent to the driveway, can accommodate up to 200 people and is ideal for wedding ceremonies or summer picnics.

I returned on a wonderful summer day as a bride was about to walk down the patio stairs and over the lawn towards the permanent white gazebo where the ceremony was to take place. Tables shaded by umbrellas were ready for the reception. Several opulent buffet stations were set up in the different rooms, extending the theme of the solarium's mural.

The Pan Pacific

(800) 533-6465
(415) 929-2064
FAX: (415) 929-2067
www.panpac.com

500 Post Street
San Francisco, CA 94102

Contact: Sue Robbins (Director of Catering & Sales)

Specialties: Elegant, contemporary hotel featuring extraordinary versatility and service

Food: California Fusion cuisine (lunch, from $35; dinner, from $55)

No. of Guests: sit-down, to 350 (280 with dancing); cocktails, to 600; minimum attendance required

Price (location): no charge with food and beverage minimums; ceremony charges may apply
Extra Charges: gratuity

Payment Terms: 30% non-ref. deposit, balance due 72 hours prior to event	**Changing Room:** yes
	Dance Floor: yes
Credit Cards: major credit cards	**Parking:** limited valet
Lead Time: 1 week to 1 year	**Music:** amplified permitted
Rental Time: 4 hrs.	**Restrictions:** no rice, etc.; music in Terrace
Wheelchair Access: yes	Room must end by 11 pm

Picture yourself soaring 21 stories in an enclosed glass elevator to the top of an elegant, luxurious hotel set in the heart of downtown San Francisco. On top is the magnificent Terrace Room with its panoramic view, used for ceremonies, rehearsals, weddings, and other special occasions. This brightly lit room, with its club style atmosphere, has an art deco-inspired working fireplace, inset coffer ceilings with crown moldings, a marble bar, and an adjoining outside Solarium, perfect for a dessert buffet or a haven for cigar aficionados. At sunset, the reflections off the high-rise buildings give the illusion of the sun setting in the East, not the West. It's magical.

Just as beautiful are the rest of the Pan Pacific contemporary architectural details and Asian accents. The lobby, situated two floors above the hustle and bustle of downtown, has a tranquil setting. The bronze sculpture by American artist Elbert Weinberg was inspired by Matisse's "Joie de Dance" and has become the backdrop of many photos. The Olympic Ballroom and pre-function area on the second floor have been recently updated with Tuscan color carpets of sage, terra cotta, and buttercup, which compliment the exquisite rose-colored Portuguese marble. The champagne and gold colored ceilings add height to the illustrious oversized brass and crystal chandeliers. Dimension and beauty are added to the room by its back wall of beveled glass, recessed columns, and the beautiful woven wall fabric imported from England. "Set for a wedding, it just has that certain quality," says Sue Robbins, veteran Catering Director.

I think that it's their team of specialists' attention to detail and personalized service that create that quality. I find their service and California Fusion menus, designed and prepared by renowned executive Chef Michael Otsuka, to be impeccable. Their commitment to excellence is why clients and industry professionals alike recommend the Pan Pacific over and over again. "The Pan Pacific – elegance defined."

The Plumed Horse
Classic Dining & Banquets
14555 Big Basin Way
Saratoga, CA 95070

(408) 867-4711
FAX: (408) 867-6919
plumed@plumedhorse.com
www.plumedhorse.com

Contact: Banquet Director

Specialties: Tasteful, elegant gourmet restaurant in the romantic setting of Saratoga Village

Food: Classic Continental with predominant French and California influence (menus from $12)

No. of Guests: 7 private rooms, from 16 to 110; entire restaurant, to 250 seated

Price (location): setup fee, $50 - $100; ceremony, $300; Sundays, $750 (incl. setup fee)
Extra Charges: gratuity, corkage fee, cake-cutting fee, $100 for your own band or DJ

Payment Terms: $500 deposit (ref. up to 90 days prior), balance due at end of event
Credit Cards: major credit cards
Lead Time: 24 hrs. to 2 years
Rental Time: day, 5 hrs.; evening, unlimited
Wheelchair Access: yes

Changing Room: yes
Dance Floor: yes
Parking: ample, valet service available
Music: amplified permitted
Restrictions: no confetti, smoking patio available

The restaurant's name dates back to the middle of the last century when the village tinker built a stable for his old horse. On cold days he draped his horse in blankets and put a plumed hat on its head. On this site, The Plumed Horse opened its doors in 1952. Though a fine restaurant from the beginning, it is now one of the best restaurants in the area. Recognized for having one of the greatest wine lists in the world, The Plumed Horse has been awarded the "Grand Award" by *The Wine Spectator* since 1987 and enjoys AAA's Four Diamond status. It has received the DiRoNA (Distinguished Restaurants of North America) award for "the most tasteful standards, delicious food, great wines and spirits, and extraordinary service."

The main dining room is my favorite, reminiscent of a French country restaurant, with an open-beam ceiling, cozy fireplace, and a well-appointed wine cellar. The adjacent rooms, varying in size, are as tastefully done with rich mahogany, elegant silk panels, mirrors, stained and etched glass, and brass fixtures. The Oak Room has a bar, kitchen, access to an outdoor patio, and audio/visual equipment. The Cellar is a rustic, warm room that hosts weekly wine tasting events and offers private dining. A spacious elevator provides access to all floors from the parking lot.

I attended a Christmas party at The Plumed Horse and was impressed with the delicious food and outstanding service, the best I have ever experienced in California. During the day or on Sunday when the restaurant is closed, you can rent the entire facility. The banquet director assists you with every little detail and can provide additional services. Candles and table decorations are included in the price.

The Queen Anne Hotel
A Guest House With European Tradition
1590 Sutter Street (at Octavia)
San Francisco, CA 94109

(800) 227-3970
(C) (415) 621-3223
FAX: (415) 487-9247

Contact: Sales Office or Laura Parente of Premier Catering (C)

Specialties: Queen Anne Victorian building

Food: Old world classical and new world creative cuisine (lunch, from $12 ($300 min.);
            dinner, from $25 ($500 min.))
No. of Guests: sit-down, to 80; cocktails, to 150

Price (location): $1,500
Extra Charges: none

Payment Terms: 50% deposit, balance due
                      1 month prior to event
Credit Cards: major credit cards
Lead Time: 1 week to 1 year
Rental Time: 6 - 8 hrs., overtime available
Wheelchair Access: yes

Changing Room: yes
Dance Floor: available
Parking: hotel parking lot (fee)
Music: amplified permitted until 10 pm
Restrictions: smoking in designated areas;
                    alcohol provided by caterer

This "Painted Lady" Victorian building has overcome its rather stormy 100-year history and is now more beautiful than ever. The one-time girls' finishing school became an exclusive gentlemen's private club. Then, narrowly escaping the 1906 earthquake fire, it became a home for young working mothers. Subsequent owners did very little to keep the place in shape until it was purchased by the K.R.V. Company. They spent a year restoring its former elegance and furnishing it with American and British antiques.

The hotel has 48 guest rooms and suites and several rooms for events and conferences that can accommodate from 15 to 150 people. The salon and library with the use of the parlor are perfect for parties and weddings. Next to the salon is a small courtyard. There are fireplaces in the lavishly furnished public areas. A boardroom with seating for 10 is available for business meetings, luncheons, or dinners. Audio-visual equipment is available.

The accommodating hotel staff is very proud of this beautiful Victorian.

Their exclusive full-service caterer is Premier Catering, providing a range of service from informal to fine dining. I had the pleasure of attending a private tasting of beautifully prepared and presented hors d'oeuvres. These were followed by an entree of Salmon Coulibac – a filet of salmon with mushrooms and spinach wrapped in pastry, baked to perfection, and topped by a white butter sauce. The food is delicious; their hotel "a guest house with European tradition."

Ralston Hall
College of Notre Dame
1500 Ralston Avenue
Belmont, CA 94002

(650) 508-3501
FAX: (650) 508-3774

Contact: Event Coordinator of Ralston Hall

Specialties: Completely furnished Victorian mansion with elegant ballroom, several parlors, formal dining rooms, and antique gallery ideal for photography

No. of Guests: sit-down, to 200

Pricing: $3,000 - $4,500
Extra Charges: overtime ($300/hr.), wedding rehearsal ($100/hr.)

Payment Terms: $500 security deposit, full payment due 6 months prior to event
Credit Cards: Visa, MasterCard, Discover
Lead Time: 1 month to 1 year
Rental Time: 8 hrs.
Wheelchair Access: yes

Changing Room: yes
Dance Floor: large
Parking: ample
Music: amplified permitted
Restrictions: no rice, etc.

Ralston Hall, a registered National Historic Landmark, was built between 1864 and 1867. It is fully furnished, primarily with furniture dating back to that period. The building was formerly the country estate of William C. Ralston, a financier and founder of the Bank of California. Today, Ralston Hall belongs to the College of Notre Dame and is one of the most elegant and beautiful places on the Peninsula.

The first floor is available for corporate events, weddings, receptions, fund-raisers, photo shoots, and filming. The east wing includes the Ballroom, the Ballroom Annex and the Cipriani Parlor, while the west wing includes the formal Large Dining Room, Small Dining Room, Sun Porch, Ralston Parlor, and Chinese Room. The attractive interior lends itself to many beautiful photo opportunities. In front of the hall is a large, oval garden with a lovely fountain, providing many lovely spots for wedding ceremonies. Ralston Hall is a perfect site for weddings. As I watched the caterer set up for the reception inside, the guests were in the garden enjoying champagne and hors d'oeuvres after the ceremony in the rays of the late afternoon sun.

The 8-hour rental period includes 2 hours for setup, 5 hours for the event, and 1 hour for breakdown. The services of one security person are included in the price. Ralston Hall provides a very experienced and helpful coordinator. Since it is a valuable landmark, several restrictions apply to the inside of the building: no lighted candles, no balloons, and no tacks or tape.

Round Hill Country Club

(925) 934-8211
FAX: (925) 831-8291

3169 Round Hill Road
Alamo, CA 94507

Contact: Catering Department

Specialties: Spacious, Mediterranean-style country club for weddings, Bar/Bat Mitzvahs, anniversaries, and any special celebration

Food: Fresh, seasonal California cuisine with Mediterranean flair (menus from $32)

No. of Guests: President Dining Room: 25 - 100; Vista Ballroom: sit-down, 230; cocktails, to 300

Price (location): $200 - $1,000
Extra Charges: gratuity, valet service, coat check

Payment Terms: $1,000 deposit, balance due 2 weeks prior to event
Credit Cards: no
Lead Time: 1 - 12 months
Rental Time: 4 hrs., overtime available
Wheelchair Access: yes

Changing Room: yes
Dance Floor: large, built-in
Parking: valet
Music: amplified permitted
Restrictions: no rice, etc.; no photos on golf course

Surrounded by large oaks amidst the rolling hills and beautiful residential homes of Alamo is the splendid Round Hill Country Club. Centrally located in Contra Costa and within a mile of the freeway, this hidden jewel has been facilitating events for over 36 years.

The Mediterranean accents and soft, muted contemporary tones and colors complement newly appointed modern furnishings. The banquet wing is designed separately from its luxurious golf course, giving privacy to their special events. The spacious, comfortable breezeway, with large picturesque windows, is adjacent to the Vista Ballroom and lends itself for flowing smoothly from a reception area to the cocktail and dining areas.

Executive Chef Peter Overly specializes in American/ Mediterranean-style cuisines. In addition to his flexible, well-planned menus are the Round Hill Country Club's beverage packages. I find that the price-per-person beverage package, along with no cake cutting fees, are a rarity and a delightful feature – a perfect way for clients to budget their money!

While I was observing the President Dining Room setup for a wedding buffet and the Vista Ballroom setup for an elegant sit-down reception, I could not help but notice the accommodating staff working together as a finely-tuned team. A banquet manager was present to oversee that the room and staff were in place in plenty of time before the guests arrived. Even the placement of the guest book and the treatment surrounding it were done with such attention to detail.

From the time you enter the Round Hill Country Club until the conclusion of your event, the experienced personnel helps you plan and orchestrate an organized and personalized event.

San Jose Museum of Art

(408) 291-5376
(408) 291-5390

110 S. Market Street
San Jose, CA 95113-2383

FAX: (408) 294-2977
rental@sjmusart.org
www.sjmusart.org

Contact: Lorran Bronnar or Betty J. Ewing

Specialties: Modern art museum with national and international 20th century art

No. of Guests: Wendel: 150 seated; 250 standing; New Wing: 120 seated, 450 standing; entire museum: 250 seated, 1,000 standing
Pricing: entire museum, $6,000; Wendel, $1,500; New Wing, $4,500; additional time, $500/hr.
Extra Charges: setup, rentals, holiday use, liability insurance, refundable security deposit

Payment Terms: 30% non-ref. deposit, balance due 1 month prior to event
Credit Cards: all credit cards
Lead Time: 10 days to 18 months
Rental Time: 5 hrs. (see text)
Wheelchair Access: yes

Changing Room: yes
Dance Floor: Historic Wing
Parking: valet, street, or garage
Music: jazz, classical quartet; amplified negot.
Restrictions: no red wine, dark chocolate or berries

On the northeast side of San Jose's palm-shaded plaza stands the San Jose Museum of Art. The Historic Wing, built of golden sandstone, dates back to 1892 and is now a registered California historic landmark. This wing formerly housed the post office, the main library, and became the San Jose Museum of Art in 1974. In 1991 the new state-of-the-art wing was completed, combining the historic and new with marble, granite, and smooth sandstone blocks. Through an unprecedented collaboration with the renowned Whitney Museum of American Art in New York, the museum has on loan four major exhibits from the Whitney until the end of the century. At the time I visited the museum and met with its marketing director, a temporary exhibit of the distinguished American glass artist, Dale Chihuly, took my breath away. You can still admire three of his dramatic blown-glass chandeliers which have been acquired by the museum.

Events are held in the modern and airy, two-story-high lobby with 30-foot windows, the open Skybridge Gallery overlooking the lobby, and the newly remodeled Historic Wing. The multimedia center is perfect for computer or media demonstrations, and the covered portico stairs at the entrance outside can be used as well. Food is not permitted in the galleries, but docents are available for guided tours during an event. The corporate events department will help with your needs and go so far as to suggest special exhibits which might be appropriate to the event theme. I had an opportunity to attend a concert and reception, and loved the modern, elegant atmosphere.

References think it's a fabulous place and love working with the accommodating staff. The museum is available from 5 p.m. to 10 p.m. (Tue. - Sun.) and 9 a.m. to 10 p.m. (Mon.). Additional time is available for a fee. The Charlotte Wendel Education Center is now available for daytime events and meetings.

Saratoga Country Club

(408) 253-0340

FAX: (408) 253-4056
lthibeault@saratogacc.com
www.saratogacc.com

21990 Prospect Road
Saratoga, CA 95070

Contact: Linda Thibeault

Specialties: Light, airy dining room with adjacent deck overlooking golf course with view of Silicon Valley; ceremony site

Food: Regional American cuisine (menus from $26.75, includes cutting & serving wedding cake)

No. of Guests: sit-down, to 240 (min. 100); cocktails, 300

Price (location): outdoor ceremony site, $800; indoor reception facility, $800
Extra Charges: gratuity

Payment Terms: 2/3 room rental deposit, cater. deposit 120 days prior, balance due day of event	**Changing Room:** yes
	Dance Floor: built-in
Credit Cards: no	**Parking:** ample
Lead Time: 1 - 12 months	**Music:** amplified permitted
Rental Time: ceremony, 2½ hrs., recep., 4½ hrs.	**Restrictions:** no rice, etc.; all beverages to be purchased from country club
Wheelchair Access: yes, but not for rest rooms	

Judging from the many referrals I received, the clubhouse of the Saratoga Country Club is very popular for any kind of event. It is located on Prospect Road in the hills of Saratoga. The light-colored banquet room exudes an elegant family feeling with pretty carpeting and a permanent octagonal dance floor. White trellises and several large plants can be used as room dividers. The adjoining deck overlooks the golf course and parts of Santa Clara Valley.

Up the hill, about 20 yards from the clubhouse, is a lawn area surrounded by boxwood hedges and rose bushes. A white gazebo is a perfect site for ceremonies and provides a great view of the valley.

Each year, the experienced event manager prepares a detailed booklet of helpful guidelines for planning weddings. Her well-planned worksheets clearly map out the bride's plans as they pertain to the club. I'm sure that her knowledge and strong attention to detail has ensured enjoyable wedding days for many nervous brides and their mothers.

At a wedding I observed at the clubhouse, the food was well displayed and delicious. Polite waiters offered hors d'oeuvres before the luncheon and refilled the champagne glasses. The event coordinator oversaw the event and made sure everything was perfect.

Saratoga Foothill Club
(408) 867-3428

Private Women's Club
20399 Park Place
Saratoga, CA 95070

Contact: Dianna Espinosa

Specialties: Historic landmark built in 1915; clubhouse and garden

No. of Guests: June - October, 185; November - May, 150

Pricing: wedding and reception, $800; corporate dinners, $400
Extra Charges: refundable security deposit, parking ($50), certificate of insurance

Payment Terms: $200 deposit, balance
                due 4 weeks prior to event
Credit Cards: no
Lead Time: 1 week to 2 years
Rental Time: 1 day
Wheelchair Access: yes

Changing Room: yes
Dance Floor: hardwood
Parking: nearby, small fee
Music: amplified permitted indoors only
Restrictions: no rice, etc.; no beer,
                no hard liquor

The Saratoga Foothill Club, a women's club, is the oldest social organization in Saratoga. In 1915, the well-known architect, Julia Morgan, designed the club and supervised its construction. It is a timeless redwood structure with a pergola, and is listed in the *National Register of Historic Landmarks*.

This club is quite attractive. The landscaped garden can be used during the summer. A spacious entrance hall leads to the main hall with a large stage. An adjacent, smaller room with a large fireplace is perfect for a buffet setup. A large professional kitchen is available for the caterer. This attractive structure gives a lovely impression; a shiny hardwood floor, large, sparkling windows, and a renovated ladies room show the constant upkeep by its members. Over the last few years, the facility's board has restored it to the arts and crafts period of 80 years ago with authentic furniture, lamp fixtures, and other objects of the era.

Since the club is still actively used by its members, several rules must be observed (listed above). Clients must carry homeowners insurance. The facility is available from 9:30 a.m. to 9 p.m., and only one event is scheduled per day. Because it's so attractive at a very moderate price, it's in high demand. After making an appointment you can visit the club on Monday evenings at 7 p.m. and meet the manager, Dianna Espinosa.

The church parking lots across the street must be rented for each event.

Seascape Resort
Beautiful Events by the Monterey Bay
One Seascape Resort Drive
Aptos, CA 95003

(831) 688-6800
(800) 929-7727
FAX: (831) 685-3059
channing@seascaperesort.com
www.seascaperesort.com

Contact: Wedding Coordinator

Specialties: Resort on the Monterey Bay with ocean-view banquet rooms and ceremony site on bluff overlooking beach

Food: Generous portions of fresh California cuisine with Mediterranean influence

No. of Guests: sit-down with dance floor: Seascape room, to 270; Riviera room, to 120; 5 smaller rooms, 50 to 90
Price (location): from $70 per person (see text)
Extra Charges: gratuity, beverages, changing room

Payment Terms: $1,000-$2,000 non-ref. dep., 50% due 60 days prior, balance due 14 days prior
Credit Cards: major credit cards
Lead Time: 10 days to 2 years
Rental Time: 5 hrs.
Wheelchair Access: yes

Changing Room: suite for additional charge
Dance Floor: yes
Parking: ample
Music: amplified permitted
Restrictions: no rice, etc.

You think you're on vacation as you enter the open lounge with its magnificent view. This ocean-front luxury resort, built in 1993, features 284 rooms (studios, 1- and 2-bedroom suites) equipped with fireplaces, kitchenettes or full kitchens, private balconies, and spectacular views of Monterey Bay. Seascape was designed as a full-service resort for leisure guests, meetings, and private functions. The resort is an answer to a couple's desire for an elegant, oceanfront setting. The ceremony site is on a bluff overlooking cypress trees and the Monterey Bay. A champagne toast and appetizers can be served here immediately after the ceremony so the guests can watch as photographs are taken. For the reception, you can choose from seven attractive banquet rooms, depending on the size of your party. Each room has large windows, and four have outdoor balconies. Spacious pre-function areas are perfect for bar setups, guest-book signing, etc.

One beautiful autumn day, the catering department invited me for lunch at the Sanderling Restaurant. The food was deliciously prepared, attractively presented, and served by courteous staff. The competent catering director and catering manager have worked in the event industry for many years, know what setup works best, and will help with every detail. You can compose your menu from menu suggestions or have it custom-designed to include even old family recipes. The location price includes hors d'oeuvres, sit-down or buffet meals, ceremony and reception sites, a deluxe, white lattice arch, dance floor, and security services.

One bride told me how much she loved the romantic setting, how organized and beautiful everything was, and how her guests enjoyed staying there. A corporate client mentioned the excellent food and complimented the accommodating and knowledgeable staff.

Shadowbrook

(831) 475-1222

FAX: (831) 475-7664
office@Shadowbrook-Capitola.com
www.Shadowbrook-Capitola.com

1750 Wharf Road
Capitola, CA 95010

Contact: Wedding Coordinator

Specialties: Romantic, beautiful indoor/outdoor restaurant overlooking Soquel River

Food: Creative Continental cuisine; seafood a specialty (menus from $16.95)

No. of Guests: 12 - 225

Price (location): $600 for entire restaurant on Saturday; $200 room charge for other days
Extra Charges: service charge, cake-cutting fee, coffee, $500 for ceremony

Payment Terms: deposit of min. food/bev. cost 30 days after booking; balance due at end of event	**Changing Room:** yes
	Dance Floor: yes, with stage
Credit Cards: all credit cards	**Parking:** 2 free parking lots
Lead Time: 24 hours to 18 months	**Music:** amplified permitted indoors only, acoustical allowed outside
Rental Time: 9 am to 3:30 pm	
Wheelchair Access: yes	**Restrictions:** primarily daytime weddings

While I was walking down the steep, winding path surrounded by lush, blooming flowers and shrubs, I was suddenly taken by the aroma of a wonderful mixture of herbs. I learned later that I had taken the back approach to the restaurant, near the chef's herb garden. The "official" approach leads you down past the cable car for guests and the waterfall to the entrance of this restaurant, voted "most romantic restaurant," by readers of *San Francisco Focus* magazine.

In 1920, the first log cabin was built as a summer home on the hillside overlooking Soquel River. The next owners added the Fireside Room, reminiscent of a Swiss chalet. In 1947, the doors of the restaurant opened for the first time. A subsequent owner added the deck by the river and installed additional antique furnishings. It has now been under the same ownership since 1978, and it's obvious how much the owners enjoy the site. They added more annexes and patios, and the structural improvements withstood the 1989 earthquake with virtually no damage. A waterfall was re-installed, the large hillside was completely landscaped, and two full-time gardeners were assigned to its care. A third gardener oversees the many indoor plants, cleaning the abundant leaves of the different palms and vines climbing around the posts and beams.

The professionally trained wedding coordinator will help you plan your event. In summertime the ceremonies are usually held outside, while in cooler weather the stone fireplace in the Fireside Room and the atrium area of the entry lounge are favorite spots. Smaller receptions are usually held in the room of your choice, while larger ones can occupy one entire level. I immediately fell in love with this charming and cozy restaurant, and booked a table right away for my husband's birthday. The food and service were excellent, as was the large selection of fine wines.

The Shannon-Kavanaugh House
"The Anchor of San Francisco's Postcard Row"
722 Steiner Street
San Francisco, CA 94117

(415) 563-2727
FAX: (415) 563-0221
mjs@s-j.com
www.s-j.com

Contact: Thomas Zickgraf (Director)

Specialties: The ultimate San Francisco experience for those looking for a touch of history

No. of Guests: Dining Room: sit-down, 25; Main Parlor: sit-down, 36; cocktails: 65 - 70

Pricing: from $1,200; accommodations, from $175; garden apartment, $175; Victorian cottage, $275
Extra Charges: food, staff, rentals

Payment Terms: 50% non-ref. deposit, balance due 3 weeks prior to event
Credit Cards: major credit cards
Lead Time: to 1 year
Rental Time: 4 - 6 hrs.
Wheelchair Access: no

Changing Room: yes
Dance Floor: no
Parking: valet
Music: amplified permitted
Restrictions: no rice, etc., no smoking

What could be more San Franciscan then hosting an affair at The Shannon-Kavanaugh House, the historic Victorian "anchor" of San Francisco's famous "Postcard Row"? Built in 1892, this meticulously restored Queen Anne-style Victorian, located in the Alamo Square district, is set against the breathtaking San Francisco skyline. This beautiful home, built by carpenter Matthew Kavanaugh, was eventually subdivided and condemned until Michael Shannon "rescued" it in 1975. Michael graciously began conducting historical tours, which motivated him to begin the long journey of restoration. As one of the most photographed homes in San Francisco, it has been featured in scores of print, TV ads and films, including *The Dead Pool*, *Invasion of the Body Snatchers*, and *Full House* (TV series). The 4-story interior is exquisitely furnished with antiques and contemporary furniture manufactured by Shannon & Jeal.

As soon as I entered the pristine Shannon-Kavanaugh House, I was enveloped by the warmth and nostalgic atmosphere created from the illuminating brass and copper, gaslight chandeliers and the great hall staircase. For an intimate ceremony, the Main Parlor is exquisitely furnished and equipped with an analog and digital, play-itself Pianomation™ piano. The Grand Dining Room's warm interior, pewter accents, Victorian paintings, and beautifully restored fireplace is inviting for a formal sit-down dinner. The French doors of the Victorian-style kitchen open to a flower-filled balcony with a splendid view of the skyline. The Garden Apartment and Victorian Cottage, with private entrances, can also be rented for one night or as short-term rentals Thomas Zickgraf, Director of the Shannon-Kavanaugh House, works with industry professionals to provide a variety of fine foods, beverages, and entertainment for intimate ceremonies, social gatherings, high-powered corporate affairs, or weekend getaways for anyone wanting a touch of history.

Sheraton Palo Alto

(650) 328-2800
FAX: (650) 324-9084
catering@pahotel.com

625 El Camino Real
Palo Alto, CA 94301

Contact: Catering Department

Specialties: Picturesque, Spanish-style hotel with flowing water and flower gardens

Food: International and California cuisines (menus from $29)

No. of Guests: sit-down, to 350; cocktails, to 450

Price (location): none
Extra Charges: service charge, cake-cutting fee, corkage fee, ceremony setup

Payment Terms: $1,000 to reserve, estimated balance due 10 days prior to event	**Changing Room:** yes
	Dance Floor: yes
Credit Cards: major credit cards	**Parking:** ample
Lead Time: 1 week to 1 year	**Music:** amplified permitted
Rental Time: 5 hrs., overtime available	**Restrictions:** no rice, etc.; smoking
Wheelchair Access: yes	in designated areas

This picturesque hotel with flowing water and flower gardens makes it a favorite place for hosting events and accommodating out-of-town guests and family. This 4-star hotel, converted from Holiday Inn to Sheraton Palo Alto in July of '98, is proud of their customer service, a trademark of Sheraton Hotels.

The Piazza is a Spanish-style atrium with a glass dome, tile floors and stucco archway – an ideal place for ceremonies. On either side are two banquet rooms, the Oak/Sequoia and Justines. The Oak/Sequoia Room can be divided into two smaller rooms, while Justines opens out onto a beautifully manicured garden and patio area with a pond of Koi fish, bridges, and waterfalls. Adjacent to this lovely landscaped area are the pool and courtyard where their famous Sunday brunch is served. In a separate wing is the Reception Room, with two chandeliers and faux bronze doors that open onto a private access lawn and gazebo area. For a formal affair, the Cypress Ballroom, with grand chandeliers and Chinese antiques displayed in softly lit shadowboxes set in the walls, can accommodate both large and small groups.

I was able to sample Chef Pierre Arce's delicious California cuisine. From corporate theme buffets to customized wedding menus, Chef Arce is flexible in accommodating different tastes. Longtime Banquet Manager, Mickey Pineda, assistant Linda Abidi, and the staff specialize in personalized service and creative ideas.

With their recently renovated rooms and suites, and future plans to add 200 more units, the Sheraton Palo Alto has your special day completely covered.

Shrine Event Center

(925) 294-8667
FAX: (925) 294-8666
beets@beetscater.com
www.beetscater.com

170 Lindbergh Avenue
Livermore, CA 94550

Contact: Read Phillips

Specialties: Spacious, contemporary hall with stage; utmost flexibility in meeting clients' needs

Food: Beets Fine Catering (see page **71**)

No. of Guests: sit-down, to 450; cocktails, to 1,000

Price (location): $725
Extra Charges: service, upgraded rentals, insurance waiver

Payment Terms: 50% 2 months prior, balance due day of event
Credit Cards: Visa, MasterCard
Lead Time: 3 days to 1 year
Rental Time: 5 hrs. for parties
Wheelchair Access: yes

Changing Room: yes
Dance Floor: yes
Parking: ample
Music: amplified permitted
Restrictions: no rice, etc.

The Shrine Event Center, built in 1990, was designed specifically for large events. The interior of the center is done in light colors and includes a 7,000 square foot auditorium with a large curtained stage, bar room, and several meeting rooms for groups of 30 to 1,000. When I visited the center, track lighting was being installed to create a more intimate atmosphere. The newest addition is beige cotton swags extending across the ceiling and to the floor on opposite sides of the room. A large parking lot and easy access make this location perfect for corporate events, theme parties, and trade shows. The Livermore Rodeo had crowned their rodeo queen at the center the week before my visit.

This is also a popular wedding location where more than 80 were celebrated in 1997. Photos in their portfolio show how many different looks the hall can take on depending on the event. For example, the new swags can be enhanced with ribbons, and room dividers can separate the ceremony from the reception area. Meeting and banquet tables are available, as well as linen, china, glassware and silverware. Upgraded chairs can be rented for an additional $1 each.

Much of each event's success is due to the work of in-house caterer, Read Phillips, owner of Beets, a catering company offering innovative food with your budget in mind. I witnessed Read's versatility firsthand during an open house at Shrine Event Center. Several stations displayed picnic food, Cajun and Arabian ethnic foods, and a salad bar.

Spectrum Gallery
A Space for Art and Events
511 Harrison Street (at First Street)
San Francisco, CA 94105

(415) 495-1111
FAX: (415) 882-9999

Contact: Thomas Roedoc

Specialties: Art gallery with spectacular view, designed for events, artwork included

No. of Guests: sit-down with dancing, 100 - 400 (all in one room)

Pricing: Saturday & Sunday, $3,250; Friday night, $2,250
Extra Charges: dance floor, facility technician, pin-spot lighting on dining tables

Payment Terms: 50% non-ref. deposit,
      balance due 90 days prior to event
Credit Cards: no
Lead Time: 2 weeks to 2 years
Rental Time: 5 hrs. plus setup/breakdown
Wheelchair Access: yes

Changing Room: yes
Dance Floor: parquet
Parking: ample
Music: amplified permitted
Restrictions: none

Spectrum Gallery is a dream come true. Thomas Roedoc combined his vision with experience and hard work to create a fine art gallery designed specifically for events. A former wedding and event coordinator, Thomas built Spectrum with all the features one can only imagine for a spectacular event: a 20-foot-high wall of windows facing downtown (just 4 blocks away); beautiful large-scale paintings on all the walls; a 1,200-square-foot caterer's area (open to all), abundant on-street and lot parking nearby, a stage (if needed) and dance floor, tables and chairs, a bridal dressing room, a coat-check room, microphone, and spacious rest rooms.

Thomas is especially proud of the sophisticated lighting system. He can pin-spot each table, light the buffets, and wash the dance floor with colored gels (each separately dimmable), adding drama and altering the mood to suit each phase of the event. Since the Gallery opened its doors in 1990, it has hosted over 800 events. And it's always spotlessly clean! With its high ceilings (16-24 feet) and amazing lighting, tall centerpieces look very dramatic against the twinkling backdrop of the San Francisco skyline. There are electrical outlets everywhere, a 16-foot-wide projection screen, and 17 Bose speakers providing whisper-clear sound for background music and toasts. The gallery is versatile enough (Thomas nicknamed it the "Chameleon Room") for theme events as well as traditional receptions and ceremonies. The rental price includes tables and chairs, lighting and sound, janitorial services, and a greeter/parking director. There are no restrictions on decorations or sound, and Thomas is always available to help with planning.

Thomas Fogarty
Winery and Vineyards
19501 Skyline Blvd.
Woodside, CA 94062

(650) 851-6772
FAX: (650) 851-5840
tfwinery@aol.com
www.fogartywinery.com

Contact: Brooke Greene

Specialties: Contemporary winery with beautiful views overlooking vineyards and bay

No. of Guests: Hill House and Pavilion, to 220 seated; Board Room, to 20; Redwood Room, to 40

Pricing: weekends: Nov. 16 - April 14 and all Fridays, $3,500; April 15 - Nov. 15, $5,400;
corporate rates, $500 - $2,500
Extra Charges: extra tables and chairs, wine, champagne, insurance waiver

Payment Terms: 50% deposit, balance + $500 security deposit due 4 months prior to event
Credit Cards: major credit cards
Lead Time: 2 weeks to 12 months
Rental Time: weddings, 8 hrs.; corp., 4 or 8 hrs.
Wheelchair Access: yes

Changing Room: yes
Dance Floor: inside Hill House only
Parking: limited, valet included for weddings
Music: amplified permitted with limitations
Restrictions: no rice, etc.; wine from winery only

I was quite taken with the Fogarty Winery during my first visit. Located on Skyline Boulevard in the Santa Cruz Mountains, the winery offers breathtaking views overlooking the San Francisco Bay all the way to the East Bay hills. Its modern structures adapt beautifully to the surrounding vineyards, and its fine wines and champagnes are among the best in the area.

Several areas are available for parties, weddings, and receptions. The Hill House, with its redwood walls and oak floors, is built on three levels. After extensive remodeling, the main room, with bar and fireplace, is now level with the large covered deck, enclosed with glass and seating up to 220 guests. The Redwood Room on the upper floor, surrounded by a tiled terrace, seats 40 at wooden barrel tables with leather chairs. The smaller board room is comfortably furnished, and a selection of audiovisual equipment is available. The Pavilion, the newest structure adjacent to the Hill House, is a spacious, tiled and covered terrace that can be used for outdoor events or ceremonies. The lawn area, surrounded by trees and flower beds, is the most elevated site and can accommodate from 150 to 200 people.

Fogarty is a marvelous place for parties, weddings, wine tastings, and business retreats. Its modern kitchen is well equipped for preparing even elaborate gourmet dinners. All structures face the valley, providing a spectacular view of the vineyards and the bay.

Due to its location in a neighborhood, amplified music must be carefully monitored, and bands must be chosen from the preferred band list. Carpooling is recommended due to limited parking space. Winery visits are by appointment only.

Villa Montalvo
California's Historic Estate for the Arts
15400 Montalvo Road
Saratoga, CA 95070

(408) 961-5814
FAX: (408) 961-5850

Contact: Kerry Prescott (Wedding Rentals Manager)

Specialties: Elegant Mediterranean-style villa with beautifully landscaped gardens for ceremonies, receptions and special events

No. of Guests: to 200; over 200 requires special arrangements and additional fees

Pricing: Oval Garden/Love Temple ceremonies, $1,400 - $1,950; Montalvo Circle: reception (6 hrs.), $6,700; ceremony/reception (8 hrs.), $7,500; fees over $3,200 are tax-deductible
Extra Charges: certificate of insurance, valet service required for over 200 guests

Payment Terms: 50% non-ref. deposit, balance & security deposit due 60 days prior to event	**Changing Room:** yes **Dance Floor:** yes
Credit Cards: Visa, MasterCard	**Parking:** ample
Lead Time: 3 months to 1 year	**Music:** amplified permitted until 10 pm
Rental Time: 2 - 8 hrs.	**Restrictions:** no rice or bird seed
Wheelchair Access: yes	

Set in the middle of 175 acres surrounded by lush landscaped gardens, this sprawling estate is probably the most beautiful place for events on the Peninsula. The Mediterranean-style Villa Montalvo was built in 1912 by Senator James Duval Phelan as his country home. The gum tree, wood-paneled walls provide an elegant, yet warm atmosphere. Large French doors open to the spacious front verandah where most of the receptions are held, overlooking beautifully landscaped gardens, and beyond them, the valley 800 feet below. This mansion was the senator's favorite home and a center for social activities with many artists and politicians among the guests. Now a nonprofit art center featuring the West Coast's oldest artist residency program, a gallery, children's educational activities, and year-round performances, it is still one of the most sought-after locales for events in the Bay Area. The drive up the hill past the manicured lawns and beautiful flower beds is breathtaking.

The villa and the adjacent buildings are perfect for many kinds of events. Wedding ceremonies are performed in the Oval Garden where wisteria covers the surrounding walkways. Flower beds with rose bushes and hydrangeas contribute to the romantic aura. Another ceremony site is the Love Temple at the base of the lawn, enclosed by wrought iron gates, with a brick walkway and surrounded by Mediterranean gardens. The Spanish Courtyard is a perfect site for post-ceremony toasts and hors d'oeuvres, with its fountain in the center, rose beds, boxwood hedges, and vine-covered columns.

Booking the Montalvo Circle Reception entitles you to a 6- or 8-hour time slot and use of the downstairs and adjacent gardens, as well as full meal and bar service. Inquire about the many possibilities for corporate meetings and events.

The Vintage Room and Courtyard
at Stanford Barn
(by appointment)
Palo Alto, CA

(650) 325-4339
(800) 440-4458
FAX: (650) 325-8068

Contact: Ulrike vom Stein

Specialties: Attractive, historic brick building with courtyard

Food: California Cafe Catering

No. of Guests: indoors: sit-down, 160, cocktails, 300; courtyard: sit-down, 150, cocktails, 200

Price (location): Fri. - Sun., $1,600; Mon. - Thu., $500 to $1,000; courtyard, $500
Extra Charges: extra rentals, dance floor, certificate of insurance

Payment Terms: 50% non-ref. deposit, balance due 60 days prior to event
Credit Cards: major credit cards
Lead Time: 24 hours to 1 year
Rental Time: 8 hrs., 1 event per day
Wheelchair Access: yes

Changing Room: yes
Dance Floor: yes
Parking: ample
Music: amplified permitted
Restrictions: no rice, etc.

The Stanford Barn has quite a history. Built in 1886, this attractive three-story brick building served as a winery. The adjacent smaller building at the rear, which is now the Vintage Room, housed the steam engine that ran the machinery. The entire building was so solidly built that it survived the 1906 earthquake undamaged. In 1916, Herbert Fleishhacker leased the land for his Holstein cows and converted the winery into a milking barn. Used primarily as a barn until 1961, the property is now owned by Stanford Barn Enterprises, who renovated and revitalized the historic property.

I really like the Vintage Room. The ivy-covered red brick building with its large windows and French doors creates a warm feeling. The columns inside are enhanced with grapevine garlands and "B" lights. New carpeting and comfortable chairs provide a cozy, yet elegant feeling. A large antique bar stands along the rear wall. I saw the room dressed up for a wedding, with a beautifully decorated buffet and colorful flower decoration, but it also lends itself perfectly for company parties, especially holiday events. The gazebo, a permanent structure on one side of the courtyard, can be used as an arch or chuppah for a wedding ceremony. For larger events the courtyard can be tented. Ulrike has many years of restaurant, catering, and event experience, and is very easy to work with, always open to new ideas and suggestions.

California Cafe Catering, located across the courtyard, is the exclusive caterer of the Vintage Room.

All decorations must be pre-approved.

The Westin St. Francis Hotel

(415) 397-7000
FAX: (415) 403-6891
www.ByRecOnly.com/westinstfrancis

335 Powell Street
San Francisco, CA 94102

Contact: Amie Kraft (Catering Manager)

Specialties: Historic grand hotel on Union Square, featuring banquet rooms and accommodations with sweeping views overlooking the San Francisco Bay Area

Food: California and International cuisine; full Kosher catering under strict rabbinical supervision is available

No. of Guests: Borgia Room (ceremony): 100 seated, 130 standing; Colonial Ballroom (dance floor): sit-down, 260; Victor's Palace (dance floor): sit-down, 150; Alexandra's (dance floor): sit-down, 250

Price (location): $1,200 - $1,500 (ceremony room); prices depend on season and availability

Extra Charges: gratuity, valet service

Payment Terms: 30% deposit, balance due 72 hours prior to event
Credit Cards: major credit cards
Lead Time: subject to availability
Rental Time: to 12 hrs.
Wheelchair Access: yes, except Borgia Room

Changing Room: bridal suite
Dance Floor: yes
Parking: limited valet; many lots in vicinity
Music: amplified permitted
Restrictions: no smoking

Grace and grandeur are the first impressions that come to mind when I think of the Westin St. Francis – a luxurious, historic landmark hotel on Union Square with a cable car stop at the front door. The $55 million restoration has returned the St. Francis to the traditional, exquisite style and elegance of 1904. It sparkles inside and out. From the time you meet with Amie Kraft, resident event expert, until your menu is prepared by an award-winning culinary team, led by Executive Chef Bernd Liebergesell, the Westin St. Francis staff will dazzle you.

The ambience of the banquet rooms creates romance and fantasy. The Colonial Ballroom with its picturesque murals, elegant balconies, moldings, and gold leaf trimming is stunning. Decorated with candelabra and dressed for an event, the ambiance will send you back to a nostalgic place in time. On The Imperial Floor (32nd level) is Victor's Palace, fashioned after a Russian czar's residence. Every aspect of this room creates a lasting impression. From the finger towels and perfume in the restrooms to silver champagne buckets, specialty custom linens, crystal stemware, and fine china, your event will never be forgotten. Special menus and white-glove service add to the royal treatment, and the views of the city are overwhelming. The popularity of Victor's Palace led to the addition of adjacent Alexandra's, also offering magnificent views. Opened in 1998, Alexandra's is decorated in rich cabochon jewel tones of ruby, garnet, amber, gold and silver, and offers the same luxurious experience as Victor's Palace.

The St. Francis' central location is footsteps away from world-class dining, shopping and entertainment. The Main Building's guest rooms exude old-world charm, with many rooms overlooking Union Square. The Tower guest rooms are spacious and more contemporary, with dramatic views of the entire city, making it the ultimate destination to host an elegant event.

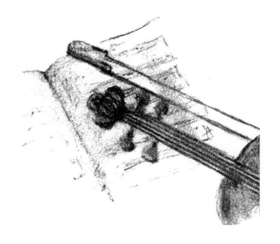

MUSIC

NOTES

INTRODUCTION

At a garden party I attended, a harpist was playing in a corner next to a fountain. The soft tones traveled throughout the small garden and gave the party a relaxed and festive ambience.

Have you ever thought of entertaining your guests with the musical interludes that the lords would arrange for their dinner guests? Some musicians specialize in "center stage" performances. This would definitely add a special touch to your event. So would a slide show of the bride and groom when they were young, accompanied by the appropriate background music. Several DJs provide this service.

Choosing the right music source is very important as it certainly is a memorable aspect of every event. And you should consider your guest list when making your decision. A DJ whose specialty is hard rock might be an appropriate choice for a prom, but for a wedding you might want to select music that also appeals to the older generation. For a Bar or Bat Mitzvah, you should hire someone who can entertain youngsters as well. Be aware that event sites usually have rules regarding music volume; locations in residential neighborhoods are particularly strict. Churches and synagogues have policies regarding what is appropriate ceremony music.

Music should be planned for the entire course of the event, climaxing sometime before the end. The DJ or band leader is the perfect person to guide you through the event and make it flow. Only soft music should be played during dinner, while the dance music should begin during dessert. Since the performers take short breaks, ask them to provide music during these intervals. All of the musicians appearing in the guide said they would act as master of ceremonies and will dress according to the event.

A good **band** or **DJ** should be able to get people onto the dance floor. They should closely observe the party see if the selected music is being enjoyed by the guests and be able to switch on the spot.

Some DJs, musicians and bands can provide music for both the wedding ceremony and the reception. One or two performers may perform during the ceremony, then be joined by others to play background music during dinner. Then the entire group will appear for dancing. This service is referred to as **progressive entertainment**. Some musicians will even change their attire during the course of the event.

Impromptu **audience requests** can most often be honored if the requested music is not obscure. DJs are best at handling audience requests as they are not limited by style of music and also have huge music libraries to choose from. Give them a "do not play" list to ensure that inappropriate music is not played. A DJ told me a horror story about a colleague who played a favorite song of the groom's parents, only to shortly discover that the groom's father had passed away only weeks before the wedding. This put a damper on the entire evening.

Some musicians will prepare special arrangements or compositions, or will learn music specially for your occasion.

Some bands will carefully plan the details with you and will send you sample **audio** or **video tapes** containing a cross-section of the music they can play. I know of a band that offers private auditions to prospective clients. On the other hand, most bands perform at public venues, which is the best way to see them in action. Some of the more famous bands prefer not to book more than a half year in advance as they often go on tour.

If you want ideas about the type or style of music to have, you can call upon the services of an **entertainment agency**. While this might prove more costly, it could turn out to be money well spent. Agencies have a large selection of talent to choose from and will help find what you want. The agencies reviewed in this guide can get practically any type of musician or entertainment for you, from bagpiper to classical quintet. Talent agencies are licensed by the Labor Commission and bonded by the State of California. They take up to 25% of the total price; your deposit sits in escrow until the contract is fulfilled. **Production companies** are also good resources for talent. In addition to entertainment, they also provide lighting, props, and other production services. These companies are not bound by the business rules applied to talent agencies and are often more expensive.

A word of caution about agencies and DJ companies. I've heard more than once that overbooking has led to sending substitutes to an event. You can avoid this possibility if you insist on meeting the DJ assigned to your party or by recording the band leader's name in the contract. This will give you some recourse if your party doesn't flow as smoothly as anticipated.

Money Matters

Prices usually depend on the number of musicians and performance time. Show bands charge higher prices. Progressive bands give you more for your dollar.

The *most expensive* time is December. Bands are often booked a year in advance and can command at least twice the normal rate during the holidays.

Extra charges: An additional charge by musicians may apply if your location or event schedule requires them to set up well in advance of their performance. Also, they often arrange in their contract to have you provide food for them during breaks. If you prefer that they not drink alcoholic beverages, note that in your contract.

Money Saving Tips

- Weekdays are always less expensive.
- You can avoid early setup charges if the band plays in a room adjacent to where the cocktail reception is being held.

Note

Businesses are listed in the order of agencies, bands, DJs, soloists (flute, guitar, harp, piano), and strings.

AGENCIES

Angel Entertainment
(formerly An Angel's Touch)
P.O. Box 3754
Walnut Creek, CA 94598

(925) 937-4277
(800) 836-5559
FAX: (925) 947-2592
Jessica@Angelevent.com
www.AngelEvent.com

Contact: Jessica Siegel

Service Area: Greater Bay Area

Specialties: Musicians, DJs and entertainers for all occasions

Price Range: medium to high
Extra Charges: may apply for travel or early setup

Payment Terms: 50% deposit, balance due
1 week prior to event
Credit Cards: Visa, MasterCard

Lead Time: same day to 1 year
Playing Time: 1 - 6 hrs.
Audience Requests: yes

Fate has certainly played an important role in Jessica's life. As a violin student in high school, she was caught in the harp room that was off limits to non-harp players. The only excuse she could come up with was that she wanted to play the harp. Now she has a master's degree in music education and harp performance, and is known as one of the finest harpists and music educators in the area.

While she performed at weddings and parties, guests would approach her for recommendations of other musicians, and Angel Entertainment grew quite naturally over the years. She applies the same high standards to the agency as she has set for herself as a performer. The musicians who work for her music service are extremely professional and talented performers. Through her friendliness and honest work she has become the preferred provider for several popular wedding and special event locations in the Bay Area.

She enjoys combining her musical skills with working with people and appreciates the feedback she gets about her work. She loves getting to know her clients and is great at working with brides. Jessica's reputation is based on providing excellent service, quality, courtesy, and professionalism.

During my last visit to her office, Jessica showed me the many sample tapes and promotional materials that she sends out to her clients. Each performance is evaluated after the event.

The Entertainment Connection
Talent Agency
1202 Lincoln Avenue, Suite 101
San Jose, CA 95125

(408) 275-6325
FAX: (408) 275-1902
entconnect@aol.com
www.TECProductions.com

Contact: Read Zaro

Service Area: West Coast (Bay Area and Northern California a specialty)

Specialties: Full service talent agency providing entertainment for all occasions

Price Range: medium price for bands: $1,700 - $3,000; DJs, from $450
Extra Charges: travel beyond 60 miles of San Francisco

Payment Terms: 25%-50% deposit depending on act, balance due day of event
Credit Cards: Visa, MasterCard, Discover

Lead Time: 1 day to 1 year
Playing Time: depends on artists
Audience Requests: yes

Founded in 1972, The Entertainment Connection is one of the few state-licensed and bonded talent agencies included in this guide. Such a business is restricted in the percentage it can add to the band's or entertainer's fee. The money remains in escrow until the contract is fulfilled, thus protecting clients and musicians from a bad deal. Read Zaro, the company's president, is well respected by clients as well as by the bands and entertainers he represents. He describes his business as very personalized, encouraging personal contact between each band leader and client, and you are guaranteed to get the group you requested. The DJs, who own their own companies, are subject to strict requirements: the group must have at least one year of solid experience, a tape, a song list, and a professional photograph. Read spot-checks his performers regularly. His second company, Bel-Aire Productions, provides the sound, technical know-how, and can oversee the flow of entertainment for any size event and for fairs, festivals, and corporate events. Most of the large high-tech companies in the area are among his satisfied customers.

If you don't have any special music in mind, Read can help you find the entertainment that best suits the activity. You can watch videos or listen to tapes to help you make your selection. He can also locate any band for you. He is always very nice and helpful, and stresses that he never sends performers other than the group contracted for. Some of the other types of entertainment he provides are modern or classical music, dance troupes, celebrity look-alikes, comedians, magicians, jugglers, mimes, clowns, and fun for children.

Innovative Entertainment

(415) 552-4276
FAX: (415) 552-3545
peter@inn-entertainment.com
kristen@inn-entertainment.com

888 Brannan Street, Suite 615
San Francisco, CA 94103

Contact: Peter Berliner or Kristen Radakovich

Service Area: National and International

Specialties: Full-service entertainment agency for every musical and entertaining aspect of the event

Price Range: varies from single entertainers and DJs to large orchestras and bands
Extra Charges: travel beyond Greater Bay Area, staging, lighting, lodging

Payment Terms: 50% deposit; balance due prior to event
Credit Cards: no

Lead Time: 1 day to 3 years
Playing Time: 1 hr. to full event coverage
Audience Requests: yes

From strolling violinists or a harpist at the ceremony, to a jazz trio during cocktails, to a romantic orchestra during dinner, and followed by an electrifying party dance band, Innovative Entertainment will produce every aspect of your evening's entertainment. "From soup to nuts," sums up Peter Berliner, owner and producer.

After his band disbanded back in 1975, Peter received a request to help book a band for an event, which gave him the idea of starting an entertainment agency. That was 23 years ago; the rest is history. Setting exceptionally high goals for himself, he opened an office in Sacramento, booking musical entertainment for county fairs, large Nevada casinos, and corporate headliners all over the world. In 1992, he opened his studio in San Francisco, closing the office in Sacramento in 1994.

I enjoy working with Innovative Entertainment because I know they take good care of my clients. As the representatives of many bands, including Encore, Dick Bright's SRO, the Dick Bright Orchestra, and Pride and Joy, they work only with a select group of acts, which I can depend on being of the highest professional and entertaining quality. From beginning to end, Peter takes care of everything, including lighting, staging, sound, security, and lodging. I feel additionally secure knowing that he will find a replacement in the case of an unforeseen emergency. They are licensed and bonded, thus protecting both the client and the band. "It's a party insurance. We take care of people – service on top of service," professes Peter.

Music Resource
A Complete Entertainment Service
422 Pine Street
Sausalito, CA 94965

(415) 331-7007
FAX: (415) 331-7778
SFbeat@sirius.com

Contact: Joseph Jordan or Coleman Burke

Service Area: Greater Bay Area and beyond

Specialties: Entertainment coordinators providing full service party and event production with emphasis on music and entertainment

Price Range: $250 - $10,000, depending on number of entertainers
Extra Charges: travel beyond Greater Bay Area

Payment Terms: 50% deposit, balance due day of event
Credit Cards: no

Lead Time: depends on entertainment
Audience Requests: yes

The idea for this company was born when Coleman Burke, leader of the well-known band, Pride and Joy, found himself being asked to provide music when his band was booked. He founded Music Resource (formerly MusicWorks) with his associate Joseph Jordan, who had worked several years for another music production company. The two make a great team.

The company provides affordable music for weddings as well as private and corporate events. Coleman, by trade, and Joseph, by interest, closely follow the music scene, and together have over 25 years of experience. They pride themselves in providing creative entertainment and are constantly on the lookout for fresh new talent. The company can arrange for all types of entertainment, as well as sound equipment, lighting, staging, and set designers. They see themselves more as music coordinators, letting the clients choose, but giving advice when asked. Audio and video tapes of and promotional material about the entertainers are available upon request.

Clients and peers alike compliment their excellent and ethical service.

Music Resource represents Pride and Joy, Northern California's perenially favorite party band.

North Bay Entertainment

(707) 224-0241
(707) 224-0364

1475 Fourth Street, Suites 2B & 2C
Napa, CA 94559

FAX: (707) 224-1376
northbay@wine.com

Contact: Thomas Schoenberger

Service Area: Greater Bay Area

Specialties: Full service agency providing all styles of music, from classical quartets to gospel choirs

Price Range: bands, $1,500 - $5,000/4 hrs.; DJs, $125 - 150/hr.
Extra Charges: travel beyond Wine Country

Payment Terms: 50% deposit, balance
                              due day of event
Credit Cards: no

Lead Time: 1 day to 1 year
Playing Time: 2 - 4 hrs.
Audience Requests: of course

"They are always on top of things and always come through. Their service is impeccable," raves one of their clients. That was the first of numerous recommendations I received about North Bay Entertainment, founded in 1991 by Thomas Schoenberger. An archaeologist by training and a composer, Thomas has studied music in the U.S. and Europe. He plays piano, violin, trumpet, guitar and flute. He also played in a band in college. He was motivated to start his own business after he was hired to improvise sonatas for a party, dressed up as Mozart.

Thomas wanted to create a new way of doing business for a music agency. Clients can talk to the musicians before sending tapes, and a staff member is present at many events to make sure everything is perfect. There are no hidden costs, gratuity or commission, and his consultation is complimentary.

Thomas has strict criteria for the performers he represents. In addition to being accomplished musicians, they must be punctual and responsible; speak intelligently and dress appropriately, and be well versed in social etiquette.

North Bay Entertainment offers an Atmospheric Division based in Marin and two Disc Jockey Divisions (East Bay & Sonoma), in addition to other offices in San Francisco and Santa Rosa. They are the exclusive agency for such high-level performers as Tim Hockenberry, The Bob Dalpe Orchestra, and the lovely, ethereal recording artist/pianist, Faranak. The company is the exclusive musical agency for the Big Four Napa/Sonoma Valley 4-Star Resorts (Auberge du Soleil, Meadowood Resort, Silverado Country Club, and Sonoma Mission Inn and Spa).

Thomas will not book strippers, rap music or "questionable" entertainment.

Rudolfi
Artists in Music
862-A DeHaro Street
San Francisco, CA 94107

(415) 550-1872
FAX: (415) 550-8027
Rudolfi@best.com
www.rudolfiartists.com

Contact: Peter Rudolfi

Service Area: Greater Bay Area, Napa, Sacramento, Monterey

Specialties: Unique combinations of instruments for classical music; large number
of dance bands: Swing to Contemporary

Price Range: various price ranges, from soloists to 18-piece bands
Extra Charges: travel, special lighting, augmented sound

Payment Terms: 50% deposit, balance
due 1 week prior to event
Credit Cards: no

Lead Time: 1 week to 1 year (subj. to availability)
Playing Time: 2 - 5 hrs. (2 hr. min)
Audience Requests: customized play lists

"Live music on the most special day of your life can be as beautiful and magical as the day itself. You and your guests see and hear the musicians creating the sound while also interacting with them. The songs you know are reinterpreted in a unique signature style." These are Peter's feelings about the spirit of live music at an event.

Peter is a composer, cellist, agent, and innovator. In the late 1970's, when classical musicians were playing only in concert halls, Peter found that this style of music also worked well in a wedding and party atmosphere. This inspired him to gather other kinds of musical groups and performers that fulfilled his vision. Today he offers a full-service agency with both classical soloists and ensembles as well as numerous popular dance bands.

Peter spends time reviewing, auditioning, and evaluating each group. Their ability to perform well and also conduct business are both important qualifications for representation at his agency. As a music expert, he provides a large selection of artists and performing groups from which a client can choose. Prior to meeting clients in person, Peter conducts a telephone interview. He inquires about the type of function, interest in music, number of guests, and type of audience that will be listening or dancing so that he will be completely prepared for the meeting. His studio wall is filled with cassettes, videos and CDs. Peter is very knowledgeable and welcomes the opportunity to educate a client about different instruments and combinations that work well together. You are able to compare many bands in one visit while taking your top choices home for extended listening. Peter has established a great repertoire of musical talents. He is comfortable letting you talk directly with the band or DJ, and may even be able to arrange for you to see them during a live performance. There is considerable value for you in being able to save time by previewing many performers at one time and in one place. Just knowing that Peter can find a last-minute replacement is of considerable assurance to any nervous bride or groom.

BANDS

A Swinging Affair

(707) 528-2342
FAX: (707) 566-0293
vocalist@sonic.net

(by appointment)
Santa Rosa, CA

Contact: Claire Victor

Service Area: Greater Bay Area and Wine Country

Specialties: Finger-poppin' music from Cha-Cha to Bossa to Swing, and more

Price Range: $950 - $2,500 depending on number of musicians and time
Extra Charges: early setup, parking, extensive travel, lighting

Payment Terms: 50% non-ref. deposit, balance due at start of event	**Lead Time:** 24 hrs. to 18 months
	Playing Time: 3 - 6 hrs.
Credit Cards: no	**Audience Requests:** always welcomed

"Add a jigger of moonlight to a touch of class, sprinkle with piano ivories, then shake with catchy rhythms and serve with lush vocals on top for a sensory delight sure to please the most discerning ear," is lead vocalist Claire Victor's recipe for A Swinging Affair. This just about sums them up.

Claire's vast experience as a jazz singer with some of "the greats" as well as co-founder of the dance band "The Mix" makes her an authority on what ingredients are needed to make a great band. A Swinging Affair is just that. From their smooth polished rhythm to their finger-poppin' beat, they are a solid, yet versatile group. Their music not only entertains but also gets you in the mood.

Located in Sonoma County and tailor-made for the wild, yet sophisticated sounds of the cocktail set, they are no strangers to Wine Country weddings and corporate events. They can arrange a solo piano or vocalist, or up to a 7-piece band for a romantic ceremony, elegant cocktail reception, or a rockin' celebration. Claire can also comfort you with expert advice and scheduling tips.

Satisfied clients claim, "They can do anything, ANYTHING!" Claire invites you to make your next affair "A Swinging Affair…with rhythm that is hot, music that is cool, and a band that knows how to have fun."

Bobbe Norris & Larry Dunlap
Music Performance & Production
P.O. Box 1028
Pacifica, CA 94044

(650) 359-5996
FAX: (650) 359-2314

Contact: Larry Dunlap

Service Area: Greater Bay Area and beyond

Specialties: Dance and background music (Standards, Motown, Swing, Latin, Jazz, Top 40s, Classical); solo piano to 18-piece band; piano ceremony music (optional flute, vocalist)

Price Range: solo piano, from $200; 5-piece band, from $1,150
Extra Charges: travel, early setup, extensive consultation

Payment Terms: 50% non-ref. deposit,
                 balance due day of event
Credit Cards: no

Lead Time: 24 hours to 9 months
Playing Time: 2 - 6 hrs.
Audience Requests: yes

Bobbe Norris and Larry Dunlap are two well-known names in the Bay Area jazz and entertainment scene. As a piano-vocal duo or with bands of up to 18 musicians, they have performed at the Monterey Jazz Festival and as far away as Canada, the Bahamas, and throughout Europe. When I last interviewed them, they had just recorded their latest album, and Larry had recently performed one of his compositions with a school orchestra in San Jose.

Bobbe, with her wonderful, rich contralto voice, was well on her way to stardom when she decided to quit the scene after a record company advised her to sing in styles that wouldn't show her true talents. Larry played piano during high school and pursued a degree in composition. He has written for bands, and has performed and recorded with Cleo Laine and John Dankworth. He was also musical director for the Pointer Sisters and is considered one of the top piano players in the area. When Larry met Bobbe, he encouraged her to sing again. They have recorded several albums together and individually, and were featured together in the *San Francisco Examiner* and in *California Jazz-Now*.

Accompanied by bass and percussion players, Larry at the piano and Bobbe as vocalist set the mood for a wonderful jazz evening at Garden City. Bobbe truly glows while performing and likes playing musical games with husband Larry during the performance.

Their clients speak very highly of them, commenting on their versatility, accommodating style, and professionalism. "They have a great beat. Every song they play is danceable!" A fellow musician even went as far as saying, "Larry is one of the business' 'heavy weights' and Bobbe is one of the best jazz singers in the area."

Body & Soul

(510) 527-1685 (Kevin)
(510) 464-3018 (Deborah)
webmaster@bodynsoul.com
www.bodynsoul.com

(by appointment)
Richmond, CA

Contact: Kevin or Deborah

Service Area: Greater Bay Area and beyond

Specialties: 8-piece band playing a wide range of very danceable Funk, Soul, and R&B

Price Range: from $1,800
Extra Charges: travel beyond immediate Bay Area, lights, early setup, overtime

Payment Terms: 30% non-ref. deposit, balance due 90 days prior to event	**Lead Time:** 2 weeks to 1 year
	Playing Time: 3 - 5 hrs.
Credit Cards: no	**Audience Requests:** yes

So you want a band that sounds like the real thing? How about a band that not only authentically covers a wide range of danceable Funk, Soul, and Rhythm and Blues from the '60s to the '90s, but will also gladly fulfill requests for any tune you desire. You've found it in Body & Soul.

In existence since 1994, Body & Soul pride themselves on their loyalty to the original song. They like to play and sing the version familiar to everyone. Their ability to combine their upbeat style while playing '60s Motown with the same energy as contemporary '90s makes this band ideal for any crowd that likes to dance. After hearing just a few songs, I could tell that they keep the young in the groove and the old in the mood.

All of Body & Soul's musicians have been professional performers for many years and come from many genres. This comes in handy when entertaining a mixed range of ages. With three lead vocalists in front of a solid rhythm section consisting of keyboards, guitar, bass, drums, and a horn section, this is a well-balanced band. This combination not only creates a full sound but also allows flexibility to perform various styles in different arrangements.

Kevin McCarthy, band leader, bassist, and webmaster, with 27 years of experience on the local music scene, has created a dynamic party band. Lead vocalists Deborah Coley (jazz and ballads) and Calvin Taylor (soul, funk and ballads) are "the perfect complement to each other," as Kevin describes. With the addition of Peter Frankel (vocalist for Motown, Stax-Volt, R&B, and Rock) and backed by the rhythm section, you have an ultra-tight band each with distinct styles.

Ecstatic clients agree, "This is a group of personable, talented professionals whose upbeat music will have everybody dancing."

Classic Sounds

(408) 866-2594
(Phone & FAX)
www.cambrianpark.com/bbsounds

(by appointment)
Campbell, CA

Contact: Mark Russo

Service Area: Greater Bay Area and beyond

Specialties: Trio to 12-piece orchestra playing a variety of Swing, Big Band, Ballad, Waltz, Rhumba, Latin, Disco and Rock

Price Range: trio (flute, cello, violin), from $400; 12-piece orchestra, from $2,200; smaller ensembles available
Extra Charges: travel beyond 1 hour

Payment Terms: 50% deposit, balance due 1 week prior to event
Credit Cards: no

Lead Time: 1 month to 1 year
Playing Time: 1 - 6 hrs.
Audience Requests: yes

There is just something about the sound of a full orchestra that enriches a classic, elegant social affair, such as a wedding. Mark Russo's Classic Sounds, with their variety of music and diverse styles, adds just that touch.

A graduate of the Berkelee School of Music in Boston, Mark Russo is fluent in classical, jazz and blues styles. He has been a woodwind instructor since 1990 and a faculty member at the Community School of Music and Arts. As a professional musician, he has toured with many well-known artists like Vic Damone, Mel Torme, George Kirby, and Albert King. An Indie Award nominee and KKSF play list artist, Mark currently has 2 Christmas albums, "Instrumental Christmas" and "Season's Silhouette," on the market.

Mark performs with a number of local and Bay Area talents. His group, Classic Sounds, can perform as a trio for the ceremony, provide a jazz pianist for the cocktail reception, then progress to an 12-piece orchestra for the reception. Their classy setup and crisp sound are matched by their stylish performance. At a wedding I attended, the brass section had the rich sound of a big band without being overpowering. Debbie Sarti's dreamy renditions of "Fly Me to the Moon" and "Wish Upon A Star" were magnificent. Once dinner was over, they jazzed up with a dance session mixed with rock, pop, salsa, and a variety of contemporary favorites, bringing a classic sound to the classic event.

Clients and vendors rave about Mark's accommodating manner and talent. "I cannot think of anyone who cares more about his music and clients, and the guests realize this when he plays."

Cool Jerks
The Entertainment Connection
1202 Lincoln Avenue, Suite 101
San Jose, CA 95125

(408) 275-6325
FAX: (408) 275-1902
entconnect@aol.com

Contact: Read Zaro (exclusive agent)

Service Area: Greater Bay Area, Northern California

Specialties: Motown, R&B, Funk, Soul, Rock 'n' Roll

Price Range: from $3,200
Extra Charges: travel beyond 60 miles

Payment Terms: 50% deposit, balance due day of event
Credit Cards: Visa, MasterCard, Discover

Lead Time: 4 months to 1 year
Playing Time: 4 hrs.
Audience Requests: yes

For over 15 years the Cool Jerks have been putting on a sizzling performance. This 9-piece band combines a cool rhythm section and hair-raising horn section, accompanying energized lead vocalists Dave Robinson and Julie Moreno – a powerful combination. David, a professional singer for over 24 years, joined Cool Jerks in 1996. His electrifying vocals mixed with his funky dance moves are balanced by Julie's sensational, wide vocal range. Julie has been singing with the band since 1993.

The Cool Jerks' energy is contagious. During a special event at the San Jose Fairmont, people couldn't stay away from the dance floor. The group's combined dance steps, together with David Robinson joining the crowd on the dance floor, contributed to a truly dynamic show. What impressed me was that, throughout the evening, a sound-check person was always present, calculating the vocals against the music. Each song was adjusted to enhance the musicians or the vocalists. This made the sax lead-in to Julie Moreno's rendition of "Since I Fell for You" a sensational performance. This party band delivers the best in Motown, R&B, Soul, Rock 'n' Roll, and even a bit of Big Band Swing to round things out.

Enthusiastic fans comment: "The Cool Jerks fit any location you need them to. They'll play mellow when you want and rock the place when needed." "The horn section's dance medley is worth the entertainment alone." "The night of your party, remember to book them for next year or you'll lose out."

The Essentials

(415) 499-5643
GPizzino@aol.com

(by appointment)
San Rafael, CA

Contact: Greg Pizzino

Service Area: Coast to Coast

Specialties: 5- to 8-piece band playing R&B, Rock 'n' Roll, Soul, Motown, Standards (Sinatra, Bennett)

Price Range: $500 - $3,500, from 3-piece to 10-piece band
Extra Charges: travel beyond Bay Area, early setup

Payment Terms: 40% non-ref. deposit, balance due day of event
Credit Cards: no

Lead Time: 1 week to 1 year
Playing Time: 1 - 4 hrs.
Audience Requests: yes

I met The Essentials during the early days of my research and have continued to receive recommendations about them. Most of the band members have been together for over ten years. Bassist Greg Pizzino, who has assembled the band's repertoire over the years, is the contact person. Steve Mayer, keyboardist, has written the band's horn charts, which are highly praised by musicians and listeners alike. Tim Bickel, on drums, has been the band's driving rhythmic force for years. Lorn Leber, guitarist and formerly with the Jerry Garcia Band, is a talented player who is well versed in all styles of music and adds immensely to The Essentials' mix. The band has recently added a new dimension to their presentation with vocalists Larry Batiste and Keta Bill. Larry and Keta, well-known musicians in the Bay Area, have performed with such groups as Zasu Pitts and Big Bang Beat. The horn players on their demo tape and heard at live performances, are from such groups as Huey Lewis and the News, and Toni, Tone, Tone.

Their music is smashing, and what makes them special is their wide variety of styles. They have a large repertoire of over 200 songs since their primary activity in earlier years was playing in clubs. Now the business focuses on playing for corporate and private events. However, they still make club appearances, so it's easy for prospective clients to get a taste of their performances. The place was packed when I heard them. They played mostly jazz, and almost all the guests moved to the beat. They can play a wide variety of music for events, particularly weddings. A classical duo can perform music for the ceremony on saxophone, keyboard, flute and guitar. A jazz trio can play during the meal, followed by a full-blown band for dancing.

Clients think they are a polished, talented, and versatile group, and very easy to work with. Joel Selvin of the *San Francisco Chronicle* and David Plotnikoff of the *San Jose Mercury News* hail the band as one of their Bay Area favorites. The group has recorded two albums.

The Full Tilt! Band
Live Music for All Occasions
(by appointment)
San Anselmo, CA

(415) 331-5221
(415) 459-3223
FAX: (415) 459-5115
www.ByRecOnly.com/fulltilt

Contact: Donna Spitzer

Service Area: Greater Bay Area

Specialties: 4- to 6-piece Variety Band playing Swing, Classic Rock, Blues, Jazz, Contemporary

Price Range: $1,200 - $1,800
Extra Charges: travel beyond 1 hour, early setup

Payment Terms: 50% non-ref. deposit, balance due week of event
Credit Cards: no

Lead Time: 1 day to 1 year
Playing Time: 1 - 6 hrs.
Audience Requests: yes

The Full Tilt! Band was setting up for a wedding when I first saw them. They were quite an impressive sight in their tuxedo attire, including Donna, the petite, blond band leader. I've heard about them several times since then. Just the other day, a mansion coordinator remarked, "Oh, the Full Tilt! They're among my favorite bands."

Donna is a former Montessori school teacher. She used to perform with a choir, and in theaters and cabaret shows as a singer and actor until 1988 when she started her own band. Her band members have worked with such famous artists as Van Morrison, Jerry Garcia, James Brown, and Celine Dion. The band's drummer has a background in New Orleans-style and Afro-Haitian music. The band is popular with the West Coast swing dance clubs around the Bay Area. Many of the male band members are strong lead vocalists as is Donna on lead female vocals. While the band plays in clubs and for public events, their main business is now performing for private and corporate functions. I heard them at a summer street fair in San Rafael along with many passersby who stopped to watch and listen to their professional entertainment.

Donna is proud of her customer service. She will send out a song list, a demo tape, and will meet the client in person or consult over the phone. The band will learn special songs, charging for this only if the requests are numerous.

The Garage Band
Weddings, Corporate & Special Events
1202 Lincoln Avenue, Suite 101
San Jose, CA 95125

(408) 275-6325
FAX: (408) 275-1902
entconnect@aol.com

Contact: Read Zaro (exclusive agent)

Service Area: Greater Bay Area

Specialties: Music from the '40s to the '90s

Price Range: from $2,400
Extra Charges: travel beyond 60 miles

Payment Terms: 50% deposit, balance due day of event
Credit Cards: Visa, MasterCard, Discover

Lead Time: 4 - 6 months
Playing Time: 4 hrs.
Audience Requests: yes

While doing research for the previous edition of the guide, it seemed that the Garage Band was the most popular source of entertainment, even more popular than eight years ago when I received several recommendations about them. They are a very versatile 6-piece band with a great female lead singer. I thoroughly enjoyed listening to them at the Fairmont Hotel in San Jose. Their transitions from one song to the next are especially smooth. I also heard them at a friend's wedding. My husband and I danced so much to the smashing music from yesterday and today that I was sore for the next few days.

The band emphasizes their ability to play just about every request if the music is on hand, which is quite likely since they come well prepared to every job. They read the crowd well and take breaks when appropriate to the flow of the event.

The Garage Band is so named since they started in a garage in 1984. The garage is now a recording studio. All band members are professional players who have performed in bands since their college days.

The band also offers a horn section as an option. Their exclusive agent is Read Zaro who can send their demo tape to you. He can also provide you with a performance schedule, song list, and pictures.

The Jazz Workshop
Octet and Big Bands
P.O. Box 2544
Sunnyvale, CA 94087

(408) 739-2788
(Phone & FAX)
pager: (408) 322-7715
Workshop@accesscom.com
www.jazzworkshop.com

Contact: Clay Buckley

Service Area: Northern California

Specialties: 3- to 16-piece band playing Big Band, Swing, Jazz, Latin, Dixieland, Motown, R&B, Oldies, Rock 'n' Roll, contemporary music; string quartet or harp

Price Range: from $375
Extra Charges: none

Payment Terms: 30% non-ref. deposit, balance due day of event
Credit Cards: no

Lead Time: 2 - 3 months
Playing Time: unlimited
Audience Requests: yes

Most of the members of the Jazz Workshop, with bassist Clay Buckley, have been playing together since 1986. This extraordinary octet and big band is well known for its versatility and broad musical range. They have played at the Garden City Jazz Club, Cafe Jazz, and at most of the major Bay Area hotels. They have also performed at the Paul Masson and Mirassou wineries, the Gilroy Garlic Festival, and numerous outdoor events and concerts in Northern California. The group was honored with an invitation to play at a Foothill College-sponsored fund-raiser in 1995 before such distinguished guests as former President Bush and Colin Powell.

To be flexible, The Jazz Workshop offers several options: a 5-piece wedding band, playing Swing tunes or tunes from the '60s and '70s; a jazz quartet playing Jazz standards; a Dixieland group; a strolling banjo to 6 pieces playing music of the '20s and '30s. The "Dixie Cats" come attired in straw hats, red vests and bow ties. An octet or big band with up to 16 pieces can be provided at an extremely reasonable cost.

I heard them play in parks in the area. All the spectators enjoyed their performance, featuring the music of Glen Miller, the Dorseys, Benny Goodman, Woody Herman, Duke Ellington, Nat and Natalie Cole, Billy Joel, James Brown, and Aretha Franklin.

A customer who had hired them for a '20s theme party told me that The Jazz Workshop had perfectly matched the dance music repertoire to the theme. Newlyweds told me about the beautiful music they had played at their wedding. From time to time you will read about The Jazz Workshop in local newspapers; the *San Jose Mercury News*' Leigh Weimers wrote, "They do everything but windows!"

The Joe Sharino Band
California's #1 Party Band
P.O. Box 2343
Oakhurst, CA 93644

(831) 722-4344
(Bay Area Office)
www.JSBand.com

Contact: Joe Sharino

Service Area: Greater Bay Area and Western U.S.

Specialties: 4- to 9-piece high energy band specializing in music from the '40s to '90s (Pop, Rock, Motown, Funk, Disco, Country, Big Band and Swing); audience participation

Price Range: Saturdays, $3,800 - $4,800; Fridays & Sundays, $2,900 - $3,700; higher in December
Extra Charges: travel beyond Bay Area, custom songs written for event

Payment Terms: 50% deposit, balance due day of event
Credit Cards: no

Lead Time: 2 months to 1 year (try anytime)
Playing Time: 2 - 6 hrs.
Audience Requests: yes

The Joe Sharino Band is one of the most popular dance bands in the South Bay. They have received 12 "Best Band" awards from such publications as the *San Jose Mercury News*, *Metro Magazine*, *Good Times* magazine, and from KGO radio in San Francisco. The band has appeared in national telecasts on Showtime, NBC, and ABC. The band was recently chosen from among 90 Bay Area bands as the "House Band" for the San Francisco Forty Niners, and they perform at most home games at the stadium. Joe and the band have performed for virtually every major corporation in the Bay Area, the California State House of Representatives, and at nearly 250 weddings. They have also played at major casinos in Lake Tahoe and Las Vegas.

The band is known for its high-energy dance music and for their ability to involve the audience. Joe gets people to sing along and keeps the dance floor full. Joe reads the audience well, and their wide variety of styles makes it easy for them to please everyone. He told me that they play longer sets and take fewer breaks than other bands.

Joe celebrated his 25th year in business in March 1998, and with all his success, he hasn't changed a bit. He is very nice and accommodating, will help schedule the flow of the event, and can write a custom song for a wedding or corporate event. Included in the price is early setup, lights and sound, and taped music or CDs played before the band starts and during the breaks.

Joe had invited me to the Cocoanut Grove where the band played each Friday in August. The place was packed as was the dance floor. You just couldn't help but move with the beat. Joe's feel for the audience, his musicality, his ability to fill almost all requests, and his personality and good looks make him so popular.

Larry Lynch and the MOB
Featuring 5 Decades of Great Dance Music
1202 Lincoln Avenue, Suite 101
San Jose, CA 95125

(408) 275-6325
FAX: (408) 275-1902
entconnect@aol.com

Contact: Read Zaro of The Entertainment Connection (exclusive agent)

Service Area: Greater Bay Area

Specialties: Music from the '40s to the '90s; Rock, Big Band, Swing, Motown, and Disco; dinner music

Price Range: from $2,500
Extra Charges: travel beyond 60 miles

Payment Terms: 25% deposit (50% in Dec.), balance due day of event
Credit Cards: Visa, MasterCard, Discover

Lead Time: 3 months (but try anytime)
Playing Time: 4 hrs.
Audience Requests: yes

From the '40s to the '90s, Larry Lynch and the Mob have one of the widest arrays of popular musical selections of any dance band. Lead male vocalist and drummer, Larry Lynch was formerly with the Greg Kihn Band for nine years and a vocalist on their #1 hit *Jeopardy*. He has toured the world with many top-hit bands, including Peter Gabriel, Tom Petty & The Heartbreakers, the Rolling Stones, Journey, and many others.

Since 1985, Larry has led the MOB, a 5-piece, energetic dance band. Lauren Alexander, lead female vocalist; Robbie Dunbar on lead guitar and vocals; Jonathan Bassil on bass, and Tim Strandberg, on saxophone and keyboard bring their extensive, live performance experience to the band.

Seeing them perform live, you can feel their energy. For an upscale wedding I attended at Ralston Hall, the tables could not get cleared fast enough to expand the dance floor to accommodate a dance session of Hava Nagila. From that moment on, the dance floor was packed. The MOB kept up the momentum by their selection of music and smooth transition from one song to the next. You know people are having a great time when even the few guests still seated were singing and clapping their hands to the music.

Reviews from their clients are nothing less than outstanding. One client expressed, "You really made the party; just hope we didn't wear you out." On the down side, "This band is always booked!"

Magnolia Jazz Band
From Elegant Trio to Dance Combo
P.O. Box 2739
Sunnyvale, CA 94087

(408) 245-9120
FAX: (408) 746-0570
robbie@magnoliajazz.com
www.magnoliajazz.com

Contact: Robbie Schlosser

Service Area: Greater Bay Area

Specialties: 3- to 7-piece band playing traditional jazz, Dixieland, hits of the '20s, '30s and '40s, and Swing (Benny Goodman, Glen Miller, Duke Ellington)

Price Range: $700 - $2,000
Extra Charges: travel beyond Bay Area, early setup

Payment Terms: 50% deposit, balance due day of event
Credit Cards: no

Lead Time: 1 week to 1 year
Playing Time: min. 2 hrs., no max.
Audience Requests: yes

The Magnolia Jazz Band is well established in the Bay Area music scene, having performed at thousands of events since 1975. The band specializes in Swing-era standards and Dixieland favorites. Their music can be upbeat, danceable, or serve as an elegant background. You can hire every size group, from a strolling trio to a 7-piece dance combo.

The Magnolia Jazz Band was recommended to me several times. I have listened to them at various parties and always thoroughly enjoy their music. Robbie Schlosser, a former science teacher and now the band leader, is well respected by customers and peers. He is very friendly and accommodating, and can help you with music selection. Each event is discussed and customized during a personal meeting – from the wedding ceremony, to background music during dinner, to upbeat dance music. Robbie compares the band to a good waiter who always provides what the customer wants. Most of the musicians have been playing with him for a long time.

To see the band live, request a performance schedule from Robbie. Ask for their event calendar, demo cassette, buy one of their recordings, or visit them on the Internet.

Merging Traffic

(408) 270-4407

(by appointment)
San Jose, CA

Contact: Richard Santi or Maureen Minhoto

Service Area: Greater Bay Area

Specialties: 3- to 8-piece versatile band, featuring Top 40s, Big Band, Swing,
            Ballroom, Rock, Motown, Disco, Funk, Ethnic, Classical; wedding ceremonies

Price Range: $1,100 - $2,600 for 4 hours
Extra Charges: none

Payment Terms: 1/3 deposit, balance
                due day of event
Credit Cards: no

Lead Time: 1 day to 2 years
Playing Time: 2 - 8 hrs.
Audience Requests: yes

Merging Traffic, an important component of the private and corporate event scene in the Bay Area, was recommended to me several times. Through continually high-quality performances and their warm and honest personalities, they have made many friends among peers and clients alike. Maureen and Richard, the heart of Merging Traffic, have been together since 1980. They used to play in nightclubs and built a large repertoire of songs during that time. Today they prefer to play at parties and weddings because of the more intense response. I attended one of the private auditions that they hold about every four to six weeks for prospective clients. They feel this demonstrates their talent better than a sample tape, and they are able to get to know their customers.

Maureen, lead singer, is very pretty and, despite her petite size, has a wonderful, strong alto voice. Richard plays the electronic keyboard that can generate various instrument voices, giving the band more depth. There are usually 3 to 8 performers; however, on request, the band can have as many as 12 professional musicians.

At parties, they adjust their music to the mood of the guests. Sometimes they play up to two hours continuously, depending on the mood. They only take breaks during natural pauses, such as the cake-cutting ceremony. They specially learn songs for their clients; Maureen once asked a Jewish neighbor for help with Hebrew pronunciation. The band has the largest repertoire of ethnic songs I have come across.

Jim & Morning Nichols
The Nichols Band
(by appointment)
Pacifica, CA

(650) 355-4535
FAX: (650) 359-3056
morning@nicholsmusic.com
www.nicholsmusic.com

Contact: Jim or Morning Nichols

Service Area: Greater Bay Area

Specialties: Dance music (Classic Rock, Swing, Jazz, Latin, some ethnic); up to 17-piece band; solo guitar and versatile voice

Price Range: from $200 for solo
Extra Charges: none

Payment Terms: 25% - 50% deposit, balance due day of event
Credit Cards: no

Lead Time: 1 week to 1 year
Playing Time: 1 - 4 hrs. plus
Audience Requests: yes

Jim and Morning Nichols are a delightful couple and versatile, dedicated musicians. You can't go wrong in hiring them for your party because not only are they great musicians but also very easygoing and accommodating. For example, when Morning was asked if she would perform the BRO song at my last party, her answer was simply, "Sure!" The pair can perform with any size group, and can provide music for the ceremony, dinner and dancing. After talking to their clients, they will turn their ideas into the entertainment that never fails to meet their clients' expectations.

Morning has performed extensively at a variety of concerts, clubs, and festivals, including the Monterey Jazz Festival and the Mabel Mercer West Coast Cabaret Convention. Jim has played with Kenny Rankin, Tom Waits, and other artists, and has appeared on television ("The Tonight Show"), radio, recordings, and at clubs. He has also performed at Carnegie Hall. Morning and Jim have released three CDs with GSP Recordings, which have received extensive national air play. Together they co-lead the Nichols Band. Jim's brother, John, is the lead male vocalist and bass player, and their fine drummer also sings. Other talented musicians join the Nichols to perform at a wide variety of musical engagements, such as the Black & White Ball in San Francisco and the Fillmore and Union Street fairs. Since 1994, they have annually toured France, England, Germany, and Finland.

I had such a wonderful time talking to Morning and Jim, and listening to the songs they performed in their home just for me. I later heard them perform with Smith Dobson at Garden City, a jazz club in the South Bay. The audience cheered wildly. Jim is considered one of the best local jazz guitarists. Morning has a beautiful voice and sings even complex jazz sequences with ease. She also excites her audiences by singing rock 'n' roll and rhythm and blues. Sample tapes are available.

Eddie Pasternak
Guitarist/Band Leader
(by appointment)
Oakland, CA

(510) 655-5783
(Phone & FAX)

Contact: Eddie Pasternak

Service Area: Greater Bay Area

Specialties: "Big Band" to the "Big Chill" eras; interpretations of Jazz, Swing, Latin standards, Motown, R&B, Rock 'n' Roll

Price Range: $250 - $500/musician depending on time, day, size of band, and distance
Extra Charges: none

Payment Terms: 50% non-ref. deposit, balance due day of event
Credit Cards: no

Lead Time: 1 week to 1 year
Playing Time: no min / no max
Audience Requests: yes

A highly experienced guitarist and bandleader, Eddie Pasternak presents polished wedding performers and music that appeals to guests of all ages. Over the past two decades, Eddie has made a success of hundreds of wedding ceremonies and receptions.

Eddie performs as a soloist as well as in a variety of ensemble settings, ranging from duos to large dance bands. Working with the Bay Area's finest musicians, he will create an ensemble that is specific to your musical taste and that will perfectly complement your event.

"Your wedding reception is probably the biggest party you'll ever plan. I can help you create the right atmosphere for your celebration," comments Eddie. During the wedding ceremony and early in the reception, he generally plays romantic classics, songs easily recognized, and with the warmth and sentiment appropriate to the moment. As the festivities progress, he gets the guests up and dancing with music ranging from the Big Band to the Big Chill eras, with an added pinch of Caribbean Spice and Salsa Picante. You can be sure that, throughout the event, his band will perform with unflagging musicality and enthusiasm.

References think he is one of the best guitarists in the area. They love his professional approach, his reliability, and his personality.

Richard Olsen Orchestras

(415) 831-3367
FAX: (415) 831-3995
richband@sirius.com

(by appointment)
San Francisco, CA

Contact: Richard Olsen

Service Area: Coast to Coast

Specialties: Versatile Big Band playing a variety of music from Swing to Motown, from '70s to contemporary; 5- to 17-piece bands; duos, trios, and strings for background or ceremony

Price Range: $500 - $10,000
Extra Charges: travel, early setup

Payment Terms: 50% deposit, balance
due day of event
Credit Cards: no

Lead Time: 3 days to 1 year
Playing Time: 2 - 4 hrs., overtime available
Audience Requests: yes

Slim's nightclub named Richard Olsen's Orchestra "the Bay Area's most versatile Big Band." When I listened to them at an event at the California Academy of Sciences, the dance floor was constantly full. During a break I heard some people asking, "You play so well, how come we haven't heard you before?" I saw Richard and his band again this year at the event, and the caterer told me how they had checked out several bands and couldn't find any better.

Almost 20 years ago Richard, an accomplished saxophonist, clarinetist, flutist and singer, started as the leader of a rock band. His current band has been together for over 10 years. Most of his advertising is by word of mouth. His clients are society and corporate people who have been enjoying his fine music for a long time. He has also played for every major hotel in the city. Besides his own Big Band, Richard can provide combos of four or five musicians performing everything from Swing, to Latin, Country/Western, Disco, and Contemporary Rock. String combos perform Broadway show tunes, and strolling, dancing and background music. Solo instruments, such as piano, guitar, harp, violin, and banjo, are also available.

During a long conversation Richard told me about his work and his ethics. Depending on the event, he will adjust the volume so people can talk. He can easily anticipate what has to be done from his years of experience and by working with the other vendors to coordinate the entire event; for example, not playing dance music while the hot food is being served. "We are here to work together for the client the best we can, not outdoing each other" is his motto. Tuxedos are his band's usual attire.

At one very elegant wedding reception, he provided 12 violinists, standing on pedestals, serenading guests during dinner, followed by a 17-piece Big Band for dancing.

Richie Begin and the Soul University

(831) 426-9040

(Phone & FAX)

P.O. Box 4121
Santa Cruz, CA 95063

www.ByRecOnly.com/souluniversity

Contact: Richie Begin

Service Area: Northern California

Specialties: Progressive entertainment from Swing to Soul

Price Range: $800 - $2,500
Extra Charges: travel beyond Bay Area

Payment Terms: 50% deposit, balance due day of event
Credit Cards: no

Lead Time: to 1 year
Playing Time: 1 - 4 hrs.
Audience Requests: yes

Progressive entertainment from wedding ceremony, to piano for the cocktail hour and trio for dinner, to a full dance band for the reception and party, Soul University is an all-in-one, versatile band.

Richie Begin, former lead singer and founder of "The Cool Jerks," has been a consummate entertainer and band leader for over 12 years. In addition to composing, he has been a columnist for *Good Times* magazine in Santa Cruz for 12 years. The name "Soul University" honors the history of Soul music in America, spanning the last three decades. Richie's energizing personality is reflected in his performance, and his trademark – a red tuxedo jacket with matching red patent leather shoes.

Soul University is comprised of band members from many famous West Coast bands, including Tower of Power and Miami Sound Machine. Their enduring popularity stems from their versatility as a source for all of the evening's musical needs, from Big Band and Swing favorites to boogie dancing, to Motown and Soul tunes. Perhaps it's Richie's "Al Green voice" together with Lori Hofer's harmonizing vocals that keep the audience wanting more.

I had the opportunity to listen to Soul University at an elegant wedding at the Spectrum Gallery. Their blend of instruments and vocals kept the crowd on the dance floor all night. Even the bartender from behind the bar couldn't help but play air guitar along with the band.

Shtetlblasters
From Jerusalem to Motown
(by appointment)
Berkeley, CA

(510) 287-2540
FAX: (510) 215-6554
sounds@microweb.com
www.microweb.com/sounds

Contact: Michael Gill

Service Area: California

Specialties: Multi-faceted 7-piece band specializing in traditional Jewish music and R&B

Price Range: from $1,800
Extra Charges: travel beyond Bay Area

Payment Terms: 25% non-ref. deposit, balance due day of event
Credit Cards: no

Lead Time: 1 month to 1 year
Playing Time: 4 hrs.
Audience Requests: yes

The Shtetlblasters' logo, an electric guitar silhouette playing on a rooftop, is illustrative of this band's multi-faceted repertoire. Their name ("shtetl," Eastern European Jewish villages, and "blaster," a portable tape player) is a play on words that describes the band's soulful music, including Ashkenazic (Eastern European Jewish, including Klezmer), Sephardic (Ladino), Mizrachi (Middle Eastern Jewish), and American musical styles.

From traditional Jewish to Motown, the Shtetlblasters bridge two cultures. The band members, all of whom sing, are Michael Gill (keyboards and woodwinds), Achi Ben Shalom (acoustic guitar), Jan Padover (Middle Eastern and Latin percussion), Callie Thomas (vocals), Bruce Barth (electric guitar), Scott Urquhart (bass guitar), Brad McKeague (drums and percussion), and Rick Ellis (percussion). Together they add texture and just the right pitch to every piece.

This progressive band can be split into different sections, from traditional or contemporary music for the ceremony, to jazz music for cocktails, to authentic Israeli folkdance instruction, to a rocking party band for the reception.

Playing since 1990, the Shtetlblasters are great at reading the room, from leading the guests in Israeli folk dancing to switching to easy listening so that guests can converse during dinner. They compose many of their own songs and welcome the opportunity to learn a special first dance for the bride and groom. One of the many times I worked with them, they surprised the entire room by a cappella serenading the bride and groom with "Always in Love," a special song composed by Scott. A reference commented, "Their high-energy renditions of big band tunes and popular dance hits are contagious."

Spats
Patti Lyles Band
P.O. Box 67275
Scotts Valley, CA 95067

(831) 335-7767
FAX: (831) 335-7326
spats@scruznet.com
www.pattilylesproductions.com

Contact: Patti Lyles

Service Area: Greater Bay Area

Specialties: Multi-instrumentalist entertainers from the Big Band Era to the contemporary sounds of today; Jewish weddings, Bar/Bat Mitzvahs; disc jockey services and expert planning

Price Range: 3- to 6-piece band, from $900
Extra Charges: travel; early setup

Payment Terms: 50% non-ref. deposit, balance due day of event
Credit Cards: no

Lead Time: 1 day to 1 year
Playing Time: 2 - 6 hrs.
Audience Requests: yes

Spats' top hat and cane logo representing "The Ultimate Entertainer" is indicative of the Patti Lyles Band. Spats is a group of talented, multi-instrumentalists and vocalists, each of whom is versed in different musical styles from the '20s Big Band Era to Smash Mouth/Alternative Rock, giving them one of the largest repertoires of any band I know. Their inclusive DJ services ensure that there is never any "white noise," only continuous music throughout the evening. "We are not a generic or typical wedding band," says Patti, lead vocalist.

Patti's background adds greatly to this successful party band. In 1982, she owned a band named Touch of Gold, a house band for Hyatt Hotel in Burlingame. Her extensive experience as an entertainment contractor gave her the luxury of handpicking some of the top musicians in the industry – musicians well-versed, multi-talented, professional and reliable – to represent Spats. Having coordinated so many events, she's like a magician taking care of the "smoke & mirrors" details each event has behind the scenes. This is critical to a band since they usually set the pace of the event. Patti meets with her clients at a convenient location to discuss the schedule of events and timeline. She even provides the schedule to the client's various vendors!

Patti's powerful singing voice and entertainment ability as master of ceremonies, highlighting all the special moments, is Spats' trademark. "A solid, all-around professional band," clients rave.

Swing Fever

(415) 459-2428
FAX: (415) 459-8964
SwingFev@sirius.com
www.SwingFever.com

(by appointment)
San Rafael, CA

Contact: Bryan Gould

Service Area: West Coast

Specialties: Swing, Big Band, music of the '30s and '40s in small band form, Latin, R&B; 3- to 8-piece band; solo guitar, or flute and guitar for ceremonies

Price Range: $1,000 - $3,000
Extra Charges: travel beyond Bay Area, early setup

Payment Terms: 50% deposit, balance due 3 days prior to event
Credit Cards: no

Lead Time: 1 day to 18 months
Playing Time: 2 - 6 hrs.
Audience Requests: yes

Founded in the late '70s by trombonist Bryan Gould, Swing Fever is well known among Glenn Miller and jazz lovers in the Bay Area. They have performed at many jazz festivals and have appeared at the last four Black & White Balls in San Francisco, the San Francisco Art Institute's 125th anniversary dinner, the Napa Valley Wine Auction, Willie Brown's mayoral inauguration, and at countless corporate and private functions. Bryan recently told me that they have now played for more than 700 weddings. You can catch their performances at clubs around the Bay Area, and their second album, featuring Duke Ellington trumpeter Clark Terry, is currently available in local stores.

The members of the core band, consisting of five pieces (saxophone, trombone, guitar, bass, and drums), have been together for a long time. The group can be enlarged to include seven pieces and a female vocalist. One of the more well-known members is Harold Jones (drums) who worked for Count Basie and Sarah Vaughn for many years, as well as for Natalie Cole. Bryan (band leader and trombonist) has show business in his blood; his father was a well-known San Francisco showman and promoter.

The band was the featured entertainment at a restaurant in the North Bay. Many of the restaurant patrons were lured to the dance floor, and I found myself lightly tapping my fingers and feet to the swing beat. Bryan, with the perfect voice for Swing music, had great rapport with the audience. Their professional sound puts them alongside the famous bands of the Swing era.

An hour-long cassette tape and a video are available to prospective clients. Their swing repertoire includes about 1,200 songs. Since the band plays only swing, jazz, Latin and R&B styles, Bryan can offer tapes of other bands to his clients through his booking agency, Swing Fever Entertainment.

The Tim Wallace Band
Weddings, Parties and Special Events
(by appointment)
Redwood City, CA

(800) 303-2263
(650) 365-7100
(Phone & FAX)
tim@twmusic.com
www.ByRecOnly.com/timwallace
www.twmusic.com

Contact: Tim Wallace
Service Area: Greater Bay Area

Specialties: 6-piece versatile dance band playing all styles: '40s to '90s, Motown, Jazz, ballroom dance and classical music; several duos for wedding ceremony

Price Range: 6 pieces, from $1,500; duos, from $350
Extra Charges: travel beyond Bay Area, early setup

Payment Terms: $500 deposit, balance due day of event
Credit Cards: no

Lead Time: 1 week to 18 months
Playing Time: 1 - 8 hrs.
Audience Requests: yes

Tim was dressed in his black tuxedo when he met with me. While playing one of his tapes, he showed me his extensive portfolio with pictures of ceremonies, receptions, and corporate events. Also included are his extensive song list, sample schedules for receptions, and even a map to the site for the musicians. A large section of the portfolio is dedicated to evaluation questionnaires, expressing his clients' satisfaction, and many letters of recommendation. The clients I talked to praise him highly, and event coordinators, who found Tim through my book, rave about his work and his accommodating manner. They think he is a wonderful musician who keeps the party going. They also love the mood he creates as he involves the guests, even in group dances.

With several classical duos (guitar and flute, and keyboard with flute or saxophone), Tim provides entertainment for the ceremony and the reception. His band has two to six pieces and includes a female vocalist. The band can bring along a small lighting system. The timing of their breaks depends on the flow of the event; CDs are played during the breaks. Tim's thorough consultation ensures a smooth-running event. For Bar/Bat Mitzvahs, he offers candle-lighting ceremony music and can even provide toys to amuse the children.

Tim began playing piano at eight, and played flute and saxophone throughout high school, college and the military. He toured the western U.S. and Germany while a member of the 6th Army Band stationed at the Presidio. I listened to the band play in a park. In spite of the sweltering heat, many people enjoyed the quality music until the end, and quite a few even danced.

Wally's Swing World
The Entertainment Connection
1202 Lincoln Avenue, Suite 101
San Jose, CA 95125

(408) 275-6325
FAX: (408) 275-1902
entconnect@aol.com

Contact: Read Zaro (exclusive agent)

Service Area: Greater Bay Area, Northern California

Specialties: Big Band, Swing, '40s-'50s Standards, '50s Rock

Price Range: from $2,800
Extra Charges: travel beyond 60 miles

Payment Terms: 50% deposit, balance due day of event
Credit Cards: Visa, MasterCard, Discover

Lead Time: 4 months to 1 year
Playing Time: 4 hrs.
Audience Requests: yes

If you are looking for a hot band that can perform all the classics and satisfy every age, enter Wally's Swing World. Wally's "little Big Band" recreates the magic of American music's Golden Era. From Wally Trindade's slick dinner jacket, vintage microphone and electric guitar, to his silky Sinatra-like voice, young and old can't help but be impressed. This versatile band crosses generations by swooping the audience with "I've Got You Under My Skin," then rocking them on the dance floor with "Splish Splash."

The tuxedo-clad members fit the bill with a swinging three-piece horn section (trumpet, tenor sax and alto sax), a rocking upright bass, a fedora-sporting piano man, and a cool-handed drummer. They pride themselves on being capable of playing it all, from Big Band, Swing, Jump Swing and Lounge, to Rock-a-Billy, Latin and Salsa. Their repertoire ranges from Glen Miller, Benny Goodman, Tony Bennett and Frank Sinatra, to Bobby Darin and Elvis Presley. Their versatile combination inspires people to comment with enthusiasm: "Once you seem them, you'll want to book them." "We simply didn't want them to stop playing."

At a fund-raiser for over 500 on a cold San Francisco spring evening, Wally's Swing World warmed up everyone in the giant tent. Their sound was smooth and silky for the cocktail hour, then tight and robust for the dancing. Once people hit the floor, I had a hard time getting close enough to watch the band.

Wally's Swing World had been performing regularly throughout the Bay Area long before this recent craze of Swing emerged. Wally began singing at age six and has been a professional musician most of his life. With a degree in Jazz music, he is fully capable of writing the arrangements for the band. In 1995, Wally's Swing World opened for Chris Isaak and, to date, they perform regularly at various clubs and other venues throughout the Bay Area, as well as at weddings and other events.

The Zydeco Flames

(415) 457-5767
(510) 527-2036
www.zydecoflames.com

P.O. Box 1653
San Anselmo, CA 94979-1653

Contact: Frank Bohan or Bruce Gordon

Service Area: International

Specialties: 5-piece band playing Zydeco; solo or smaller ensembles playing Jazz and Blues; background music during ceremonies and cocktail hours

Price Range: from $2,500, depending on place and date
Extra Charges: travel, early setup

Payment Terms: 50% deposit, balance due day of event
Credit Cards: no

Lead Time: 1 day to 6 months
Playing Time: 1 - 4 hrs.
Audience Requests: yes

On the last day of the Sacramento Jazz Jubilee, we fortunately didn't have to wait too long to enter the tent where the Zydeco Flames were performing. The five band members electrified the crowd who were clapping and moving to the rhythm while anyone who could find room was dancing. I thought, "What a perfect band to include in my guide!" About a week later I ran into Frank Bohan, Zydeco Flames' guitar player and booking agent, at a coffee shop. That's when I learned that the word "zydeco" came from the French phrase, "Les haricots ne sont pas salées." When "les haricots" is pronounced with a Creole accent, it sounds like "zydeco." The Creoles used this expression to describe the music that the French had brought to the area. It means, "The green beans are without salt." So the Creoles spiced it up with other, more rhythmic melodies to give it punch and snap. This tempting music is very popular today, broadening the variety of danceable music.

Frank explained that including "Flames" in their name stemmed from their desire "to be hot, to set people on fire. It is a happy music with an infectious beat." The group has been together since 1990. Bruce Gordon, on accordion, and Lloyd Meadows, with his rubboard and great voice, were the group's founding members. Guitarist Frank Bohan, bass player Timm Walker, and William Allums, on drums, perfected the group that has become so popular during the past few years that they have been invited to play at festivals and numerous fairs all over the country. A highlight was playing for President Clinton at a fund-raising event in 1996.

A jazz club owner told me how much he thought of not only their music, but also their professional attitude. A newspaper article describes their music as "an amalgam of traditional Cajun, boogie, blues and soul...with punchy accordion-based melodies, powerful blues-style vocals, and funky, irresistible layered rhythms." Their music is available on four recordings.

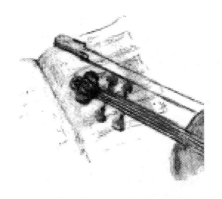

DISC JOCKEYS

Adrian Cavlan Mobile Music
The Entertainment Connection
1202 Lincoln Avenue, Suite 101
San Jose, CA 95125

(831) 469-3900
FAX: (408) 275-1902
ac@got.net
www.weddings-online.com/acmm

Contact: Adrian Cavlan or Read Zaro

Service Area: Greater Bay Area, Monterey Bay

Specialties: DJ with particular interest in elegant presentation; music from the '40s to the '90s; unique ceremony music; ethnic music from throughout the world

Price Range: from $695
Extra Charges: parking over $10, extra equipment installations as requested

Payment Terms: 50% deposit, balance due day of event
Credit Cards: Visa, MasterCard

Lead Time: 1 day to 1 year
Playing Time: 2 - 8 hrs.
Audience Requests: encouraged

For the last three years, both *Metro* and *Good Times* readers' polls have voted Adrian the best DJ in Santa Cruz County. And justifiably so because he is one of the classiest DJs around. Clad in his elegant black tuxedo, his normal attire, he speaks well and clearly, and makes sure he knows the correct pronunciation of everyone's name. I know this from firsthand experience. A personal meeting with the client is very important to him as his goal is "to create a unique and memorable reception for each individual bride and groom." He will make suggestions for the formal dances and do whatever it takes to make the event a success. With his sensitivity towards etiquette, he emphasizes that the selection of music should be classy and appropriate, yet not stilted. After the cake-cutting ceremony, he notices that the guests tend to loosen up and responds accordingly. Adrian will work with the facility coordinator to learn about specifics and rules. A worksheet that he prepares with the client during the consultation accompanies him on the day of the event to ensure that no details are missed.

Adrian's CD collection boasts of over 25,000 songs. He owns all his excellent equipment, and 3-way speakers, mostly hidden in attractive consoles. He has access to special lighting and additional equipment to accommodate parties of 500 to 5,000 people. He offers a sample song list of appropriate songs for parties, ceremonies and receptions, but is glad to play anything the client requests.

Clients describe Adrian as a class act, and one commented on how well he tied together the different aspects of the wedding reception. Another client remarked on the wonderful rapport Adrian established with the guests and how quick he was to pick up on everything that was going on. Everyone I spoke to said they love working with this easygoing and friendly entertainer.

California Music Express
"Your One-Stop Music Connection"
(by appointment)
San Ramon, CA

(925) 803-1697
(408) 732-1697
FAX: (925) 244-1997

Contact: Paul Binder

Service Area: Greater Bay Area and beyond

Specialties: Professional disc jockeys for all occasions

Price Range: $575 for 4 hrs.
Extra Charges: party props, lighting

Payment Terms: $100 deposit, balance due day of event
Credit Cards: Visa, MasterCard

Lead Time: 2 days to 2 years
Playing Time: min. 4 hrs.
Audience Requests: yes

Owner Paul Binder has always loved music. While a high school student, he played in a band, and during college he worked as a DJ for extra money. Most of his staff of 12 DJs have been friends since college. Paul, who has a business degree, bought a DJ company in 1984, gave it a new name, and made it what it is today – one of the most highly respected companies in the Bay Area.

During an extensive consultation at their San Ramon office, Paul's staff will help select music for the ceremony, whether it is classical, traditional, or contemporary. They will also suggest music for the reception depending on the age of the guests and the part of the country they come from. If your favorite song is not currently in his large music library, they will find it for you. He will assign a DJ who is a specialist in your choice of music. Each DJ arrives an hour before the event to talk to vendors and check the schedule to make sure announcements will be done on time. After so many years, the DJs are masters at reading a crowd and projecting the right sound and volume.

Paul has also been a featured speaker at the 1994, 1995, and 1997 International DJ Expo, speaking on topics such as sales, training, and corporate games. He has a monthly column in *DJ Times* magazine in which he reviews the latest in state-of-the-art DJ equipment, giving California Music Express the jump on all new equipment and an edge in the mobile disc jockey industry. Paul describes his DJ staff as "interactive" entertainers, who entertain beyond what is considered standard in the industry. Among their services are karaoke, party props, and lighting. All equipment is hidden in consoles, compact and self-sufficient. They bring backup systems and include a wireless microphone for speeches and toasts. With years of experience and vast music knowledge, it is no wonder that references praise California Music Express' versatility and tremendous assistance in organizing an event.

Denon & Doyle
Disc Jockey Company
1300 Galaxy Way, #7
Concord, CA 94520

(925) 944-5021
(800) 944-9585
FAX: (925) 827-3308
denondoyle@aol.com
www.djay.com

Contact: Brian Doyle

Service Area: Greater Bay Area and beyond

Specialties: Music from the '20s to the '90s, specializing in mixed adult age groups; event coordination

Price Range: $500 - $750
Extra Charges: overtime

Payment Terms: 50% deposit, balance due day of event
Credit Cards: all credit cards

Lead Time: 1 day to 6 months
Playing Time: min. 3 hrs.
Audience Requests: yes

Denon & Doyle was the most recommended DJ company during the time of my research. Brian, the founder and owner, was formerly a DJ on several radio stations playing country music and classic rock for many years. Founded in 1984, the company now has 18 DJs. Brian is very nice and accommodating person who gave me many recommendations for the guide. The key to their success is that all of them are partners, and quite a few have been with the company for many years. A brochure with their pictures and resumes is included in their introduction folder. All are very nice men, dressed elegantly in tuxedos. Most of them have either a college degree or are working on one. They use professional equipment, play mostly CDs, and use wireless microphones.

A video prepared from past performances will help you choose the right DJ. Especially for weddings, Brian will help you with the design of the whole event. He even designed a special wedding planner with hints and timing ideas. The DJ will work with the caterer and the other professionals to announce the cake-cutting ceremony, etc., and contribute to the smooth flow of the event. All of the DJs pride themselves on playing the right music for mixed events and, most important, on how they read the crowd. They adapt the music and the sound system from soft cocktail music during arrival of the guests and the dinner to extremely upbeat songs to lure people to the dance floor.

I was able to experience Brian's professionalism firsthand when he served as MC and DJ at my BRO party in February 1995. He scheduled the performers, picked the perfect music during breaks, and kept on top of the entertainment portion of the party so I wouldn't have to.

Special lighting effects are free of charge.

Hey Mr. D.J.
Exceptional Entertainment
P.O. Box 26694
San Jose, CA 95159

(408) 223-1400
fun1@best.com
www.heymrdj.com

Contact: Rich Amooi

Service Area: San Jose, South Bay and Peninsula

Specialties: Great music and personality

Price Range: $750 - $1,150
Extra Charges: ceremony music

Payment Terms: 50% deposit, balance
                    due 3 weeks prior to event
Credit Cards: no

Lead Time: to 18 months
Playing Time: 3 - 6 hrs.
Audience Requests: yes

"He senses the mood and lights the fire" is how a professional photographer sums up Rich Amooi, owner and operator of Hey Mr. D.J.

With over 18 years experience and a former on-air radio personality, Rich uses his knowledge of music and his personality to carry what he calls the "art of wedding entertainment." Using the best available equipment in the industry and wireless microphones, Rich acts as the musical host, tailoring his voice and energy to set the tone. He states, "It's almost a science." The flow, the music, and motivating the crowd are all part of making it fun. Using his huge library of CDs featuring thousands of songs from all eras, Rich customizes the music to the specific event. He uses the personal client meeting, a 5-page planner, and the guests at the event as his guidelines.

The name of his services, Hey Mr. D.J., is quite the icebreaker. More often than not, when guests shout out "Hey, Mr. D.J., can you play… ," then discover the name of his company, they are left with a lighthearted feeling. Rich looks forward to every event, and people notice. It is no wonder that he is recommended by many local hotels, banquet facilities and event professionals, including other disc jockeys. You hire him, you get him. As a commitment to excellence, he is fully licensed and insured, and carries a full backup system just in case. As Rich says, "Let the fun begin!"

Music A La Carte

(408) 395-6266
raffi@musicalacartedj.com
www.musicalacartedj.com

(by appointment)
Los Gatos/Monte Sereno, CA

Contact: "King Raffi" Nalvarian (Owner)

Service Area: Greater Bay Area

Specialties: A variety of music – '40s to '90s, Swing, Disco, Pop, Country, New Wave and Modern Rock; ceremony music is available

Price Range: $895 - $1,095
Extra Charges: lighting, karaoke, ceremony, overtime

Payment Terms: 50% non-ref. deposit, balance due 1 week prior to event	**Lead Time:** 1 - 18 months
	Playing Time: 5 - 7 hrs.
Credit Cards: no	**Audience Requests:** yes

At the moment you meet with "King Raffi," owner of Music A La Carte, you can feel his high energy level and fun spirit. "It's all about having a good time. We keep it moving," says Raffi. Clients and vendors alike couldn't agree more.

Locally born and raised, Raffi Nalvarian got the name "King Raffi" from being the class prankster in high school. Every time he was called to the principal's office, classmates would chant, "King, King, King…" Starting out as a Public Relations Marketing major and becoming an on-air radio personality, Raffi is a part-time DJ for LIVE 105. With over 13 years of experience, Raffi is well-versed in music and reading a crowd. He gets the audience involved and paces the event for a continuous party for both young and old. "My goal is to get people exhausted – I want them to feel like part of the memory."

One humorous comment, which I am sure most couples can relate to, is: "Besides being a terrific MC and choosing extremely cool music, you somehow managed to get our modern music-hating parents out on the dance floor several times. In fact, they are still singing praises about you, which should be a huge compliment to you since they were very much against us getting a DJ in the first place."

Nickelodeon

(408) 298-7710
FAX: (408) 867-9345
Reachcarl@aol.com

P.O. Box 7491
San Jose, CA 95150

Contact: Carl W. Mindling

Service Area: Greater Bay Area

Specialties: Versatile DJ providing music from the 1930's through today;
keeps the dance floor consistently full

Price Range: from $1,100, depending on date, time, and location
Extra Charges: none

Payment Terms: 30% deposit, balance
due day of event
Credit Cards: major credit cards

Lead Time: 1 week to 12 months
Playing Time: 4 - 5 hrs.
Audience Requests: encouraged

"Carl is just the best," was a comment I heard from several people who work in the party and wedding business. Clients were just as pleased and commented, "Our office wants him every year," "very dependable," "has a feel for crowds," "I love working with him."

I have known this friendly and helpful man for years. Carl has been perfecting his style since he started as a DJ in 1968. His professional sound equipment and constantly updated CD library are concealed in custom-built consoles which are easily arranged to fit the available space. His system is organized by computer to allow immediate access to the desired music. Setup always takes place before the event. He now carries a pager, since "you cannot imagine how many last minute changes I get. It's worth it to me if my clients can reach me anytime by pager. Vendors who are easy to reach can often set a client's mind at ease."

Nickelodeon is a one-person company offering very personalized service. When you contract with Carl, he himself will be present at your event, playing the music and serving as master of ceremonies. If he is booked, he will recommend other, highly respected DJs in the area. He places a lot of emphasis on pre-event planning during a personal consultation to help ensure a successful party. His strong point is his ability to include difficult requests without losing the majority of the dancers. Many of his wedding clients are now looking to Carl to provide their ceremony music. One of the big advantages he can offer for ceremonies is a wireless lapel microphone for the person performing the ceremony.

Most of Carl's business comes from referrals and longtime customers.

One Night Stand–VIP
Mobile Disc Jockey Entertainment
P.O. Box 6747
San Mateo, CA 94403

(650) 571-5940
(925) 833-0414
FAX: (650) 571-7644
jtomdjs4u@aol.com

Contact: Tom Nelson or Brent Anderson

Service Area: Northern California

Specialties: Skilled entertainment specialists, trained in customizing and tailoring events to the individual

Price Range: packages from $400
Extra Charges: light show, props, prizes, overtime, travel charges may apply

Payment Terms: $100 non-ref. deposit, balance due 2 weeks prior to event
Credit Cards: major credit cards

Lead Time: last minute to 2 years
Playing Time: 3 hrs. min.
Audience Requests: welcomed

With superior customer service as their main objective, Tom Nelson of One Night Stand and Brent Anderson of VIP joined forces from across the bay to form One Night Stand–VIP. With state-of-the-art equipment and the same philosophies about conducting business, Tom operates the Peninsula while Brent operates the East Bay location. Their team of longtime, dedicated entertainment specialists is located around the bay, giving them the opportunity to match the right person with the event and minimizing the possibility of ever getting stuck on the opposite side of the bay. They have a very comprehensive, customized wedding planner to assist with every facet of your event.

In working with One Night Stand–VIP, what stands out is their flexibility in accommodating schedule variations. They work closely with the other vendors and make sure that everyone is present before making announcements. Their DJs are trained by shadowing experienced specialists. Tom and Brent look for professionals who are comfortable performing in front of live crowds, polite, even when they receive off-the-cuff comments, and accommodating to their clients. All the details are handled by Tom or Brent during the planning stages, and you will always have the opportunity to meet the DJ assigned to your event. Each event specialist is equipped with a base collection of 400 CDs of the most requested songs of all times plus selections that reflect the event they are servicing.

For events that call for interactive entertainers, they provide novelty props such as party hats, inflatable props, toys, fog & bubble machines, and lighting effects such as strobe lights, mirror balls, and police beacons. Their talents were tested when they met the challenge of entertaining a deaf girl and her friends for her Bat Mitzvah. They coordinated their activities and music with lighting to the beat of the music. For the August '96 blackout, all the DJs rented or bought generators to save the day. Not all the weddings in the hotel were as lucky. "Quick thinking is what it is all about."

Sound Trax
Mobile Disc Jockey
(by appointment)
Mountain View, CA

(650) 969-4235
FAX: (650) 903-0928
sndtrax@ccnet.com
www.soundtraxdj.com

Contact: Rens Boorsma

Service Area: Greater Bay Area

Specialties: Music for all ages and all events, from the Big Band era to today; music for wedding ceremonies

Price Range: from $600
Extra Charges: overtime

Payment Terms: $150 deposit, balance due prior to event
Credit Cards: no

Lead Time: 24 hours to 14 months
Playing Time: 4 hrs.
Audience Requests: yes

Rens worked in the DJ industry for more than 10 years before starting his own company in 1994. During that time he toured Air Force bases in Europe for three years on his own. He wouldn't start his own business until he was able to purchase a top quality sound system with crystal clear tones. That beauty is pictured on the brochure he sends to prospective clients. Two wireless mikes are available for guests to use. Rens always brings along a second system, used mainly for ceremony music but can also serve as a backup system. His music, most of which is on CDs, dates back to the Big Band era and continues up to today's newest hits. For company parties and school dances, he can provide a light show with more than 10 different lighting effects and a smoke machine.

A personal meeting during which he gets to know his clients and their preferences is mandatory. Rens will make suggestions about the music or about the timeline important to the flow of the event. He will tell you when and where he is performing so that you can see him live. Rens is a very versatile DJ and will play whatever the client wants, even music provided by the client. He will talk as much or as little as requested, and saves his jokes for a fun-loving crowd. Once or twice during the reception he will ask the bride and groom for feedback.

Due to his extensive experience, accommodating personality, his ability to work the crowd, and his excellent equipment, Rens' business is booming. He is at the top of the list of highly respected event coordinators who warmly recommended him for my book. One company hired him immediately for their next event after seeing how he brought so many people to the dance floor, unlike any DJ before him. Clients find him "absolutely wonderful!" One bride told me how well he handled the non-English-speaking relatives from Europe and complimented him on getting the crowd going in his easygoing, sensitive manner.

Star Sounds
"Music, just for the fun of it!"
(by appointment)
Menlo Park, CA

(650) 324-4927
(650) 855-1968
FAX: (650) 324-8609
reitmanr@starsounds.com
www.starsounds.com

Contact: Richard Reitman

Service Area: Greater Bay Area

Specialties: Music custom-designed for event and mood; Big Band, Motown, Jazz, Pop, Rock

Price Range: $595 - $695 for 4 hours
Extra Charges: travel beyond 1 hour

Payment Terms: $100 non-ref. deposit, balance due day of event
Credit Cards: no

Lead Time: 1 month to 1 year
Playing Time: 4 - 8 hrs.
Audience Requests: encouraged

Richard turned his passion for great music and parties into a second business. An MIT graduate and information systems manager by day, Richard has developed top-quality professional audio systems for Star Sounds. Since founding his business in 1983, his library has grown to over 3,000 CDs and over 40,000 song titles, ranging from Glen Miller to Hootie and the Blowfish and the Top 40s hits. His top-quality professional equipment, including backups and wireless microphones, is neatly organized.

Richard consults extensively with his clients. He sends them album and song lists, and makes suggestions appropriate to the age of the guests and the type of event. At the event, he actively solicits requests from the guests. Sometimes his wife Diane accompanies him, getting the crowd going and acting as MC. They tend to stay away from heavy metal but every other type of music is available. The couple has entertained groups as small as 20 and as large as 2,500.

I had a chance to see Richard and Diane in action, and really loved their work. Since the host and hostess knew the type of music they wanted, but not many album and song titles, Richard designed an evening of music and refined it to include requests from the guests. Due to unexpected rain, the garden party moved to the garage, which did not leave much room for Richard's equipment. He was very cooperative and creatively made do with the limited space. During dinner, the music was soft enough for conversation, and during dancing it was just perfect. Diane brought maracas and tambourines, and encouraged people to dance. There could not have been a better DJ for this event.

Top Tunes DJ's

(650) 878-DJ4U
(800) TOP-TUNES
FAX: (650) 757-4703
www.toptunesdjs.com

(by appointment)
San Francisco, CA

Contact: Carl Hilsz

Service Area: Greater Bay Area and beyond

Specialties: Weddings and corporate events; compact disc music from the '40s to the present; consultation service

Price Range: from $325
Extra Charges: none for setup or breakdown

Payment Terms: 50% deposit, balance due before event
Credit Cards: Visa, MasterCard

Lead Time: 1 day to 2 years
Playing Time: no min.
Audience Requests: yes

When you meet Carl and his associates, you soon find out how much they love the business. Carl provides music for all kinds of events; however, his favorite events are weddings. He loves to work with bride and groom and help them with the music selections. He showed me the computer printouts of their large music library; the song list which he is always updating contains over 30,000 titles on CDs. Top Tunes will obtain any music not currently in their library. All of their equipment, which they consider the best in the industry, is hidden in unobtrusive, custom-built consoles.

Top Tunes loves entertaining and encouraging people to dance and have fun. They can read the crowd and get people involved. They are also glad to simply act as master of ceremonies with a more conservative approach. With their diverse range of experience, Top Tunes specializes in personalizing your event.

Celebrating their 10th year in business, Top Tunes is recommended by many hotels and reception locations in the Bay Area. Top Tunes is a member of the National Association of Mobile Entertainers and Chamber of Commerce. References we called upon raved about their performances. They also commented on their great personalities and how they get exactly what they want – an elegant, laid-back, or animated performance that keeps the party going.

SOLOISTS

Marian Concus
Flute
P.O. Box 391328
Mountain View, CA 94039

(650) 969-9308
schweitz@mediacity.com
www.mediacity.com/~schweitz

Contact: Marian Concus

Service Area: Greater Bay Area

Specialties: Classical, popular, and ethnic music; soloist or with other musicians

Price Range: first hour, $150; each additional hour, $75
Extra Charges: travel beyond 1 hour, parking, audience requests

Payment Terms: 50% non-ref. deposit, balance due after performance
Credit Cards: no

Lead Time: 6 months, sometimes less
Playing Time: 1 - 4 hrs.
Audience Requests: yes

Following undergraduate studies at UC Berkeley, Marian was awarded a fellowship to study in Paris, France, with Michel Debost, the former principal flutist of Orchestre de Paris. She later returned to the US and received a Bachelor's Degree from the New England Conservatory of Music in Boston. She has recorded in Paris as well as in the US, both alone and with other musicians. Her diverse releases include eclectic love songs, Klezmer music, popular background music for TV and film, and contemporary classical compositions.

Marian is an excellent flutist. She performed Opus 125 by Furstenau for me, which she played with compassion and great virtuosity. Well known in our area, she is a member of the Fremont Symphony and the Santa Cruz County Symphony, and has performed with the San Jose Symphony. She has appeared with Composer's, Inc. at the Modern Art Museum in San Francisco. Marian was a featured soloist at the opening of the Center for the Performing Arts in Mountain View. "[A] flutist with a nice deep tone and expressive manner," was how the *San Francisco Chronicle* described her.

As a soloist or with other musicians, Marian can perform a concert or play for special events. For events she usually plays classical or popular background music, although her repertoire also contains a few waltzes and Israeli dances. She will audition live or provide a tape for her customers. Special musical arrangements or requests are available for an additional fee.

Paul Binkley
Classical and Jazz Guitar
(by appointment)
San Francisco, CA

(415) 282-0840
pbinkley@aol.com

Contact: Paul Binkley

Service Area: Northern California

Specialties: Classical and Jazz guitar music; two guitars, duo with flute,
               trio with flute and cello, mandolin

Price Range: $200 for 2 hours; each additional hour, $50
Extra Charges: travel beyond 40 miles, extensive personal consultation

Payment Terms: 50% deposit, balance
                  due day of event
Credit Cards: no

Lead Time: 1 day to 2 months
Playing Time: 2 - 4 hrs.
Audience Requests: yes

Paul and I had met before a wedding. I admired the flowers while he, elegantly dressed in a tuxedo, unpacked his guitar. As he warmed up, I was so attracted by the wonderful sounds that I walked over to find out a little about him before asking him for an interview. After learning that he had studied at the San Francisco Conservatory of Music and played there for events while pursuing his studies, I definitely wanted to include him in the guide.

Besides performing at private functions, Paul is a guitarist with the San Francisco Symphony, Opera, and Ballet. He is also a guitar instructor at Mills College and was a featured soloist on the school's centennial album, which was rated one of the ten best classical albums of the year by *The New York Times*. He has also recorded several albums with other musicians.

Paul often performs classical music and Neapolitan songs on the mandolin. He is a member of the Modern Mandolin Quartet with whom he has recorded four CDs and many samplers for Windham Hill Records. Paul also appeared on the Grammy-winning recording of Prokofiev's *Romeo and Juliet* with the San Francisco Symphony under Maestro Michael Tilson Thomas. Paul and a friend, a well-known jazz guitarist, performed at the donors' dinner for the opening of the new library in San Francisco. Paul often performs classical music and Neapolitan songs on the mandolin.

Paul is not only a wonderful and passionate guitarist, but also a very nice and accommodating person. One bride told me about the many compliments she received on his wonderful performance.

Karen Kirk Thielen & Beaux Mélanges
Harp & Vibraphone Solo or Duo
(by appointment)
Menlo Park, CA

(650) 328-HARP
(Phone & FAX)
pkmthielen@aol.com

Contact: Karen Julie Kirk Thielen

Service Area: Greater Bay Area

Specialties: Harpist alone or with vibraphone, playing classical harp, Spanish and Irish music, and Pop

Price Range: solo: $225 for first hour; each additional hour, $70; duo: $375, each additional hour, $120
Extra Charges: travel beyond 30 miles

Payment Terms: $100 deposit, balance due 2 weeks prior to event
Credit Cards: no

Lead Time: 1 week to 1 year
Playing Time: 1 - 4 hrs.
Audience Requests: yes

Karen's resume is impressive: a Spanish Government scholarship to study Spanish harp music, finalist in an Alpha Delta Kappa Fine Arts grant competition, and several awards from the University of California. Karen is Principal Harpist with the Monterey Symphony Orchestra, Principal Harpist with Opera San Jose, and Second Harpist with the San Jose Symphony. She has also substituted several times with the San Francisco Symphony, Opera, and Ballet. Karen is the faculty harp instructor at San Jose State and Santa Clara University. One of her more exciting performances was in March 1991 when she was harpist for Luciano Pavarotti in his Pebble Beach concert. While she played in the hospitality tent for the World Cup soccer events, Plácido Domingo came up to her and thanked her for her wonderful performance. I had met Karen at a law office party and liked her playing and her nice appearance so much that I had to include her in my book.

Karen prefers the classics for setting an elegant mood. However, she will play music appropriate to any event. If a client requests some special pieces, she will master them and even adapt music from other instruments for an additional fee.

Karen and her husband Peter are a harp and vibraphone duo under the name of Beaux Mélanges. Peter works for the San Jose Symphony as percussionist and substitutes frequently with the San Francisco Ballet. Their light and tender music is perfect for outdoor as well as indoor weddings or parties. The two instruments are lovely for Christmas songs. As a duo they perform classics, opera tunes, popular songs, and Spanish and Irish music. A video tape is available upon request.

Dan Levitan

(510) 795-8004

Harpist
33419 Turnstone Place
Fremont, CA 94555

Contact: Dan Levitan

Service Area: Greater Bay Area

Specialties: Harp music, from Classical to Pop; background music

Price Range: first hour, $200; each additional hour, $75
Extra Charges: travel beyond 30 miles of Fremont, platform

Payment Terms: 50% non-ref. deposit, balance due 2 weeks prior to event
Credit Cards: no

Lead Time: 1 day to 1 year
Playing Time: 1 - 4 hrs.
Audience Requests: yes

Dan invited me to an hour-long, lunchtime concert at an office building in downtown San Jose. His harp music floated through the covered courtyard and drifted into the offices. Dan is a wonderful performer who will tackle the most difficult pieces and interpret them with great accuracy and musicality. His talent was obvious as he played his own transcription of Mozart's Piano Sonata K545, Magistretti's transcription of "Theme and Variations of Paganini," and the modern Harp Concertino by Castelnuovo-Tedesco. His repertoire also includes popular selections, such as "Evergreen" and "Love Story" which I enjoyed listening to.

One of the best harpists in the area, Dan has performed with just about every professional and community orchestra in Northern California. He is a virtuoso, solo harpist, and is Principal Harpist of the San Jose Symphony Orchestra, Marin Symphony Orchestra, and the Fremont Newark Philharmonic. He competed in the San Francisco Opera principal harp audition in 1989 and was asked to perform with their orchestra for the entire season. Dan has won several first-place awards in harp competitions. He also has participated in two international harp competitions in Israel and on the Isle of Man in the UK. He received rave reviews for his solo performance of Ginastera's neoclassical Harp Concerto with the San Jose Symphony and was deemed "the night's high point...turning the concerto into a flight of beauty and excitement."

Dan's three commercial recordings are his "10th Anniversary Concert" (his first solo CD), "Moonlight" (solo harp and flute & harp on cassette), and "Shades of Love" (voice, flute and harp, also on cassette).

Besides being a wonderful artist, Dan is also very friendly and personable. He establishes an immediate rapport with the audience and goes out of his way to accommodate his clients.

Anna Maria Mendieta
Harpist (Solo or Ensemble)
(by appointment)
San Francisco, CA

(415) 584-3167
FAX: (415) 586-3001

Contact: Anna Maria Mendieta

Service Area: Greater Bay Area and beyond

Specialties: Classical, Renaissance, Impressionist, and Baroque to Contemporary, Popular, New Age, and Show Tunes

Price Range: ceremony/reception, from $300
Extra Charges: sound equipment, props, customized recording to CD or cassette

Payment Terms: 50% non-ref. deposit, balance due 1 month prior to event
Credit Cards: no

Lead Time: to 9 months
Playing Time: 1½ - 7 hrs.
Audience Requests: yes

Anna Maria Mendieta creates the atmosphere at all the events at which she performs. Her natural grace and beauty accentuate her remarkable musical performances. Classically trained at the age of 7 at the San Francisco Conservatory of Music, Anna Maria gave her first solo recital when she was 8 years old and began playing with orchestras at age 13. Since receiving her music degree from the College of Notre Dame in Belmont, CA, she has performed at several venues from Davies Hall in San Francisco to The Kennedy Center in Washington, D.C. Her long list of prestigious concerts include performances for former President Gorbachev and the King and Queen of Spain, including an invitation to play for President Clinton. Anna Maria has appeared on television, in motion pictures, and was featured on national radio. Her albums, including "Enchanted Christmas" and "Broadway-Center Stage," among others, are released by Sugo Records.

Her fame as a concert harpist and soloist is matched by her many years of experience as a wedding harpist. "It's a perfect balance," says Anna Maria. Her ability to play from memory gives her the freedom to watch and count each person in the procession. This allows her to perfectly time the processional music to each attendant. For the prelude, she alternates styles of recognizable music to please all age groups. As she says, "It sets a warm atmosphere for the guests."

What I think distinguishes Anna Maria is her excitement about every wedding at which she performs. Her flowing gown always matches the color scheme of the wedding, and her staging props allow her to either be part of the scene or just melt into the background. What's magical is her coordinated background music during key points in the ceremony. To create drama, Anna Maria softly plays short phrases of music during the vows and the ring exchange. At the conclusion, as a brief moment of meditation, she gradually builds the volume, gracefully singling out these special moments. It's so romantic, like watching a love scene.

Chris Huson
Pianist
(by appointment)
Mill Valley, CA

(415) 381-2660

Contact: Chris Huson

Service Area: Greater Bay Area and beyond

Specialties: Jazz, "Chicago" Blues, Boogie-Woogie, Brazilian music; solo or with bass and/or drums

Price Range: solo piano, from $125; trio, from $450
Extra Charges: travel, equipment

Payment Terms: 50% deposit, balance
                         due day of event
Credit Cards: no

Lead Time: 1 day to 1 year
Playing Time: 1 - 5 hrs.
Audience Requests: yes

Chris comes highly recommended. He is both a very versatile piano player and a very nice person. He knows all of his music by heart, and when I asked him how large his repertoire was, he answered modestly, "Three nights," which translates to 10 to 12 hours. Chris enjoys playing a variety of styles and loves trying something new. This led him to playing gospel music on a church organ in Oakland for several years. He learned Latin tunes from a salsa group, and Brazilian music, his favorite, from a Brazilian band. From listening to Chris play, you can't help but notice how much he enjoys his music. At the first BRO party, Chris so admired the tone of the beautiful piano provided for the evening that he played for us while we cleaned up, right up until the instrument was picked up.

Chris has performed at the 1987 All Star Baseball game, the Golden Gate Bridge's 50th anniversary celebration, the Great American Music Hall, and at numerous San Francisco marathons. He has worked with Chevy Chase, opened for Steve Martin, and appeared on the Merv Griffin Show. I heard Chris perform at an open house. His lively, yet unobtrusive background music– a mixture of jazz, blues and bossa nova – gave the event a more elegant touch. Clients love the variety of music he can play, alone or with other musicians. In one of Herb Caen's infamous columns, Chris' performance at Moose's is described as "a plethora, that's what it is, and plethora lithen to."

Chris puts a lot of heart and soul into his playing. He performs for corporate and private events as a soloist or accompanied by a bassist. Chris can play for a ceremony and provide background music during dinner. He can also add drums and saxophone to perform dance music in many styles (see "Specialities" above).

Alan Steger
Pianist
P.O. Box 15466
San Francisco, CA 94115

(415) 387-3057

Contact: Alan Steger

Service Area: Greater Bay Area and beyond

Specialties: Large variety of Standards, Show Tunes, Pop, Jazz, Latin, Blues, some Classical; wedding and holiday music; solo, duo, trio, quartet and quintet

Price Range: from $125
Extra Charges: travel, electronic keyboard, PA system

Payment Terms: 50% deposit, balance due day of event	**Lead Time:** same day to 1 year
	Playing Time: 1 - 6 hrs.
Credit Cards: no	**Audience Requests:** yes

With over 1,000 tunes, Alan has one of the largest repertoires. I heard him perform at the Cypress Club in San Francisco, where he played piano as part of a trio. They drew repeated applause from diners and bar guests. His soulful piano playing was admired by many that stopped to watch him play. Every so often I would catch someone stop themselves between a cocktail and conversation to grab a quick dance step or hum the last bar to a tune.

Alan's very rhythmic and strong harmonic sense of standards comes naturally to him. He began to study piano as a child. When he was 11, he played with a band, and at 13, played piano on a children's TV show. He became interested in jazz at 16 and put himself through college with his music. Shortly after moving to California in 1973, he began working with many bands, accompanied singers, and played solo piano in restaurants around the Bay. In the '80s, in addition to working with vocalists Tony Martin and Della Reese, he was hired by Viking Cruise Lines as a musical director while he continued to teach piano and music theory to private students. He has performed with the swing group, The Chicago Six, backed the Ink Spots and vocalist Rosalind Kind, and served as rehearsal pianist for vocalist Eddie Fisher. Alan is currently appearing in a variety of performance formats: with the Dan Hicks Bayside Jazz group, with the Oakland East Bay Symphony at pops concerts, and monthly, as a duo with bassist, as part of Stanford Hospital's music program. He also occasionally appears at such San Francisco venues as Stars Restaurant and The Hotel Huntington.

Alan has arranged hundreds of songs for himself and other Bay Area vocalists, including Denise Perrier, and will gladly transcribe music for his clients. Many professionals describe Alan as a well-rounded musician who plays many different styles and is well respected by the customers. For your own listening pleasure, you can see Alan perform solo piano every Sunday at Scott's Seafood Restaurant in Jack London Square, Oakland.

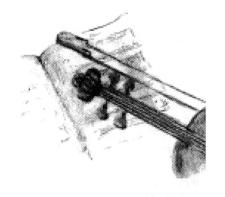

STRINGS

Hillmont String Quartet

(510) 236-6410
KeithH1036@aol.com

5910 N. Arlington Blvd.
San Pablo, CA 94806

Contact: Keith Herritt

Service Area: Greater Bay Area

Specialties: Light classical, popular music and jazz for parties and weddings

Price Range: $425 - $870
Extra Charges: travel beyond Bay Area

Payment Terms: 50% part. ref. deposit, balance due day of event
Credit Cards: no

Lead Time: 1 week to 8 months
Playing Time: 1 - 4 hrs.
Audience Requests: yes, if music is available

The Hillmont String Quartet, in existence since 1985, got its name from Hillmont Street, where one of its members lived at the time. I heard about them from a wedding consultant whose clients had used them quite often. No wonder, since all quartet members are very accomplished musicians who play with symphony or chamber orchestras in the area.

The Hillmont String Quartet is now in the unusual position of having three violinists filling the two violin positions included in a string quartet. Because of career and family demands, Aenea Keyes, Ann Krinitsky and Lili Byers are job-sharing the violin chairs. Aenea has played at Carnegie Hall, Lincoln Center, and the United Nations, as well as in Europe and Japan. She is also a talented improvisor and composer. Ann, similarly multi-talented, recently took leave from her playing and her conducting position with the Berkeley Youth Orchestra to perform in Hawaii for a year. Lili, a founding member of the Quartet, also plays with and serves as personnel manager of the Women's Philharmonic. Keith Herritt, the Quartet's violist, is also a music administrator with the Santa Rosa Symphony. Michael Knapp, the group's cellist, is one of the few players of that instrument to excel in both the classical and jazz styles. On request, the quartet can include vocalists, flutists, and brass players in their performance.

I listened to the Quartet at a rehearsal at Lili's house, which provided a good overview of their music. A Beethoven country dance and portions of sonatas by Tartini and Bach were excellent. Clients highly recommend them for their dependable service and appropriate, pleasing music.

The Jasmine String Quartet

(by appointment)
San Jose, CA

(408) 377-4647
(408) 255-1633
(408) 978-1361
FAX: (408) 445-2971
oneachord@aol.com

Contact: David or Susan Stein, Rebecca McCormick or Irene Trapp

Service Area: Greater Bay Area

Specialties: Light classical and romantic music, some popular selections

Price Range: $560 for 2-hr. min.; $180 each additional hour
Extra Charges: travel fee may apply; new song arrangement fee

Payment Terms: 25% non-ref. deposit,
                  balance due prior to event
Credit Cards: no

Lead Time: up to 1 year
Playing Time: 2 - 5 hrs.
Audience Requests: no

The members of the Jasmine String Quartet are all professional musicians and have been performing together since 1982. The quartet has performed in recitals at the Lick Observatory and the Mount Hermon Christian Conference Center. In July 1991, they performed with John Denver in the Paul Masson Summer Series.

Rebecca McCormick and Susan Stein (violinists) are members of the San Jose Symphony. David Stein (cello and piano) is a member of the Monterey Symphony and is musical director of the Children's Theater in Palo Alto. He is also an accomplished, professional pianist. Irene Trapp (viola and vocal) sings professionally and has many albums to her credit. She is a mezzo-soprano whose style ranges from classical to popular music. For a $50 doubling fee per person, Irene and David can perform a vocal or piano selection for your celebration.

The quartet maintains a consistently high standard of excellence in their work. This was reflected in the positive recommendations of their references who indicated that the quartet's professional sound and classical music added a special touch to their event.

Demo tapes are available upon request.

Musica Viva　　　　　　　　　　　　　　(510) 524-5203
String Quartet - Strolling Violin - Gypsy Violin & Piano
(by appointment)
Berkeley, CA

Contact:　　　Donna Lerew

Service Area:　Greater Bay Area

Specialties:　String Quartet: Classical to Viennese waltzes; Romantic Strolling Violin;
　　　　　　　　Gypsy Violin and Piano Combo

Price Range: Quartet, from $500; Solo Violin: first hour, $150; ea. add. hour, $100;
　　　　　　　　Gypsy Violin & Piano, from $300
Extra Charges: travel beyond 1 hour

Payment Terms: $100 non-ref. deposit,　　| **Lead Time:** 1 day to 9 months
　　　　balance due on or before day of event | **Playing Time:** 2 - 4 hrs.
Credit Cards: no　　　　　　　　　　| **Audience Requests:** yes

"The beautiful music provided just the simple elegance we desired on our special day." "You helped make our event truly magical!" "You added a special touch to our wedding." These are just a few of the many thanks Musica Viva has received.

It is no wonder audiences and guests alike rave about their performances. All the members, outstanding Bay Area professional musicians, have performed at many venues – wineries, symphonies, operas and ballets throughout the Bay Area, including San Francisco Opera House, Davies Hall, Pacific Union Club, Grace Cathedral, and the De Young Museum. With years of practice and working together as an ensemble, Musica Viva's skill is peerless. The quartet's wide variety of traditional and light classical music adds an extra touch of elegance to any event. Their music is so robust you actually believe you are hearing more than four musicians.

Donna Lerew, first violin, made her debut at the age of seven. She studied with some of the world's foremost violinists and graduated with awards from the Eastman School of Music and Paris's Ecole Normale, where she studied on a Fulbright Scholarship. Since then, Donna has played with the National Symphony, the San Francisco Ballet, and the San Francisco Opera. She is currently active as a teacher and strolling violinist in the Bay Area and concertmaster of the Fremont Symphony Orchestra. Newspaper critics talk about "her dancing bow, which leaps with electric intensity, leaving the audience spellbound." Donna performs with emotion, capturing the very heart of the music.

Whether Donna's strolling violin is playing a romantic ballad, or the quartet is performing the classics, or a custom program of gypsy and popular music is arranged, you can rest assured that this music will add an enchanting touch to any event.

The Nob Hill String Quartet
The Nob Hill Salon Orchestra
(by appointment)
Oakland, CA

(510) 835-1382
(415) 332-5428
jten@crl.com

Contact: John Tenney or Teressa Adams

Service Area: Greater Bay Area and beyond

Specialties: String quartet: elegant classical and popular music
Salon orchestra: the best danceable American and Continental music from 1890 to 1940

Price Range: 3 - 5 pieces for 2 hours, $475 - $800
Extra Charges: nominal travel charge beyond 25 miles

Payment Terms: 50% deposit, balance
due day of event
Credit Cards: no

Lead Time: 1 week to 1 year
Playing Time: 2 - 5 hrs.
Audience Requests: yes

The Nob Hill String Quartet is very well known throughout the Bay Area. All its musicians are versatile, have impressive resumes, and have played and recorded with many other groups, including Van Morrison with whom they have toured and recorded. Quartet cofounder John Tenney is at home in any style of music and can write custom arrangements if desired. Co-founder Teressa Adams played the entire San Francisco run of "Phantom of the Opera" and is principal cellist with the Midsummer Mozart Orchestra. She received a Grammy award for "Best Local Studio Musician – String Category." The Quartet's references could not praise them enough.

John and Terry also offer the Nob Hill Salon Orchestra. Fifty years ago, such groups would play the best American and Continental dance music: fox trots, waltzes, rags, blues, and Charlestons. They consisted primarily of violins, cellos, and piano, and performed in elegant restaurants and exclusive homes from tea time to evening. The Nob Hill Salon Orchestra continues the tradition today; it can be a wonderful feature of Victorian weddings, anniversaries, and art deco or "Gatsby-era" theme parties.

John and Terry can provide music for parties, wedding ceremonies, and receptions. Besides the Quartet and the Salon Orchestra, they offer trios and duos, strolling violinists, and ensembles with flute and harp. Promotional packages that include demo tapes are available on request.

PHOTOGRAPHERS

NOTES

INTRODUCTION

Memories of your wedding are preserved in your mind, your heart, and in your wedding album. You want to recall the events of that important day by looking at the pictures, and you want to share them with your friends. Therefore, you should choose a photographer whose style and personality most appeal to you.

Spend some time looking through the portfolios of several photographers. View both complete wedding and preview albums to get a good overview of their work and style. If the pictures stir up some excitement in you about your wedding day, then you have found the right photographer. It might be someone who does beautiful portraits, or someone who captures the event in candid shots.

The highly skilled photographers in the area do a great job. If their rates seem high, keep in mind that half their fee covers their overhead expenses (film and developing; proofs, final prints, and the album). Remember that photographers have a long day of hard work as they accompany you from the wedding ceremony to the end of the party. They spend an additional 20 to 30 hours consulting and editing. The larger format cameras, which are expensive, produce higher quality prints, especially for enlarging portraits. 35mm cameras allow greater ease of movement and can zoom in closer for candid moments.

This might come as a surprise, but most photographers will plan a wedding with you and make sure that all the pictures you want are taken during the event. Many use a worksheet to help them keep track of what needs to be done. One woman complained to me that the photographer had forgotten to take a picture of her and her parents during the event and ended up charging extra for a subsequent studio session. Just because you saw a picture from one of the sample albums, don't assume that the photographer will take the identical shot at your event. List all "must-have" photographs prior to the wedding day. Careful planning can avoid disappointments.

Now, here's what can happen when you don't hire a professional photographer. At one wedding I attended, it was obvious that the photographer was inexperienced. She stood right in front of us during the ceremony, barring the view for many guests, ran out of film when the couple was showered with rose petals, and got caught by the Hava Nagila dancers in the middle of the floor. She was also not properly dressed. (A true professional always dresses like a guest so as to appear unobtrusive.) If a friend is shooting your wedding, make sure he or she brings along enough film. Friends of ours who shot their friends' wedding ran out of film before the cake-cutting ceremony.

Remember to confirm the following items in your contract: date, location, arrival time, total amount of time the photographer will be present, package plan, and the name of the photographer assigned to your event. If you hire a photographer for a shorter amount of time, inquire about the other events he or she has scheduled for that date. If your wedding runs late, the photographer may have to leave for another appointment.

Some photographers tend to "take charge" of the wedding so that they can get all the pictures done quickly. Some might become rude if your guests don't readily cooperate with them. Ask references about these kinds of behavior.

It is customary these days to have many pictures, especially formal shots, taken before the ceremony for several reasons: your makeup is fresher, and you'll have more time to spend with your guests. If you are planning to get married in a church or synagogue, find out about their particular rules concerning photography.

Make sure your photographer and videographer work well together. Conflicts may arise if the photographer prefers to use available light only, while the videographer wants to use big strobe lights while taping.

Most photographers offer **package plans**. Some also offer **à la carte** arrangements, customized to your particular requests.

Previews are the initial prints, made from the negatives, from which you make your selections. Most photographers have previews ready between one and three weeks. Several photographers will include the previews for free with your album order. Most photographers keep all the **negatives**. Some might sell them to you after a few years.

Camera format tells you the type of cameras the photographer uses. The larger, mid-size cameras produce larger negatives, and better quality pictures, and are great at producing poster-size photographs. The smaller 35mm cameras are easier to handle and are more suitable for candid photography.

Money Matters

Prices vary depending on the amount of time the photographer spends at the wedding, the number of prints, and on the type of album.

Money Saving Tips

Ask your photographer if he or she offers gift certificates in case your guests are wondering about a gift for you. This is just like registering for wedding gifts at a store.

Art of Photography
by Karen Bates
(by appointment)
Oakland, CA

(510) 530-5265
(call for FAX number)

Contact: Karen Bates

Service Area: Greater Bay Area

Specialties: Weddings and portraits

Price Range: from $1,600
Extra Charges: travel beyond Bay Area, parking

Payment Terms: 50% deposit, balance
                        due 30 days prior to event
Credit Cards: Visa, MasterCard
Lead Time: 1 week to 1 year

Package Plans: à la carte
Time Present: 5 hrs. to full coverage
Previews Ready: 2 - 3 weeks
Camera Format: 2¼, 35mm

Karen was highly recommended to me by colleagues and other wedding industry professionals. Easygoing and full of humor, she is fun to work with and has a special knack for making her subjects feel relaxed in front of the camera. As a former dance instructor, Karen has a great eye for composition. She is recognized for her architectural and environmental styles of photography. Even her posed shots look lively. Her artistic flair, great ideas and excellent use of space make the pictures even more exciting, and her clients have come to respect the artistry and creativity in her work. With all of these qualifications, it's no wonder she is highly in demand and booked well in advance for Saturday weddings.

Karen's goal is to present her client with a perfect storybook album that captures the happiness and romance of the special day. She encourages her clients to be available for pre- or post-wedding photographs so as not to interrupt the flow of the event, and also offers engagement sittings. She is particularly helpful when it comes to logistics and when dealing with the emotions of the day. You can be assured of her presence at the event since she never subcontracts to other photographers. She shoots on a medium format camera, and is always accompanied by an assistant.

Karen also travels extensively throughout the US, Mexico, UK, and Scandinavia, teaching and lecturing at schools, conventions, and seminars. She has won several awards for her work which has been displayed in international exhibitions. Her work was recently accepted into the Loan and Traveling Loan Collection of the Professional Photographers of America, recognition awarded to those exhibiting the highest level of photography in the country. This year she received the coveted Master of Photography degree and is also a Photographic Craftsman.

Bartnikowski & Price
Wedding Photography
135 Cowper Street
Palo Alto, CA 94301

(650) 326-9567
FAX: (650) 326-6247
terrasoul@nanospace.com
www.sacredspace.com

Contact: Mary Bartnikowski or Michael Price

Service Area: Bay Area, Napa, Monterey

Specialties: Exclusively weddings; black and white portraiture

Price Range: $2,450 for entire day (includes custom 5"x5" prints in Art Leather albums); album with pictures, $495 - $1,240; engagement portrait session, $225
Extra Charges: travel

Payment Terms: $600 non-ref. deposit, balance due 1 week prior to event
Credit Cards: Visa, MasterCard
Lead Time: 1 week to 1 year

Package Plans: 1 plan
Time Present: full coverage
Previews Ready: 4 weeks
Camera Format: 2¼

Mary and Michael have been partners in wedding photography for over 15 years. After photographing over 500 weddings, they are masters at capturing any type of wedding situation. They treat each wedding like a film unfolding with their cinematic eye. Mary has a tender way of relaxing even the most camera-shy groom into smiling radiantly. Her trained eye catches those peak moments without intruding on the flow. Michael's easygoing nature is transferred into the relaxed photos he delivers with precision and sharpness. He seamlessly blends in while stalking the laughter and anticipating the bloom of the moment. Candid photojournalism is their specialty.

Mary and Michael approach each wedding as an artistic endeavor. Their passion for perfection is evident in each of the more than 400 images they give the bride and groom to keep. They specialize in honest coverage without holding the couple hostage for photographs. References cherish their photos because they are so "beautiful and sensitive in their content." They commented on their unobtrusive way of covering a wedding, and compliment the many pictures they didn't even realize were taken.

Ben Janken Photography
Distinctive Weddings
(by appointment)
Oakland, CA

(510) 482-9041
FAX: (510) 482-9086
www.sfweddingphoto.com/janken/janken.htm
www.weddings-online.com/pho/BenJanken

Contact: Ben Janken

Service Area: Greater Bay Area

Specialties: Weddings, events, portraits

Price Range: $900 - $7,000
Extra Charges: travel beyond one hour

Payment Terms: 50% deposit, balance due at pickup of previews
Credit Cards: Visa, MasterCard
Lead Time: 1 month to 1 year

Package Plans: 4 plans and à la carte
Time Present: 3 hrs. to full event coverage
Previews Ready: 2 - 3 weeks
Camera Format: 2¼

When I first met Ben, his business was equally divided between wedding and commercial photography. Being a "people person," he had always enjoyed wedding and portrait work. Over the last few years, his wedding business has taken off so much that he has had to refer many clients to other photographers. As I browsed through his latest photos, I noticed the improvement in the quality of his work. He has become a master at "coaxed candids." A great example of such a picture shows a couple embracing on a balcony of the Flood Mansion, with the stunning backdrop of the Golden Gate Bridge bathed in the wonderful warm glow of the sunset. Ben's experience and skills are obvious in his work. His high-quality prints have wonderful, natural and crisp colors.

While talking to him, I felt I was being well taken care of. I had the same feeling when we worked on my family portrait. All he did was make one suggestion, and the sitting was over in no time. Upon seeing the portrait, our friends and relatives remarked, "A professional at work." Ben's clients feel the same way: they praised his excellent pictures; his organizational skills; his warm, relaxed personality, and his ability to make everything run smoothly. They also think his pictures are very professional, lively, and fun to look at.

Ben believes it is very important to plan a wedding carefully. He works closely with the couple, records the requested pictures on a worksheet, learns the names of the relatives, and assists in planning the event, all the while getting to know them better. To further strengthen his skills and improve the quality of his pictures, Ben meets regularly with a group of photographers to talk about and critique each other's work.

Bruce Forrester Photography, Inc.

(415) 388-3686
FAX: (415) 388-3687

809 Spring Drive
Mill Valley, CA 94941

Contact: Bruce or Susan Forrester

Service Area: Greater Bay Area and beyond

Specialties: Weddings, events, people

Price Range: $1,600 - $6,000
Extra Charges: travel beyond 45 miles

Payment Terms: 1/3 deposit, 1/3 due day of event, balance due at pickup
Credit Cards: Visa, MasterCard (for reprints only)
Lead Time: 1 week to 18 months

Package Plans: several flexible plans
Time Present: full event coverage or custom
Previews Ready: approximately 2½ weeks
Camera Format: 35mm

Town & Country's "The Bride's Guide to Planning the Perfect Wedding" listed Bruce Forrester as "one of the country's very best first-class photographers." Bruce earned a BA in fine arts from the San Francisco Art Institute. He began his career as the staff photographer for the monthly society publication *Revue West* and then became the primary Northern California photographer for *Women's Wear Daily*. Bruce has exhibited in several galleries and the San Francisco Museum of Modern Art. His photography has been published in over 30 countries worldwide, and a book of his black & white photographs has been published for children.

In business for over 20 years, Bruce has photographed over 600 weddings with minimal advertising. His commitment to excellence is of the highest level. Backup equipment and an assistant always accompany Bruce. His excitement and passion are seen in the tremendous amount of film he shoots at any event. The use of 35mm format is conducive to Bruce's photojournalistic style.

In working with Bruce, I find that he never misses a step. He is passionate about capturing every moment, and it shows in his final albums. Since he feels no two weddings are alike, he has no preconceived agenda. From portrait to candid, he shoots in color and black & white, stretching his creativity during every wedding. One client commented, "He hiked all the way out into the middle of a vineyard to capture a shot."

The time he spends with his clients in creating the finest albums available is his way of "personalizing his work of art."

Camerawork

(831) 464-1244
www.dquijanophoto.com

3290 Fairway Drive
Soquel, CA 95073

Contact: Daniel Quijano

Service Area: Peninsula, South Bay, specializing in the Monterey Bay area

Specialties: Wedding, portrait, professional and art photography

Price Range: from $1,500
Extra Charges: travel beyond 50 miles

Payment Terms: $500 - $800 non-ref. deposit, balance due day of event
Credit Cards: Visa, MasterCard
Lead Time: 2 weeks to 2 years

Package Plans: 4 plans; albums à la carte
Time Present: 5 - 8 hrs.
Previews Ready: 1 week
Camera Format: 2¼ (35mm on request)

"You have to have him in the book because, aside from being a great photographer, he's also a fun person to be with," one florist told me. Daniel Quijano is an all-around photographer. He received a master's degree in photography from San Francisco State University and is an instructor at Cabrillo College. In addition to professional and art photography, weddings are an important part of his business. To give his clients his best, he will accept only one event per day.

Dan thinks that the key to a beautiful wedding album is a very thorough consultation. The first one lasts about an hour and a half, during which he discusses everything: different kinds of approaches, candid or formal preferences, and which family pictures should be included. He can help plan the wedding day and coordinate the entire event. He learns the names of the family members and makes sure everything goes smoothly. "It will reflect in my pictures, and I only want to give the best."

Dan's portfolio speaks of his experience; it contains beautiful formal portraits, candids, and even funny pictures. His favorites are natural, outdoor pictures that create a special mood. References recommend him highly. They have nothing but praise for his work and told me how his help made everything so much easier.

"Daniel is so accommodating he even offered to wear a period outfit for a Renaissance theme wedding." Clients and vendors alike find his personality and flexibility perfect assets for a day filled with emotions and schedule variations.

Willis Preston Campbell
Master of Photography
1015 Cedar Street
Santa Cruz, CA 95060

(831) 425-5700
FAX: (831) 425-2220
wpc@wpcphotography.com
www.wpcphotography.com

Contact: Willis Preston Campbell

Service Area: Greater Bay Area

Specialties: Weddings and portraits

Price Range: $750 -$5,000
Extra Charges: travel beyond 25 miles

Payment Terms: $750 - $900 non-ref. deposit, balance due in 3 installments
Credit Cards: major credit cards
Lead Time: 3 - 12 months

Package Plans: 3 plans and à la carte
Time Present: 2 hrs. to full day coverage
Previews Ready: 3 weeks
Camera Format: Hasselblad 2¼ and Canon 35mm

Willis' studio and office are located in a remodeled Victorian house in downtown Santa Cruz where you can view his beautiful portraits and wedding albums. His name, however, is as well known in the Bay Area as it is down the coast as far as Carmel and Monterey.

Willis has been in business for over 26 years, 21 of those at his current location. He received his Master of Photography degree in 1994. His pictures are perfect; the composition and quality of his prints show the experience and knowledge of a true professional. His albums include portraits, fun candids, and illustrative work. He certainly captures the moment and the fun of the wedding day with imaginative, well-composed pictures.

With so many years of experience, Willis understands the importance of planning a wedding, and he does his best to make sure the event runs smoothly. He learns the names of the immediate family, stays in the background, and follows the flow of the event. His goal is to create a wedding day story. Willis believes in treating everyone the way he himself would like to be treated. He usually works with an assistant.

One client told me that he selected Willis because of his excellent work and professionalism. He thought his best work was his informal pictures in which he captures the spontaneity of the event.

Dawn Photography

(650) 348-3655

FAX: (650) 348-5258
deardawn@batnet.com
www.ByRecOnly.com/dawnphotography

1147 California Drive
Burlingame, CA 94010

Contact: Dawn Deardorf

Service Area: Greater Bay Area and beyond

Specialties: Weddings; family and child portraiture; boudoir photography

Price Range: full coverage, from $1,375; à la carte, from $600
Extra Charges: none

Payment Terms: $400 deposit, balance due based on customized payment plan
Credit Cards: major credit cards
Lead Time: 1 week to 18 months

Package Plans: 4 plans and à la carte
Time Present: 3 - 12 hrs.
Previews Ready: 2 weeks
Camera Format: 2¼

Dawn was always interested in photography. In 1987, with encouragement from friends whose weddings she had photographed, she began working with a well-known wedding photographer in the area. After about a year, she felt she had learned enough to open her own business. She continues to sharpen her skills by taking weekend courses and seminars from various nationally known photographers. Some of her best work adorns the walls of her studio, including photos that have won Awards of Merit from Professional Photographers of the Greater Bay Area.

Dawn emphasizes personalized service and conducts extensive meetings with her clients at her studio, in their home, or at the wedding site. She will return phone calls promptly, learn the names of relatives, and goes into such detail as learning the bride's color scheme. She is willing to travel and has photographed weddings in New York and Hawaii. She values the engagement photo session, included in most of her plans, as a great way to get to know the couple. Dawn will go the extra mile, even literally, for her clients. One bride told me that she accompanied them to the beach to take some wedding pictures. She also informed me that most of her friends had hired Dawn for their weddings. One friend liked a photo of herself so much that she used it for her Christmas cards.

Dawn's style is romantic and portrait-oriented, but she also includes many candids in her work. Black & white pictures are available on request. An evaluation form sent to clients after the event is further proof of her excellent service.

Deanna Graham Photography

(Formerly William Ball Photography)
(by appointment)
Los Gatos, CA

(408) 356-3540
FAX: (408) 356-2118
www.deannagraham.com

Contact: Deanna Graham

Service Area: Greater Bay Area

Specialties: Weddings and environmental portraiture

Price range: from $2,100
Extra Charges: travel beyond 25 miles

Payment Terms: $1,000 deposit at engagement session, balance due at pickup of previews
Credit Cards: Visa, MasterCard
Lead Time: 6 - 12 months

Package Plans: 4 plans
Time Present: to full coverage
Previews Ready: 2 weeks
Camera Format: 2¼ portrait, candid 35mm

Photography has been Deanna's longtime love. One day she decided to pursue her passion and sold her successful business, took photography classes, attended professional seminars, and began working with the well-known photographer, William Ball, from whom she eventually purchased the business. Eight years later, she is now well known in her own right and ranks high among the group of wonderful women photographers in the Bay Area.

I have always loved and admired her work, filled with rich tradition and romance. Her outdoor portraits are very sensitive and very much in tune with nature. I saw an engagement picture of a couple in a park in autumn. The brown hues of the leaves are so vivid that you almost can imagine the rustling sound and the scent of the leaves. Another favorite of mine is of a wedding in the wine country. The bride is feeding grapes to her new husband in the vineyard while in the background the sun is setting over the golden California hills. I like Deanna's feminine approach as well as her wonderful family and children portraits. Last year, several of her wedding photos were featured in the national publication *Elegant Bride*. At the end of the wedding a fantastic display of fireworks entertained the guests. Deanna caught the couple in the departing Rolls Royce driving through an arch of fireworks.

Deanna also has a talent for putting her clients totally at ease. Her warm, vivacious personality and her creativity guarantee a successful photo session. She always tries to include an outdoor engagement sitting, which lets her become better acquainted with the client and helps set the tone for what she will capture on the wedding day. She works with an assistant and uses color or black and white film. During each wedding, she strives to capture the essence of romance. She will shoot more candids or more portrait-style pictures, depending on the client's wishes. Her goal is to create an album or wall portrait that will be enjoyed and admired for years to come.

Rufus Diamant
Celebrations Photography & Video
5999 Westover Drive
Oakland, CA 94611

(510) 530-4480
FAX: (510) 763-0804
RDiamant@verio.com
www.ByRecOnly.com/rufusdiamant

Contact: Rufus Diamant

Service Area: Greater Bay Area

Specialties: Photography and videography for weddings and Bar/Bat Mitzvahs

Price Range: Photography, $1,550 - $2,350; videos, from $1,800; $500 discount for both stills & video
Extra Charges: travel beyond East Bay, black & white photography

Payment Terms: $350 non-ref. deposit, balance due at pickup of album
Credit Cards: no
Lead Time: 1 week to 1 year

Package Plans: 5 flexible plans
Time Present: 6 hrs. to full event coverage
Previews Ready: 5 - 10 days
Camera Format: 2¼; video: digital

Rufus' extensive portfolio is evidence of a very experienced photographer. His background in fine arts and several years of filming educational and political documentaries have influenced his cinematic approach. His priority is documenting the event and including formal pictures. He wants to be thought of as a guest rather than as the domineering photographer running the show. Putting people at ease and moving quickly are his main concerns. He meets with the bride and groom before the wedding to get to know them and their families, and to learn their requests.

It's fun to look at Rufus' candids. They totally capture the moment and portray the mood of the event. You can almost hear the hora music or the shrieks accompanying the bouquet tossing. His group pictures, though posed, are far from ordinary. The way he puts a group together makes the photo much more exciting than having everyone stare at the camera saying "cheese." For formal pictures, he prefers nature or architecture as background over a studio setting in order to bring out character and feeling.

Rufus offers video services in addition to photography. His videos are very natural in tone, partly due to eliminating glaring lights. They capture the action, but are also conversational and relaxed, fitting in easily with a variety of wedding styles. If you would like both photos and a video of your event, he will bring along a videographer who uses his same photojournalistic approach.

Clients love Rufus' work, highly recommend him because he is easy to work with, unobtrusive during the event, and sensitive to his clients' needs and wishes. Working with multi-cultural couples accounts for nearly half of his business.

Peter Diggs
Photography
(by appointment)
San Francisco, CA

(415) 648-2266
FAX: (415) 648-6313
diggsp@pacbell.net
www.diggsphotography.com

Contact:　　Peter Diggs

Service Area:　International

Specialties: Everything from weddings to commercial photography

Price Range: $2,500 - $4,150
Extra Charges: travel beyond ½ hour

Payment Terms: 1/3 non-ref. deposit, 1/3 one week prior, balance due at pickup
Credit Cards: no
Lead Time: 1 week to 6 months

Package Plans: 5 plans
Time Present: flexible
Previews Ready: 1 week
Camera Format: 2¼

He simply says "Peter here" when he answers the phone. Just as simple are his package plans and his business approach, as I learned when he photographed the cover of one of my guides. His pictures, however, are so beautiful and interesting that it's hard to tear yourself away from looking at them. Peter showed me a magazine that featured his pictures of tables covered with food and wine, photographed in a light similar to that seen in the art of the old European Masters. While traveling, he enjoys doing art photography of mostly simple, yet striking objects. An exhibit documenting his last trip to China is displayed in his hallway.

Peter's wedding photography reflects the same high quality. He must have a gift for dealing with people, because, even in his portraits, his subjects look more comfortable than I have ever seen. Peter calls it "making people look like they really are. They should not look into the camera with the intention of being photographed but rather see themselves in a mirror." He most often uses only available light, explores different angles, changes perspective, and always seems to be in the right place at the right time. My favorite picture is of a bride who is pictured at an angle, raising her glass to a friend in the background. The low rays of the sun are reflected in the glass and in her hair while everything else remains in the shadows.

Everyone I spoke to about Peter liked him a lot. His great sense of humor and creativity enable him to come up with amusing effects. One black & white picture of a bride and groom in a rather serious pose has a slight twist of humor to it and is titled "Who says wedding photography has to look like – wedding photography?" While enjoying the reputation of a great artist, he is very professional and considerate towards his clients. He always makes sure to request a list of the people who should be photographed.

Eliot Khuner Photography

(510) 524-3569
FAX: (510) 524-0969
eliot@EKPhoto.com
www.EKPhoto.com

1052 Monterey Avenue
Berkeley, CA 94707

Contact: Eliot Khuner

Service Area: Silicon Valley to Wine Country

Specialties: Weddings, fine art black & white portraiture

Price Range: from $2,500
Extra Charges: black & white film

Payment Terms: $500 non-ref. deposit;
balance due 1 week prior to event
Credit Cards: Visa, MasterCard
Lead Time: 3 months to 1 year

Package Plans: 4 flexible plans
Time Present: 5 hrs. to full event coverage
Previews Ready: 2 weeks
Camera Format: 2¼ medium format

Capturing people and relationships is the essence of Eliot's photography. In viewing his work, it is obvious that fine art portraiture is his medium. He creates timeless pictures by capturing the "real person" – the feelings, personality, and relationships. His traditional style places emphasis on the faces, lighting, and emotions, in both candid and formal portraits.

From talking to Eliot you get a real sense of his knowledge and experience in the dynamics of covering such an important day. "I am honored when families choose me to be the eyes through which they will see this special day forever," says Eliot. He simply loves photographing milestone events, evident by the tremendous number of pictures he takes at every wedding. His candids capture the spirit of the moment, the black and white portraits are timeless, and his beautifully lit formals appear 3-dimensional.

Eliot's father gave him his first camera at the age of 13. By the age of 14 he was taking pictures for the school yearbook, developing his talent for candid portraiture. He opened his portrait business in 1976 and, after shooting his sister's wedding, expanded his business to include weddings in 1978. With his relaxed disposition, Eliot blends in well at events. Except for his wedding day assistant, Eliot Khuner Photography is a one-person operation. From your initial visit to the final design of your album, Eliot creates a sense of comfort and familiarity.

"Your photographs really capture the spirit of the moment." "The pictures looked like stills from a movie." "Eliot would finish any photo project beyond our expectations." These are just a few of the comments I received from Eliot's clients. Visit his website for a look at the depth of his photographic talent.

Ets-Hokin Studios

Photography
(by appointment)
San Francisco, CA

(415) 255-8645
FAX: (415) 255-7018
www.etshokin.com

Contact: Studio Manager

Service Area: International

Specialties: Alternative study weddings, professional photography

Price Range: from $6,500
Extra Charges: none in Bay Area

Payment Terms: 1/3 on booking, 1/3 two weeks prior, balance due at pickup of contact sheets
Credit Cards: Visa, MasterCard
Lead Time: 1 - 18 months, date dependent

Package Plans: custom
Time Present: full day coverage
Previews Ready: check with studio
Camera Format: 35mm, 2¼, large format on special request

While enjoying a successful career in commercial photography, Joshua Ets-Hokin turned to wedding photography as another outlet for his creativity and as a way of working with his favorite subjects – people. Contrasting with his beautiful, professional, still-life creations are his artistic recordings of the different dynamics experienced at weddings. A wedding for Joshua is more than just a series of camera clicks; he looks at each wedding as a serious body of work. He is also honored to be part of such an intimate event, and sees himself as the observer, interfering with the flow of the event as little as possible.

Joshua's approach to wedding photography is very exciting and different from anything I've seen before. He plans the portraiture together with the couple, which might include grandfather and granddaughter, or the bride with her favorite aunt. The style of his black & white work reminds me of *Life Magazine* photos of the 1960s. His mastery of composition, using light and shadow to catch expressions and movement, shows many subtle moments often missed in the course of a hectic day. His portfolio shows rather unique and interesting photos, such as one groomsman coming down a slide while the others are gathered around to watch. Triptychs (three consecutive photographs) portray movement or a changing facial expression. The selected prints are mounted on archival board and presented to the client in two linen covered boxes, enclosed in a matching slipcase.

Brides I talked to told me how they had wanted something different from traditional wedding photography. They were completely in awe of Joshua's work and also commented on his cheerful personality and how great it was to work with him. Joshua's photographs are often found in magazines throughout the Bay Area and across the country.

In addition to full-day coverage, weekend and overnight quotes are also available.

D. Douglass Fraser
Illustrative Photography
7023 Stockton Avenue
El Cerrito, CA 94530

(510) 524-6170
(Phone & FAX)

Contact: Don Fraser

Service Area: Greater Bay Area and beyond

Specialties: Specializing in people: weddings, portraits, corporate work, fine art photography

Price Range: from $1,400
Extra Charges: travel beyond Bay Area

Payment Terms: $500 non-ref. deposit, 50% 30 days prior to event, balance due at pickup
Credit Cards: Visa, MasterCard
Lead Time: 1 - 18 months

Package Plans: 4 plans
Time Present: 4 hrs. to full event coverage
Previews Ready: 1 - 2 weeks
Camera Format: 2¼

Viewing weddings from the inside, capturing events as they unfold without altering them describes Don Fraser's illustrative photographs. "An informal approach to formal photography," comments Don.

As a landscape photographer, Don blends his artistry of painting, inherited from his family of accomplished painters, with the modern technology of film. His experience in film, corporate portraiture, and commercial labs has added to his natural ability to communicate with and relate to people. He opened a photographic studio 13 years ago in the town of El Cerrito that specializes in portraits and upscale weddings.

Always working with an assistant, Don uniquely "double-lights" many of his photographs, giving them a 3-dimensional quality. His method separates the subject from the background, enhancing details and eliminating shadows. It looks like people are coming out of the pictures. "My creativity depends on keeping an edge," sums up Don.

I find Don's extensive knowledge of light the key to his fine art photography. He has an uncanny ability to diffuse light, eliminate glass glare, and sculpt faces to bring out the individuality and elegance of his subjects.

Don takes the time to consult with his clients on colors, styles, and the best locations for capturing and complimenting the individuals. He maintains a low-key approach, shooting from behind the scenes. One of his biggest compliments, he is proud to say, was someone mistaking him for one of the guests. His clients commented on his wonderful pictures, his competent and professional approach, and his unobtrusive way.

Genesis Photography

(650) 967-2301
FAX: (650) 967-3772
info@genesisphoto.com
www.genesisphoto.com

185 Moffet Blvd.
Mountain View, CA 94043

Contact: Ana Matos

Service Area: Greater Bay Area

Specialties: Large format traditional and environmental portraiture;
photojournalistic, hand-mounted, archival quality, black & white

Price Range: from $2,200
Extra Charges: travel depending on distance

Payment Terms: 1/3 non-ref. deposit, 1/3 60 days prior, balance due 15 days prior to event
Credit Cards: Visa, MasterCard
Lead Time: 1 month to 1 year

Package Plans: 4 flexible plans
Time Present: full event coverage
Previews Ready: 7 - 10 days
Camera Format: 8x10, 4x5, 2¼, 35mm

You can't help but be blown away by Genesis' professional photography studio. Their investment in equipment is paramount to most Bay Area photographers. The sleek entryway is a gallery of photos. The consultation room is perfectly lit for viewing their quality albums and photos. Down the hall are two large camera rooms equipped with 8x10, 4x5, 2¼, and 35mm cameras, and backdrops and equipment for wedding, portrait, and commercial shoots – all evidence of their high degree of technical proficiency. To maintain better quality control, they process all black & white film and custom print all their photographs on-site.

What impressed me most was how neat and organized they keep their customer records and pictures. They even developed their own computer program that effectively documents client history, location, payment plans, and specific needs and requirements. They are able to pull pictures from various event locations at the click of a mouse – a perfect way to view a prospective event site. As Vinnie puts it, "You can't be creative unless you are organized."

Owner Vinnie Isola's style and approach are followed closely by photographers Norine and Christina, while they each call upon their own creative energy. Their unobtrusive style combines an exquisite timeless and environmental portraiture with photojournalistic black and white action. Clients meet with Ana and view the individual albums of each of the photographers available for their wedding date. She handles all the scheduling and other administrative tasks while lending a sensitive ear to the client.

Consistent among the photographers' work is the fine balance of highlights and shadows. Their black & white printing is done according to archival standards, then beautifully hand-mounted. The color process is carefully monitored for quality assurance. Their photographs are elegant reflections of people, emotions, and relationships. It's powerful work; you have to see it!

Glenn Jay Photography
& Choice Photographic Associates

Laurelwood Shopping Center, 3154 Campus Drive
San Mateo, CA 94403

(800) 73-CHOICE
(650) 573-3355
FAX: (650) 573-0609
(209) 948-1035
FAX: (209) 948-1066

Contact: Glenn Jay or staff

Service Area: Northern California

Specialties: Weddings, Bar/Bat Mitzvahs, social photography, portraits

Price Range: $700 - $4,000
Extra Charges: travel beyond 50 miles, parking, tolls, valet/bell tips for equipment handling, overtime

Payment Terms: 3 installments
Credit Cards: major credit cards
Lead Time: 2 - 12 months

Package Plans: à la carte, album packages
Time Present: 2 - 7 hrs.
Previews Ready: 10 days
Camera Format: 2¼, 35mm upon request

Glenn Jay is a second-generation wedding photographer who, at an early age, began an apprenticeship with his father on wedding and Bar/Bat Mitzvah assignments. He photographed his first wedding at the age of 17. In 1978, with 12 years of experience, he moved his business from Arizona to its San Mateo location. Glenn Jay Photography is the oldest studio in San Mateo, celebrating its 20th year in business.

The photos in Glenn's portfolios are beautiful and were obviously done by an experienced photographer. Glenn has received several awards from the Professional Photographers Association of the Greater Bay Area. He also leads workshops for the association. His clients comment on his wonderful, high-quality photos, as well as his personality and great way of handling people and making them feel relaxed.

Glenn spends a lot of time consulting with his clients and prepares an extensive information package for them. Regardless of your photographer's talent, the logistics and wedding day schedule are critical to the success of your investment. There is a lifetime guarantee on all photographs and albums. An engagement portrait session and 11x14 photo are included in each plan.

In 1991 Glenn established Choice Photographic Associates, the first and only professional wedding photographer's cooperative in the Bay Area. It was created to both meet the demand he could not personally provide and offer a range of high-quality professionals at reasonable prices. The customer can save time by selecting from several experienced photographers, from Santa Cruz to Sacramento, who are priced according to their proven talent – a wide variety of professionals for a wide variety of tastes. Their second location is 2776 Dry Creek Way, Stockton, CA 95206.

Jere Visalli Photography

(415) 331-1223

jere@visalli.com
www.visalli.com

(by appointment)
Sausalito, CA

Contact: Jere Visalli

Service Area: Greater Bay Area and beyond

Specialties: Creative photographs that reflect your personality and style, photographed in a non-obtrusive, low-key manner

Price Range: 6 hours coverage, from $1,800
Extra Charges: none

Payment Terms: $500 at booking, 2/3 one month prior to event, balance due at pickup
Credit Cards: Visa, MasterCard
Lead Time: immediate to 1 year

Package Plans: 4 flexible plans; à la carte
Time Present: 2 hrs. to full event coverage
Previews Ready: 10 days
Camera Format: medium format, 35mm

"Vision Art," a term coined by Jere's wife Carol, is indicative of Jere's photographic style. With use of both medium format and 35mm cameras, Jere perfectly blends photojournalistic and formal moments to reflect his client's tastes. With the use of his medium format camera he utilizes his environment and the architecture around him to tell the story. As a visionary, he always looks for ways to capture the essence of the person in his or her surroundings. One picture that caught my interest showed a portrait being taken, while from the side a candid portrait was also being taken. Another picture, shot from across the yard, showed a bridesmaid misting a bride's face on a hot sunny day. "Reactions right there with the action," says Jere.

Jere's inspiration came from his father, an amateur photographer. His training came from assisting his brother-in-law, a professional photographer, until 1990 when he opened his own studio in Sausalito.

His low-key and non-obtrusive manner is evident in the rare moments and emotions captured on film. Jere is totally adaptable to the client's needs. He uses a variety of films and processes such as black and white, infrared to create fantasy, and sepia-tone to enhance the mood. "Weddings are colorful and black and white is tradition – a little of both in one shot," says Jere. For a slight glow, Carol adds subtle hand coloring to add highlight to some of the black and white images. I believe tradition, variety and spontaneity make up Jere's collection of beautiful "Vision Art."

Juliet Varnedoe Photography

(415) 552-5099

FAX: (415) 552-5098
stelzman@sirius.com
www.julietstelzmannphoto.com

1810 Harrison Street, #8
San Francisco, CA 94103

Contact: Juliet Varnedoe

Service Area: Bay Area and beyond

Specialties: Natural light portraiture and unique candids

Price Range: from $3,000
Extra Charges: travel beyond ½ hour

Payment Terms: 1/3 down, 1/3 one month prior, 1/3 day of the wedding
Credit Cards: no
Lead Time: 1 week to 1 year

Package Plans: 3 packages, custom
Time Present: 5 - 8 hrs.
Previews Ready: 2 weeks
Camera Format: 2¼

Striking use of natural light. Each photograph documents the day. Mood is created through the shadows, light, and motion. One particular photo that captured my attention was of the bride and groom's first dance. The background's blurred movement and action coupled with the dancers focused my attention on the emotion they were feeling at that moment. Another picture of a bride surrounded by a group of guys in a cigar-filled room brought me back to a place in time – the speakeasy. Many of Juliet's photos can stand alone as beautiful gallery pieces. Her assortment of color and black & white albums are sure to fit any individual style.

Juliet has been a fine art photographer since 1987, and has spent the last 4 years shooting weddings. Her major was English literature and music, but after moving to California in 1985 she decided to pursue fine art photography as another creative outlet. For two years, she worked as a fashion photographer's assistant, completing catalogues for Macy's and Gumps. Upon compiling her own portfolio, she was admitted to the San Francisco Art Institute and obtained a master's degree in fine art photography.

Juliet's style is a personal documentary of the day. Her personal interaction and direction from the start allows the day to unfold after the ceremony. She is careful not to disturb the essence of the day. The unfolding of the event appeals to Juliet's eye. One client commented, "Juliet brought out our personality and caught the exact moment. There was a series of pictures of me dancing with my father. Each one could have been framed and given as a present. Both pictures told of our relationship and personalities." Another client said, "Her technique was unique; even the posed photos looked like candids. You saw the personality and not the pose."

Martina Konietzny
Photography
(by appointment)
Emeryville, CA

(510) 652-6563
Martina@sirius.com
www.sirius.com/~martina

Contact: Martina Konietzny

Service Area: International

Specialties: Naturalism and abstract vision in color and black & white

Price Range: from $3,500
Extra Charges: none in Bay Area

Payment Terms: several installments
Credit Cards: no
Lead Time: to 2 years

Package Plans: custom
Time Present: full event coverage
Previews Ready: 2 - 3 weeks
Camera Format: 2¼, 35mm

Martina and I met at Seattle Street Cafe where her 18 large black & white prints on permanent display were purchased by the owner. I had seen Martina's wedding portfolio before, but now I was amazed at what she showed me – a body of work that definitely places her among the finest candid photographers in the area. One of her portfolios is a small show box with her work in smaller dimensions, all archivally printed and matted on museum board. This box became an instant hit with many clients who ordered her work in this size. Weather doesn't matter; I saw such a fun picture of a couple under an umbrella.

With a solid background in art, including a BFA from the S.F. Art Institute and MFA from S.F. State, Martina has shown her work in solo and group exhibits and has won several awards and competitions. When you talk to Martina, you can't help but notice how much she loves her profession. She puts so much effort into learning the important details that she usually meets with the couple several times. She will recommend a location for the engagement photo session according to the preferences and hobbies of her clients. She came up with the idea of the new library as a setting for my portrait. Before I arrived, she had arranged the photo session with the library's supervisor and scouted out the best spots. I watched her make instant friends with everyone, with her accommodating and sweet manner and dark twinkling eyes.

Each album is individually designed, and Martina offers a satisfaction guarantee with her service. Clients love her great work and her warm personality. They commented on how well she handled odd family dynamics and how well she blended in with the crowd. Besides her beautiful wedding work, her portfolios also show unique portraits of children and adults. Martina prefers to photograph her subjects the way they like to see themselves.

Martina took the fabulous picture on the front cover of this guide.

Scott Lasky

Photography
(by appointment)
San Jose, CA

(408) 363-0654
(Phone & FAX)
LaskyPhoto@aol.com

Contact: Scott Lasky

Service Area: Greater Bay Area

Specialties: Weddings, Bar/Bat Mitzvahs, portraits

Price Range: $600 - $1,200 (includes previews)
Extra Charges: travel beyond 1 hour, album

Payment Terms: 1/3 non-ref. deposit, 1/3 due
2 weeks prior, balance due at pickup of previews
Credit Cards: no
Lead Time: 2 weeks to 18 months

Package Plans: à la carte
Time Present: 4 - 8 hrs.
Previews Ready: 2 weeks
Camera Format: 2¼

Like so many photographers, Scott began his career shooting his friends' weddings. Raised in Los Angeles, he received his Bachelor of Arts degree in physics at San Diego State University, with emphasis in optics. Now, after more than 12 years of running his own studio, Bar/Bat Mitzvahs make up about half of his business. He has many portfolios that show his talent. His pictures are well composed and their quality is excellent. Looking through his portfolio again, I found that his work has become more candid and fun. My favorite picture shows the bridegroom kissing the bride while bridesmaids and groomsmen watch. One of the men had sneaked behind a bridesmaid and gave the shocked-looking girl a kiss on the cheek.

Scott will plan the formal photos with the couple during an initial meeting. He does not run the show, is very calm and will do whatever the couple wants. If bride and groom prefer not to see each other before the wedding, Scott is willing to go to one or both homes, as well as to other sites, to take family pictures before the event. He will coordinate closely with the caterer, band, and videographer. Scott is a very nice person, and you can see from his pictures how relaxed his subjects feel.

You can create your own package, which includes Scott's time at the event, the number of photos taken, and the finished albums. The previews are complimentary.

Customers were pleased with their albums and commented on his nice, accommodating way.

LensArt
of Lafayette
3437 Mount Diablo Blvd.
Lafayette, CA 94549

(925) 284-4120
FAX: (925) 284-4694

Contact: Terri or Robert Scheid

Service Area: Greater Bay Area and beyond

Specialties: Weddings and portraits

Price Range: from $2,000
Extra Charges: custom-made album, travel beyond 1 hour

Payment Terms: 1/3 deposit, 1/3 halfway,
1/3 one week prior to event
Credit Cards: Visa, MasterCard
Lead Time: same day to 2 years

Package Plans: 3 plans and full coverage
Time Present: 5 hrs. min.
Previews Ready: 1 week
Camera Format: 35mm, 2¼, view camera

I met Terri and Rob in their attractive Lafayette studio. After knowing each other for several years they married in early 1995, so they're quite aware of the needs, wishes, and pressures of couples about to be married. Rob has been a photographer for many years, while outgoing Terri did event coordination. She has been Rob's photostylist since 1988 and is now also doing photography. One of her portraits of a bride with three flower girls is so romantic that other clients wanted to purchase it. Terri and Rob usually attend events together, thereby complementing each other's work, for example, by photographing the same subjects from different angles.

I was treated as if I were a client as I sat on a comfortable couch sipping a cup of tea. Terri described their services, from the first meeting to the final album. I saw their photo checklist as well as a wide variety of their work. Their previews are presented individually for easier comparison and album page composition. I saw previews of a wedding that were gathered in a very pretty box decorated with tassels and ribbons. Terri usually decorates the box with a personal item, such as a flower from the bouquet. I also saw a beautiful picture of a Wine Country wedding. My favorite was of a bride and groom exchanging private vows before the ceremony under a majestic tree in Yosemite, shot at a distance to accommodate their wish for privacy.

Clients commented on the quality of their candids and the extra effort they put into their work. They feel that Terri and Rob are quite personable and pleasant to work with. One event coordinator of a large hotel recommended them to clients, who were all very pleased.

Richard Mayer
Photography
(by appointment)
Belmont, CA

(650) 508-1201
FAX: (650) 508-1203
bebopphoto@aol.com
www.sfweddingphoto.com/mayer/mayer.htm

Contact: Richard Mayer

Service Area: Greater Bay Area and beyond

Specialties: Weddings, garden weddings; natural light photography, Bar/Bat Mitzvahs, portraits; public relations; black & white photography throughout day; watercolor portrait

Price Range: $1,800 - $5,000
Extra Charges: none in Bay Area

Payment Terms: $550 deposit, 50% 2 weeks prior to event, balance due at pickup
Credit Cards: major credit cards
Lead Time: 4 weeks to 1 year

Package Plans: 4 plans and custom plan
Time Present: 6 hrs. to full event coverage
Previews Ready: 3 weeks
Camera Format: 2¼

Richard studied photography at the Academy of Art College in San Francisco. His first experience in the field was as a free-lance photojournalist. He continued taking classes from leading photographers and also taught seminars for the Professional Photographers of the Greater Bay Area, as well as classes in advanced photography for the City of Berkeley.

Garden weddings are Richard's specialty, and he loves using nature or attractive buildings as backdrops. He uses natural light as much as possible for indoor shots. One of my favorite pictures shows a long hallway of a hotel with light entering through several dormer windows while a bride looks out one of them. He also has clever, whimsical ideas for group shots, especially for Bar/Bat Mitzvahs which are a lot of fun. He calls upon his photojournalistic background to record the event. He makes people feel relaxed, works quickly, and his formal picture sessions seldom last longer than 20 minutes. Richard blends in well with the crowd. He gives 100% effort to each event and aims to please everyone. His work for weddings and Bar/Bat Mitzvahs includes planning the event's agenda. During the last meeting, Richard discusses all the important details with you and even learns the names of close relatives.

You can visit him at his studio in Belmont and browse through his extensive portfolio, which is evidence of his expertise and his love of people and his job. Clients choose him over others for his well-balanced, beautiful work and his very accommodating way. I also talked to many event professionals who love working with him and recommend him highly. Richard offers discounts on engagement pictures and for the early return of previews. Black & white photography can be provided throughout the event for an additional charge. A watercolor portrait of one of his pictures can be ordered.

Don Melandry
Certified Professional Photographer
1334 Carlotta Avenue
Berkeley, CA 94703

(510) 526-5130
DMelandry@aol.com

Contact: Don Melandry

Service Area: Greater Bay Area and beyond

Specialties: Weddings, Bar/Bat Mitzvahs, portraits

Price Range: $995 - $2,000
Extra Charges: travel beyond 1 hour, parking

Payment Terms: $300 non-ref. deposit, balance due 2 weeks prior to event
Credit Cards: no
Lead Time: 1 month to 1 year

Package Plans: 4 plans and à la carte
Time Present: 4 hrs. to full coverage
Previews Ready: 1 week
Camera Format: Hasselblad 2¼

Before starting his own business, Don was a photographer for a Berkeley newspaper, documenting everything from civic leaders to social events. His desire to learn all about his subjects continues to today. During an extensive meeting with the bridal couple, he asks about their hobbies, learns details about the guests, and compiles a list of photographs to be taken at the event. Knowing such details, Don once flagged down a passing fire engine and requested that it serve as a backdrop for a picture, since the bride's father was a fireman. For another couple who met while bike riding, he suggested photographing them leaving the reception on bicycles.

One of Don's best photographs enhances the entrance to his home. This photo of a couple in the foyer of a Peninsula church received an award, as has his other work, from the Professional Photographers of the Greater Bay Area. The amount of thought that he puts into each picture is quite obvious when browsing through his portfolios.

Don's clients comment on his calming effect, his professional, yet laid-back approach, his impromptu ideas, and his great work. One bride told me that just about all her friends had hired him for their weddings.

For best results, Don will assemble the wedding album himself. He is willing to sell you the negatives three years after the event. For couples booking weddings, he offers a complimentary portrait sitting on their first anniversary or with their first child, whichever comes first.

Theodore H. Mock

Photography
415 University Avenue
Palo Alto, CA 94301

(650) 321-5574
FAX: (650) 321-6592
odettem@earthlink.net
www.mockphoto.com

Contact: Theodore or Odette Mock

Service Area: Greater Bay Area

Specialties: Weddings and company parties; indoor and outdoor portraits

Price Range: $1,150 - $5,995; à la carte, $150/hr., plus charge for previews
Extra Charges: none in Bay Area

Payment Terms: 35% deposit, balance due at pickup up previews	**Package Plans:** 5 plans
	Time Present: ½ hr. to full coverage
Credit Cards: major credit cards	**Previews Ready:** 7 - 10 days
Lead Time: 6 - 12 months	**Camera Format:** 2¼

Theodore and Odette Mock's studio in downtown Palo Alto is almost an institution. Daughters and sons, photographed during their senior year, return for their weddings and later for family or executive portraits. The owners are always friendly and helpful, waiving to passersby and opening the door even during off hours. Theodore is the artist, whose beautiful pictures decorate the walls, showing his clients how much love and care he puts into his work. After receiving a degree in graphic design, Theodore pursued his love of photography as a business. His graphic design experience is visible in his work where background and people form an integrated whole.

His wife Odette can assist in planning a wedding. An album with photographs of the popular churches and ceremony locations in the area, showing background and natural lighting, help in decision making. A very thorough pre-event consultation is conducted about a week before the event. Odette accompanies her husband to most events. She told me that she has considered attaching wheels to her heavy bag, in which you can find everything from safety pins to makeup. She hands out tissues, powders shiny cheeks, and knows how to pin corsages and fluff the bride's dress before she walks down the aisle. During post-production activities, Odette is in charge of retouching wrinkles and blemishes on the faces of the older generation.

One client I spoke with hires Theodore for every family event. Another client commented, "He floats around with the crowd, almost like a family member. He does wonderful portraits and candid shots."

All packages include an engagement sitting shot in black & white film.

Nagareda Studio

(408) 971-6456

FAX: (408) 292-3984

NagaStudio@aol.com

201 East Jackson Street
Japantown/San Jose, CA 95112

Contact: James Nagareda

Service Area: Greater Bay Area and beyond

Specialties: Weddings, family portraits, commercial photography, black & white photography

Price Range: packages, $750 - $2,800; portraits, $50 plus prints
Extra Charges: travel beyond 20 miles

Payment Terms: 50% deposit, balance due at pickup of previews
Credit Cards: no
Lead Time: 1 week to 1 year

Package Plans: 6 plans
Time Present: 1½ hrs. to full coverage
Previews Ready: less than 2 weeks
Camera Format: 2¼

James fell in love with photography while working in camera shops. He owned a photo studio in Santa Barbara before moving to San Jose to finish his degree in molecular biology. His former hobby has now become his profession. James is a very nice, calm and polite young man, brought up in the Japanese tradition. When I visited his studio he offered me coffee and sweets, commenting that this way of treating his clients is such a part of him that he would consider it rude not to do it. He works with his clients to achieve exactly what they want and is not hesitant to make suggestions. James speaks Japanese and is well known at the Buddhist temple next door.

His portfolio shows pictures of Asian weddings, wedding portraits in the stylized Japanese tradition, as well as brides in authentic kimonos of heavy silk. He provided the gown rental company with photographs of these expensive gowns. Some of his work is displayed on his studio walls. Among the photos of children and weddings are also those of fashion models and album cover designs. Wedding portraits can be shot in his studio or in a nature setting. To create perfect lighting effects, James will always be accompanied by an assistant. With his high-tech equipment, he can manipulate photographs, opening eyes or making people disappear. His clients think he does a fantastic job. References recommend him highly and think his prices are quite reasonable.

James' extensive commercial work is well known throughout the Japanese community in San Jose. His commercial clients include Sony and Honda, among others. His prints received special recognition during a recent international competition sponsored by Wedding & Portrait Photographers International.

On Location Photography

(408) 245-1444
FAX: (408) 245-4421

1102 Lautrec Terrace
Sunnyvale, CA 94087

Contact: Mary-Jo Seese

Service Area: Greater Bay Area

Specialties: Weddings and portraits (studio and on location)

Price Range: $1,750 - $2,700
Extra Charges: travel beyond 25 miles, retouching

Payment Terms: $1,000 deposit, balance
due at pickup of previews
Credit Cards: no
Lead Time: to 1 year

Package Plans: 3 plans
Time Present: 7 hrs. to full coverage
Previews Ready: 1 week
Camera Format: 2¼

One large portfolio filled with thank-you letters documents Mary-Jo's 18-year successful career. It began in 1980 when she apprenticed to one of the well-known wedding photographers in the Bay Area. After working for him for several years, she opened her own studio.

Mary-Jo was one of the first photographers I visited, who was then, as she is today, one of the great women photographers in the area. Easygoing and fun to be with, she is extremely organized when it comes to her work. Her dedication to delivering the best product possible starts with the consultation. You can see her beautiful work exhibited in her studio and in several portfolios.

The photos in one of the albums that she shows to clients demonstrate how different dresses and materials photograph. Light cotton prints and satin dresses tend to look washed out, while stronger colors in dresses and flowers give a much more cheerful look. Her most beautiful portraits are photographed against a natural background with natural light. However, a studio backdrop is always brought along for unforeseen circumstances.

Several of her photographs document family milestones; engagement, wedding, mother and child, and cute children's pictures tell of the continuing close relationship with Mary-Jo. Her references gave her glowing recommendations: "Mary-Jo is terrific. She is extremely efficient, on time, was here during the entire event, was very kind, pleasant to have around, and delivered a beautiful product."

Andrew Partos
(510) 841-6727

Photographer
2208 Blake Street
Berkeley, CA 94704

Contact: Andrew Partos

Service Area: Greater Bay Area, Mendocino to Monterey

Specialties: Uncontrived photos of people on significant occasions; celebrations; portraits

Price Range: $500 - $3,500
Extra Charges: significant travel expenses, extended coverage

Payment Terms: deposit and contract secure services, balance due at pickup
Credit Cards: no
Lead Time: to 18 months

Package Plans: 4 plans
Time Present: limited or complete coverage
Previews Ready: 2 - 3 weeks
Camera Format: 2¼

Born in Hungary and raised in Australia, Andrew studied theatre at UC Berkeley. He went on to pursue photography, first at the California College of Arts and Crafts and later at the Rochester Institute of Technology, where, besides earning a degree in photographic illustration, he was also a *Life* magazine photo contest winner.

I saw a copy of the album from his sister's wedding, the first he ever photographed. All the love and effort put into the photography was immediately apparent in the album, which was presented as an illustrated children's fairy tale. Even this early in his career, he captured some wonderfully artistic shots. For the more than 20 years since then, he has been perfecting his style and very personal touch as a full-time photographer.

Displayed in his studio are a variety of images from his professional work and personal travel. His pictures tell a story: beautiful portraits reveal relationships between his subjects, much more than just sweet smiles in front of the camera. You can read so much meaning into the gaze between mother and bride, or father and son. I also loved a group shot displayed on the wall which showed the fun the subjects were having. His lighting technique gives even artificially lit photos the quality of natural light. Bar/Bat Mitzvahs are another specialty.

Andrew's clients love the wonderful pictures that reflect his natural approach and how well he works with available light. Clients also comment on his sensitive, patient manner and on his unobtrusive, yet effective presence. One Jewish bride appreciated his familiarity with the customs involved in the Jewish wedding ceremony and reception because he didn't miss a shot.

John Eric Paulson
Master Photographer
2995 Leigh Avenue
San Jose, CA 95124

(408) 559-5922
www.geocities.com/soho/gallery/7738

Contact: John Eric Paulson

Service Area: Western States

Specialties: Weddings, Bar/Bat Mitzvahs, portraits

Price Range: $2,000 - $20,000
Extra Charges: none

Payment Terms: 30% deposit, balance
                  due 10 days prior to event
Credit Cards: major credit cards
Lead Time: to 1 year

Package Plans: custom plans
Time Present: full event coverage
Previews Ready: 3 weeks
Camera Format: 2¼

The first time I met John, he told me of his desire to be one of the best wedding photographers. His reputation now extends beyond California, and in 1994 he received the Gallery Award from Kodak, having scored the highest in the wedding print category in the state. The winning photo showed a bride and groom in the winter snow of Yosemite Valley. John's creations are inspired by famous painters. This specialist in environmental wedding portraits likes to reflect the couple's love for each other amid nature or grand architecture. John takes a lot of pride in his work. His emphasis is on portraits, which include dramatic back lighting. His candid reception shots, however, thoroughly capture the excitement of the event.

John's clients like the fact that he spends considerable time consulting with them. The high quality of his pictures was mentioned by several references. John is one of the few photographers who presents proofs in a multimedia show, scheduled three weeks after the wedding. Production of the custom-designed leather albums can take up to eight months. When I reviewed his work again, I found his pictures to be very romantic. He knows how to portray couples at their best, and his use of the background setting makes the photos even more beautiful.

John is a certified Master Photographer and Photographic Craftsman, and lectures on wedding and Bar/Bat Mitzvah photography throughout the United States and Canada. He does not believe in shortcuts, and caters to select couples who want the best money can buy.

Black & white or infrared film is available upon request.

Nan Phelps
Photography
(by appointment)
Berkeley, CA

(510) 528-8845

Contact: Nan Phelps

Service Area: Coast to Coast & International

Specialties: Art photography in black & white and color

Price Range: from $2,600
Extra Charges: travel beyond East Bay ($25/hr.)

Payment Terms: $500 deposit, balance
        due 2 weeks prior to event
Credit Cards: Visa, MasterCard
Lead Time: 1 week to 1 year

Package Plans: 5 plans
Time Present: 5 hrs. to full event coverage
Previews Ready: 1 week
Camera Format: 2¼, 35mm

The last time I visited Nan, I witnessed the uninhibited joy of a bride who was picking up her wedding album. You could see the delight in her face as she leafed through the pages, reliving her Wine Country wedding. Ever since we first met, I have admired this exceptional artist who is a master at capturing the entire wedding. Nan did the heartwarming pictures on the back cover of this guide. You see the joy of the bride dancing with her nieces, the bridesmaids helping the bride with her dress as they walk through the meadow, the little girl admiring the cake.

As soon as you enter Nan's studio, you know at once that this photographer is special. You won't find many large portraits on canvas, nor will you find pictures adorned with awards. What you will find, though, are candid photographs, so artistically done that you can almost smell the flowers, taste the cake, and hear the laughter. But there's another sense of which you're immediately aware: you know that you'll be well taken care of.

With a BA in fine arts, Nan began her career with a studio of drawings and paintings. She explored the possibility of adding photography in the '80s and fell in love with it. Her natural series of photos tell the story of the day. They can be realistic or have a touch of magic in the subdued sepia colors of the '20s. In her kind, quiet way she brings out the natural beauty of her subjects, makes them come alive, and creates a special mood using available lighting. She prefers to remain in the background but, at the same time, misses nothing.

Nan usually works with 3 cameras: one with film for normal lighting, one with black and white film, and one with 1,000 ASA film. Her great talent has been recognized beyond the Bay Area; she has shot weddings as far east as Tennessee and west to Hawaii. Clients and colleagues comment that Nan is an incredible photographer and rave about her artful photographs. Her clients hire her again and again for their children's photos and other family events.

Photography by Delgado
Where Dreams Come True!
1341 The Alameda
San Jose, CA 95126

(408) 287-6547
FAX: (408) 287-4816
godelgado@aol.com
www.photographybydelgado.com

Contact: George Delgado

Service Area: Greater Bay Area

Specialties: Weddings, Bar/Bat Mitzvahs, portraits

Price Range: Full Service: $2,750 - $5,750; Limited Service: $1,200 - $2,500
Extra Charges: travel beyond Bay Area

Payment Terms: $500 deposit, 50% prior
   to event, balance due at pickup of previews
Credit Cards: major credit cards
Lead Time: 1 month to 2 years

Package Plans: several plans and à la carte
Time Present: 3 - 10 hrs.
Previews Ready: 10 days
Camera Format: 2¼

Delgado was a name I heard over and over again when I first began my research. His range of photographic skills is extensive, from photojournalistic, to traditional, to classical. George is not only well known for his great work, but also for the wonderful person he is. With a twinkle in his eye and a contagious laugh, he makes even the most tense couple relax so that he can get the romantic portraits he is known for. Impeccably dressed in a black tie, George is always accompanied by an assistant and will provide a backdrop for less attractive backgrounds.

George started out as a self-taught photographer, taking journalistic portraits in the streets of Saigon. He continued his career by offering photography workshops to fellow soldiers. Back in the U.S., he pursued a BA in photography and graphic arts. George has received many awards for his work. He was acclaimed "Best Wedding Photographer in the Greater Bay Area" in a KYA Radio opinion poll. In 1991 he was awarded "Wedding Photographer of the Year" by the Professional Photographers of the Greater Bay Area, which was followed by first-place recognition for "Wedding Portrait of the Year" in 1991, 1992, and 1996, and "Best of Show, Photograph of the Year" in 1994 by the Professional Photographers of Santa Clara Valley.

While George offers a portfolio presentation in slides, you can also view a large selection of impressive candids and more traditional work in an album. He seeks out the right lighting and arranges the best poses to create beautiful portraits before the wedding vows are exchanged. Then he switches to his photojournalistic style of candid and party photography to bring out the best in his subjects. George works all over the West Coast. His clients like his excellent work and his unobtrusive manner. They also praise him for being very organized and thorough, for helping the wedding flow, and for being lots of fun.

Photography by Gebelein

(by appointment)
San Jose, CA

Contact: John Gebelein

Service Area: Greater Bay Area

Specialties: Weddings and environmental portraits

Price Range: full coverage, from $1,000
Extra Charges: travel beyond Santa Clara County

(408) 264-7523
(800) 452-1268
FAX: (408) 270-7407
John@Gebelein.com
www.Gebelein.com

Payment Terms: 1/3 non-ref. deposit, 1/3 two weeks prior, balance due at pickup	**Package Plans:** à la carte
	Time Present: hourly to full coverage
Credit Cards: Visa, MasterCard	**Previews Ready:** 2 - 3 weeks
Lead Time: 1 week to 1 year	**Camera Format:** 2¼

John prefers to let his work speak for itself. One of his walls is almost entirely covered with awards. His modesty made it take a while for me to learn that he is also a certified Master Photographer and Photographic Craftsman, one of the highest certifications a photographer can obtain. His highest honor, however, was the selection of one of his prints for the permanent collection of the International Photography Hall of Fame in Oklahoma.

John is very easygoing; he likes to talk about his hobby of country western dancing and about his trips throughout the western U.S. From these trips comes his silken image collection – soft, pictorial landscape photographs displayed throughout his house.

His albums show his different styles, including traditional pictures and candid shots. I liked his environmental portraits the best. He combines his expertise in landscape photography with human nature. Using the landscape, the light, a blooming bush, or just a picnic basket, he creates the most beautiful scenes. For busy people, John will send out several samples of his work. He will also work with you to select the right pictures for the album, and can also matte wall pictures. Through computer manipulation he can open eyes and make unwanted images disappear.

John's clients like his calm and unobtrusive presence during the event. He took so many great pictures that they found it difficult to narrow down the selection for their album.

Photography by James Fidelibus

(925) 938-3999

Master Photographer

FAX: (925) 934-8709

1727 Bonanza Street

JBStudios@aol.com

Walnut Creek, CA 94596

Contact: James Fidelibus

Service Area: Worldwide

Specialties: Weddings, portraiture, magazine and corporate work

Price Range: $2,500 - $8,000; foreign country weddings by quote
Extra Charges: travel beyond 1 hour

Payment Terms: 50% part. ref. deposit, balance due day of event
Credit Cards: Visa, MasterCard
Lead Time: 6 - 24 months

Package Plans: 5 plans
Time Present: full event coverage
Previews Ready: 10 days
Camera Format: 2¼, 35mm

The attractive studio, resembling a quaint castle, belongs to James Fidelibus, one of the most recommended photographers in the Greater East Bay. The portraits on the wall speak to his great talent, and his wedding albums are fun to look through. Besides formal pictures, there are a lot of candids that tell the true story of the wedding. Candid pictures can be quite boring if you don't know the people, but James' are just the opposite. I saw beautiful environmental and scenic outdoor portraits, where background and subject enhanced each other. He travels abroad photographing weddings – at a Loire chateau in France, a castle in Salzburg, Austria, in Northern Italy, and Mazatlan, Mexico. His albums contain great photos of people having fun. You can recognize several celebrities, from rock stars to world-famous models.

Friends told me that James is a fun person, full of humor, and easily makes people feel relaxed. He told me that it's always a great challenge to "capture the magic," and his top priority is to bring out the natural beauty of the person. He always brings lots of film so that he's ready for all situations.

James fell in love with photography while in high school and took photography courses in college. From attending many workshops and lectures and putting in a lot of time, he became Master Photographer, one of the highest accomplishments a photographer can attain. James photographed me for the back cover of an early edition of the guide, so I have firsthand experience of his work. It's a lot of fun to work with him, and the results are extraordinary.

Photography by
Rusty and Dolores Enos

131 Magnolia Avenue
Larkspur, CA 94939

(415) 924-3563
FAX: (415) 924-2434
justmarried@earthlink.net
www.weddingtips.com/enos

Contact: Dolores Enos

Service Area: Greater Bay Area

Specialties: Wedding photography and special event photography and consultation

Price Range: $1,500 - $3,700
Extra Charges: none

Payment Terms: $500 deposit, balance due 1 week prior to event
Credit Cards: major credit cards
Lead Time: 1 day to 1 year

Package Plans: 7 and customized
Time Present: 5 hrs. to full event coverage
Previews Ready: 10 working days
Camera Format: 2¼

This husband-and-wife wedding photography team is very special. Rusty and his wife, Dolores, started out to conquer the wedding photography market in 1983. Today they are very much in demand. Their many portfolios portray their wonderful work. Rusty has a great eye and is very quick to catch the right moment. One picture that shows a swan pulling at a bride's gown won the Commitment to Excellence Award. Another, which I admire, is of a couple softly lit by the light of the moon high above. Rusty considers his style to be documentary and photojournalistic, and when coupled with traditional portraits and environmental photography, the elements add up to complete the wedding album. "The albums we plan for you are sure to become your family heirlooms…timeless treasures, now and forever," says Dolores. Rusty attends workshops and seminars all over the country and is a member of the Professional Photographers of America.

Dolores assists Rusty at events. Using the coach approach, she orchestrates the traditional bridal portraits, thus shortening the picture-taking time. She truly is an asset to the whole photographic experience. When it comes to environmental engagement shoots, Dolores mirrors the bride and groom into natural, loving and emotionally-styled photographs. Dolores has a warm and loving personality and makes everyone feel very comfortable. Rusty and Dolores' mission is to produce a signature portrait for every bride and groom. As an award-winning wedding consultant, Dolores can answer any concerns you may have about your wedding.

Clients are very pleased with Rusty's beautiful pictures, Dolores' coaching and coordinating skills, and, together, their unobtrusive style.

Prichard Photography

(510) 486-0905

FAX: (510) 848-0554
twodp@jps.net
www.sfweddingphotographers.com

1806 Blake Street
Berkeley, CA 94703

Contact: Don Prichard

Service Area: Greater Bay Area

Specialties: Weddings and family portraiture

Price Range: packages from $1,100
Extra Charges: travel charges may apply

Payment Terms: $350 non-ref. deposit; 50%
6 weeks prior, balance due upon completion
Credit Cards: Visa, MasterCard, Discover
Lead Time: 1 week to 1 year

Package Plans: 4 plans
Time Present: 4 hrs. to full event coverage
Previews Ready: 2 weeks
Camera Format: 2¼, 35mm

Spontaneity – capturing the day as it unfolds rather than creating fantasy is Don Prichard's aim and approach. "Feeling the joy of the day by getting as many candid photos as possible," he explains.

With over 15 years of experience and more than 40 weddings a year, Don has refined his low-key approach to perfection. Even under the tightest of timelines or the most demanding conditions, he remains relaxed. Respectful of the couple's time with family and friends, he takes group and family pictures in an amazingly quick fashion. His portraits are always flattering, making great use of the surroundings.

Don is happy to guide wedding couples and offers helpful suggestions during the planning process. Don is quick to state, "I never forget that it is their wedding." He contributes his expertise towards helping the client lay out the final album, balancing the album between family groupings and photos that capture the uniqueness of the day.

Clients compliment Don's approach and his ability to capture what they wanted. One client expressed, "Thanks for such great pictures. We just love the way you captured it in the candids. It's like reliving all the excitement."

ProPhoto

(408) 978-7137

FAX: (408) 978-3697
inquire@prophoto.com
www.pro-photo.com

2389 Walden Square
San Jose, CA 95124

Contact: Sue Allen

Service Area: Greater Bay Area

Specialties: Weddings and portraits in color and/or black & white; digital services to create watercolor prints and other unique works of art; slide presentations at rehearsal dinner or reception
Price Range: from $1,600

Extra Charges: significant travel expenses, extended coverage

Payment Terms: deposit to secure date; 2 additional deposits towards final order
Credit Cards: Visa, MasterCard
Lead Time: 1 month to 2 years

Package Plans: à la carte
Time Present: to 8 hrs.
Previews Ready: 10 days
Camera Format: medium format

You can't help but feel at ease with Larry and Sue at ProPhoto. Their genuine concern and confident charm create a steady stream of referrals and repeat customers. ProPhoto doesn't merely shoot an event; instead, they consult with their clients until they have identified their dreams, concerns, and other important issues. With over 10 years in the business and as members of several professional organizations, including Professional Photographers of California and of Santa Clara Valley, Wedding Photographers International, and the National Association of Catering Executives, ProPhoto is consistently recommended by the top echelon of major hotels, event facilities, and organizations in the Greater South Bay.

What's unique about this dynamo team is their harmony and perfect balance as husband and wife. Their caring and fun-loving relationship puts their clients at ease and is contagiously calming on the day of the event. This is key to ProPhoto's ability to capture natural expressions, as family, friends, and guests tend to feel comfortable in front of the lens. Clients echo about how at ease they were made to feel throughout all stages of working with Sue and Larry.

Sue and Larry look at each event uniquely and endeavor to create a final product that is customized to the client's wishes. Rather than offering the traditional "package," they prefer to take a storybook approach to capturing an event and work with the client to create a flexible timeline and flow that will be conducive to creating the desired results.

ProPhoto takes pride in the amount of preliminary work and preparation they invest so that the wedding day runs like clockwork. Their years of experience have proven that these techniques enable them to create the artistry on film their clients will cherish for years to come. Larry and Sue suggest, "Leave your watches at home."

Ron Schreier Photography

(415) 242-0999
www.ronphoto.com

(by appointment)
San Francisco, CA

Contact: Ron Schreier

Service Area: International

Specialties: Capturing history; a photojournalistic approach to "real people" and "real time"

Price Range: from $2,000
Extra Charges: overnight travel and lodging, airfare

Payment Terms: $600 deposit, 1/3 due 1 week prior, balance due at pickup of previews
Credit Cards: no
Lead Time: 1 week to 18 months

Package Plans: flexible custom plans
Time Present: unlimited
Previews Ready: 3 weeks
Camera Format: 35mm

"Honest photography" truly captures Ron Schreier's photographic style. "Capturing history, freezing a moment forever is what it's all about," said Ron passionately as I was reviewing his captivating photographs.

I have been hooked on Ron ever since I met him at a wedding I coordinated for a friend. He is unique in the way he shoots what he calls "a milestone event." Several weeks prior to a wedding, Ron scouts out the event location. He evaluates the light for the time of day and reviews the client's expectations and ideas. He then shoots a roll of film, uncovering the couple's interaction and inhibitions in front of the camera. On the day of the event, the rapport he has established with the clients allows him to glide through the crowds unnoticed. Many think he is an invited guest. Ron includes unlimited time coverage in all of his wedding plans. When I asked him why he feels he needs to spend so much time with the couple, he responded, "Hours are 100% irrelevant. It's the only chance you have to capture the ambience of what was."

As a sports photographer, Ron is no stranger to the spontaneity of photographing a wedding. His father, a traditional wedding photographer, and mother ran a wedding photography studio. After graduating from Brooks Institute in Santa Barbara, Ron worked for seven years with many notable professional photographers, photographing national ads and magazines. In 1989, he moved to San Francisco and began covering weddings in his photojournalistic style. One of my favorite pictures shows two little flower girls innocently playing, parents in the background fixing decorations, while a bridesmaid is leisurely walking towards her captivated audience – a powerful photograph depicting the many elements and thoughts in that moment in time.

Ron never stops to eat at the event. He carries two cameras with color and black & white film, never misses a shot, and is always right there to capture the action. "Capturing real people in real time!"

Don Roper
Photography
740-D Sierra Vista Avenue
Mountain View, CA 94040

(650) 965-4389
FAX: (650) 965-2785

Contact: Don Roper

Service Area: Greater Bay Area

Specialties: Weddings, portraits, architecture and commercial photography

Price Range: $1,700 - $2,500
Extra Charges: travel beyond Santa Clara Valley; parking

Payment Terms: $400 deposit, balance due at pickup of previews
Credit Cards: no
Lead Time: 9 months

Package Plans: 8 plans
Time Present: 6 hrs. to full coverage
Previews Ready: 10 days
Camera Format: 2¼

As have so many others, Don became hooked on photography when he took some photography classes to fulfill requirements for his degree. He got more and more involved and finally chose photography as his profession. He now has more than 20 years of experience. He offers eight different packages, all of which include a bridal album, as well as hourly coverage of the ceremony and reception.

Don's studio is a working, no-frills photography studio with many pictures on the wall. His work is displayed in several portfolios. During an extensive meeting, all the shots and poses are discussed and recorded on a worksheet. In contrast to the formal shots of the ceremony, the ones at the reception are more candid, showing the uniqueness of each event. He prefers a low-keyed, natural approach and maintains a good relationship between foreground and background. All of his packages include a free portrait sitting.

Since Don uses local developing labs, he is able to deliver proofs and the final album much faster, without the danger of negatives being lost in the mail.

Don is a very pleasant, helpful person and is easy to deal with. His portfolios show that he not only has a talent for candid shots, but that he can take beautiful portraits as well.

Sheldon of Los Altos

(650) 948-3823
(800) 948-3823
FAX: (650) 948-1569

380 Main Street
Los Altos, CA 94022

Contact: Timothy Gill or Edward Richardson

Service Area: Greater Bay Area

Specialties: Wedding photography, portraits

Price range: 5 plans, $1,395 - $3,295; portrait sessions, from $50
Extra Charges: travel beyond 20 miles

Payment Terms: $400 deposit, 50% 2 months prior, balance due at pickup of previews
Credit Cards: major credit cards
Lead Time: to 18 months

Package Plans: 5 plans
Time Present: 2 - 9 hrs.
Previews Ready: 2 weeks
Camera Format: 2¼

After Sheldon Block retired in February 1995, Timothy Gill and Edward Richardson bought the well-established and respected photography studio in Los Altos and guarantee to continue producing the quality of service for which the studio is known. Timothy, who has been working with Sheldon since 1988, has a degree in fine arts with a major in photography. This certified professional photographer is a member of Wedding Photographers International with over 12 years of experience. Besides attending seminars and classes, he is pursuing his Master of Photography degree. The style of his pictures is very similar to Sheldon's: they are perfect and beautiful. Timothy devotes much time and effort to each assignment and will even learn the names of the members of the wedding party.

Edward has been photographing weddings professionally since 1986 and joined Sheldon's staff in 1991. I looked through the previews of one of his recent weddings at Pebble Beach. I bet the bride and groom had a difficult time making their selections because both the portraits and candid shots were fabulous. The group shots were interestingly arranged against the beautiful background, and the candids of the reception reflected a close-knit family.

With me as a model, Timothy demonstrated the newest technology used primarily for portraits. A computer stores the photographed image on a floppy disk. Pictures are displayed on the computer screen in color or black & white, and can be printed. You can see your image right there, saving you a second trip to the photographer.

Michael Steinberg
Photography
P.O. Box 2567
Saratoga, CA 95070

(408) 867-3077
www.michaelsteinberg.com
www.ByRecOnly.com/steinberg

Contact: Michael Steinberg

Service Area: Greater Bay Area

Specialties: Weddings

Price Range: $1,200 for coverage, additional charge for albums and photographs
Extra Charges: none in Bay Area

Payment Terms: 50% deposit, balance due 1 month prior to event
Credit Cards: major credit cards
Lead Time: to 1 year

Package Plans: 1 custom plan
Time Present: full coverage
Previews Ready: 14 working days
Camera Format: 2¼

"Michael is special. You have to include him in your book," said the event coordinator of one of the most beautiful locations in the Bay Area. The photographs, obviously done by an artist at work, convinced me at once. In addition to his beautiful portraits, his camera is always ready to capture a glance between bride and flower girl, or the intimate hug between mother and son. One of my favorite pictures exhibited in his studio is a bride and groom embracing in a dimly lit hallway. On the opposite wall, a workman is talking on the phone next to his bicycle. I love Michael's work because it shows so much emotion and, at the same time, fun, like the newlyweds with babies in their arms and surrounded by toddlers.

Michael has a degree in journalism and worked as a free-lance photographer for *National Geographic Magazine* and for the Associated Press. Commercial and corporate work, as well as fashion photography, contributed to his well-rounded experience. One of his photographs of Ray Charles was selected by *American Photo Magazine* as one of the top 100 celebrity photos worldwide.

Michael's journalism background is reflected in his work. "Each album is like a film: it has a beginning , a middle, and an end, and is different from everybody else's." He prefers taking family pictures after the ceremony, because everybody is much more relaxed and the smiles have no hint of anxiety. Clients love his beautiful work and think he is very creative, not only for his images but also for helping assemble the wedding album. They described how he blended so well with the crowd that they completely forgot he was there.

Storybook Studio

(650) 595-5444
(408) 739-3333
FAX: (650) 595-5722
teresa@storybook.com
www.storybook.com

626 Walnut Street, Suite 205
San Carlos, CA 94070

Contact: Teresa Halton

Service Area: Greater Bay Area

Specialties: Weddings and portraiture

Price Range: $1,000 coverage of day plus photographs and album
Extra Charges: none

Payment Terms: $800 deposit, $1,800 prior to event, balance due at order
Credit Cards: major credit cards
Lead Time: 1 day to 1 year

Package Plans: à la carte
Time Present: to 8 hrs.
Previews Ready: 2 weeks
Camera Format: 2¼

Teresa fell in love with photography while still in school and has now been in business for over 11 years. A native of L.A., she moved here in 1991 and has already photographed over 350 weddings in the Bay Area. The name of her company reflects the philosophy behind her work. To Teresa the wedding album is a storybook of that most important first chapter, the most memorable day of a couple's life – the wedding day. The album should be more than just a collection of photographs; its sequence should tell a story.

The schedule is planned during an extensive consultation. Teresa is the only photographer in the studio. She will photograph the wedding with an assistant who helps her double-light every shot, watches every detail, and helps considerably to shorten the shooting time for the official pictures.

With Teresa's help, the bride and groom can create their own custom-designed album. With complete confidence in the quality of her work, which speaks for itself, she knows that the pictures will sell themselves. That is why she charges only for her time and leaves it up to the client to select the photographs, usually many more than initially anticipated.

Teresa's clients love her wonderful work, making everybody look so natural. One bride thought that all of the group pictures turned out well because they were taken so quickly that nobody had time to blink. "She was more like a friend we could trust during the event and helped us so much with putting the wedding album together."

Studio 7

(925) 934-1972
www.dennisdesilva.com

1372 N. Main Street
Walnut Creek, CA 94596

Contact: Dennis DeSilva

Service Area: International

Specialties: Capturing natural and real people and events; portraits

Price Range: average package, $3,500
Extra Charges: airfare, lodging

Payment Terms: 50% deposit, balance due day of event
Credit Cards: no
Lead Time: 1 week to 1 year

Package Plans: 3 flexible plans
Time Present: 2 hrs. to full event coverage
Previews Ready: 1 week
Camera Format: 2¼

From the time you enter Studio 7, you know Dennis DeSilva is not just an average photographer. Beautifully captured weddings and portraits of celebrities and politicians decorate his walls. In the late '70s, Dennis was sought out by an aide to George Miller who was running for Congress. Through them, Dennis met Senator Ted Kennedy who used one of his photographs on the cover of his book, *Our Day and Generation*. Through the years, Dennis has photographed many noted politicians and congressional leaders, including President Clinton and the First Lady. His portfolios show portraits of stars, including Morgan Fairchild, Nicholas Cage, Sean Connery, Clint Eastwood, Sonny Bono, Phyllis Diller, Willie McCovey, George Lucas, and Joe Fraiser. My favorite is of Herb Caen posing in front of a framed picture of *The Thinker* while reading one of his columns. Dennis is currently Mayor Willie Brown's official photographer.

A film major at San Francisco State University, Dennis has always had a natural eye for the camera. The very first photograph he submitted to the Professional Photographers of the Greater Bay Area won him a gold ribbon. In 1970, he opened Studio 7 and began photographing weddings. He views each photo opportunity as a possible memory. "Each wedding inspires me to do something better," says Dennis.

Dennis possesses a certain magic when working with people. He loosens them up, steps back, and lets them be themselves, then shoots. "I know when to shoot and when not to shoot," says Dennis. He is a master at balancing light with natural positioning. He plans and maps everything out before involving clients, allowing them to enjoy their celebration. "I am a 'memory collector'," says Dennis. "I look for the best memories to capture while you live them." I enjoy working with Dennis because he needs very little direction. He knows who and what is important to the client and utilizes the different angles and beauty of any location. Dennis is a different breed of photographer. *Please call ahead for an appointment.*

Judy Tembrock

(408) 973-1225

Photographer
(by appointment)
Cupertino, CA

Contact: Judy Tembrock

Service Area: South Bay and Peninsula

Specialties: People – weddings, portraits, family pictures

Price Range: $400 - $4,000
Extra Charges: travel

Payment Terms: 25% deposit at booking, balance due in 3 installments (last one with finished prints)
Credit Cards: no
Lead Time: to 12 months

Package Plans: custom plans
Time Present: 1 hr. to full coverage
Previews Ready: 2 weeks
Camera Format: 2¼

When the last of her four children entered school, Judy, a former elementary school teacher, found time to take photography classes at De Anza College. She enjoyed them so much that she earned a degree in photography and began her second career in 1980. She never needed to advertise as word of mouth has brought her all her customers. Her beautiful and sensitive photographs, reflecting her sweet and calm personality, have received six awards from the National Photographers of America Merit Collection.

Judy's favorite subjects are people. She begins her first visit with a blank sheet of paper, waiting to be filled with the wishes and ideas of the couple. She will then propose an outline, most often exactly what her clients had in mind. Wedding clients told me that they were very happy with her work; she had taken all the photographs they had requested, and many more, and the subjects didn't even notice when she took them. Judy always works with an assistant at weddings.

I loved her portrait of a grandfather with his little grandson. The boy hadn't wanted his picture taken, so Judy found an interesting book for him to read while sitting on his grandfather's lap, thus making him totally unaware of the photographer. During my last visit, I fell in love with a photo of a children's tea party. While conducting a Christmas photo session, Judy spotted a cute table and chairs, around which she gathered the children. To such sessions Judy will bring flowers from her garden or adorable hats to enhance the portraits.

Judy also offers black & white photography.

M. Christine Torrington
Photography
209 Post Street, Suite 812
San Francisco, CA 94108

(415) 921-6333
FAX: (415) 986-3886
christine@sfphotopro.com

Contact: M. Christine Torrington

Service Area: Greater Bay Area

Specialties: People at special events: weddings, portraits, promotions, conventions, publicity

Price Range: $550 - $3,000
Extra Charges: none

Payment Terms: 50% deposit, balance due at pickup
Credit Cards: major credit cards
Lead Time: 1 day to 2 years

Package Plans: custom plans
Time Present: 1 hr. to full event coverage
Previews Ready: 1 day to 2 weeks
Camera Format: 2¼, 35mm

Christine started out in her career by fulfilling requests from friends and others to enlarge the photos she had given them as souvenirs. Her instant success led her to move into her portrait studio on Union Square after only three years. She is as fast at taking posed shots as she is at getting the initial prints done as soon as requested, sometimes even the next day. She captures the warm, human, and amusing sides of her subjects as her photos tell the story of the event. One couple came up from Los Angeles to have Christine shoot their wedding pictures in and around their favorite San Francisco site, the Fairmont Hotel, and on a cable car in front.

Christine's services are customized to the individual client. She shoots in color or black & white, and will spend from a minimum of one hour to however long her attendance is required at an event. Since the first set of prints is included in her à la carte arrangement, clients may choose to put their albums together themselves. In response to client requests, Christine now also offers wedding packages, including one or more albums and an option to purchase the first set of prints. Much of Christine's work comes from corporations, associations, and event companies. She has been the official chapter photographer for more than a dozen hospitality industry associations, clubs, convention bureaus, and meetings industry tabloids, shooting all their local events and meetings for their monthly publications. Photographs of prominent, national figures hang on her studio walls.

Christine sees her work as an opportunity to combine her natural love and respect for people so that she can create the best record of the most special moments in their personal and business lives. Clients commented on how much they appreciated her energy and expertise. They also admired her abilities to make people feel relaxed and to do a great job in capturing the happiness of their event.

RENTALS

NOTES

INTRODUCTION

Specialty linens, fine china, and silverware add to the elegance of an event. Props, lighting and greenery further enhance the ambiance. All of these and more are available from several good rental companies in the Greater Bay Area. Standard items don't vary much in price. The only exception is dance floors, for which I found substantial differences in cost.

The life span of rental items is limited. It's worthwhile to check the condition of each item you are renting. A reputable company may even repaint the item upon its return.

Payment terms are usually a deposit and COD ("cash on delivery") for the balance due. Delivery is usually free with a certain minimum order. Rental time is generally 48 hours, which is basically a Saturday plus Sunday when the rental stores are closed. Since the store's main cost is in cleaning and handling, longer-term rentals are often not much more than weekend rentals. Check with your location to see if delivery and pickup can be done during the week since most rental companies charge additional fees on Saturday and Sunday.

Renting a tent requires some advance planning since there aren't many available and because larger ones require a special permit from the city. The better companies are aware of local regulations and will help you obtain the permit in time. Don't attempt to set up anything other than smaller canopies by yourself. Tent rental companies know how to secure a tent to withstand a cheerful wedding or party. They will inspect the proposed tent site, put it up the day before the event, and return just before the event begins to readjust the ropes.

Money Matters

Prices vary according to item, so call for price lists.

Money Saving Tips

Find out if the next or previous client renting your location plans to use the same rental items, such as tables, chairs or a tent, so you can share the cost.

A-ABCO Rents & Sells

Special Event and Party Specialist
2200 Bay Road
Redwood City, CA 94063

(650) 365-3050
FAX: (650) 365-0859

Contact: Naomi or Alan

Service Area: Greater Bay Area

Specialties: Party tents and canopies; all items needed for parties, weddings and conventions

Pricing: call for price list or quotes (see Introduction)
Extra Charges: minimal delivery charge

Payment Terms: payment upon delivery,
                net 30 days for charge accounts
Credit Cards: all credit cards

Lead Time: to 1 year
Rental Time: 2 days
Delivery: yes

A-ABCO has one of the largest inventories of rental equipment in the Bay Area. Their 11 different types of chairs include gold and white chivari chairs, and their thousands of tables come in all shapes and sizes. For your garden party the company offers umbrellas, barbecues, heaters, and approximately 100 different sizes of tents and canopies with elegant liners and leg drapes, doors with French windows, custom lighting, and portable floors, as well as oak parquet and black and white dance floors. The heating system can even be controlled by a thermostat. Their latest item is a pool truss system that safely covers swimming pools of just about any size and shape. It can provide additional guest seating or can be used to feature the band or as a dance floor. Screens and audio-visual equipment (even a bullhorn) are available for corporate events.

Their showroom displays a wide variety of china patterns and many styles of glassware and silverware set on table linen in an array of colors, patterns and sizes. Plates with a red pepper design are perfect for a casual barbecue or spaghetti feast. For the most elegant events you'll find 500 place settings of Royal Crown Derby china and fine crystal stemware. Silver-plated chafing dishes, trays, bowls, candelabra, and tea services neatly shrink-wrapped fill the shelves.

I always enjoy coming for a visit because Naomi and her staff are so accommodating and knowledgeable about helping with every phase of an event. Their friendly voices over the phone make you instantly feel that you are in good hands. Several caterers told me that the company will dispatch equipment on very short notice, even on the weekends.

Party planning is free of charge. Party professionals can assist you with every phase of your event. Sales tax is included in the rental price.

Green Valley Plant Rental
Hartmann Studios

(510) 232-5060
FAX: (510) 232-1350

100 West Ohio Avenue
Richmond, CA 94804

Contact: Mark Guelfi (President)

Service Area: Northern California

Specialties: Live plant and prop rentals; prop design and construction

Pricing: request price list
Extra Charges: delivery and pickup

Payment Terms: COD
Credit Cards: major credit cards
Lead Time: 1 day to 1 month

Rental Time: 3 days
Delivery: yes

Mark and Michael Guelfi's story sounds like "the American dream." They started with a bucket stand in San Francisco. Now Mark is president of both companies, while Michael oversees Podesta Baldocchi (see page 147).

Green Valley Plant Rental, the premier, short-term plant rental company in California, shares a large site in Richmond with Hartmann Studios. The nearly 100,000-square-foot facility includes a large greenhouse for tropical plants and an outside area for native plants. It's fun to walk among the well-tended and healthy plants. There are rows and rows of boxed hedges (totaling 2,000 feet), small and large ficus trees, beautiful red and green Japanese maples, bamboo, palm trees, ferns, giant birds of paradise, and poodled pines. The scent is reminiscent of the deep woods as you walk among the many redwoods, cypresses, and Monterey pines, some of which are over 15 years old. Plants can be arranged in decorative containers and strung with "B" lights. The company has serviced such events as the Super Bowl in Pasadena and the U.S. Golf Championship at Pebble Beach.

Hartmann Studios, founded by Bob Hartmann and now part of this large event services company, occupies the large warehouse. Its large inventory includes reproductions of San Francisco, the Golden Gate Bridge; Western, Moroccan, and Egyptian theme pieces; seasonal props, Italian statues, benches, trellises, and gazebos. You can also find theatrical lighting equipment, staging, dance floors, Astroturf, carpeting, drapery – you name it. I greatly admired the unbelievable selection of columns, some of which I've seen in romantic Wine Country scenes and in beautiful French and English gardens. New props are created in the wood and paint shop. I was surprised to learn that each prop is repainted upon its return to the studio. Design and production staff will help you with all your needs.

Manisse Designs
A Tradition in Luxurious Linens
519 Marine View Avenue, Suite C
Belmont, CA 94002

(650) 591-8332
FAX: (650) 413-1522
manisse@pacbell.net

Contact: Manisse Newell

Service Area: Coast to Coast

Specialties: Elegant, versatile linens, napkins, chair covers, and vests for attending staff

Pricing: linens from $20
Extra Charges: delivery

Payment Terms: 50% deposit, balance COD
Credit Cards: Visa, MasterCard
Lead Time: 1 day to 1 year

Rental Time: 3 days
Delivery: yes

When I first met Manisse in 1994, she had just returned from New York where she had purchased the most beautiful material to make into linens. This famous florist began her rental business when she couldn't find the right pattern and materials to enhance her floral designs. Now, wherever she goes, she is on the lookout for new treasures. Her inventory has grown substantially over the last few years. She has many damask table cloths with different patterns, such as the Gorham striped pattern, and extraordinary alabaster damask, Battenberg lace, gold leaf organza, gold lamé with welting or ruffles, and as many overlays as tablecloths. Also available are table runners and gold moirée bows. Everything can be mixed and matched, even the ruffles. All of Manisse's designs have coordinated napkins.

Her chair covers are textured damask with inverted pleats at each leg and a flat sash tied with a knot in the back. She also carries a cotton candy line: cotton tablecloths in hot pink come in larger or smaller square patterns with seat cushions fastened to the chairs with bows. A really cute idea are the vests for the attending staff that match some of the tablecloth patterns.

All linen samples are presented in a catalog, along with pictures and suggestions, that is constantly updated. A brochure of her designs is available for $50 which is credited towards your order.

I saw Manisse's linens exhibited at a conference of event professionals. All the participants where in awe of her great designs.

Party Prints
Party Linen Rental with a Flair

(650) 259-9707
FAX: (650) 259-9968

857 Hinkley Road
Burlingame, CA 94010

Contact: Alice Verby or Sharon Dolin

Service Area: Coast to Coast with emphasis on Greater Bay Area

Specialties: Decorative linen in a variety of colors and designs, with fitting sashes for chair covers; silver candlesticks with shades

Pricing: tablecloths, from $15; napkins, from $.85
Extra Charges: shipping beyond 10-mile radius, rush orders

Payment Terms: 50% deposit, balance due upon delivery
Credit Cards: Visa, MasterCard
Lead Time: 1 - 3 months, rush orders possible

Rental Time: 4 - 5 days
Delivery: yes

Alice and Sharon started their party linen rental company in 1982. They found their niche in the party and wedding business when Alice attended a party on the East Coast. The beautiful linen that was used there could not be found anywhere in our area. They began working out of their homes and quickly outgrew their first warehouse. Their office/warehouse covers 2,300 square feet and is filled to the brim.

Alice and Sharon specialize in elaborate linens, such as paislies, plaids, stripes, black & white combinations, and special designer prints, with coordinated overlays and matching napkins. Tablecloths in gold or silver lamé and in English floral chintz are but a few choices from their large selection. They also have oversizes and ruffles. After so many years in business, they can sense new trends in decorating and are constantly adding to their stock, which now comprises the largest inventory in Northern California. One of the hottest items is the sheer organdy overlay in colors of cream and white. For a Wine Country event, the overlay was placed over maize-colored satin, which was simply pure elegance. Other new items are sashes, made from the same fabric as the tablecloth, that can be used to decorate their chair covers.

Customers receive packages of swatches to ease their selection. Combination sets are priced less. Special color commissions are more expensive and require a four-week delivery time. If you live outside the area, the order will be shipped via UPS. There is a fee for lost items, burns or cuts, and large stains. Upon request, they will add new items to their inventory if they feel they can be rented in the future. A set of linen with fish as decoration was designed for the San Francisco Aquarium. They have provided linen for many parties at the Hoover Institution and for presidential fund-raisers, debutante balls, and the Napa Valley Wine Auction. They have shipped their linen as far away as Hawaii, Williamstown, and Brussels.

The Stuart Rental Company
Celebration Resources
430 Toyama Drive
Sunnyvale, CA 94089

(408) 734-9966
(800) 400-0543
FAX: (408) 734-9988
support@stuartrental.com
www.stuartrental.com

Contact: Susan Kidwell

Service Area: Northern California

Specialties: Quality tenting; extensive well-kept party furnishings from
"Northern California's Oldest, Largest and Most Professional Event Company"

Pricing: request price list
Extra Charges: delivery and pickup

Payment Terms: 50% reservation deposit,
balance due upon delivery
Credit Cards: Visa, MasterCard
Lead Time: 1 day to 2 years

Rental Time: 2 days
Delivery: charge depends on size of order

Serving Northern California for over 150 years, The Stuart Rental Company maintains a high profile in the event industry with their specialties of custom tenting, canopy rental, and assistance in event preparation and production. Their experience from working on prominent events helps them create unique and appropriate settings based on the event location and individual preferences. In recognition of their work, the company has received multiple Gala awards for tenting as well as for logistics.

The items in their large furnishings inventory are meticulously clean and well kept, and the dishes, linens, glass, and silverware are additionally protected with a protective wrap. Their wide variety of inventory includes everything from a large selection of fine specialty china, linens, glassware and chairs to catering and serving equipment, kitchen supplies, and wedding accessories, such as arches and gazebos. They are continuously adding new patterns and items that are more elegant than you would expect to be available for rental. The company supplies rentals to anywhere in Northern California; their showrooms are located in Sunnyvale and Walnut Creek.

Their large team of experienced event professionals place great emphasis on personalized service. They make it a personal commitment to maintain a positive approach in supporting events, developing the best possible event based on their client's individual needs. Their statement: "We guarantee that, within your budget, our products and team will perform to your satisfaction."

SPECIALTIES

NOTES

INTRODUCTION

This section lists businesses that offer unique services, entertainment and gifts to enhance your event, such as:

advice counseling

chocolate creations

keepsake books

murder mysteries

personalized travel designers

song parodies & skits

All About You
Sonic Portraits
(by appointment)
Monterey, CA

(831) 647-9053
sari@mbay.net
www.ByRecOnly.com/allaboutyou

Contact: Sari August

Service Area: Coast to Coast

Specialties: Song parodies, poems, and skits for all occasions

Pricing: from $250
Extra Charges: travel, out-of-state phone calls

Payment Terms: 50% deposit, balance due prior to delivery
Credit Cards: no

Lead Time: 6 weeks to 6 months
Delivery/Pickup: yes
Portfolio: samples upon request

There are many occasions for which a personalized song or poem can add a special touch to a celebration. How often are we invited to a wedding or party and can think of absolutely nothing to give the celebrants? We were invited to a 50th birthday bash, and I immediately thought of Sari's service. The wife of the celebrant and I hired her to write a song about her husband. It was a pretty big job since the responses to the questionnaire Sari sends to her clients contained a tremendous amount of information. From the initial contact to the final product, all communication was done via phone and e-mail. All the guests had lots of fun singing the song at the party.

Sari was asked to write a song for a retiring event coordinator. Although this person was admired by her colleagues, not much personal information was provided. However, Sari was able to glean enough information from the sparse responses to write a song that was well received. After the performance, her daughters hugged Sari as they told her how well she had portrayed their mother.

After writing the song, Sari records it on an audio tape and includes a copy of the lyrics. If the performance is local, she can be requested to accompany the singers. While she can write an original song, she feels that using the tune of the celebrant's favorite song or a popular tune is more fun since everyone can join in. Sari has written songs for all types of occasions, from birthdays to election victory parties. One client had the band perform a song at a formal birthday dinner on the East Coast. Another client, who provided her with a chronology of his parents' 50 years, received not one, but a medley of songs. Sari also writes customized songs for children and skits about specific themes. She wrote the lyrics for "The BRO Song" which was performed at the last BRO party and appears at the beginning of this guide.

Amy Honigman, Ph.D.
Licensed Clinical Psychologist
(by appointment)
Piedmont, CA

(925) 838-2558

Contact: Amy Honigman

Service Area: Greater Bay Area

Specialties: "Surviving the emotional demands of planning a wedding"

Pricing: $90/hr.
Extra Charges: none

Payment Terms: at time of service
Credit Cards: no

Lead Time: from 1 week
License: PSY 11755

The emotional demands of planning the "perfect" wedding can be stressful. Surviving the emotional, social and family demands can be even more of a challenge. Amy Honigman, a licensed clinical psychologist with over 20 years of experience, has helped many couples and their families regain sight of what is really important. "I love weddings and how people interpret them," says Amy. Making a wedding meaningful and memorable is her focus.

With a statistically high number of divorced families, high demanding careers, and religious and multicultural issues, it is very common for couples and families to become unfocused. Most people just need clarification and validation on the choices they make and how to effectively communicate them. "A third party to navigate," clarifies Amy.

Amy has an insightful list of some common anxieties: "The Jitters," "Relationship Changes," "Good Practice," "Working Together," "Clear Communications," "Clarifying Meaningfulness," "Delegating Responsibilities," "Strategies for Calming Yourself," "Dealing with Others," and all the stressful demands that come along with them.

As a coordinator, I frequently see the frustration brides have dealing with family issues, trying to make everyone happy and still hanging on to their ideal wedding. For every issue an engaged couple might have and every action they might take, there is very often an underlying cause. Amy's professional and intuitive manner helps couples and families unfold the real issues, focus, validate, and overcome the emotional stress.

Clients express their gratitude for Amy's ability to put things into perspective.

Mad Moon Creations

(by appointment)
San Francisco, CA

(415) 552-0919

FAX: (415) 431-8269
celebrate@MadMoonCreations.com
www.MadMoonCreations.com

Contact: Sherry M. Richert

Service Area: United States

Specialties: Customized, handmade keepsake books for once-in-a-lifetime events

Pricing: Do-It-Yourself kits, from $75; customized, from $100
Extra Charges: shipping, custom covers

Payment Terms: 50% deposit, balance
due upon delivery
Credit Cards: no

Lead Time: at least 6 weeks
Delivery: shipping available
Portfolio: yes

There is nothing like a personalized gift to express how much someone means to you. Mad Moon Creations combines photographs and quotes from friends and family, special wishes, artwork, and recollections of events in a personalized, beautifully bound book. "If it doesn't make everyone laugh and cry, then I haven't done my job," says Sherry, creator of these innovative keepsakes. As far back as Sherry remembers, she has always made personalized gifts reflecting the recipient. A life-long writer and producer of non-profit publications, she found a way of combining her love of creating personalized gifts in a hardcover book format. Sherry says it best: "At the heart of what I do is creating gifts that reflect who people are in the eyes of those who love them most. My books become a touchstone for people, something to always remind them of how much they are loved."

Poring over her beautifully bound books, I could feel the emotion and joy that is seldom expressed in a lifetime. Sherry offers a variety of ways to customize the books for showers, weddings, graduations, anniversaries, memories, Bar/Bat Mitzvahs, birthdays, or anytime when just a plain "thank you" does not amply express your gratitude. The Group Celebration Book, designed for any occasion, has at least 25 pages of organized text, scanned photographs, and interview responses from family and friends, bound by different covers to reflect each individual style. The Customized Guest Book is a collection of responses from the bride and groom to each other with pages designed for the guests to fill. The Do-It-Yourself kits are perfect for showers or individuals who wish to create their own personalized albums.

Here are some comments from Mad Moon customers: "Sandra and I were totally touched, overwhelmed and blissed-out by the wedding book you put together. A million thanks for translating all our friends' love and support into such an awesome tribute." "This book made me feel loved as no other gift could…a compendium of the devotion, affection, humor, and love of so many friends." "A gift from the heart." "Have tissues handy – these gifts are powerful stuff!"

Mama 'n Mia, Inc.
Chocolate with an attitude!
(by appointment)
Saratoga, CA

(408) 741-8256
(800) 437-1993
FAX: (408) 741-1726
sales@mamamiachocolate.com
www.mamamiachocolate.com

Contact: Lesley Carr or Eydie M. Leighty

Service Area: USA

Specialties: Whimsical chocolate art and custom designs for private and corporate events

Pricing: favors and gifts from $1
Extra Charges: shipping

Payment Terms: 50% deposit, balance due at delivery
Credit Cards: MasterCard, Visa

Lead Time: 1 week to 2 months
Delivery: yes
Portfolio: several brochures

It all began with the chocolate pizza that Eydie gave her father for Christmas several years ago. Lesley, the "Mama," was so excited about the pizza that she and her daughter (Mama 'n Mia) started their business in 1992. First, all the family members participated in chocolate tasting to find out which chocolate was the best, settling on Guittard. At the same time, they dealt with the issues of starting a business, including finding a kitchen. They decided to set up production in Washington State, where Eydie lives. They market their products nationwide from both Washington and Saratoga, where Lesley lives. I had the opportunity to visit their kitchen in Washington and saw the production of 9,000 bags of chocolate balls accompanied by white chocolate scoops as Christmas presents for a company's employees.

They now offer eight different "pizza" flavors, such as the deep-dish "Peanut Butter Ami" and "That's Nuts!" which is filled and topped with five different kinds of gourmet nuts. Food items resembling deviled eggs, baked potatoes, ice cream sundaes, and bagels have been added to the repertoire. There are also bold-colored, hand-painted flowers in clay pots and lollipop designs in many different colors and shapes, sitting in small ceramic bags. They also do themes for Halloween, Christmas, and Hanukkah. For favors for a Chinese wedding they designed picture frames, adhering to FDA guidelines by protecting the edible chocolate from the chemicals of the photograph to be inserted. In addition to their usual lines, which are constantly expanding due to Eydie's creativity and customer demand, they create personal items, such as favors and company logos, for any theme. For a company party they presented a gambling theme with board games and playing cards.

A prototype for each new item is made from a new mold and must pass the scrutiny of Lesley, Eydie and their employees before it's ready for production.

Murder On the Menu
Parties of Murder, Mystery, and Mayhem
(by appointment)
Oakland, CA

(510) 339-2800
FAX: (510) 339-8309
whodunit@murderonthemenu.com
www.murderonthemenu.com

Contact: Janet A. Rudoph

Service Area: Northern California and beyond

Specialties: Customized private and corporate murder mystery events
and other team-building activities

Pricing: from $1,500
Extra Charges: travel beyond Northern California

Payment Terms: 50% deposit, balance due
day of event
Credit Cards: no

Lead Time: 2 weeks to 2 years
Portfolio: yes

If you are looking for a completely unique way to entertain or get your guests acquainted with each other, there is really no better way to break the ice than to have a little "Murder on the Menu." From parties of ten to five thousand, everyone will be guessing and accusing while they wine and dine.

Each mystery script is custom written by professional mystery writer Janet A. Rudolph, "the Mistress of Mystery," to fit a requested theme ranging through the Roaring '20s, Fabulous '50s, or Contemporary 2000, modeled to meet your group's objective. With several professional actors on hand to direct the action, you're sure to find the culprit.

Through unusual interactive activities, individually or as a team, participants achieve specific goals and objectives. These activities involve creative problem-solving, team-building, and risk-taking. The actors, many of whom are multilingual, blend in so well that it is hard to distinguish them from the guests. Throughout the event actors and guests give out clues. Some people are even spotlighted to help the story along. It is hard not to get involved when everyone thinks they know "whodunit." One Halloween murder mystery was held at a "haunted house" in San Francisco, where the bride and groom had themselves "murdered" during their actual wedding reception.

Praised by dozens of the largest corporations throughout the country, the group is just as capable performing an intimate affair. How about an evening of mystery and intrigue for your dinner guests, a scavenger hunt weekend for your out-of-town guests, or even a mystery wedding? The possibilities are endless, the murders and suspense are masterful.

Your Personal Travel Designers

(650) 969-3104
(800) 233-0073
FAX: (650) 969-3198
pat.bill@ix.netcom.com
www.yptd.com

(by appointment)
Los Altos, CA

Contact: Pat or Bill Harding

Service Area: United States

Specialties: Designing personalized travel experience, complete with accommodations and itineraries to fit your travel style

Pricing: $149 for Deluxe Travel Planning Service (inquire about full schedule of fees and services)
Extra Charges: international calls/faxes, foreign currency drafts

Payment Terms: in advance for travel planning services; payment for travel arrangements vary by supplier
Credit Cards: depends on travel supplier

Lead Time: as soon as possible
Portfolio: extensive library
CST#: 1001477-40

Whether it's renting a villa in Tuscany or a manor house in the Cotswolds, Your Personal Travel Designers offers a tailored itinerary and a keepsake portfolio designed especially for you. Bill and Pat plan romantic escapes to the South Pacific, Mediterranean Europe and Africa, Latin America, Southeast Asia, and the wine regions of the world. Your plans can include an enchanted stay in a quaint village, an escape to a secluded hideaway, an adventure in the lush tropics, or a rejuvenating break at an exclusive retreat. Your accommodations are arranged to reflect your personalities and profile.

Their itineraries are planned in minute detail with the traveler in mind. By uncovering travel expectations, special interests, hobbies, habits, and budget, they design a personalized travel experience documented in a portfolio. Each portfolio includes an itinerary at a glance, day-by-day calendar, and details on transportation, accommodations, local contacts, planned activities, and, most importantly, options. These provide the flexibility to adapt daily activities to your mood.

While their services are not ideal for someone looking to purchase low airfares or someone traveling on a bare-bones budget, they deliver top value for your money. Their specialty is customized service, with trips spanning multiple weeks with multiple stops. Bill and Pat combine personal experience with extensive travel resources to design your customized itinerary. Their office library is comprised of everything from catalogs and brochures on leading hotels to a collection of books on charming B&B's. Personally selected travel references occupy every inch of their office shelves; files and brochures are categorized by country. They work closely with rental agencies and wholesalers to keep up with the current status of properties and sight-seeing alternatives. Pat has been a certified Aussie Specialist since 1996, and they are members of Cruise Lines International Association. By popular request, they now provide your out-of-town guests with travel accommodations and area explorations. Bill and Pat have it all covered!

TRANSPORTATION

NOTES

. . . .

. . . .

. . . .

. . . .

. . . .

. . . .

. . . .

. . . .

. . . .

. . . .

. . . .

. . . .

. . . .

. . . .

. . . .

. . . .

INTRODUCTION

It has become quite popular for the bride and groom to rent a limousine or other special means of transportation to the ceremony and reception sites. Have you ever considered traveling in antique cars to a picnic at the beach?

The minimum required rental time for limousines is usually three hours for weddings. Some companies provide non-smoking cars, and others offer the red carpet treatment with a complimentary bottle of champagne for bride and groom.

Newspaper articles have warned about limousine companies that don't have proper licenses and insurance. The TCP number provides some assurance that you are dealing with a reputable company.

To avoid disappointment on the day of your event, clarify and confirm in writing:

- specific year, model, color and condition of the vehicle
- exact address of pickup and drop-off locations
- names to contact in case of emergency on the day of the event
- whether the company is renting to you its own vehicle or subcontracting from another

Also find out the assigned vehicle's schedule and location prior to your event. Weddings are notorious for running late. Avoid having a less comparable vehicle pick you up by getting everything in writing.

Money Matters

I found no significant **price** differences among the limousine companies. Find out if the quoted price includes the driver and gratuity.

Money Saving Tips

Renting multiple vehicles or charter services from the same company can save you a considerable amount of money.

Elegant Journey Limousine
"When only the exceptional will do"
2204 Park Avenue
Santa Clara, CA 95050

(408) 249-5838
www.ejlimo.com

Contact: George Rose

Service Area: South Bay

Specialties: 1956 Rolls Royce Silver Cloud, Vintage 1956 Rolls Royce Custom Stretch Limousine, 1909 Rolls Royce Silver Ghost Convertible, 1911 Rolls Royce Horseless Carriage Limousine, Stretch and Super Stretch Mercedes Benz Limousines

Price (events): 3-hour packages, $293 - $483
Extra Charges: travel

Payment Terms: 50% deposit at booking, balance due 14 days prior to event
Credit Cards: major credit cards
Travel Included: yes (some exceptions)

Lead Time: as early as possible
Decoration: with approval
License: TCP 2730-P

Elegant Journey's limousines look like they were just delivered from the Behring Museum in Blackhawk. Color coordinated, with 24-karat gold trim, and without a speck of dust, they are the dream of many brides. The 1956 Rolls Royce Silver Cloud and the Mercedes Benz Stretch and Super Stretch Limousines are white with champagne-colored sides. The most beautiful are the magnificent vintage 1909 Rolls Royce Silver Ghost convertible and the 1911 Rolls Royce Horseless Carriage Limousine. All limousines come with complimentary champagne, red carpet service, and professional chauffeurs to provide you with quality, on-time service.

Elegant Journey Limousine, a family-owned business, has been in operation since 1979. The chauffeurs wear tuxedos for weddings and three-piece suits for other occasions. They make a point to arrive 15 minutes early for weddings. The cars can be decorated, but no tape is allowed.

George takes pride in his automobiles and the service his company provides. During my first visit, he demonstrated how they set up their Rolls Royce for a newly married couple with the elegant touch of a red carpet, complimentary champagne in a silver ice bucket, and silver goblets.

Ever since I began publishing my guides, I've heard nothing but raves about Elegant Journey Limousine.

Regal Limousine   (888) 552-5466
Make Every Occasion a Regal Occasion
480 Collins Avenue, Unit I
Colma, CA 94014

Contact: Tim Hilton or Charlie Cerini

Service Area: Northern California

Specialties: White 8- and 10-passenger Lincoln Towncar limousines, black sedans; black 6-passenger limousines, reliable customized service; clean look

Price (events): $45 - $85/hr., min. 3 hrs.
Extra Charges: 15% gratuity, parking, bridge toll, travel beyond Bay Area

Payment Terms: credit card number for security, payment in full prior to event
Credit Cards: major credit cards
Travel Included: no

Lead Time: 2 hours to 6 months
Decoration: yes
License: TCP 9346-P

The interior of the 10-passenger, white Lincoln stretch limousine still smelled like new when I saw it during the interview. Tim, one of the owners, had just dropped off a few customers and made excuses for not having vacuumed it before showing it to me. Clad in a spotless black suit with white shirt and tie, the usual attire, he is proud of his cars and the excellent service he has been providing for the past four years. All his drivers are well trained and wear the same outfit, except when tuxedos are specifically requested.

To lessen the stress of weddings, Tim makes sure that the car arrives well before departure time and will allow 3 - 4 hours between the time the first job is expected to end and the next booking. He doesn't mind picking up people as long as time permits, or taking flowers from the ceremony site to the reception. Tim treats his clients with the utmost respect. He reviews the itinerary, writes down all the addresses, and makes sure that no one has to worry about anything. He offers a complimentary bottle of champagne with champagne flutes (because they look great in pictures), sparkling cider, or soda. If he knows children will be in the party, he will bring along a special video.

This company could not come more highly recommended. Uptown Limousines, one of the most respected companies in the area, refers all wedding work to Tim. One client, who hired Tim on three different occasions, mentioned his promptness, arriving even earlier than the scheduled time. She also admired the spotless limousine and has recommended this service to many friends.

VIDEOGRAPHERS

NOTES

INTRODUCTION

Video technology is quite commonplace these days, covering school events, company picnics, corporate meetings, and, of course, weddings and receptions. Videos keep alive the memories of such an important event. They are a great way to share your day with relatives and friends who were unable to be with you and to relish a day that has passed much too quickly.

All of the references I contacted about the videographers in the guide were extremely excited and pleased with their videos. Many volunteered to send me their cassettes for review. One bride's father mentioned that he was now able see everything that had taken place in the church before he entered. One bride whose grandfather passed away two weeks after her wedding was grateful to have captured him on the video.

Inquire about a company's experience in shooting your type of event. This will weed out any newcomers to the field who might consider themselves "experienced." Take time to look at their video portfolio so you can get an idea of how they cover the type of event you are planning. Look for picture clarity, color purity, camera movement, transition between scenes, and sound quality. I personally prefer watching a demo tape of different events, while a wedding consultant friend believes the best way to judge quality is to view the tape of one event from beginning to end.

The camera plays an important role in the quality of a video. To make the most of natural light in a darker environment, a "3-CCD" or 3-chip camera yields superior results when compared to 1-chip cameras. In addition to the conventional analog camera, use of the digital camera is on the rise. Among the analog formats, ¾" Betacam is the best, followed by Hi8 and SVHS. The latter is superior to VHS, even though very good VHS equipment can produce adequate results. The digital DVCAM or DVCPRO formats are the best, followed by the smaller mini-DV digital format cameras. Digital cameras offer many benefits, especially when combined with digital editing.

Editing equipment also plays a major role in the final quality of your video. Analog editing is best in Betacam, followed by SVHS and Hi8 systems. When a digital camera is used, digital editing can avoid generation loss. Talk to your videographer about mastering formats. In a few short years, the transfer of your wedding video to DVD will be greatly affected by the mastering methodology.

In-house editing is preferable to sending the tape to an editing service.

To eliminate any disappointment the day of the wedding, find out if your church or synagogue allows videotaping during the ceremony. And ask your videographer to attend the rehearsal if he or she is not familiar with the ceremony site. Videographers recommend positioning two stationary cameras for taping the ceremony so that they are hardly noticed: one next to the altar and the other on the balcony or at an exit. One camera is usually adequate for reception coverage unless you plan to conduct many interviews.

Money Matters

Prices depend on the length of time the videographer is present, the number of cameras used, and the quality of the equipment. Videographers often include videos for the parents in the quoted price.

Creative Video Services
Professional Video Production
39899 Balentine Drive, Suite 125
Newark, CA 94560

(510) 252-9700
CRVideo@aol.com
www.cvs-weddings.com

Contact: Frank Bella or Kim Davis

Service Area: Northern California

Specialties: Videos for weddings and other occasions

Price range: packages from $1,795
Extra Charges: travel beyond the counties of San Francisco, San Mateo, Santa Clara, and Alameda

Payment Terms: 1/3 deposit, 1/3 due 30 days prior, balance due 60 days after wedding	**Package Plans:** 4 plans
	Time Present: full coverage
Credit Cards: major credit cards	**Video Ready:** 8 - 16 weeks
Lead Time: 6 months to 1 year	**Tape Format:** DVCAM (Broadcast Digital), Beta-SP

When I watched one of his wedding ceremony videos, I understood why it recently earned Frank first place in America, his third in as many years, at the Wedding Video Expo. At the 1998 Expo, CVS won five national awards for their work, including first place in America for ceremony and reception videos. What makes Frank's videos so special are not only the well-edited content, but also the intense, almost 3-dimensional clarity and the excellent sound quality. With over 17 years in the business, he has become a nationally-known authority on wedding videography, writing articles and lecturing nationwide. His company has taped more than 2,700 events. Eight crews of well-trained and well-equipped videographers will shoot no more than three events per day. Crew selection is based on the couple's personalities and wedding location.

CVS is well known within the industry for being on the cutting edge of technology. They pioneered the use of broadcast TV cameras for weddings in the early '80s, and in 1998 became the first Bay Area company to introduce Broadcast Digital recording at weddings. This new technology not only adds phenomenal depth and clarity to the images, but also features cameras that produce beautiful, natural images without the need for a lot of harsh video lights. The mixing, cutting, and production are done in their elaborate editing studio, using equipment normally reserved for network television work.

Frank is personally involved in the editing and final production of each video. He showed me the special touches he can include in his videos, such as black and white images, slow motion, and soft focus vignetting. CVS can also produce a romantic music video about the bride and groom's courtship, a combination of photographs and video clips that can be shown at the wedding. His clients appreciate his low profile during the event as well as his professional approach. One client was so impressed with the wedding tape Frank had done for him that he wanted to send it to me.

Custom Video Classics
Fine Art Videography
(by appointment)
Novato, CA

(415) 893-9929
(Phone & FAX)
www.ByRecOnly.com/customvideo

Contact: Laura Moe or Karyn Kleinman, B.M., P.A.

Service Area: Greater Bay Area and Wine Country

Specialties: Video production for weddings, Bar/Bat Mitzvahs, special events

Price range: $995 - 2,050
Extra Charges: travel beyond 45 minutes, parking, tolls

Payment Terms: 50% deposit, 25% due at rehearsal, balance due at pickup
Credit Cards: Visa, MasterCard
Lead Time: 1 week to 1 year

Package Plans: 4 - 6 plans
Time Present: full event coverage
Video Ready: 4 - 6 weeks
Tape Format: 3-chip digital & industrial SVHS

Laura has been videotaping special events, such as weddings, Bar/Bat Mitzvahs, and corporate events since 1985. Her 14 years of experience, coupled with Karyn's 20+ years of experience and degrees in music, photography, and computer science, bring to their clients a high degree of versatility and vast amount of knowledge.

Karyn and Laura keep up with the latest advances in video technology and use the new, 3-chip digital cameras along with the professional grade SVHS cameras for their event coverage. These lighter cameras require less artificial light and have a slower zoom, providing the videographer with more flexibility under low light situations. One video I saw was quite professionally done with a smooth flow, beginning with the childhood photomontage. The use of special effects gave the tape a more natural appearance. Music and sound are very important elements in the creation of a memorable, finished tape. Laura and Karyn have an extensive understanding of how music can make a tape flow, and they spend a lot of time working with their clients in choosing music that is both energetically appropriate as well as unique to each couple.

Working with clients begins with an extensive consultation. Showing wedding videos and getting feedback give Laura and Karyn a better idea of how to tailor the video to the unique needs of each client. They offer 6 wedding and 4 Bar/Bat Mitzvah packages with either 1- or 2-camera coverage. An increasingly popular option is a 10-minute photomontage, set to music chosen by the client, that is shown at the reception on a giant screen. Each of the wedding packages includes their attendance at the rehearsal in order to meet the family members and clergy, and determine camera and microphone placement. All of their work is edited in-house.

Clients love their videos and their unobtrusive presence. One of the greatest compliments that Laura has received, in addition to their good work, was, "I hardly even knew you were there."

Dream Video Productions

1910 Camden Avenue, Suite #4
San Jose, CA 95124

(800) 454-3843

(408) 559-3500
FAX: (408) 559-5197
kelly@dreamvideo.com
www.dreamvideo.com

Contact: Kelly Priest

Service Area: Greater Bay Area and beyond

Specialties: A high-level video production, blending creative elements, romance, and state-of-the-art equipment

Price range: $1,495 - $2,495
Extra Charges: none

Payment Terms: $650 non-ref. deposit, 50% due 1 week prior, balance due at finished tape
Credit Cards: Visa, MasterCard
Lead Time: 3 - 12 months

Package Plans: 3 plans and à la carte
Time Present: 2 hrs. to full coverage
Video Ready: 8 - 10 weeks
Tape Format: SVHS

"Never in my wildest dreams did I think the day would get captured like that. You brought tears, smiles, and laughter to us. The work you produced is priceless. Thank you for the incredible pricing. 'Value' is an understatement." "You were our favorite part of our wedding because you were everywhere, yet nowhere… Funny, sad, poignant, silly and beautiful moments on film. We enjoyed our wedding – but we relived it through your eyes; everything we missed you caught on tape. To say thank you will never be enough – to say you're the best in the biz is a gross understatement." These are just two of the many rave reviews about this company.

While Kelly Priest was studying broadcasting in college, one of his teachers asked him to videotape their wedding. Through referrals, he continued to videotape weddings on weekends. After videotaping about 40, he found weddings challenging and creative. He opened a studio in Los Gatos in 1990, outgrew it, then moved to his current studio in San Jose in 1996. Kelly's team of highly experienced videographers all match his style and creativity.

"Look for the truth. People should not be affected by my presence," states Kelly. Shooting from behind a pillar or with a camera tucked under his arm, he captures the chemistry between the bride and the groom in a most inconspicuous way. In working with Kelly, I appreciate the most respectful approach he has about capturing interviews. He sets a camera in an unobtrusive area so that guests and family feel welcomed, not intimidated to make any special wishes or comments.

All of Dream Video Productions' packages feature offer from 7 hours to full event coverage. When I asked why so many hours, Kelly replied, "We take the point of view of a storyteller. The day just doesn't start at the ceremony." My favorite is his "Picture Show," a montage of up to 90 photographs set to music. A captivating love story of pictures, music and a "He said/ She said" interview perfectly blended.

JBC Video
Royal Weddings & Strictly Mitzvah!
1368 Bush Street, Suite #208
San Francisco, CA 94109

(415) 563-3348
FAX: (415) 563-3524
jbcvideo@royalweddings.com
www.royalweddings.com

Contact: Joel Cook or April Lee Ellis

Service Area: Northern California and beyond

Specialties: Special event video production, video editing/duplication

Price range: packages, $600 - $3,500; inquire about hourly rate
Extra Charges: travel beyond 60 miles of San Francisco

Payment Terms: 1/3 deposit, balance due at event
Credit Cards: Visa, MasterCard
Lead Time: 2 days to 12 months

Package Plans: 6 plans and à la carte
Time Present: 2 hrs. to full coverage
Video Ready: 1 - 16 weeks
Tape Format: DVCAM, SVHS, Hi8

When I first met Joel, producer and director of JBC Video/Royal Weddings and Strictly Mitzvah! Video Productions, he had just moved from his home/office to a tiny studio in San Francisco. Now, ten years later, his is the largest and one of the most successful event video companies in San Francisco, having produced thousands of events on videotape throughout Northern California. His company is highly recommended by some of the most prestigious hotels and event professionals in the area. They admire the non-obtrusiveness and professionalism of his production crews, the candid flow, and the quality of their videos.

Joel is very proud of his staff, their talents, and team effort. "They are the backbone of the business." His experienced production teams can cover up to five events per day. The ceremony is recorded with 1 to 3 carefully positioned cameras. Strategically placed shotgun and wireless microphones ensure that the wedding vows will be clearly heard. They will document the many details of the location, flowers, cake, table settings, etc., that reflect the uniqueness of their clients' events. Instead of just following the photographer, the videographers will shoot the many candid activities which might otherwise be overlooked during the excitement of the day.

Their premier wedding packages include multi-camera coverage of the rehearsal dinner, bride and groom preparations, wedding, and reception. They also include the photo montage (photographs of the couple from childhood through their courtship, edited to music) and event montages (a recap of all the best moment of the day, edited to a favorite song). All event videos are carefully custom-edited into 1- to 3-hour movies. An extensive collection of beautiful stock footage of San Francisco and Bay Area landmarks can be edited into the video.

Joel will send out demo tapes, but encourages his clients to meet in his studio to meet their videographers and view an event video that is closely related to their own plans.

Lang Video Art

(510) 834-7550
FAX: (510) 834-7554
Langvid@pacbell.net

(by appointment)
Oakland, CA

Contact: Robert or Dana Lang

Service Area: Greater Bay Area and beyond

Specialties: Videos for weddings, Bar/Bat Mitzvahs, and corporate activities (training, communication)

Price range: from $1,200
Extra Charges: parking

Payment Terms: 1/3 deposit, 1/3 one month prior to event, balance due at pickup
Credit Cards: Visa, MasterCard
Lead Time: 3 weeks to 15 months

Package Plans: 6 plans and custom-designed
Time Present: 2 hrs. to full event coverage
Video Ready: 6 - 8 weeks
Tape Format: SVHS, Hi8, Digital S, DVCPro

A cat was pawing through the Yellow Pages of a 1984 phone book and came across Robert's ad. The cat's owner called Robert and, after learning that he was still in business after 12 years, hired him on the spot.

Robert's fascination with technical gadgets inspired him to start his video business. He bought his first camera in 1981 to record his newborn son's activities. He then began taping family reunions and friends' parties, and was soon asked to tape a wedding. After perfecting his style and improving his editing equipment at home, he started Lang Video Art in 1983. Robert is constantly updating his equipment and now has several top-of-the-line 3-chip cameras, wireless mikes, and over 75-gigabytes of hard disk space for computer editing. One bride's father was so pleased with Robert's work that he offered to send me the video.

While Robert may cut some of the reception footage, the wedding ceremony is rarely edited. He can add computer-generated special effects and titles. He pays great attention to detail and will go so far as to incorporate the color scheme in his titles. A prospective client can view his special effects, still video scenes of an event's highlights, and a montage of old photographs provided by the couple. Chances are that Robert will already have a couple's church or synagogue on tape. I particularly enjoyed learning about how he conducts interviews during the event. He learns how the guest is related to the couple and then asks meaningful questions. The interviews are conducted throughout the reception and are never boring. He uses his large selection of special effects sparingly, simply to make the work more interesting, and usually ends with a recap that includes slow motion footage. In addition to reflecting Robert's professional style, the videos are beautiful in color, fun to watch, and certainly compete with the best in the business.

Multivision Productions

(925) 687-9999
FAX: (925) 687-3946
info@multi-vision.com
www.multi-vision.com/weddings

1200 Concord Avenue, Suite 180
Concord, CA 94520

Contact: Hamid Massoud

Service Area: Greater Bay Area and beyond

Specialties: High-end videography for weddings, Bar/Bat Mitzvahs, and
other occasions; commercial videos

Price range: from $2,000
Extra Charges: travel beyond Greater Bay Area

Payment Terms: 50% deposit, balance due 1 week prior to event	**Package Plans:** 4 package plans
	Time Present: unlimited
Credit Cards: major credit cards	**Video Ready:** 8 - 12 weeks
Lead Time: 6 months to 1 year	**Tape Format:** Betacam SP, Hi8, Digital (DVCAM)

Multivision Productions was recommended to me by one of the top videographers in the area. I met Hamid in his elegant studio in Concord where I learned about his background and watched videos. Hamid has an MBA from San Diego State and keeps up with the video technology by attending classes and seminars on film and production. He started out to conquer the video market. Now, several years later, he shoots with broadcast cameras and edits in his state-of-the-art studio. His reputation that extends well beyond the Bay Area has earned him many national awards. Companies such as MCI, Safeway, Mobilnet, and Del Monte are among his clients.

The video I saw was superbly done. Recaps of the event's highlights were done in color and in black & white, and included slow motion segments, all of which made the video even more romantic. I learned that this can be achieved only with first-grade equipment. I really admired a "love story" video, which he also offers. This story, shot at Stanford University, starred an engaged couple who began by telling about how they first met and ended with how he proposed to her. Their story unfolded as they walked through the campus, stopping for hugs. The video also included footage from the groom's own video which made it look like a real movie. I could have watched it over and over again. Such a love story can be shown during the ceremony on a 6' x 8' screen.

I talked to the bride whose "love story" I saw. She raved about Hamid's creativity and spontaneity in coming up with ideas, the exceptionally high quality of his work, and about how comfortable she and the groom felt working with him.

New York Broadcast Video

(408) 997-1542
FAX: (408) 268-1596
nybvideo@aol.com

(by appointment)
San Jose, CA

Contact: Larry Brickman (Owner & Producer) or Iris Brickman (Coordinator)

Service Area: Greater Bay Area

Specialties: Video productions of weddings, Bar/Bat Mitzvahs, special events

Price range: $1,000 to $2,995
Extra Charges: travel beyond Bay Area

Payment Terms: 1/3 deposit, 1/3 1 week prior to event, balance due upon completion	**Package Plans:** 4 custom plans
	Time Present: full coverage
Credit Cards: Visa, MasterCard	**Video Ready:** 6 - 8 weeks
Lead Time: 48 hrs. to 18 months	**Tape Format:** professional grade 3-chip SVHS

Larry and Iris are a wonderful husband-and-wife team. Pictures of former clients on the walls of their studio tell of the good friends they became in the course of wedding preparations. Larry has won numerous national awards for his work. He has a degree in video and communications from New York Institute of Technology and worked several years for network and corporate television stations in Manhattan. In 1990 Larry and Iris moved to the Bay Area and started a full-time event video company.

With over 20 years of experience, Larry refers to himself as a producer. So that everything runs smoothly, Larry starts with on-site inspections, meeting with the clergy and wedding coordinator to arrange camera placement and confirm technical requirements. He supervises the entire production. He also does all the editing and can include digital special effects, black & white, and slo-motion. Photomontage, a wedding invitation segment, guest interviews, and ending montage of those special moments are included in each package. He also provides wireless microphones. The master copy of the video is presented in an attractive, custom-designed case. Gift certificates for weddings are also available. The videos I saw are of high quality, with clear, crisp colors that reflect Larry's excellent qualifications and his professional equipment. Clients commented on the spectacular video and were surprised by the extensive coverage since they completely forgot that Larry was there.

I saw Larry in action as he videotaped one of our BRO parties. Even while he worked, it was fun interacting with him. He did an excellent job capturing the spirit of the event on tape and producing the video with titles and appropriate music.

Iris, a former psychologist, is the soul of the company. She cares about each customer, providing personal service and support. She helps create the plan of their dreams and assists in finding other resources.

Ron Garcia Studios
Videography
(by appointment)
San Jose, CA

(408) 253-2532

Contact: Ron or Michele Garcia

Service Area: Greater Bay Area, except San Francisco

Specialties: Videography for weddings, receptions, and other special occasions

Price range: $1,095 - $1,795
Extra Charges: travel beyond 1 hour

Payment Terms: 1/3 deposit, 1/3 1 month prior, balance due on delivery	**Package Plans:** 3 plans and à la carte
	Time Present: full coverage
Credit Cards: no	**Video Ready:** 3 weeks
Lead Time: 1 week to 1 year	**Tape Format:** ½" SVHS, VHS

1999 marks Ron's 18th year as a wedding and special event videographer. His background in photography makes him very sensitive to working as a team with the still photographer. His eye for lighting and composition, combined with the latest in SVHS, is obvious in his video style. He offers up to three manned cameras and one still camera.

Ron considers a detailed consultation essential to the success of the video. He introduces the couples to his packages and discusses their wedding plans. While he showed me his lovely videos, he told me that respect for the wedding ceremony is very important to him. He always attends the rehearsal to decide on the number of cameras and the type of wireless microphones that will be unobtrusive during the ceremony. "There is always the possibility of a special situation, like taping the bride's mother playing piano during the ceremony." Music, still photos and interviews can be edited in appropriate places. Ron uses a natural approach toward showing the emotion of the day, the interaction of the guests, and the fun and laughter. I observed the unobtrusive way he videotaped my friend's wedding.

Ron's clients love his work and say he is very sensitive to the mood of a wedding. He works hard, is very honest, and his prices are quite reasonable. The best compliment for him is when couples say, "We love the work, and we didn't even notice you were there."

Thomas Hughes Video Productions

(415) 925-8600
FAX: (415) 454-9237

39 Corte Morada Way
Greenbrae, CA 94904-1311

Contact: Anita Hughes

Service Area: National

Specialties: Weddings and photo montages

Price range: packages, $900 to $3,400
Extra Charges: travel beyond Greater Bay Area

Payment Terms: $250 non-ref. deposit; 90% 2 weeks prior to event; balance due on completion
Credit Cards: Visa, MasterCard
Lead Time: to 1 year

Package Plans: 4 plans; à la carte
Time Present: ceremony only to full coverage
Video Ready: 2 - 4 months
Tape Format: VHS, DVCAM, Hi8

What began in 1983 as a perfect way to record the sights and sounds of family and friends gathering on the most important days of their lives evolved into a highly skilled and very respected professional video production company. From the time clients meet with Anita Hughes, it is evident that Thomas Hughes Video Productions has a genuine concern about providing a quality wedding videotape tailored to the client. Uncovering the client's style and taste is of utmost importance. "Video is so personal. It's a real collaboration and commitment," comments Thomas.

Their understated style of capturing an event is consistent among all Thomas Hughes videographers. During the editing process the story is beautifully customized for the particular client. Information about the event and family, and special requests and notes, such as lighting and things to look out for, are noted in the client's file prior to the wedding. This information is crucial in producing a story that reflects the personalities and elements of the day. Once the event is recorded, it is digitally edited on the computer to expand and enhance certain elements. The imaginative use of dissolves from one moment to the next create amazing segments to maximize an emotion or mood. You can really relive the feeling of the moment.

"Many spend a fortune on the design of the room, so it's important that it is documented and captured, not distorted," explains Thomas. Their professional and very respectful manner is one of the many reasons I can recommend Thomas Hughes Video Productions. They always take additional steps to uncover any obstacles and familiarize themselves with location and vendors before the event. They are team players with all of the vendors and clients.

Video Madness

900 S. Winchester Blvd., Suite 11A
San Jose, CA 95128

(888) 588-8433
(408) 441-1619
FAX: (408) 260-1025
bigbelly@best.com
www.videomadness.com

Contact: Bob Farnsworth

Service Area: Greater Bay Area and beyond

Specialties: Complete digital shooting, editing and digital mastering (DVD-ready)

Price range: packages from $995
Extra Charges: big screen video presentation; engagement videos; CD-ROM and DVD transfers

Payment Terms: 50% deposit, 2nd payment 10 days prior to event; balance due on completion
Credit Cards: all credit cards
Lead Time: 1 - 18 months

Package Plans: 5 plans; custom options
Time Present: 6 hrs. to weekend coverage
Video Ready: 8 - 12 weeks
Tape Format: Hi8, Mini-DV; DV-Cam

"I am so happy we hired Video Madness" commented one of my brides after discovering that her fiancé, while escorting his parents down the aisle, had been too nervous to hear the tenor she hired as a surprise to sing "Sunrise, Sunset."

Owner Bob Farnsworth studied liberal arts, film and photography at RIT, and music at the renown Eastman School of Music in New York. His diverse array of skills brings both technical and artistic abilities together. "The Marriage of Art & Technology." The use of 3-chip digital cameras and nonlinear, firewire-based digital editing make sure that they stay on the forefront of technology. "It's about forever," comments Bob.

Video Madness has been a full-time, full-service, digital videography company for over 10 years, with highly qualified and professional videographers. They have filmed over 2,000 weddings in the Bay Area, with over 500 filmed in the new, cutting-edge digital format. They use primarily 3-chip digital cameras but offer 3-chip analog cameras as a high-quality, less expensive choice. The 3-chip analog cameras provide wonderful color reproduction and superior low-light performance, while the 3-chip digital cameras offer unparalleled picture and sound quality. It is always a pleasure and relief knowing that Video Madness will be videotaping one of my client's weddings. Their low profile and discreet manner, leading to recommendations by photographers and coordinators, are surpassed only by their beautifully captured event videos. Bob's editing of the music to certain moments and emotions is done with extreme precision. I even melted while viewing a video of a wedding couple whom I didn't know.

A client's comment: "The only time I remember him being there was either making me laugh or comforting me." From one groom, whose video was a surprise: "I didn't realize a videographer was filming until we were presented with the final tape. He captured everything!"

VideoVid

(800) 695-0045 (pager/message)
(650) 578-9776 (direct/message)

1951 O'Farrell Street, #412
San Mateo, CA 94403

videovid@slip.net
videovid@hotmail.com
www.ByRecOnly.com/videovid

Contact: Vidur Sood

Service Area: Napa to Monterey

Specialties: Digital quality film and non-linear digital editing

Price range: Digitally-edited packages, from $1,000
Extra Charges: travel charges may apply

Payment Terms: 1/3 deposit, 1/3 due before event, 1/3 due upon delivery
Credit Cards: major credit cards
Lead Time: 1 day to 1 year

Package Plans: custom packages à la carte
Time Present: up to 8 hrs.
Video Ready: 2 - 12 weeks
Tape Format: Digital, Hi8

With technology so fluid, Vidur has the ability and flexibility to create whatever you imagine could be created using digital equipment and computers. While an undergraduate at Stanford University, Vidur was technical director for the university's Instructional TV Network using multiple cameras to broadcast engineering classes to Silicon Valley computer companies. After graduation, he set off to become editor for a children's TV show in India, an interest he shares with his parents. On his return, he worked at Oracle Corporation as a programmer until he began VideoVid in 1993. His extensive experience, knowledge, and background have placed Vidur on the cutting edge of video technology.

Upon meeting Vidur, you can't help but feel comfortable. His interest in the client is truly genuine, and the quality of his service and product is unbeatable. Colors stay true, and peak emotional moments are captured in seconds with his digital camera. The computer then extends those moments by calculating between frames to generate new ones, producing a completely smooth and seamless effect.

His expertise is unparalleled. By taping and editing the events himself, Vidur knows exactly what special effect or splice is needed to trigger the same mood. His connection with the event becomes personal. One scene that comes to mind is of two young children with their teddy bears dancing, which is synchronized perfectly to the music, "Without Love, There Is Nothing."

Vidur customizes all of his packages to fit the type of day and client. From the onset, he establishes a rapport with his clients. Vidur quotes, "Actors never act." He strongly feels that if the clients and their guests are comfortable with him, their video will appear natural. Working with him, I've seen how he glides through the crowds, always anticipating the moments and capturing the ambience of the day in the most unobtrusive fashion.

Wedding Memories
Video Service
1950 Olivera Road, Suite One
Concord, CA 94520

(800) 676-5262
(925) 676-6000
FAX: (925) 676-6179
www.weddingmemoriesvideo.com

Contact: Susan Lamb (ext. 104)

Service Area: Greater Bay Area

Specialties: Wedding and commercial videography

Price range: $520 - $1,085
Extra Charges: travel beyond 1 hour

Payment Terms: 50% non-ref. deposit,
              balance due week prior to event
Credit Cards: major credit cards
Lead Time: 1 week to 1 year

Package Plans: 5 plans, also à la carte
Time Present: 4 hrs. to full event coverage
Video Ready: 1 - 8 weeks
Tape Format: SVHS

From customizing packages and attending pre-production meetings to sitting in on the editing session, you are involved in creating your own video at Wedding Memories, a division of Lamb Productions. With a degree in communication, owner Mark Lamb and his highly professional broadcast experience team have been producing high-quality, clear image videos for 14 years.

Susan Lamb presents all aspects and terms of wedding videography. She assists you in selecting a plan or customizing one to fit the event. Susan discusses the wedding day agenda, music selection, video montages, and much more. "Between your ideas and our experience, your video will be perfect," says Susan.

Clients love the superb videos, underscored with wonderful music, and felt they received much more that anticipated – all without even noticing they were being filmed. "They were everywhere, but in no way were they bothersome." "Their customer service was great, from the telephone interview to the end of our event."

Zoom Video Productions
Video Services
3768 Benton Street
Santa Clara, CA 95051

(408) 248-4408
FAX: (408) 557-9077

Contact:　　Michael Izumi

Service Area:　Greater Bay Area

Specialties: Weddings, events and corporate videos

Price range: $1,300 - $2,000
Extra Charges: travel beyond 30 miles, use of video projector

Payment Terms: $600 non-ref. deposit, balance due upon completion
Credit Cards: no
Lead Time: 1 month to 1 year

Package Plans: 4 plans and à la carte
Time Present: 5 hrs. to full coverage
Video Ready: 4 - 8 weeks
Tape Format: Hi8, VHS, SVHS, Betacam SP, Digital

Michael was recommended by several professionals who appeared in previous editions of the guide. One well-known florist had hired him for his own wedding and proudly showed me the video. I also heard comments like, "We fell in love all over again watching it!" and "You have been such a pleasure to work with."

As one of the few who pursued videography in college, Michael received a BA in broadcasting from San Jose State University. While a student, he worked for KNTV Channel 11 and later became a full-time news camera man, a position that afforded him extensive experience in news production and editing. After six years, Michael decided to pursue a full-time career of producing weddings and corporate videos and became a video contractor for Intel and Hewlett Packard. A highlight of his career was shooting a documentary of the 1996 U.S. Figure Skating Championship held in San Jose.

Michael is easy to get along with. He is very modest and has no intention of stealing the show. His goal is to document the event, complementing the photographer rather than appearing competitive. He shoots with professional Sony Digital 3-chip cameras, and always has two cameras available for the ceremony and one for the reception. He can provide a video projector at the reception to show your guests childhood pictures and wedding day highlights, edited to music. Editing is a major component of his work. He can personalize the video with music montages, titles, and special effects, editing with a digital, non-linear editing system.

THE MARRIAGE LICENSE

Requirements:
- Must be 18 years of age. Persons under 18 must have written consent from parent or legal guardian and permission from a California Superior Court Judge).
- Bride and groom must apply together.
- Bring proper identification – Valid Driver's License, Passport, Military ID, or Certified Copy of Birth Certificate (accompanied with photo ID).
- Provide parents' names, mother's maiden name, and their place of birth.
- If divorced within the last 6 months you must supply a copy of the final judgement decree.
- Widows or widowers must supply a certified death certificate of the spouse
- As of Jan 1, 1995, blood tests are no longer required.

Things to note:
- You do not need to be a resident or US citizen to obtain a marriage license.
- Some county clerks offices accept only cash or money orders.
- Some offices are closed during the lunch hour; all offices are closed on holidays.
- Allow up to 1 hour for a marriage license to be issued.
- Marriage licenses vary between counties.
- Always call to get updated information.
- Same sex marriages are not recognized in California.

Public License or Regular Marriage License:
- License is public record.
- License is valid up to 90 days after issuance.
- Can be married any place in the State of California.

Confidential Marriage License:
- Couple must be living together as husband and wife; some counties require proof.
- License is valid up to 90 days after issuance.
- Can only be married in the county in which license was issued.
- No one can view the license without a court order.

WHERE TO GET A MARRIAGE LICENSE

Alameda County
Municipal Court
39439 Paseo Padre Parkway, Room 100 – 1st floor
Fremont CA
510 795-2328
8:30 am – 4:30 pm
$67.00 Public License / Confidential – N/A

Alameda County
Superior Court - Hayward
24405 Amador Street, Room 108 1st floor (Jackson and Winton Ave)
Hayward, CA
510 670-5060
8:30 am – 4:00 pm
$67.00 Public License / $78.00 Confidential License

Alameda County
Clerk Recorder's Office
1225 Falon Street, Room 100 (at 12th & 13th Street)
Oakland, CA 94612
510 272-6363 / www.co.alameda.ca.us
8:30 am – 4:30 pm
$79.00 Public License / Confidential License – N/A – come together – fee includes one certified copy

Alameda County
Superior Court - Pleasanton
5672 Stoneridge Drive, 2nd floor
Pleasanton, CA
925 551-6895
8:30 am – 4:30 pm
$67.00 Public License / Confidential License – N/A
Both present – divorced within last two years you need a copy of the judgment

WHERE TO GET A MARRIAGE LICENSE

Contra Costa County
Clerk Recorder
822 Main Street (1 block west of court house)
Martinez, CA
925 646-2956
8:00 am – 4:00 pm
$64.00 Public License – Cash Only / $69.00 Confidential License – If divorced with 12 months must provide paper

Marin County
County Clerks
3501 Civic Center Drive, Room 247
San Rafael, CA
415 499-3003
9:00 am – 4:00 pm
$70.00 Public License / $82.00 Confidential License

Monterey County
Clerk Office
240 Church Street, #305 (3rd floor west wing)
Salinas, CA
831 755-5450
8:00 am – 3:30 pm
$54.00 Public License / $64.00 Confidential License

San Francisco County
County Clerk's Office
Marriage License Bureau
25 Van Ness, Ste. 110 (at Market)
San Francisco, CA 94102
415 252-3282
8:00 am – 4:00 pm
$69.00 Public License / $69.00 Confidential License Cash/Money Order

WHERE TO GET A MARRIAGE LICENSE

San Mateo County
Hall of Justice and Records
Recorder's Office
400 County Center, 6th floor
Redwood City, CA 94063
650 363-4712
8:00 am – 4:00 pm
$78.00 Public License / Confidential License - N/A - Cash Only

Santa Clara County
Superior Court Building
Recorder's Office
170 Park Center Plaza (at Park Ave and Almaden)
San Jose, CA
408 288-9143
9:00 am – 4:00 pm
$73.00 Public License / $78 Confidential License - Cash Check or Charge Card add'l $8.00

Santa Cruz County
Clerks Office
701 Ocean Street, Room 230
Santa Cruz, CA 95060
831 454-2470
8:00 am – 4:00 pm
$55.00 Public License / $60.00 Confidential License

RECOMMENDED WEDDING FAIRES

Schedule of Wedding Faires
in the Greater Bay Area

1999

East Bay

Party & Wedding Faire
produced by Dale Tomy Associates
January 17 – San Ramon Marriott Hotel
February 7 – Walnut Creek Marriott Hotel
February 21 – Modesto Centre Plaza
March 7 – Concord Sheraton
September – San Ramon Marriott Hotel
For information and future dates please call (925) 370-9823.

Winter Wedding Faire
produced by Bridal Network
January 10 – Claremont Resort
For information and future dates please call (510) 339-3370.

Marin

Bridal & Party Showcase
produced by Just Married Productions
January 31 – Marin Center Exhibit Hall
April 19 – Marin Embassy Suites Hotel
For information and future dates please call (415) 924-3563

Napa

Bridal & Party Showcase
produced by Just Married Productions & The Main Event
March 28 – Napa Valley Expositions
For information and future dates please call (415) 924-3563
                                        or (707) 253-8160.

RECOMMENDED WEDDING FAIRES

Schedule of Wedding Faires
in the Greater Bay Area

1999

Peninsula

The Bridal Extravaganza
January 9 & 10 – Santa Clara County Fairgrounds, San Jose
January 17 – Airport Marriott Hotel, Burlingame
August 22 – Marriott Hotel, Santa Clara
For information and future dates please call (408) 360-9333
or visit www.bestbridalshow.com

San Francisco

Palace Wedding Faire
produced by Bridal Network
March 7 – Sheraton Palace Hotel
For information and future dates please call (510) 339-3370

INDICES

Business Index

Geographical Index

Alameda

Compass Rose   187

Alamo

Round Hill Country Club   219
Rozelle, Katrina   64

Aptos

Seascape Resort   223

Atherton

Divine Catering   82
Holbrook Palmer Park   198

Belmont

Flowers by Julie   133
Manisse Designs   142
Mayer, Richard   319
Ralston Hall   218

Benicia

Captain Walsh House   183

Berkeley

Eliot Khuner Photography   309
Faculty Club, The   193
Fleurs de France   130
Instead of You   112
Janèl Clair Design   164
Melandry, Don   320
Musica Viva   292
Partos, Andrew   324
Phelps, Nan   326
Prichard Photography   331
Shtetlblasters   263
Trumpetvine   97

Burlingame

Cheese Please   77
Dawn Photography   305
Kohl Mansion   201
Party Prints   348
Plan Decor   146
Unique Bride   40

Campbell

Belle Fleur   125
Classic Sounds   249
Inviting Ideas   163
Not Just Cheesecakes   63
Rosies & Posies   148
Trudys Brides   39

Capitola

Bonne Bouche Catering   74
Shadowbrook   224

Colma

Regal Limousine   366

Concord

Denon & Doyle   272
Englund's Catering Service   83
Multivision Productions   376
Wedding Memories   382

Corte Madera

Event of the Season   84

Cupertino

Lily Dong Couture Bridal   36
Tembrock, Judy   339

Daly City

Tosca Productions   117

Danville

Crow Canyon Country Club   188
Pleasant Thoughts   168

El Cerrito

Fraser, D. Douglass   311
Patricia Gibbons Floral Designer   144

Emeryville

Konietzny, Martina   316
LeDuc, Paula   88

San Jose

San Juan Bautista

San Mateo

San Pablo

San Rafael

San Ramon

Santa Clara

Subject Index

A

art gallery   191, 228

B

bakeries   53, 54, 60, 61, 64
bands   246 - 268, 293
banquet facilities   179, 205, 216
bartenders   47
bed & breakfast   183, 206
beverage service   47
bouquet preservation   127, 132, 135, 137,
        146, 147, 150, 169
bouquets. *See* flowers
bridal accessories   33, 34, 35, 36, 37,
        38, 39, 40, 111, 116
bridal gifts   138
bridal salons   33, 34, 37, 38, 39, 40
bridesmaids dresses   33, 34, 37, 38, 39, 40

C

cake tops   161
cakes   53 - 65
    cheesecakes   58, 59, 63
    Kosher   59
    special occasion   53, 54, 56, 57,
        58, 59, 60, 63, 64
calligraphy   103, 159, 161, 162,
        164, 166, 171
caterers   71 - 98
    event coordination   73, 75, 81, 82,
        87, 88, 89, 92, 96
    take-out service   74, 97
centerpieces   58
chocolate   358
clubs   186, 189, 193, 203, 207, 211, 213
conference centers   200, 207
counseling professional   356
country clubs   188, 194, 202, 219, 221
cuisine
    California   72, 73, 76, 77, 78, 80, 83,
        84, 86, 89, 91, 92, 93, 94, 95,
        97, 179, 183, 184, 186, 187, 189,
        193, 196, 200, 203, 204, 213, 214,
        215, 217, 219, 223, 226, 231, 232
    Continental   86, 93, 186, 188, 203,
        205, 216, 224
    Deem Sum   98

ethnic   73, 75, 80, 92, 187
French   77, 85, 95
international   79, 85, 89, 179,
        185, 226, 232
Italian   77, 195
Kosher   80, 86, 232
Mediterranean   72, 73, 78, 84, 86, 89, 217
organic foods   74
Pacific Rim   73, 77, 79, 84, 85, 87
regional American   79, 80, 83, 85, 87, 89,
        185, 193, 199, 205, 221
seasonal   71, 74, 78, 88, 89
South-of-the-Border   87
vegetarian   73, 76, 94, 185

D

dessert buffets   53, 54, 59, 61,
        62, 65, 76, 78
disc jockeys   270 - 279
DJs. *See* disc jockeys
dresses. *See* wedding gowns

E

entertainment agencies   239 - 243
entertainment, special   355, 359
estate   198, 214
ethnic weddings   103, 110, 112, 116, 118
etiquette   108, 168
event center   227
event coordinators   103 - 119, 137, 142

F

favors   57, 58, 103, 109, 161, 162
flowers   125 - 154
    architectural designs   143
    contemporary design   133, 136, 141, 150
    dried   148
    European garden   127, 131, 132, 137,
        139, 142, 146, 147, 153, 154
    freeze-dried   150, 169
    garden look   130, 133, 134, 135,
        138, 144, 150
    Japanese style   127
    silk   148
    tropical   143
flute   282

IF YOU WANT TO BECOME A WEDDING CONSULTANT

June Wedding, Inc.®

An Association for Event Professionals

JWI is an internationally renowned organization whose members are wedding/corporate/special event consultants and vendors who are highly skilled and trained. They are considered the leaders in their specific fields and have met the criteria of having professional business licensing, health and other legal and insurance permits.

JWI provides a home study or on-site training and education course for the event professional who wants to develop and fine tune skills, techniques, and service, thus increasing proficiency and revenue. The JWI courses are also taught quarterly at Norwalk Community Technical College in Norwalk, Connecticut and at The College of San Mateo in San Mateo, California (www.smcccd.cc.ca.us/smcccd/cce).

Please visit our website www.junewedding.com and browse our

"Certification Programs"

For more information, contact robbi@junewedding.com.

ORDER FORM

Would you like another copy as a gift to a friend?

Just fill in the address below and send a check of $25.00 (includes tax & shipping) to:

Adobe Creek Publishing
24439 NE 19th St.
Redmond, WA 98053

For an additional $5.00 we will gift-wrap the guide and include a gift card!

Please send

By Recommendation Only
Party and Wedding Guide
to the Greater San Francisco Bay Area
including Monterey Bay

Name . . . .

Address . . . .

City/State/Zip . . . .

For more information call (425) 836-3763.

Send your comments and questions via e-mail to

johanna@ByRecOnly.com

RECOMMENDATION FORM

Adobe Creek Publishing
24439 NE 19th St.
Redmond, WA 98053

From:

. . . .

. . . .

. . . .

Phone: (   )
. . . .

☐   I would like to recommend the following business ...

☐   I disagree with your recommendation of ...

. . . .

Phone: (   ) . . . .

My experience with the above firm is as follows:

. . . .

. . . .

. . . .

. . . .

. . . .

. . . .

(use other side for more space)

RECOMMENDATION FORM

. . . .

. . . .

. . . .

. . . .

. . . .

. . . .

. . . .

. . . .

. . . .

. . . .

. . . .

. . . .

. . . .

. . . .

RECOMMENDATION FORM

Adobe Creek Publishing
24439 NE 19th St.
Redmond, WA 98053

From:
. . . .

. . . .

. . . .

Phone: ( ) . . . .

☐ I would like to recommend the following business ...

☐ I disagree with your recommendation of ...

. . . .

Phone: ( ) . . . .

My experience with the above firm is as follows:

. . . .

. . . .

. . . .

. . . .

. . . .

. . . .

(use other side for more space)

RECOMMENDATION FORM

. . . .
. . . .
. . . .
. . . .
. . . .
. . . .
. . . .
. . . .
. . . .
. . . .
. . . .
. . . .
. . . .
. . . .

photography by Ron Schreier

Tosca J. Clark, author of *By Recommendation Only*, is a certified wedding consultant. Born and raised in the Marina district of San Francisco, she married her high school sweetheart Tom in 1991. Tosca and Tom currently reside in Daly City, CA, where they are busy raising their beautiful son Gavin and operating Tosca Productions, a full wedding and special events consulting company.

Tosca brings new energy, experience, and extensive knowledge of the events industry to this edition. Her high expectations and commitment to quality ensure the continuing excellent reputation of the guide.